D0898194

JOURNAL FOR THE STUDY OF THE NEW TESTAMENT SUPPLEMENT SERIES
105

Executive Editor
Stanley E. Porter

Editorial Board
Richard Bauckham, David Catchpole, R. Alan Culpepper,
Joanna Dewey, James D.G. Dunn, Craig A. Evans, Robert Fowler,
Robert Jewett, Elizabeth Struthers Malbon, Dan O. Via

Sheffield Academic Press

The Bible, the Reformation and the Church

Essays in Honour of James Atkinson

edited by
W.P. Stephens

Journal for the Study of the New Testament
Supplement Series 105

BS
500
.B54830
1995

Copyright © 1995 Sheffield Academic Press

Published by Sheffield Academic Press Ltd
Mansion House
19 Kingfield Road
Sheffield, S11 9AS
England

Typeset by Sheffield Academic Press
and
Printed on acid-free paper in Great Britain
by Bookcraft
Midsomer Norton, Somerset

British Library Cataloguing in Publication Data

A catalogue record for this book is available
from the British Library

ISBN 1-85075-502-7

JESUIT - KRAUSS - McCORMICK - LIBRARY
1100 EAST 55th STREET
CHICAGO, ILLINOIS 60615

CONTENTS

6   *The Bible, the Reformation and the Church*

PREFACE

This volume marks James Atkinson's eightieth birthday and comes from the wide circle of his friends as a token of their esteem for him. Its theme represents the main emphases in his work as a preacher and teacher of the Bible, as a scholar of the reformation, and as a minister of the church of Christ. In his memoir, Anthony Thistelton offers both a sketch of his life and an appreciation of his work which show how well the title reflects the person we desire to honour.

We write as those who work in one or more of these fields and in that way we represent his interests, if not always his position. We write as friends and, in several cases, as past or present colleagues. By a happy providence we have an essay on Luther by Robert Stupperich, now in his ninetieth year, who was one of James Atkinson examiners in the University of Münster. (His essay has been translated by friends and former colleagues in Sheffield, Hamish and Sheena Ritchie.) That is paralleled by an essay (and subject index) from Carl Trueman, for whom James Atkinson was an examiner in Aberdeen almost forty years later. Rarely can a *Festschrift* have included contributors separated in age by more than sixty years, and associated with the person honoured in this distinctive way.

The relationship between the Bible, the reformation and the church in James Atkinson's life and work is reflected in this book. Biblical scholars link the Bible to the reformation and the church, and reformation scholars link the reformation to the Bible and to the church, both in the past and in the present. We hope that they will stimulate one whom we honour for himself and for his work and ministry, and also make a contribution worthy of him in these three areas.

Peter Stephens
Aberdeen
All Saints' Eve 1994

ABBREVIATIONS

ARG	*Archiv für Reformationsgeschichte*
BNTC	Black's New Testament Commentaries
CD	K. Barth, *Church Dogmatics*
CO	G. Baum, E. Cunitz and E. Reuss (eds.), *Johannis Calvini opera quae supersunt omnia*
DP	H. Kusch (ed.), *Marsilius of Padua, Defensor Pacis*
EvQ	*Evangelical Quarterly*
HTR	*Harvard Theological Review*
Int	*Interpretation*
JAAR	*Journal of the American Academy of Religion*
JSNTSup	*Journal for the Study of the New Testament*, Supplement Series
JSOT	*Journal for the Study of the Old Testament*
JSOTSup	*Journal for the Study of the Old Testament*, Supplement Series
LW	*Luther's Works*
NovT	*Novum Testamentum*
NTS	*New Testament Studies*
OO	*Desiderii Roterdami Opera Omnia*
PL	*Patrologia Latina*
S	M. Schuler and J. Schulthess (eds.), *Huldreich Zwingli's Werke*
SBLDS	SBL Dissertation Series
SJT	*Scottish Journal of Theology*
SNTSMS	Society of New Testament Studies Monograph Series
THKNT	Theologischer Handkommentar zum Neuen Testament
ThWNT	G. Kittel and G. Friedrich (eds.), *Theologisches Wörterbuch zum Neuen Testament*
TLZ	*Theologische Literaturzeitung*
TSK	*Theologische Studien und Kritiken*
TZ	*Theologische Zeitschrift*
WA	*Weimarer Ausgabe*
WABR	*Weimarer Ausgabe: Briefwechser*
WATR	*Weimarer Ausgabe: Tischreden*
WBC	Word Biblical Commentary
Z	*Huldreich Zwingli's Sämtliche Werke*
ZNW	*Zeitschrift für die neutestamentliche Wissenschaft*
ZTK	*Zeitschrift für Theologie und Kirche*

LIST OF CONTRIBUTORS

C.K. Barrett is Emeritus Professor of Divinity in the University of Durham.

David J.A. Clines in Professor of Biblical Studies in the University of Sheffield.

Donald Coggan was formerly Archbishop of Canterbury.

Patrick Collinson is Regius Professor of History in the University of Cambridge.

Benjamin Drewery is Honorary Research Fellow in the University of Manchester.

†Basil Hall was formerly Professor of Ecclesiastical History in the University of Manchester.

Alister E. McGrath is Research Lecturer in Theology in the University of Oxford, Lecturer in Historical and Systematic Theology at Wycliffe Hall, Oxford, and Research Professor of Systematic Theology at Regent College, Vancouver.

J.I. Packer is Sangwoo Youtong Chee Professor of Theology at Regent College, Vancouver, Canada.

John W. Rogerson is Professor of Biblical Studies in the University of Sheffield.

W.P. Stephens is Professor of Church History in the University of Aberdeen.

Robert Stupperich is Emeritus Professor of Church History in the University of Münster, Germany.

Anthony C. Thiselton is Professor of Christian Theology in the University of Nottingham, and Canon Theologian of Leicester Cathedral.

Carl R. Trueman is Lecturer in Historical Theology in the University of Nottingham.

Robert C. Walton is Emeritus Professor of Church History in the University of Münster, Germany.

JAMES ATKINSON: THEOLOGIAN, PROFESSOR AND CHURCHMAN

Anthony C. Thiselton

Professor James Atkinson was born in Northumberland on 27 April 1914. The son of Nicholas Ridley Atkinson and Margaret Bradford, and the elder brother of Sir Robert Atkinson, he was educated first at Tynemouth High School, near to his family home in the area of Newcastle and the North East coast of England. He then continued his studies at St John's College in the University of Durham, and has always retained a deep affection for Durham.

Over the years James Atkinson has held many distinguished appointments. He has been Lecturer and Reader in Theology in the University of Hull, Professor of Biblical Studies and Head of Department in the University of Sheffield, Canon Theologian of Leicester and of Sheffield Cathedral, President of the Society for the Study of Theology, a member of L'Académie Internationale des Sciences Religieuses, and Founder and Honorary Director of the Centre for Reformation Studies in the University of Sheffield. He is currently also Special Professor in Reformation Theology in the University of Nottingham. For many years he also served in English Parish Ministry, as Precentor and then as Canon of two English Cathedrals, and as a member of the General Synod of the Church of England representing the universities of the Northern Province of England.

In more than one sense of each term, therefore, James Atkinson stands as theologian, professor and churchman. He thinks and writes not only as a theologian of the church, but also as a theologian in the world of the university, with its emphasis on rigour and intellectual integrity. For him theology remains both a vehicle of Christian self-critical reflection and proclamation and, no less, also a continuous re-orientation toward truth and submission to the constraints of truth wherever this is to be found. Theology is both *ecclesial*, in that it serves the church, and also *extra-ecclesial*, in that it corrects and continually reforms the church by recalling it to its proper task. In a parallel way, the office of professor has assumed different forms and aspects in the life of James Atkinson. He has served in two British universities as Professor, and as Visiting Professor in Chicago. He has held a Chair of Biblical Studies and is a Special Professor of Reformation Theology. He taught both biblical studies and Reformation theology in the University of Hull.

As a churchman, Professor Atkinson began his ordained ministry as a curate in the Diocese of Newcastle and later his work included a parish incumbency in Sheffield and also Cathedral appointments. He represented the Church of England in the Preparatory Committee on Anglican–Roman Catholic Relations in Rome, and in Anglican–Lutheran consultations. To understand his life and theology, we need fully to appreciate the deep interaction and interpenetration which drew together these three roles of theologian, professor and churchman. Indeed 'roles' here does not entirely suggest the right idea. For all three constitute different modes of outreach of a single vision and above all of a warm pastoral heart which overflowed in service to God and to others along these three contextually distinguished dimensions invited by work respectively as theologian, professor and churchman.

As well as demonstrating the applicability of the three terms 'Theologian, Professor and Churchman', a further comment may be made concerning the admirable propriety of the title *Bible, Reformation and Church* which the Editor proposed for the volume which offers our congratulations to James Atkinson on his eightieth birthday.

First, James Atkinson's love of the *Bible* has always glowed with its brightest light not only when he expounded its content, but also when he spoke in Luther-like terms of his special fondness for the Gospel of John. Indeed he very often quoted or paraphrased Luther's own words on this, so often that transparently he spoke for Luther here, and Luther spoke for him. Luther declared, 'John's Gospel is the one, fine, true, and chief Gospel, and is far, far to be preferred to the other three', since, together with Paul and 1 Peter, this Gospel 'shows you Christ'.[1] To see Christ in the Bible remains the touchstone of operative biblical interpretation, for it is to Christ that the biblical writings bear witness.

Second, the *Reformation* brought about not only a recovery of the

---

1. *Luther's Works*. XXXV. *Word and Sacrament* (Philadelphia: Fortress Press, 1960), 'Prefaces to the New Testament', p. 362 (= LW 35.362).

witness of the biblical writings to Christ, but also a rediscovery of the primacy and priority of divine grace. If John, for Luther and for James Atkinson, sets forth the centrality of Christology, then Paul, also for them, most clearly expounds the priority of grace. Yet the biblical text with which I most closely associate the entire motive force of James Atkinson's life and work comes from the words of Jesus in the Synoptic Gospels: 'Freely you have received; freely give' (Mt. 10.8). This sentence has ever been on his lips, whether as an exclamation that he gladly took on extra commitments to address a small village congregation, or that he gladly spared extra time to help a student with an academic or personal problem, or as a reminder to another that God's own generosity left no room for niggardly reserve in one's own response to the demands of life.

Once again Bible and Reformation belong intimately together. James Atkinson delighted in the title 'Professor of Biblical Studies'. In Sheffield Cathedral in a sermon to students in rag week, he once described the appointment to this Chair as 'the proudest moment in my life'. It was not only that his beloved Luther had also done all his major work in an office of the same title. That no doubt played its part. But the theological issue was greater: only by returning again and again to the biblical texts could the *fallible* church receive *continuous* reformation, of which the most 'Reformed' church still stood in need every moment of every day.

I have already introduced the relevance of our third term, therefore, in the title to this volume, namely *Church*. In one of his many books on the Reformation, *The Great Light: Luther and the Reformation*, James Atkinson asserts, 'The *ecclesia reformata* is always the *ecclesia reformanda*'.[2] Hence not only the Bible as the touchstone of interpretation and correction must be allowed to speak, but divine calling, which calls all Christian people, whether clergy or laity, to their proper vocation, places a special task on the presbyters and pastors of the church in ministering to its nurture and welfare. If John witnesses to Christ, and if Paul points to the priority of grace, then for Luther and for James Atkinson it is 1 Peter that presents the pastoral charge: 'Tend the flock of God that is your charge not by constraint but willingly' (1 Pet. 5.2).

Such a charge is not dependent on constraint, because 'Freely you have received; freely give'. But with what is the pastor to nourish the

2. J. Atkinson, *The Great Light: Luther and the Reformation* (Grand Rapids: Eerdmans, 1968), p. 21.

congregation? Here, once again, the three threads of Bible, Reformation and Church are woven together, and then interwoven yet again with triple vocation as theologian, professor and churchman. For James Atkinson showed a concern for the purity of the ministerial word which reflects other words from Simone Weil. She writes, 'The need of truth is more sacred than any other need'. Yet falsehoods are so shamelessly paraded as truth that people drink as 'from a contaminated well'. But busy laypeople have neither the time nor the resources to check out whether the 'word' is pure and true. Hence, she declares, 'One has no right to give them spurious provender'.[3] Such a defence of the need of the ordinary layperson for the life-giving authentic message of Christ, not 'spurious provender', could fire James Atkinson into becoming an articulate, polemical and awesome critic of those who caused the little ones to stumble by offering empty husks or poisonous falsehoods in the pulpit, replacing the Gospel by mere sophistry, self-opinion, or a debased theological coinage under the pretence of 'relevance'. Hence, theologian, professor and pastor join as one for continuous reformation of the church and its preaching on the basis of the gospel disclosed in the biblical writings.

Early Years at Durham

James Atkinson entered St John's College, Durham, when Canon Charles Wallace was College Principal and Canon Oliver C. Quick was Professor of Divinity. Oliver C. Quick (1885–1944) was in process of preparing his manuscript to be published as *Doctrines of the Creeds* in 1938. He discussed the subject-matter with his theology students, who included the young James. A younger contemporary of James, Canon Neil L. Pritchard, has warm memories of conversations with him in St John's College. One day Neil Pritchard asked James what the Professor of Divinity was like. He recalls his reply: 'As a matter of fact', James observed, 'I recently had a tutorial with him at his house, and he was very reasonable. He has a habit of emphasising points rather strongly, and at one stage he picked up the poker. I thought he was threatening me with it, but he simply poked the fire.' Three years later, when Neil Pritchard was in his fourth year, a first year student asked him diffidently what Professor Quick was like. Anxiously he explained, 'I hear he once

---

3.   S. Weil, *The Need for Roots: Prelude to a Declaration of Duties towards Mankind* (London: Routledge & Kegan Paul, 1952), p. 35.

threatened a student with a poker'. Such is the stuff of academic or college myth or legend, with its transmission of oral traditions, and their processes of development and embellishment.

Canon Pritchard also recalls the warmth, enthusiasm and sheer kindness with which James Atkinson, as an older student, assisted him on his arrival as a fresher. This outgoing warmth has remained a constant feature both of Professor Atkinson and of St John's College Durham, as a Christian foundation within the University. It is no accident that until 1993 James Atkinson remained a distinguished member of the Governing Council of his old College, serving with such other notable figures in this capacity as Professor H.E.W. Turner, Professor Sir Kingsley Dunham and Bishop Stephen W. Sykes, a former Van Mildert Professor of Divinity at Durham and up to 1994 President of the Council. At its meeting following his retirement from the Council at the end of 1993 the Council honoured him by electing him as one of its very few Honorary Fellows.

In addition to completing the BA in Theology and also a further postgraduate Diploma, James Atkinson became Captain of Boats at St John's College. The Old Johnian of 1937 reports the congratulations of the Principal, Canon Charles Wallace, to James for leading the Boats with the comment: 'St John's crews have had an extraordinarily successful time and have steadily forced their way to the Head of the River. The College is the proud holder of no less than seven cups, won at the York Regatta, in University Races, and at the Durham Regatta.'

The Reverend John Tredennick, who at the age of eighty-seven still travels from Cornwall to St John's Durham for reunions most years, recalls that he and James paid a heavy price for this success at York. So vigorous had been their rowing, that the hard seats of College chapel were unendurable on their return. After the first very painful chapel service, they discovered that a judicious application of surgical spirits could to some small degree facilitate concentration on the liturgy and sermon.

None of this, for all its aspect of narrative interest, fails to shed light on the character of the young James. He has always put his heart and soul into everything; he is always warm, outgoing and caring. Even the episode of Oliver Quick's poker, when stripped of legend, suggests that we may presuppose a lively engagement of minds between two men, each of whom held firm and robust convictions. Although it would be much later in life, after a deep and serious engagement with Luther, that

Luther's words would carry their full force as a description of James Atkinson, already we may catch premature glimpses of Luther's view of faith as 'a living, daring confidence in God's grace...[which] makes men glad and bold and happy in dealing with God and with all his creatures'.[4] We shall return to the fuller statement of Luther's view later, and its function as a commentary on James Atkinson's life and theology.

Durham itself has always held a symbolic significance for James Atkinson which embodies a theological content. A faith that is sturdy, robust, and marked by the common-sense reasonableness which characterizes the very best in Anglican tradition may be said in some sense to cohere with the character and temperament of Northumbrian people. Northumbrians are loyal and warm, but never soft. They are proud in the sense that they leave no room for the inward-looking self-pity, which, in theological terms, reflects the very worst traditions of self-centred pietism. A sense of proportion is often retained by an incisive, frequently dry humour that punctures self-importance.

This pride in the distinctiveness of Northumbrian traditions often invited a historical comment on the distinctive character of British Christianity. James Atkinson frequently attacked the fallacy of the popular myth that the 'conversion of England' followed only the initiative of Pope Gregory's commission to Augustine of Canterbury in AD 597. Celtic Christianity flourished in the North well before that date, and Lindisfarne, Jarrow and Durham still stand as witness to the traditions of Aidan, Cuthbert, Chad, Bede and other Northern saints before Roman traditions assimilated Celtic ones. The key point here is that 'English Christianity' did not first acquire a distinctive identity under Henry VIII but long before.

Parish and Cathedral: Newcastle and Sheffield

In 1937 James Atkinson was ordained to the parish of Holy Cross, Newcastle-upon-Tyne. With characteristic energy, he threw himself into a busy ministry of preaching, visiting and pastoral care; but he found time to teach himself German and Hebrew, and to work toward the Durham MA. He achieved this Master's Degree in 1939. In the same year he married Laura Hindhaugh, a vivacious, generous, warm Northumbrian, as James was. She was to be his close companion and

---

4.   'Preface to the Epistle of St Paul to the Romans', in LW 35.370-71.

support until her premature death around the time of his appointment as Professor at Sheffield.

During these Newcastle years, a close friendship sprang up between two fellow curates on different sides of the city. James' closest friend was Prebendary François A. Piachaud, who recalls: 'James Atkinson had a nature that elicited friendship...He was always a delightful companion—serious of purpose yet with a keen sense of humour, a wonderful mimic, expert at pricking the bubble of pomposity or dullness never totally absent from the self-important engaged in affairs of the world of the church.'

Even in those years of his curacy, Prebendary Piachaud writes, James Atkinson assumed a leading role in initiating corporate discussions among a group of five or six fellow-curates of varying shades of churchmanship. This group, he recalls, 'set about planning a comprehensive reform of the church, from the teaching of theology to church administration. Things now taken for granted, but then novel, almost daring, were included, from church unity to the application of Christianity to social and economic structures.' Truth, for James Atkinson, remained all-important, and in those years he combined an increasing love of Scripture with a submission to truth wherever it might be found. This manifested itself most of all, as his many friends testify, in his preaching and teaching, as well as in his faithfulness and diligence as a pastor. By contrast, at certain levels in the diocesan structures and formal church programmes of the day, a certain dimension of superficiality could sometimes be detected. The group of five or six younger clergy, Prebendary Piachaud insists as a mark of affection, dubbed their Bishop, Provost and Archdeacon, in private, as 'the world, the flesh, and the devil'. While his engagement with truth was intense, James Atkinson enjoyed humour, and certainly he should not be portrayed as narrowly over-earnest. François Piachaud observes: 'He was a deeply-loved figure. [With Laura] their home was a centre of intense happiness, vitality, outgoing joy, and inspiration.'

François Piachaud rightly points out that throughout his life James Atkinson's burning concern for the continuous reform of the Church had nothing whatever to do with a rebel's criticism of due authority. Indeed James Atkinson's work on Luther stresses again and again that, as he expresses it in his preface to Luther's *Disputation against Scholastic Theology*, 'in Martin there is nothing of the rebel. He hated revolution and revolt, enthusiasm and excitement: he traced in these the hoof of Satan and not the fingers of God.' But this does not entail sitting silently by when the gospel is obscured by 'human theories...and perversions'.[5] In Paul's words, 'Who is made to fall (σκανδαλίζεται) and I do not burn with indignation (πυροῦμαι)?' (2 Cor. 11.29).

These were years in which James Atkinson devoured theological works while sustaining an outstanding ministry of preaching and pastoral care. François Piachaud introduced him. for example, to the writing of John Oman, and he was already working on the commentaries of the early Fathers on John.

In 1941, during the war years, James Atkinson moved to Sheffield. He was appointed Precentor of Sheffield Cathedral from 1941 to 1944, and became Vicar of St James and Christopher from 1944 to 1951. He would later continue his close association with Sheffield Cathedral when, on his return to Sheffield in 1967 as Professor of Biblical Studies, he also became Canon Theologian of the Cathedral.

The Very Reverend Ivor Neill, who was Provost of the Cathedral from 1967 to 1974, writes of the sense of keen anticipation on the part of the Cathedral congregation when they learned that their former Precentor would return as Canon Theologian and Professor. He observes: 'The news of James Atkinson's return to Sheffield was met with unqualified pleasure in Cathedral circles... There was that about him that won the hearts and attention of those he came to know. He had a personal humility and grace that never dwarfed anybody, and he was friend and counsellor both to clergy and laity. He was a good listener, a man of great understanding, a man of deep caring and always uncompromising regarding truth'.

Others, in addition to the Provost, underline the special note of preaching in the ministry of James Atkinson in the parish and in the Cathedral in Sheffield. Ivor Neill notes: 'He once spoke of the pulpit as "that sacred square yard which one trod at one's peril", and that was his attitude to preaching'.

Over these years scholarship and research never failed to nourish an effective parish and Cathedral ministry. The exposition of the thought and theology of the Fourth Gospel as undertaken by the Church Fathers represented a major focus of scholarly work. This study was formally supervised at Durham by Professor (later Archbishop) Michael Ramsey, and in 1950 the University of Durham conferred on him the degree of Master of Letters for this research.

---

5.   J. Atkinson, *Luther: Early Theological Works* (Library of Christian Classics, 16; London: SCM Press), pp. 262-63.

Research and Teaching on Luther in England and Germany

The degree of MLitt established James Atkinson's formal credentials in research, and in 1951 he was appointed as the first Sir Henry Stephenson Fellow in the University of Sheffield. He held this post until 1954. His work on John, begun because, in Luther's words, this Gospel above all others sets forth Christ, nourished an ever increasing focus on Christology. But of all the writers on the Fourth Gospel, it seemed to James that Luther, more than any other, had captured the centrality of this Christological focus. Hence he turned ever more deeply and in ever more detail to Luther's thought and to Luther's writings.

We need to remind ourselves that the definitive Weimar edition of Luther's works, begun in 1883, includes numerous substantial volumes (some in parts) spanning issues concerning the Bible, theology, Luther's letters, and his Table-Talk. In addition to its supplements the American edition in English translation covers at least fifty-five solid volumes. James Atkinson set himself the task of fully engaging with all this material, as well as secondary sources. The Professor of Biblical Studies at Sheffield during this period was the first Chair-holder of the Department, namely Professor F.F. Bruce. I vividly recall F.F. Bruce's comments on how, after years of busy parish ministry, the opportunity of spending all day, every day, with Luther re-vitalized and re-transformed James Atkinson's heart and mind. F.F. Bruce observed: 'It was almost as if Luther took him over. He lived Luther, thought Luther, and breathed Luther'.

That none of this was achieved without careful critical evaluation can be seen not only from the magisterial publications on Luther's theology which later emerged, but also in the successful years spent in Germany at Münster immediately following on the Sheffield Fellowship which culminated in the conferring on him of the degree of Doctor of Theology by Münster University *magna cum laude*. This German doctorate included the intimidating *Rigorosum*, in which the candidate is closely questioned for some five hours over the whole range of theological sub-disciplines from Hebrew and biblical exegesis to historical and contemporary theology, in addition to the presentation of a substantial original thesis. During this period, a happy relationship was established with Professor Ernst Kinder, and academic advice was also received from Professor Robert Stupperich.

In 1956, after the award of the DTheol degree, James Atkinson was appointed initially as Lecturer in Theology and subsequently as Reader in the University of Hull. There he taught both biblical studies and Reformation theology, but because of his proven work on Luther, he was invited to edit his first major work, namely Luther's *Early Theological Works* published in 1962 as volume XVI of SCM's distinguished *Library of Christian Classics*. (Regrettably, this invaluable series is available in 1994 only from the American publishers, Westminster Press of Philadelphia). This Luther volume contains Luther's *Lectures on the Epistle to the Hebrews* (1517–1518), his *Disputation against Scholastic Theology* (1517), *The Heidelberg Disputation* (1518) and his *Answer to Latomus* (1521). Each is introduced with careful explanatory and theological comments by the editor, who has also translated Luther's texts into English. The translation takes meticulous account of textual-critical questions about the Latin and the Weimar edition. The treatise *Answer to Latomus* differs from George Lindbeck's translation in the American edition, which was being prepared simultaneously. Very careful attention is given to the setting of each text, even of each section, within Luther's life and the development of his thought.

Naturally enough, in this volume James Atkinson calls attention to 'Luther's fresh formulation of the person and work of Christ' in his work on the Epistle to the Hebrews. 'It was Luther's Christology that set him apart from contemporary theology and eventually shaped the new evangelical theology'.[6] I say 'naturally enough' because it was this aspect of Luther's thought, perhaps above all others, that brought about the radical deepening of faith and even closer integration between theology and life to which Professor F.F. Bruce referred in the comment noted above concerning the years of intensive Luther studies from 1951 to 1955. It also reflects part of James Atkinson's personal faith, life and theology, that in his introduction to the *Disputation against Scholastic Theology* he observes that the best among the scholastics 'taught men to think', but that, as this work began to harden into a supposedly more rigid tradition, both Erasmus and Luther found themselves opposing 'the hot-heads on one side and the die-hards on the other'.[7] Finally, in the introduction to Luther's *Answer to Latomus* (1521) we find issues which are reflected in James Atkinson's work as a teacher at Hull and at Sheffield. Life had brought constraints in the shape of imprisonment at the Wartburg, but by this time 'Luther had developed into a great

6.   *Luther: Early Theological Works*, p. 23.
7.   *Luther: Early Theological Works*, p. 251.

university teacher'.[8] He addresses the university and the Church 'by an appeal to Scripture, tradition and reason'.

While he was still at Hull, James Atkinson produced his books *Rome and Reformation* (1966) and volume 44 of the American edition of *Luther's Works: The Christian in Society*, published by Fortress Press under the general editorship of H.T. Lehmann. On the very first page of the introduction James Atkinson cites one of his favourite, most often repeated, quotations from Luther—favourite, no doubt, because it throws emphasis on the work of God, but assigns a role, even if a humble one, to the Christian preacher and writer. It comes from Luther's *Second Sermon* of 10 March 1522. Luther declares: 'All that I have done is to further, preach and teach God's Word; otherwise I have done nothing. So it happened that while I slept or while I drank a glass of Wittenberg beer...the papacy was weakened...I have done nothing; the Word alone has done and accomplished everything...I let the Word do its work.'[9] This is the basis of preaching and ethics. How people live depends on how they respond to the unceasing activity of the living God. Here lies the key to Luther's theology of the Christian in society and to James Atkinson's own teaching, life and theology.

Professor of Biblical Studies at Sheffield

James Atkinson was appointed to the Chair of Biblical History and Literature at Sheffield in 1967. Professor F.F. Bruce had held this Chair from its foundation in 1947 to 1959, when he became Rylands Professor of Biblical Criticism and Exegesis in the University of Manchester. Professor Aileen Guilding, who had been Senior Lecturer at Sheffield, succeeded to the Chair in 1959, but suffered a steady decline in health. By 1966–67 the Department had reached its lowest ebb since the first year or two of its foundation.

The Appointing Committee for the Chair rightly perceived in James Atkinson the quality which the former Provost of Sheffield, the Very Reverend Ivor Neill, correctly called his capacity 'at all times to draw the best out of people'. But James Atkinson, on his side, had reservations about a Chair of 'Biblical History and Literature' which supposedly and naively offered 'objective' or phenomenological biblical study, as if

8.   *Luther: Early Theological Works*, p. 309.
9.   J. Atkinson, *Luther's Works*. XLIV. *The Christian in Society* (Philadelphia: Fortress Press, 1966), p. xi (= LW 44.xi); cf. LW 51.77.

this could be achieved by excluding 'theology' from the discipline! The innocent naivety of such an assumption was carefully explained by the candidate with characteristic warmth, conviction and grace, and the Department placed on a new footing as the Department of 'Biblical Studies'. At James Atkinson's request his title became 'Professor of Biblical Studies'.

The Department needed the very qualities which James Atkinson could bring: personal warmth; colourful vivacity and energy; humour, care for others, vision, and above all the quality of encouraging younger colleagues and students in the worth-while character of serious intellectual and theological enquiry. The Department had reached a decisive turning-point, from which it has never looked back.

At the commencement of one of the greatest achievements of his life, however, a tragedy befell James Atkinson. His wife Laura suffered a fatal car accident. There is no need to enlarge on the details, other than to observe that over the years that followed, many were the bereaved or widowed who found in James an understanding and sensitive heart to their grief, and a wonderful ministry of renewed hope, of strength, and of new trust in God in the darkness. Here James Atkinson the pastor drew both on his own experience and on his close understanding of Luther and the Bible. Had he not translated and edited as his first major publication *Luther: Early Theological Works* in which *The Heidelberg Disputation* of April 1518 set in contrast a *theologia crucis* and a *theologia gloriae*?

Thus, with Luther, James Atkinson could speak of 'the hinder parts of God...the passion and the cross' (*Thesis* 20).[10] 'The theologian of glory says bad is good and good is bad. The theologian of the cross calls them by their proper name' (*Thesis* 21).[11] 'As long as a man does not know Christ, he does not know God as hidden in sufferings. Such a man, therefore, prefers works to sufferings, and glory to a cross... But God is not to be found except in sufferings and in the cross... The people of the cross say that the cross is good and that works are evil...' (*Proof* 21). 'Christ is his wisdom, his...all, as it says in 1 Cor. 1.30' (*Proof* 25).[12] 'Lean not on thine own understanding (Prov. 3.5)...Do what in you lies'

---

10. M. Luther, *The Heidelberg Disputation*, in J. Atkinson, *Luther: Early Theological Works*, p. 290.

11. *Luther: Early Theological Works*, p. 291.

12. *Luther: Early Theological Works*, p. 294.

(*Further Proofs* 13 and 23).[13] One of his most recent works, entitled *The Darkness of Faith* (1987), explores this theme further, rightly according to Luther's stress on the darkness of faith in the context of a *theologia crucis* the due status within recognized classics of practical Christian spirituality.

As Professor, James Atkinson made a powerful impact on his students at Sheffield, who regarded him with affection and respect. At the beginning of each academic year he would give an introductory talk in which he welcomed incoming undergraduates to the Department. He conceded that theology and biblical studies were among the simultaneously most demanding and most rewarding of all university disciplines. Yet he reassured his students with the words: 'We are all fellow-learners together, even if we have spent a life-time in the subject. For to be a "learner" is the meaning of the Greek work for a "disciple", and we can never progress beyond that.' He also stressed especially to them: 'I am always here; my door is always open'.

James Atkinson was as good as his word. He always arrived in the University Arts Tower, whatever the weather, before 8.45 each morning of the week, and never left until after 5 pm. If he left his room, there was usually some such note on the door as 'In Library; back at 10.30'. He was a role-model for work and self-discipline, and the students respected this. Their affection for him, drawn out by the warmth and openness of his personality, served to bond and to focus a sense of community within the Department, ensuring that such events as Departmental dinners were successful and supported by all staff and virtually all students. It was known that he could be awesome to any student who was consistently self-indulgent or lazy. Allusion might well be made to the habit of sponging on the taxpayer or on parents for a free ride under false pretences. But to the vulnerable or weak, the Head of Department offered encouragement and strength. In cases which required fine judgment at an Examiners' Meeting, he regularly repeated his motto that his colleagues should 'temper justice with mercy'.

Professor Atkinson fully trusted his younger colleagues in the Department. Even the students would observe in the early 1970s that he was clearly 'proud of his young men'. It is not least because of his warm personal encouragement that three of this small staff gained promotion as Reader or as Senior Lecturer under his Headship during the 1970s, and of the six of us who served under him during that decade, three are

13. *Luther: Early Theological Works*, pp. 303 and 306.

currently Professors in British Universities, one became a Reader, and two hold senior posts in America. He never 'demanded' a stream of publications; none of us felt ourselves to be under undue pressure. But such was his warmth and personal character that a climate was produced in which all *wished* to be highly productive in research and publication, and to raise the profile of the Department.

One conspicuous result of this was the founding, initially, of the *Journal for the Study of the Old Testament*, largely but not exclusively due to the vision and initiative of Professor David J.A. Clines. David Clines observed to me at the end of one long vacation: 'We have spent the entire summer working on publications commissioned by other people for their commercial benefit. Why don't we found our own press?' In due course Professor Clines, together with Dr David Gunn and Professor Philip Davies, produced the first issue in typed format in a very small room in the Arts Tower on relatively primitive equipment on a shoe-string budget. As one looks through the issues, with addition of the *Journal for the Study of the New Testament* (for which Dr David Hill became co-editor and I assisted as Advisory Editor) and then subsequently monograph supplements, each stage stands as a sign of some new advance: the first issue with 'justified margins' in both columns of the page; the advance to print-format; the improved binding; the spreading international network; the founding of Sheffield Academic Press as a major world-wide enterprise. But part of it all was the vision of a Head of Department who backed his 'young men' to make their own mark in their own way, knowing always that they had his support and encouragement. By the time that Professor John Rogerson succeeded James Atkinson as Head of Department in 1979, the Department of Biblical Studies at Sheffield had become a force to be reckoned with on the national and international league-table. With John Rogerson's arrival the Department was poised to execute John Rogerson's own vision: it became a magnet for overseas research students in biblical studies from throughout the world.

In 1972 Professor Atkinson became Public Orator of the University of Sheffield. Shortly afterwards he was also appointed Dean of the Faculty of Arts. Neither appointment caused surprise. James Atkinson passionately believed that as Head of the Department of Biblical Studies he had the duty and privilege of presenting the public face of the Department at virtually every major public event of the University. He attended most Inaugural Lectures; never missed a Civic Service or

Degree congregation; attended, in effect, every Senate and Faculty Board, every appropriate Committee. He regularly took lunch in the Staff Club, where he was known by members of every Department and Faculty. In short, he became in every sense a public and esteemed figure in the life of the University as a whole. He strongly believed in the idea of the University as a meeting of minds from all disciplines, to which Christian theology and biblical studies made an essential and distinctive contribution. As Public Orator, he spoke on behalf of the award of Honorary Degrees with a combination of impressive rhetoric, humour, and sometimes allusion to Augustine, to Luther, or to other great figures of the Church, in a manner wholly appropriate to the occasion. The words 'Chancellor I present to you as eminently worthy...' always constituted a stately and climactic conclusion.

Showing the concerns of Luther and Calvin for the education of the laity and vocations in the everyday world, Professor Atkinson also spent considerable time and energy on teaching extra-mural evening classes. He also held a firm grasp of issues in other Departments during his period as Dean of Arts, grasping nettles about staff appointments (including cessations of unsuitable appointments) which predecessors in the past had failed to tackle. He was universally respected for his vigour and integrity as Dean.

The observer might be left dumbfounded about how one man could achieve so many tasks in university life, and yet still continue his own theological work alongside regular preaching and pastoral care. The personal cost must have been considerable, but the answer remains simple. His life was transparently stamped by Luther's definition of Christian faith in his *Preface to the Epistle to the Romans* of 1522, to which I have alluded more briefly. Luther declares:

> Faith is a living, daring, confidence in God's grace, so sure and certain that a man would stake his life upon it a thousand times. This confidence in God's grace...makes men glad and bold and happy...Hence a man is ready and glad, without compulsion, to do good to everyone, to serve everyone, to suffer everything in love and praise of God who has shown him this grace.[14]

It would be hard to find a finer summary of James Atkinson's life and thought.

---

14. 'Preface to the Epistle of St Paul to the Romans', in LW 35.370-71.

The Centre for Reformation Studies and Beyond

At the age of sixty-five in 1979, James Atkinson retired in accordance with University Ordinances from his Chair and Headship of Department. As Emeritus Professor he served for an interim period as a Consultant for Latimer House Research Centre, Oxford, but his heart and home remained in Sheffield. After prolonged negotiations about premises, the University of Sheffield sponsored the founding of a Centre for Reformation Studies, of which Professor Atkinson became founder and Honorary Director. The Centre maintained active links with several University Departments. For example, in co-operation with the Department of Music under Professor E. Garden, a presentation of the relation between Reformation theology and Bach's music constituted one of the Centre's main successes.

It is a tribute to James Atkinson's tenacity that over the years he has sustained an effective range of courses, conferences, lectures and over-seas tours, all under the auspices of the Centre, sadly, against the back-ground of a hard struggle to retain even minimal facilities. The scramble for space afflicts almost every British university as each tries to achieve more 'productivity' with relatively diminishing financial resources, and Sheffield was no exception.

Nevertheless, while an outreach to the Sheffield region was sustained with considerable effort, the dimensions of James Atkinson's work became increasingly national and international. The year before his formal 'retirement' he became President of the Society for the Study of Theology. In 1980 he was elected to L'Académie Internationale des Sciences Religieuses. Throughout these years he also remained a loyal and invaluable member of the governing Council of St John's College in the University of Durham. During my period as Principal of St John's College, I recall that he only ever missed one meeting, for unavoidable reasons. As a Council member he gave the same whole-hearted attention and support to the College, which he loves, as he did to the Department in Sheffield. In particular, typically he won the affection of our students and support staff. As a good Northumbrian, he was no less concerned with the hopes and fears of receptionists, secretaries, bedders and school-leavers than with the work of the senior College Officers.

It is fitting to conclude this tribute by commenting on the stream of books from this and from earlier periods which, meanwhile, continued to make their impact on the wider world. For here we see how James

Atkinson's life and his theology cohere as one. I have already spoken of the books which he produced mainly during his period as Reader in the University of Hull, especially *Luther: Early Works* (Library of Christian Classics, 1962); *Rome and Reformation* (Hodder & Stoughton, 1965); and *Luther's Works*. XLIV. *The Christian in Society* (American edn, 1966). Probably the most influential and most widely-used of all, however, remains his *Luther and the Birth of Protestantism* (Pelican edn, 1968; trans. into Spanish in 1971, and into Italian in 1982). With this we may closely associate his two books *The Great Light: Luther and the Reformation* (Paternoster Press and Eerdmans, 1968, vol. 4 in 'The Advance of Christianity' series edited by F.F. Bruce) and his work *The Trial of Luther* (Batsford, 1971).

In his latest and most recent period, over the last decade, James Atkinson has noted with appreciation the positive evaluations of his own work on Luther which have been offered by a number of Roman Catholic specialists in the field. Increasingly he has come to see the role of Luther not simply or primarily as adversary against the Roman tradition, but as Reformer and Corrector who addresses the one Catholic Church from within a common tradition; in effect, a voice which paved the way for Vatican II ahead of its time. Hence the book *Martin Luther: Prophet to the Church Catholic* appeared in 1983, while in *The Darkness of Faith* (Darton, Longman & Todd, 1987) Luther's theology of the cross speaks at a level of an ecumenical spirituality which addresses all Christians. The 1983 work, we may remind ourselves, appropriately celebrated the five-hundredth anniversary of Luther's birth. Several shorter studies addressed specific issues indicated by their titles, including for example *Church and State under God* (Oxford: Latimer Studies, 1982) and *Christianity and Judaism* (Oxford: Latimer Studies, 1984).

All these studies call attention to strengths in Luther's theology which, if they had been heeded in later years, would have delivered the Church from pitfalls, whether in Protestant pietism, in Protestant Scholasticism, in Roman Catholic theology prior to Vatican II, or in charismatic or Pentecostal traditions within the Protestant community. Thus for example in his introduction to Luther's early commentary on Hebrews, James Atkinson observes:

> Luther emphasises faith as the work of God and not man's own... He removes it out of the realm of psychological subjectivism altogether... His emphasis here, if remembered, would have safeguarded against much

of the later misunderstanding of Protestantism on faith, and particularly how its opponents have tended to think of it. Luther keeps faith closely linked to the mercy of God and to the grace of God.[15]

This comment comes from James Atkinson's earliest major work on Luther, and is repeated and elaborated in *Martin Luther: Prophet to the Church Catholic* published twenty-one years later in 1983. I heard him expound the theme orally at the Islington Conference, London, in 1963. His sparkling exposition of Luther's influence on the English Reformers left his audience spellbound.

Six Themes in James Atkinson's Work as Theologian

In addition to this understanding of Luther as Prophet to the Church Catholic, I may suggest six further major themes which, along with others, ran throughout James Atkinson's theology and also unite as one his theology and his life.

1. James Atkinson inherits from Luther the view of theology as exegesis and critical exposition of Scripture. In *The Great Light* (1968) he writes:

> It was his work on the Bible that saved him. He was working on his lectures on the Psalms in the summer of 1513 when the familiar phrase of Psalm 31 'deliver me in thy righteousness' began to disturb him. He had always thought of the righteousness of God in its obvious meaning... He poured over the Bible to find if that, after all, was its real intent. Rom. 1.17 excited him... He still read this through scholastic spectacles... And then, as he wrestled, he realised that Paul was now arguing another case... 'When I realised this I felt myself absolutely born again. The gates of paradise had been flung open, and I had entered. There and then the whole of scripture took on another look to me'... Luther's soul was eased by an unyielding and uncompromising faith in the Bible. He wanted every man to look again with fresh eyes at God's work for man as recorded in the Bible; to see the facts for himself.[16]

James Atkinson sought to live out this aim in his work as Professor of Biblical Studies at Sheffield. He chose to lecture on the exegesis of the Greek texts of John and of Romans. The highest accolade he could give to an undergraduate was to write against an exegetical comment in an

---

15. *Luther: Early Theological Works*, p. 25.
16. Atkinson, *The Great Light*, pp. 19 and 20.

examination paper, 'Really understands Paul'. The contrast between his
exegetical method of placing students in a position to 'see with fresh
eyes' stood in contrast to some of the more consciously 'value-neutral'
hermeneutical goals of some other colleagues. The difference of approach
provided me with vivid methodological examples when discussing pre-
understanding, historicality, and Barthian interpretation in my own
advanced course on hermeneutical theory. My question: 'What are the
possible strengths and possible limitations of each method?' never failed
to provoke lively discussion among Sheffield students, with thinly veiled
allusions to their teachers.

2. This should not be taken to imply any lack of historical or linguistic
rigour in James Atkinson's work. Indeed theological, lexicographical,
historical and conceptual thinking must always be, to borrow one of his
favourite terms, 'precise'. It is often fashionable to play down an emphasis
on the role of words (as opposed to symbols, pictures or deeds) in
Reformation traditions. But understanding is articulated and tested in the
public domain in language. Thus in his section on 'Luther in his Study'
in *Martin Luther and the Birth of Protestantism* the author underlines
that 'All the terms he touched underwent a transformation', whether we
are thinking of 'sin' or 'freedom' or 'grace' or scholastic traditions, or
some other terminology.[17] How 'faith' is understood depends, as
Wittgenstein constantly stressed, on how the language about faith is
used. Both in his commentaries and most especially in his translation of
the Bible into living German, Luther wrestled constantly with issues of
meaning. James Atkinson shared the view, rightly, that all the tools
offered by humanist and Renaissance learning were essential for
Luther's work as Professor, as teacher and as translator, just as every
tool of the academic trade must be utilized critically and carefully today.
Professor Atkinson remains a meticulous scholar, part of whose passion
for truth embraces matters of sheer accuracy about sources, manuscript
variants, chronology, lexicography and conceptual clarity. He regularly
exhorted his students: 'Be more precise'.

3. James Atkinson's theology also reflects Luther's high respect for
due authority, not least in the secular state, and correspondingly his
intense dislike of egocentric egalitarianism in politics or in religion,
especially in a form which employs a legitimating appeal to charismatic
enthusiasm. We have already noted the comment, which he subsequently
repeats in different forms, that 'in Martin there is nothing of the rebel.

17. Atkinson, *Luther and the Birth of Protestantism*, p. 82.

He hated revolution and revolt, enthusiasm and excitement.'[18] Professor
Atkinson shared Luther's view of the Peasants' Revolt. He observed
that Luther 'appealed to the laity, that the noble would lead and the
peasant heed...only in the interest of the unadulterated gospel'.[19] In the
figure of Carlstadt he saw the disastrous alliance of ecclesiastical and
political radicalism. At Christmas in 1521, when Luther was absent from
Wittenberg, we are reminded in *Martin Luther and the Birth of
Protestantism*, Carlstadt

> wore lay clothes to perform the ceremony [of the mass]...denounced
> images and pictures and stirred up townsfolk to demolish and burn them.
> He opposed the baptism of infants...ridiculed theological learning...threw
> aside his priestly and academic roles...tossing his head in the airy clouds
> of communism and mysticism and appealing to his own inspiration. This
> was disastrous.[20]

In his chapter on The Peasants' War, the author continues:

> The Peasants' War was closely related to the ecclesiastical radicalism which
> broke out at Wittenberg as a result of the fanaticism of Carlstadt. Luther...
> quelled these disturbances by the sheer weight of his sensible preaching.
> But the Wittenbergers were theologically aware in a way in which the
> peasants were not...[21]

Thomas Müntzer then pushed matters further. 'He claimed to hold
secret intercourse with God and to be the recipient of supernatural
revelations.'[22] Müntzer encouraged attack on civil authorities on this
basis. Luther wrote on behalf of the God-given power of secular rulers
in his work *On the Secular Power* (1523): 'His intention was to guard
the civil authority, as he had sought to guard it from the overreaching
aggression of the Roman hierarchy'.[23] James Atkinson makes his own
evaluation clear. Luther's 'cool common sense' stands in contrast to the
'mad pseudo-theological visionaries' who appealed to some supposed
charismatic or prophetic authority of their own in order to further an
egalitarian politics of violence.

Two further important theological issues lie behind this verdict, which
we may identify as a fourth and a fifth theme in James Atkinson's own

18. *Luther: Early Theological Works*, p. 262.
19. *Luther: Early Theological Works*, p. 263.
20. Atkinson, *Luther and the Birth of Protestantism*, pp. 221-22.
21. Atkinson, *Luther and the Birth of Protestantism*, p. 237.
22. Atkinson, *Luther and the Birth of Protestantism*, p. 238.
23. Atkinson, *Luther and the Birth of Protestantism*, p. 239.

theology. The fourth relates to the special role of the law and of the state
to curb evil; the fifth reaches the very nerve-centre of a theology of
grace. For the charter of the Peasants' Revolt wedded a series of
'Christian claims' to a list of 'rights'. James Atkinson concedes that
certain 'claims' may indeed be just in themselves but only as a *general
appeal to justice, not as 'Christian' claims*. He powerfully declares:
'No *claims* of any sort can be Christian claims. For Christianity can only
give, serve, minister' (his italics).[24]

4. The fourth theological theme, then, concerns the role of the state
and of the law to curb evil. It is no accident that James Atkinson edited
the forty-fourth volume of the American edition: *Luther's Works*. XLIV.
The Christian in Society (1966). In his introduction to Luther's Treatise
*To the Christian Nobility of the German Nation concerning the Reform
of the Christian Estate* (1520), the editor explains how this treatise laid
the axe to the root of the social and political thought which had
dominated the West for a thousand years. He writes: 'Luther removed
the medieval distinction between clergy and laity and conferred upon the
state...the right and duty to curb evil no matter where it appeared'.[25]

This brings us to the two most controversial aspects of James
Atkinson's work as theologian, both of which come under this present
heading. The first concerns Luther's view of the two kingdoms. Luther
did not mince his words. He writes:

> If anyone attempted to rule the world by the gospel, and to abolish all
> temporal law and the secular sword on the plea that all are baptised and
> Christian...he would be loosing the ropes and chains of the savage wild
> beasts and letting them bite and mangle everyone... A man who would
> venture to govern an entire country of the world with the gospel would be
> like a shepherd who should place in one fold wolves, lions, eagles, and
> sheep together and let them mingle freely with one another, saying 'Help
> yourselves and be good and peaceful toward one another...' For this
> reason one must carefully distinguish between these two governments
> [these two kingdoms]...the one to produce righteousness; the other to
> bring about internal peace and prevent evil deeds (*Temporal Authority: To
> What Extent it Should be Obeyed* 1523).[26]

James Atkinson openly advocates this currently unfashionable view.
During the Miners' Strike of the early 1970s Professor Ninian Smart

24. Atkinson, *Luther and the Birth of Protestantism*, p. 241.
25. LW 44.120.
26. *Luther's Works*. XLV. *The Christian Society II* (Philadelphia: Mühlenberg
Press, 1962), pp. 91-92 (= LW 45.91-92).

visited the Department of Biblical Studies in the University of Sheffield. Both held passionate convictions about the strike; both contended for justice. But it gradually emerged that while the issue for Professor Smart was whether a fair day's wage was given for a fair day's work, the issue for Professor Atkinson was whether a fair day's work was given for a fair day's wage. His background in the North East added to his sympathy for the miners; but this did not exempt anyone from observing the boundaries of due law and order. This very concern, however, also influenced the way in which James Atkinson, as Professor, defended the weak and vulnerable. When he saw himself as sometimes standing *in loco parentis*, this was not to patronize the student, but to offer protection and defence, or to curb evil where evil held sway, as a properly appointed authority. For at the root of a doctrine of the two kingdoms lies a realistic doctrine of human fallenness and sin, and a rejection of the illusory optimism of liberal humanism.

The other side of this doctrine, still under the fifth heading, concerns a revaluation of the relation between presbyters and laity, and an attack on clericalism. Once again, behind James Atkinson's convictions as theologian stands a treatise, or several treatises, from Luther, in this case especially Luther's work *On the Appointment of Ministers* (1523). Luther insisted here that the term 'priest' applies to all Christian believers. There are indeed those who are called 'to preside over the sacraments of the Word among the people', but these 'neither can nor ought to be called priests'. Luther viewed this as a 'borrowing from heathen ritual' or 'a relic from Jewish practice...' According to the Gospel writings, Luther urged, they would be better named 'ministers, deacons, bishops, stewards, presbyters'. James Atkinson had less terminological reservations about the word 'priest', provided that its proper meaning was understood. But he insisted: 'The clergy are not distinguished by some indelible character given at ordination, but they are set apart to do the particular work of a priest within that community of which they are all alike constituted members by virtue of God's calling'.[27]

The arrogance of the supposed 'spiritual estate' of popes, bishops, priests and monks, as against the 'secular estate' of princes, lords, artisans and peasants, James Atkinson found difficult to overlook. In human life, the warm-hearted Professor would overflow in his teaching sometimes with anecdotal examples drawn from church life. His unforgettable tale

---

27. Atkinson, *The Great Light*, p. 58.

about an Anglican bishop who wore matching purple stock, purple shirt, purple this and that, 'even...[dramatic pause for emphasis]... purple socks' seemed fair game. But there were also plenty of stories about monks and nuns. One Irish Roman Catholic priest commented quietly in my ear: 'I have never met before such a saintly, lovable, godly, wonderful, bigoted man in all my life'.

5. The fifth strand in James Atkinson's work as a theologian reveals the basis for this indignation over implicit claims for privileged spiritual status. Everything flows from divine grace, freely given. Hence, as Paul expresses it: 'What have you that you did not receive? If then you received it, why do you boast as if it were not a gift?' (1 Cor. 4.7).

If any biblical text might be identified as James Atkinson's own, it is 'Freely you have received; freely give' (Mt. 10.8). I made this observation at the beginning of this tribute, but repeat it because it says everything about the man and his living and thinking. This was the source of his energy, his joy, his infectious enthusiasm for the Bible and for theology, and of the gladness which he always seems to show in giving of his time and of himself. I have always envied him his unpharisaic capacity never to measure how much he gave or how much he did.

Although this is a tribute to honour a great Churchman, Professor and Theological Scholar, it would be a mistake to paint a picture so utterly unflawed as to seem artificial, unreal and unconvincing. With some hesitation, therefore, we may perhaps raise one question. Could this very central nerve 'freely you have received; freely give' sometimes conceivably offer in certain circumstances a potential trap? James Atkinson lived out the Sermon on the Mount. When he was due to preach on a major occasion, but also received a cluster of invitations to teach a small evening class or address a small group of students, he would quote to himself 'Give to him who asks' (Mt. 5.42). Since God has given without stint in measure 'pressed down and running over', who cannot share this unmeasured loving and giving? But what if one's time for preparation remains limited, even when one stays up late and rises very early to be constantly at one's desk?

With great affection one or two of my former colleagues and I recall times of such immense pressure, when our Head of Department would ask with great humility and diffidence whether we might suggest something very *brief* to stimulate his mind on a given topic! Nine times out of ten, at very least, his preaching and lecturing were unsurpassed and spellbinding. But from time to time he clearly was tired, and was 'thinking on his feet'. Yet this was for the sake of the gospel. And who could say what should have been omitted from that daunting list of commitments? History tells of many blessings brought about because the right person was there to speak at the right time. Moreover, I should not have liked to be the one omitted from the list. For me, he always kept his word: 'Whenever you need me, I am here'.

6. What better reflection and example could introduce the climactic, perhaps central theme of James Atkinson's theology? In Luther's words, everything serves the single goal of 'setting forth Christ'. If James Atkinson drove himself gladly to spend and to be spent in the service of God and of others, was this not because it was the way of Christ himself? Once again, he lectured on Romans to communicate to his students the reality of divine grace; he chose to lecture on John, to communicate the reality of Christ. But just as in John, the word would have remained empty without the deeds of the enfleshed life, so, too, students would see Christ before them in life as well as in thought.

If the reader insists in looking for possible blemishes it may be honest to concede that James Atkinson's approach to the Fourth Gospel remains controversial. He made much of the view that John's direct access to the Jerusalem traditions accounts adequately for many of the differences that mark it off from the Synoptists' dependence on Galilean traditions. He held this view with conviction and passion, and some colleagues felt that students were insufficiently exposed to its problems. But James Atkinson gave only as much attention to the technical questions of 'New Testament Introduction' as was essential in order to grasp the meaning and message of the content of the New Testament in its proper historical, social and linguistic context. He approached New Testament studies in the very opposite way to that once identified and deeply lamented by Professor Daniel Hardy when he observed, on the occasion of some interviews for a University appointment, 'Most of the candidates in New Testament seem to have chosen a research field which allows them to do everything except get to grips with what the New Testament is about'. On this matter James Atkinson and Dan Hardy share a common, if not always fashionable, vision.

James Atkinson has never merely followed some 'school', whether it be ecclesial party or some fashion in biblical studies. His one single focus, as he quotes the words from Luther, is that 'I and mine will contend for the sole and whole doctrine of Christ, who is our sole master'.[28]

I have left until the very end mention of one further vehicle through which James Atkinson furthered this end. Many are those throughout Britain, Germany, America, and beyond, who have recognized his careful handwriting on an envelope and opened a letter with keen anticipation. Some things are too intimate to place in the public domain. But I know that I am not alone in being warmed by James Atkinson's deeply sensitive letters which also witness to his infectious and robust, joyous, confident, trust in the mercy and calling of God in Christ. On my desk is a letter which begins 'My dear Tony' and ends with an exegetical and theological comment on the Greek text of 1 Thess. 5.24: 'Faithful (emphatic word order) is he who is calling you (present tense) and he also will carry it through'. Even in private letters, James Atkinson remains to the end a visionary and faithful theologian, professor and churchman.

This final allusion to letter-writing also completes our survey of the seven modes of discourse through which James Atkinson fulfilled his vocation as theologian, as professor and as churchman. He spoke through (1) exegetical commentary on biblical texts, (2) theological work on specific themes, (3) lectures on Christian doctrine, (4) sermons, (5) disputation for the reform of the church, (6) material of a kind that pupils of Luther or of Barth called 'table-talk', and (7) letters of spiritual counsel. I cannot believe that the parallel with those seven modes of discourse in *Luther's Works* arises from mere accident, still less from deliberate imitation. Each mode of discourse plays a constructive part uniting together the singleness of purpose of the man, the mind, and his ministry, and in furthering his work as theologian, professor and churchman. In each rings out the central theme: 'Freely you have received; freely give'. Here is the focus that draws into one James Atkinson's words and deeds, his heart and mind, and, in effect, Bible, Reformation and Church.

28. Atkinson, *Luther and the Birth of Protestantism*, p. 254.

PAUL AND THE INTROSPECTIVE CONSCIENCE

C.K. Barrett

It may seem ungracious to resurrect a controversy in which two distinguished theologians engaged a quarter of a century ago, a controversy which, at least in explicit terms, seems in these days to awaken few echoes. Perhaps it should be regarded as settled. But it calls to mind not only two of the most important New Testament theologians of our own age but also the greatest theologian of the first Christian generation (and perhaps of any generation) and another who comes not far short of him. And I doubt whether the last word on the matter has been said yet. It is probably true that it has been obscured by more recent controversies, not identical with it but related to it, and these cannot be entirely excluded from this discussion.

Everyone knows that in 1976 (a year later in Great Britain) Krister Stendahl republished in *Paul among Jews and Gentiles*[1] a paper which had previously appeared in the *Harvard Theological Review* (56 [1963]); it had originally been published in Swedish in *Svensk Exegetisk Årsbok* (25 [1960]). This was 'The Apostle Paul and the Introspective Conscience of the West'. The publication in *HTR* provoked a vigorous response by Ernst Käsemann in one of the lectures printed in *Paulinische Perspektiven*.[2] This volume was later (1971) translated into English,[3] and Dr Stendahl printed a rejoinder in an appendix to *Paul among Jews and Gentiles*.[4]

---

1. (Philadelphia: Fortress Press, 1976), pp. 78-96.
2. (Tübingen: Mohr [Siebeck], 1969), pp. 108-39.
3. *Perspectives on Paul* (Philadelphia: Fortress Press, 1971).
4. See pp. 129-33.

Dr Stendahl's starting-point (and I cannot in this paper go very much further than his starting-point) may be given best in his own words.

> Especially in Protestant Christianity—which, however, at this point has its roots in Augustine and in the piety of the Middle Ages—the Pauline awareness of sin has been interpreted in the light of Luther's struggle with his conscience. But it is exactly at that point that we can discern the most drastic difference between Luther and Paul, between the 16th and the 1st century, and, perhaps, between Eastern and Western Christianity.[5]

This is not merely a matter of psychology, for 'Paul's statements about "justification by faith" have been hailed as the answer to the problem which faces the ruthlessly honest man in his practice of introspection' (p. 79). What then are the roots of Paul's doctrine of justification by faith, and is the doctrine rightly regarded as central in his understanding of the Gospel? The questions may be given historical and theological sharpness if they are reworded as, Did Luther understand or misunderstand Paul? In answering the need of those who, like himself, asked, 'How can I find a gracious God?' did he, as an interpreter of Paul, and did the Protestant tradition as a whole, lead the seekers astray?[6] The doctrine of justification did not arise out of the troubles of Paul's conscience (which was 'robust', p. 80); and it was rather his way of vindicating his mission to the Gentiles, a theme worked out with special force and clarity in Romans 9–11, chapters which thus constitute essentially Paul's *Heilsgeschichte*.

It must be remembered that Dr Käsemann's reaction to this is contained in one of four lectures on Paul delivered in America, where Dr Stendahl's lecture had recently been published and might be expected to be especially influential. The title of the lecture is 'Rechtfertigung und Heilsgeschichte im Römerbrief', and one suspects that the theme may have been settled independently of the essay. Dr Käsemann could see that what he had to say about justification and *Heilsgeschichte* would be nullified if Dr Stendahl's thesis were accepted, and therefore felt obliged to attack it, though without offering the detailed exegetical reply that Dr Stendahl evidently felt that he had a right to expect.[7] To some extent this deficiency is made up in Dr Käsemann's commentary on Romans

5. *Paul among Jews and Gentiles*, p. 79.
6. *Paul among Jews and Gentiles*, pp. 82-83.
7. *Paul among Jews and Gentiles*, p. 131.

(of which Dr Stendahl speaks with great respect[8]), but only to some extent. I have noted only two references to Dr Stendahl in the commentary. His name does not appear in the general bibliography. His article 'Rechtfertigung und Endgericht'[9] is mentioned in the bibliography to 2.1-11 (p. 49) but it is not taken up in the exposition that follows. 'The Introspective Conscience' occurs in the bibliography to 9.6-13 (p. 251) and again in the argument (pp. 254-55), but the point at issue is the relation between justification and *Heilsgeschichte*; on this see below. In any case, Dr Stendahl supports his view with the observation that though we read much of righteousness and justification in Romans and Galatians, there is little of them elsewhere in the Pauline corpus. Dr Käsemann, however, both in *Perspektiven* and in the commentary maintains the centrality of justification in Paul's thought and its importance as a key to his writings.

It could hardly be said that the two primary contestants had said everything that is to be said on the issue, though as far as I am aware little has been done to follow it up since 1977. There have been not a few articles and books on Paul, including a group of major commentaries on Romans, but though 'the introspective conscience of the West' has become a familiar phrase this application of it has tended to fall out of sight.[10] This is partly because it may seem to have been absorbed in the discussion of the Law generated by E.P. Sanders and taken up many others.[11] If the Law was a covenant of grace, what room was there for a tormented conscience? What could it be but an unnecessary aberration? Perhaps on this matter also there is more to be said, though here only allusively. I have touched briefly on the main issue in one or two other places,[12] but it seems a suitable theme with which to salute one who is expert in both biblical and Luther studies.[13]

Did Paul have an introspective conscience? The answer is that he

8.   *Paul among Jews and Gentiles*, p. 129.

9.   *Lutherische Rundschau* 11 (1961), pp. 3-10.

10. See however J.M. Espy, 'Paul's "Robust Conscience" Re-examined', *NTS* 31 (1985), pp. 161-88.

11. The discussion begins with E.P. Sanders, *Paul and Palestinian Judaism* (London: SCM Press, 1977), which is still of fundamental importance.

12. See M.D. Meeks (ed.), *What Should Methodists Teach?* (1990), pp. 41-42, and *Paul: An Introduction to his Thought*, to be published by Geoffrey Chapman in 1994.

13. And I do not forget that James and I first met at a gathering of the Luther-Akademie at Goslar in 1953.

certainly did, but the question before us is not immediately settled by this answer. A conscience is nothing if not introspective; there is nowhere else it can look but within, that is, into an awareness of previous actions (which of course must include words and thoughts) and of their relation to some accepted standard of right and wrong. A conscience operating in this way is implied in 1 Cor. 4.4, where the verb σύνοιδα is the etymological partner of the noun συνείδησις and the sentence is properly translated, 'I have nothing on my conscience', that is, I can see in my remembered actions (in the area under consideration) nothing that I now believe to be wrong.[14] Such passages must not be over-interpreted or taken outside the field to which they belong. Paul means that in his dealings with (for example) the Corinthians he has no regrets. What he has done he would in like circumstances do again. His words make no claim to total moral perfection. Paul assumes too that others equally have consciences and may legitimately pass judgment on his (as well as their own) behaviour. Thus he commends himself to the consciences of all (2 Cor. 4.2): let them judge fairly how he has conducted himself. They may not judge correctly, for conscience in itself is not infallible. There were in Corinth those who passed a judgment different from his own on Paul's apostolic conduct. There are those whose conscience is weak, those for example who judge that to eat meat that has been offered in sacrifice to an idol is to participate in idolatry and is thus a wicked act which is displeasing to God. They are mistaken: to eat εἰδωλόθυτα is not in itself wicked but indifferent. The conscience of the weak is in error, but the conscience of the strong is deficient too, because it fails to tell them that wilful disobedience to whatever is believed—however mistakenly—to be God's will, and to act with love-less disregard of others, are both sinful.[15] These passages are of great importance, not only because they show that the conscience, though important, is a fallible moral guide, but because they point beyond conscience to a higher, to the only absolute, authority. The point is made explicitly by a fuller consideration of 1 Cor. 4.4 in its context: 'To me it is a matter of the smallest importance that I should be examined by you, or by any human assize; nay, indeed, I do not even examine myself. For though I have nothing on my conscience it is not by that that I am justified. He who examines me is the Lord.' It is not the verdict of my

14. Cf. Acts 23.1; 24.16. These sentences may or may not have been spoken by Paul; they show an understanding of συνείδησις current in Pauline circles.
15. See 1 Cor. 8–10; Rom. 14; 15.

conscience or the verdict of the moral examination conducted by others that I should be either pleased or distressed about. There is only one Judge, and it is his verdict that I must dread—unless I have good reason for doing otherwise. The same point is made in a different way in 1 Corinthians 8, where it is clear that the conscience of one Christian declares, It is wrong to eat εἰδωλόθυτα, and of another, This is an adiaphoron; eat what you please. It is clear that the conscience of one of these fellow Christians is mistaken and misleading. The truth is with God.

To say this is not to say that conscience is of no importance or that its judgments may be ignored. A human being's 'conscience is not so much the bar at which his conduct is tried, as a major witness, which may be called on either side as the case may be'.[16] This is the meaning of Rom. 2.15-16, where the conscience plays its part not in directing behaviour during a person's lifetime but on Judgment Day (the day when God judges the secret things of all—hidden from others and to some extent from themselves). The conscience bears witness jointly with the Law[17] to wrongdoing. The operation of the conscience is described in the clause that follows—their inward thoughts in mutual debate accuse or else excuse them. In this thought, and in the use of the word συνείδησις, Paul is following Stoic models.[18]

The conscience then is essentially (but it cannot be claimed that Paul's use of the word is rigidly consistent) not judge but witness, and a forensic process will normally begin only with some external judicial authority to set it in motion. This will most evidently happen at the Last Day, at Judgment Day, and it is God who holds assize and summons the witnesses. But since God is always Judge (whatever else he may be) his presence will always have the same effect of setting judgment in motion. Did Paul know this for himself? That he had an introspective conscience has been claimed simply on the basis of the observation that conscience is always and necessarily introspective since there is nowhere else for it to look: my conscience examines and assesses my behaviour, including of course its inward motivation. We must now go on to ask, Did the

16. C.K. Barrett, *The Epistle to the Romans* (BNTC; London: A. & C. Black, 2nd edn, 1991), p. 51.

17. συμμαρτυρεῖ—Paul does not say with what or whom the conscience bears joint testimony, but it is hard to understand anything other than the Law.

18. For a wide range of material see C. Maurer, *ThWNT*, VII, pp. 897-906.

inward investigating gaze of his conscience cause Paul acute unhappiness, a sense of hopelessness, of perdition?

Dr Stendahl considers Rom. 7.7-25, a paragraph that has divided interpreters in more ways than one.[19] It is important to remember that Paul did not set out in this paragraph to present a psychological analysis of the soul in its sickness. His intention is to answer the question, made inevitable by 7.1-6 and other passages, Is the Law sin? It is so closely associated with sin that it might seem to be identified with it. The question has to be taken seriously, but there is no doubt about the answer: μὴ γένοιτο (Rom. 7.7). Yet there is more to say, The Law, holy, righteous, good, spiritual as it is, proves to facilitate the entrance of sin and becomes its agent. The evil I would not do, yet practise, is the work of sin which dwells within me. Dr Stendahl rightly makes, with great emphasis, the point that the paragraph contains 'a defence for the holiness and goodness of the Law'.[20] From this he proceeds to an evaluation of the anthropological references in Romans 7 as 'means for a very special argument about the holiness and goodness of the Law. The possibility of a distinction between the good Law and the bad Sin is based on the rather trivial observation that every man knows that there is a difference between what he ought to do and what he does. This distinction makes it possible for Paul to blame Sin and Flesh, and to rescue the Law as a good gift of God. "If I now do what I do not want, I agree with the Law [and recognize] that it is good" (v. 16). That is all, but that is what should be proven' (i.e., that is what Paul means to prove).[21]

There are, as we shall observe, questions to raise in regard to the setting of the inward struggle (note the words ἀντιστρατευόμενον and αἰχμαλωτίζοντα in v. 23) described in this paragraph, but it is hard to see how anyone can draw from v. 17 the conclusion that 'the argument is one of acquittal of the ego, not one of utter contrition',[22] as if Paul were saying, The Law is good, I am good, it is only these impersonal factors, Sin and Flesh, that cause the trouble. It need not be said that

19. For the history of interpretation see the Commentaries of C.E.B. Cranfield ([2 vols.; Edinburgh: T. & T. Clark, 1975, 1979] I, pp. 340-47), U. Wilckens ([3 vols.; Zürich: Neukirchener Verlag, 1978] II, pp. 101-17), E. Käsemann ([Tübingen: Mohr (Siebeck), 1980], pp. 183-204), and J.D.G. Dunn ([2 vols.; Dallas: Word Books, 1988] I, pp. 378-99).

20. *Paul among Jews and Gentiles*, p. 92.

21. *Paul among Jews and Gentiles*, p. 93. The 'rather trivial observations' gave Luther years of hell.

22. *Paul among Jews and Gentiles*, p. 93.

there are details of Dr Stendahl's interpretation of the passage that are perceptive and true; but his treatment is selective. Sin worked in me πᾶσαν ἐπιθυμίαν; sin came to life and I died; sin... killed me; I am a man of flesh (σάρκινος), sold as a slave so as to be under the power of sin; what I hate [not, what I mildly disapprove], that I do; no good thing dwells in me, that is, in my flesh; sin that dwells in me; there is imposed upon me, who would do what is good and right, a law, to the effect that evil shall always attend me.

A war between two laws is raging within him, and the better part is taken prisoner by the law of sin. No wonder he cries out, ταλαίπωρος ἐγὼ ἄνθρωπος. If this passage does not depict a man profoundly conscious of division and conflict within himself it is hard to know what it is about. True, it is about the virtue of the Law. True, therefore, that the anthropological material is in a sense incidental. But it is not accidental that the anthropological material is introduced. Paul is capable on occasion of using mythological language, but he knows that in fact the scene of the battle between good and evil is the human heart, and that he had been—or was—involved in it.

I have discussed the interpretation of Rom. 7.7-25 elsewhere[23] and must not here simply repeat myself. The one exegetical point that it may be worth while to pick up is the meaning of the word *flesh*, σάρξ. It is essential to Dr Stendahl's argument that 'the "I", the *ego*, is not simply identified with Sin and Flesh' (p. 92). This will perhaps stand if the word *simply* is emphasized as strongly as possible, but it is nearer to the truth to say that σάρξ denotes not an alien body and not a part, a 'lower' or 'unspiritual' part of the self; it is rather the self devoted to itself,[24] neglectful of God and of the neighbour because it is devoted, as by nature it is, to its own interests and concerns. The clearest of all passages is Gal. 5.13-24, where the double contrast, between flesh and love and between flesh and (Holy) Spirit, is made explicit. The contrast with love indicates that flesh denotes egocentric existence; it is not a contrast with or denial of the ego but an unbridled affirmation of it. The contrast with Spirit means that the ego has no means of ejecting itself from the centre of its own existence; the most it can—in the nature of things—achieve is

23. *Romans*, pp. 130-44.

24. Cf. Luther's famous phrase, *cor incurvatum in se*; also his comment (WA 56.347) on Rom. 7.25: 'Non enim ait: mens mea servit legi Dei, nec: caro mea legi peccati, sed: ego, inquit, totus homo, persona eadem, servio utranque servitutem. Ideo et gratias agit, quod servit legi Dei, et misericordiam querit, quod servit legi peccati.'

a transformation of irreligious self-centredness into religious self-centredness, and the latter is usually more objectionable than the former, and harder to eradicate. Transformation is possible only when the ego is replaced as the controlling centre by the Spirit of God. The nature of the transformation is determined by the way in which egocentricism has previously been expressed. Of fornicators, idolaters, adulterers, catamites, sodomites, thieves, the rapacious, drunkards, the abusive, robbers, Paul can say only, ταῦτά τινες ἦτε (1 Cor. 6.11): that is what you were but have now ceased to be. The old way of life has gone. It is not so easy to point out a difference in the way of life of the man who lived under the rule of the religious flesh. The practices of religion may be little changed, if changed at all, but they acquire a new meaning. When to the Jews Paul the apostle became as if he were a Jew (1 Cor. 9.20) the religious practices that he observed he observed with a new motive, that of winning his fellow Jews for Christ.

The transformation is never described by Paul in psychological or moral terms—that is, in regard to himself. The passage just quoted from 1 Corinthians gives a clear indication of the moral transformation experienced by some of the Corinthian Christians. The change in Paul from persecutor to preacher (Gal. 1.23) might be described as a moral transformation but it was not of the same kind: before it and afterwards he believed—with good conscience—that he was acting in obedience to the will of God. The righteousness in which he was faultless (ἄμεμπτος, Phil. 3.6) certainly included obedience to Thou shalt not steal and Thou shalt not commit adultery; and if there was a sense in which he did not observe Thou shalt not kill (Acts 8.1; 26.10) it was done in the best of causes and for the glory of God. The moment of conversion[25] is described unambiguously in Gal. 1.15-16—unambiguously, but without content beyond the central fact that it meant God's manifestation of his risen Son, Jesus Christ. No moral or psychological accompaniments or consequences (beyond Gal. 1.23) are mentioned. The same is true of other references to the appearance of the risen Christ (1 Cor. 9.1; 15.8).[26] There is more information in Philippians 3, but it is almost

25. Which was at the same time a commissioning to apostolic service.

26. The narratives in Acts (9.1-18; 22.6-16; 26.9-18) describe supernatural phenomena—light, blindness, a fall, and so on—which must have been inseparable from, if they are not mythological objectifications of, inward psychological reactions, but they are not related to the conscience. Somewhat surprisingly, the words 'I am Jesus whom you are persecuting' do not elicit a prayer for pardon.

confined to the two words κέρδος and ζημία (3.7, 8; with ζημιοῦν and σκύβαλα). To reverse one's estimate of a significant feature of one's life from positive to negative is a revolutionary act which belongs to the realm of the conscience and can hardly fail to be profoundly disturbing; incidentally it casts a good deal of light on the way in which Paul understood the righteousness that is based on and arises out of law. His Jewish descent, his Pharisaic attitude to the Law, his zeal for Judaism, expressed in persecution of the church, his law-based righteousness, were credits (κέρδη) in his account, which clearly he had in the past regarded as desirable assets. The abandonment of this outlook must have caused a measure of distress—even if also of relief.

Yet Paul had a conscience; and he knew something of the torments that religion can inflict upon its devotees. The old debate about Romans 7—does it refer to Paul's pre-Christian or to his Christian life?—is an over-simplification, and Origen's compromise (*inter regenerandum*) is not the way out. Paul is writing, with the vividness and in the personal terms of one who had himself passed that way, of the relation of human life to the Law of God when this is seen *coram Deo*. Of course the Law is gracious and good, but the holiness of the Law is my condemnation, and the judge who condemns is a more formidable dicast than my conscience. It is God himself, and the Law (which indeed has other functions too) compels me to take him seriously, joined as it is by its fellow witness, conscience. Paul had always been a religious man, but it was a fresh encounter with God, taken seriously as never before because now apparent in the crucified (crucified with his own consent and approval if not by his action) yet now living Jesus, that opened his eyes to the full meaning of life as it had been, and, even after the thanksgiving of Rom. 7.25a, still was. Paul knows the terror of the Lord, exposed as he is to God (2 Cor. 5.10, 11: θεῷ δὲ πεφανερώμεθα).

It is at this point that we may turn to Luther. Important though this aspect of the question is, I shall follow the examples of both Dr Stendahl and Dr Käsemann in treating it more briefly. Dr Käsemann of course is much less concerned with the psychological issue and more concerned with the alternatives, if they are alternatives, justification and *Heilsgeschichte*.

Every student of Luther is aware of the *Anfechtungen* with which he was constantly beset. This is no place for a full discussion of the *Anfechtungen*, nor am I competent to give one; a few points only need be made. The German word is almost unavoidable; there is no English word that adequately expresses its meaning. *Temptation* is sometimes used, but it is misleading. *Depression* is worse. Rupp[27] suggests that we may 'employ John Bunyan's tremendous phrase "the bruised conscience"', and it is true that there are analogies between Bunyan and Luther (differences, too), true also that the conscience is involved in *Anfechtungen*, but a bruised, wounded conscience is rather the effect of *Anfechtungen* than *Anfechtungen* themselves. *Fechten* is *to fight*, *anfechten* is *to attack*, and *Anfechtungen* are attacks made from what-ever quarter upon the inward being and the peace of man. Luther was subject to them through the whole of his adult life; and without them his theology would have been far less profound than it was. It owed its strength to the fact that it had been fought for. Paradoxically, the adversary was sometimes the devil and sometimes God; it is bad enough when the devil questions a man's relation with God, worse still when God himself questions it.

> The whole meaning of 'Anfechtung' for Luther lies in the thought that man has his existence 'Coram Deo', and that he is less the active intelligence imposing itself on the stuff of the universe around him, than the subject of an initiative and action from God who employs the whole of man's existence as a means of bringing men to awareness of their need and peril.[28]

The familiar story of Luther's first mass gives the essentials of Luther's position in vivid form. To recite the words beginning *Te igitur clementissime Pater* was almost too much for him.

> At these words I was utterly stupefied and terror-stricken. I thought to myself, 'With what tongue shall I address such Majesty, seeing that all men ought to tremble in the presence of even an earthly prince? Who am I, that I should lift up mine eyes or raise my hands to the divine Majesty? The angels surround him. At his nod the earth trembles. And shall I, a miserable little pygmy, say 'I want this, I ask for that'? For I am dust and ashes and full of sin and I am speaking to the living, eternal and the true God.

27. G. Rupp, *The Righteousness of God* (London: Hodder & Stoughton, 1953), p. 106.

28. Rupp, *Righteousness*, p. 106. I cannot forbear to add here a reference to that profoundly theological novel, G.K. Chesterton's *The Man who was Thursday*.

'The terror of the Holy, the horrors of Infinitude, smote him like a new lightning bolt, and only through a fearful restraint could he hold himself at the altar to the end.'[29]

Conscience does indeed enter the process, but (just as with Paul) primarily as a witness, not as judge. 'Ihm [Luther] blieb in aller seiner Verwirrung sein Gewissen allein der unverrückte Massstab, nach dem er sein Verhältnis zu Gott beurteilte.'[30] But important as the conscience is he can appeal against the conscience to God.

> Der Aufrichtige muss glauben, dass ihm in der Anfechtung Gott selbst begegnet ist, er muss gewissenshalber glauben, dass das Gericht über ihn Gottes letztes Wort wäre. Und trotzdem soll er wiederum glauben, dass das Gericht über ihn nicht das letzte Wort sei, dass der Gott, der ihm in gerechtem Zorn gegenübertrat, doch nicht der 'wirkliche' Gott sei...[31]

Anfechtungen did not end with Luther's discovery of the true meaning of righteousness and justification, but they did to some extent change their character and took the form partly of the opposition he had to endure[32] and partly the nagging fear lest he, standing alone as he had so often been obliged to do, had after all been mistaken and had led half Christendom astray. He was encouraged and to some extent consoled by the reflection that many of the great men of the Bible had been in the same position. It is in this period that *Anfechtungen* are mainly the work of the devil.

The fact that *Anfechtungen* persisted to the end of his life is a clear indication that to treat them as a condition for the understanding of justification, and as brought to an end when justification is received by faith, is a serious misunderstanding, though it is a misunderstanding that has deep Lutheran roots. It is found as early as the *Confessio Augustana*.

> Quanquam autem haec doctrina contemnitur ab imperitis, tamen experiuntur piae ac pavidae conscientiae plurimum eam consolationis afferre, quia conscientiae non possunt reddi tranquillae per ulla opera, sed tantum fide, cum certo statuunt, quod propter Christum habeant placatum Deum, quemadmodum Paulus docet Rom. 5: Iustificati per fidem, pacem

29. I take the translation and the comment from R.H. Bainton, *Here I Stand* (New York: Meutor, 1955), p. 30.

30. K. Holl, *Gesammelte Aufsätze zur Kirchengeschichte*. I. *Luther* (1921), p. 24.

31. Holl, *Gesammelte Aufsätze*, p. 61; with n. 4.

32. See the passages quoted in J. Atkinson, *Luther: Prophet to the Church Catholic* (Exeter: Paternoster; Grand Rapids: Eerdmans, 1983), pp. 206-11.

habemus apud Deum. Tota haec doctrina ad illud certamen perterrefactae conscientiae referenda est nec sine illo certamine intelligi potest (XX 15–17).

The last sentence is not contained in the German text; and one looks in vain in both the Large Catechism and the Small for any suggestion that to be a true Christian one must pass through the struggle that the *Confessio* describes. Perhaps the word *intelligi* must be stressed: the fact that some have passed through the *certamen* enables the rest of Christians to understand and value the justification that they have received at less cost to themselves.

This discussion has shown that there is a difference between the experiences of Paul and of Luther on their way to and in faith. For pointing out the existence of a difference we must be grateful to Dr Stendahl. But the difference is more complicated than his description of it, and there is a resemblance which he did not observe, and which Dr Käsemann, whose interest was somewhat different, did not point out. Both Paul and Luther had introspective consciences and each of them found his conscience awakened at the point of the discovery that he stood *coram Deo*, and in the presence of a God defined in terms that were new to him. Paul, in the first Christian generation, made the discovery in the last (1 Cor. 15.8) of the resurrection appearances; for him, from the moment when God revealed his Son (Gal. 1.15-16), God could be understood only as the one who raised from death the Friend of sinners and thereby manifested a love otherwise unknown (Rom. 5.8). Before this there had been no occasion for *certamen*; there was now, and the clear evidence for it arises with (Phil. 3.7-9) and after the moment of conversion. The infant Martin Luther was baptized into the Christian tradition. It was a tradition that was in need, as few would now deny, of some kind of reformation, but at least it told him of a God who claimed him and would on certain terms accept him. They were terms that many could accept and apply; but they were terms that, as he understood them, called for perfect *contritio* and more than Augustinian ascetic discipline. His blameless behaviour as a monk corresponded to Paul's blameless righteousness of law (Phil. 3.6), but precisely because of the tradition in which he stood Luther himself knew that monastic perfection did not suffice. His *certamen* (or some aspects of it) came to an end where Paul's began, with the discovery of a gracious God.[33] For

33. No doubt—we are grateful to E.P. Sanders for emphasizing it—the gracious God was there in Judaism; but that is not where Paul found him. My own gratitude

both, the way ahead meant 'unus et idem homo simul servit legi Dei et legi peccati, simul justus est et peccat!'[34]

No more for Paul than for Luther was justification an instrument for validating the line of missionary work that he had adopted. Not that it was unrelated to the mission to the Gentiles. The doctrine and the mission ran side by side, each supporting and each deepening the other. As for *Heilsgeschichte*, it is a term that can be made to mean almost anything the user wishes,[35] and we might be better off without it. If it is construed to mean that the principle of justification was one that served its turn at a certain point—an important point—in the first century, it is misleading. If it means that justification by faith is a basic principle of God's dealing with his creatures, worked out in different ways in the story of a Paul and the story of a Luther, it is, near enough, the whole of *Heil* and the better part of *Geschichte*.

for this goes back to H.M.J. Loewe, many years ago Reader in Rabbinics at Cambridge.

34. In the passage quoted above, n. 24.

35. Käsemann, *Perspektiven*, p. 112: 'Ich habe nichts gegen das Wort "heilsgeschichtlich", obgleich mir seine Verwendung oft fragwürdig erscheint, und meine sogar, dass man die Bibel im allgemeinen und Paulus im besonderen ohne die heilsgeschichtliche Perspektive nicht begreifen kann. Umgekehrt sollte man dieses Wort nicht aus der mit ihm verbundenen Problematik herausnehmen und wie alle gefährlichen Worte möglichst genau definieren'.

JOB AND THE SPIRITUALITY OF THE REFORMATION

David J.A. Clines

In the introduction to his excellent anthology of writings on the book of Job, Nahum N. Glatzer comments that, with some notable exceptions, 'Jewish interpreters in the premodern period Judaized Job and Christian expositors Christianized him'.[1] Even in the modern period, he observes, 'the interpreter's intellectual preoccupation still tends to determine his reading of the book and causes an adaptation of Job to his own thinking or needs'.[2] For Glatzer, as for many scholars, such interpretations 'advance our understanding of the book very little' and invite merely the condemnation or the scorn of readers at the ingenuity of older interpreters in 'bypassing the stubborn soil of the book and in fashioning its hero in their own image'. In these postmodern days, however, rather than patronizing our predecessors we might do well to regard it as a tribute to the richness of the book of Job that it is amenable to so many varying readings that have engaged the sympathies and commitments of readers across many cultural divides.

It is in such a spirit that the present study of Job and the spirituality of Luther and Calvin (I will deal with only these Reformers) is undertaken. I am trying to bring my own long-standing interest in the book of Job, including the history of its interpretation,[3] into contact with some of the themes of the life-work of James Atkinson. His passion for the man Luther and for the individuality of his character and of his attitudes to life and learning have always been exciting to witness, and this essay is

---

1. N.N. Glatzer, *The Dimensions of Job: A Study and Selected Readings* (New York: Schocken Books, 1969), p. 11.

2. Glatzer, *The Dimensions of Job*, p. 12.

3. Cf. e.g. D.J.A. Clines, *Job 1–20* (WBC, 17; Dallas: Word Books, 1989), esp. pp. lxiv-lxxxiv ('Commentaries and Translations').

dedicated to him with admiration and thanks for his fashioning of a
Department of which I am proud to be a member.

The term 'spirituality', as I am using it in this paper, can be defined as
'the forms that holiness takes in the concrete life of the believer',[4] or as
'the attitude faith should take as it is exercised in the unceasing conflict
and contradiction in which a Christian is involved in daily life in the
service of Christ'.[5] It is not a term that has always been used in studies
of the Reformers, partly because some other term, such as 'the Christian
life', has been substituted for it, but partly also because the Reformers'
concern with spirituality has often been obscured by an exclusive
concentration on their theology. It is nonetheless increasingly being
urged today that casting their whole intellectual activity as a quest for a
spirituality, for a religious way of being in the world, may in fact be a
legitimate way of understanding them. Timothy George, for example,
argues that 'Calvin's life's work can be interpreted as an effort to
formulate an authentic spirituality, that is to say, a modus vivendi of life
in the Spirit'.[6]

However that may be, my specific concern here is with the question
how Luther and Calvin invoked the person of Job to express their own
perception of spirituality, that is, their understanding of the nature of the
believing life. By way of preface to a study of their representations of
Job, I shall try to establish some context for their outlooks, both in the
exegetical tradition they inherited and in the spirituality of their own time.

The Figure of Job in Pre-Reformation Spirituality

We cannot be certain of what is the earliest extant interpretation of the
figure of Job. It may that of the epistle of James, or that of the *Testament
of Job*, a work variously ascribed to the last pre-Christian century or to
the early Christian period.[7] In the epistle of James, Job is known solely

4.   So L.J. Richard, *The Spirituality of John Calvin* (Atlanta: John Knox Press,
1974), p. 1.
5.   R.S. Wallace, *Calvin's Doctrine of the Christian Life* (Edinburgh: Oliver &
Boyd, 1959), p. vii, who does not however use the term 'spirituality'.
6.   T. George, *Theology of the Reformers* (Nashville: Broadman Press, 1988),
p. 224.
7.   See *Studies on the Testament of Job* (ed. M.A. Knibb and P. van der Horst;
SNTSMS, 66; Cambridge: Cambridge University Press, 1989), esp. pp. 27-32 (in
R.P. Spittler's 'The Testament of Job: A History of Research and Interpretation',
pp. 7-32).

as an embodiment of 'patience' or 'steadfastness' (ὑπομονή), and his experience of God is characterized as that of a 'compassionate and merciful' (πολύσπλαγχνος...καὶ οἰκτίρμων) Lord:

> Behold, we call those happy who were steadfast. You have heard of the steadfastness of Job, and you have seen the purpose of the Lord, how the Lord is compassionate and merciful (5.11).

In the *Testament of Job* also, where there is a more developed portrait of Job, Job's perseverance in the sufferings inflicted on him by the Satan is one of its principal themes.[8] Here the patience of Job is expressed with three distinct terms: ὑπομονή, 'standing firm', καρτερία, 'stubbornness, toughness', and μακροθυμία, 'patience' (by which one perseveres and endures).[9]

Few modern readers, left to their own devices, would fix upon 'patience' as the most outstanding characteristic of the biblical Job's personality, or, at least, if they recognize in chs. 1–2 the 'patient' Job who accedes to the divine will, they would soon want to contrast this image with that of the 'impatient' Job in the remainder of the book.[10] No doubt the author of James had no intention of subsuming all the virtues of Job under this single heading, or of headlining the narrative of the whole book with the term. But the mere accident that this is the sole reference to Job within the New Testament ensured that in the history of interpretation this construction of the character of Job remained prominent.[11]

James was not of course the only interpreter of the character of Job available to the Reformers. Among the Christian writers on Job most influential upon them must be counted Gregory the Great, with his *Morals on the Book of Job*, and Thomas Aquinas, with his *The Literal Exposition on Job*.

The *Moralia* of Gregory[12] is of course one of the classic works of

8. C. Haas, 'Job's Perseverance in the Testament of Job', in *Studies on the Testament of Job* (ed. Knibb and van der Horst), pp. 117-54 (117).

9. Haas, 'Job's Perseverance', pp. 117-54.

10. Cf. H.L. Ginsberg, 'Job the Patient and Job the Impatient', *Conservative Judaism* 21 (1967), pp. 12-28.

11. I cite only, by way of example, one of Gregory's first sentences about Job, as a man 'who in a word, we know, received from the Judge of that which is within the reward of the virtue of patience' (*Moralia*, Epistle, 3 [= *Morals*, I, p. 8] [see n. 12 below]).

12. Gregory I (the Great), *Libri XXXV Moralium. Patrologia Latina*, LXXV,

mediaeval exegesis, expounding the threefold sense of the book:[13] a
literal sense (Job is afflicted by God in order to increase his merit[14]), an
allegorical sense (Job is the suffering Redeemer[15] and the church in its
earthly sufferings[16]) and a moral sense (Job transcends the temporal
realm and ascends to the eternal[17]). But, as befits a course of sermons
more than a work of academic theology, the issue of the spirituality of
the book of Job arises early on in his work when Gregory compares his
own physical sufferings with those of Job. He himself, afflicted by
'frequent pains in the bowels' and 'under the influence of fevers...
draw[ing] [his] breath with difficulty', thinks that perhaps 'Divine
Providence designed, that I a stricken one, should set forth Job stricken,
and that by these scourges I should the more perfectly enter into the

509-1162; LXXVI, 9-782; *S. Gregorii Magni Moralia in Iob* (ed. M. Adriaen;
Corpus Christianorum, Series Latina, 143, 143A, 143B; Turnhout: Brepols, 1979–
85); *Grégoire le Grand, Morales sur Job* (Première partie, Livres I–II, ed. R. Gillet,
trans. A. de Gaudemaris [2nd edn]; Troisième partie, Livres XI–XVI, ed.
A. Bocognano [2 vols.]; Sources Chrétiennes, 32 *bis*, 212, 221; Paris: Cerf, 1975,
1974, 1975); *Morals on the Book of Job, by S. Gregory the Great* (A Library of
Fathers of the Holy Catholic Church, 18-20; Oxford: John Henry Parker, 1844)
(cited below as *Morals*). References below are made to the Sources Chrétiennes
edition and to the Parker edition when available, and otherwise to the *Patrologia*.
   On Gregory's commentary on Job, see B. de Margerie, *Introduction à l'histoire
de l'exégèse*. IV. *L'occident latin de Léon le Grand à Bernard de Clairvaux* (Paris:
Cerf, 1990), pp. 171-81 (I am grateful to Dr Jennifer Dines of Heythrop College for
lending me this book); P. Catry, 'Epreuves du juste et mystère de Dieu. Le
commentaire littéral du livre de Job par Saint Grégoire', *Revue des études
augustiniennes* 18 (1972), pp. 124-44. The pages on Gregory's exposition of Job in
Glatzer's handbook (*The Dimensions of Job*, pp. 27-32) unfortunately do not extend
beyond a collection of typological and allegorical identifications.
   13. The threefold sense is, in Gregory's words, to 'unravel the words of the
history in allegorical senses' and 'to give to the allegorical senses the turn of a moral
exercise' (*Moralia*, Epistle, 1 [= *Morals*, I, p. 5]).
   14. 'While the innocent person is bruised by the blow, his patience may serve to
increase the gain of his merits' (*Moralia*, Preface, 5.12 [= *Morals*, I, p. 24]).
   15. '[T]he blessed Job conveys a type of the Redeemer... For there never was any
Saint who did not appear as His herald in figure' (*Moralia*, Preface, 6.14 [= *Morals*,
I, pp. 27, 26]).
   16. On Job 19.6 (= *Moralia* 14.31.38–32.39 [PL, LXXV, 1059-60]).
   17. On Job 7.15 'My soul chooseth hanging', Gregory writes: '[I]n...quitting
earthly objects of desire, they raise the mind on high' (*Moralia* 8.25.44 [= *Morals*, I,
p. 450]). Cf. also 5.40.72; 7.12.27.

feelings of one that was scourged'.[18] In so saying, he announces a self-identification with the Job of the book who 'bore the strife of the spiritual conflict'[19] and revealed his virtue and fortitude by his reaction to suffering.[20] '[E]very good man, so long as he is not smitten, is regarded as insipid, and of slight account',[21] Gregory writes, revealing as he does so, no doubt, how he construes his own state of ill-health. Suffering for Job, and hence for himself, is character-forming, but it also brings the sufferer to public attention. '[H]ad [Job] not been stricken he would never have been the least known to us';[22] and Gregory himself, as supreme pontiff, cannot be blind to the analogy.

More important, perhaps, is what is generally acknowledged as a key concept in Gregory's spirituality: that of his antithesis of interiority and exteriority.[23] In the Preface to the *Moralia* he tellingly evokes the tension in his own life between the contemplative and the active life, lamenting that 'now that the end of the world is at hand...we ourselves, who are supposed to be devoted to the inner mysteries, are thus become involved in outward cares (*curis exterioribus*)'.[24] But more broadly, and beyond his own personal experience, he sees humanity itself, which was destined for interiority, as imprisoned and exiled in exteriority:

> For man, being created for the contemplation of his Maker, but banished from the interior (*internis*) joys in justice to his deserts...undergoing the darkness of his exile, was at once subject to the punishment of his sin, and knew it not; so that he imagined his place of exile to be his home...But He Whom man had forsaken within (*intus*), having assumed a fleshly nature, came forth God without (*foris*); and when he presented Himself outwardly (*exterius*), he restored man, who was cast forth without (*foras*), to the interior life (*ad interiora*), that [h]e might henceforth perceive his losses.[25]

18. *Moralia*, Epistle, 5 (= *Morals*, I, p. 10).
19. *Moralia*, Preface, 1.3 (= *Morals*, I, p. 15).
20. '[I]t was by strokes that the report of his virtue was stirred up to fragrance... [W]hen disturbed [he] did scatter abroad the odour of his fortitude... For as unguents, unless they be stirred, are never smelt far off...so the Saints in their tribulations make known all the sweetness that they have of their virtues' (*Moralia*, Preface, 2.6 [= *Morals*, I, p. 18]).
21. *Moralia*, Preface, 2.6 (= *Morals*, I, p. 18).
22. *Moralia*, Preface, 2.6 (= *Morals*, I, p. 18).
23. See especially C. Dagens, *Saint Grégoire le Grand: Culture et expérience chrétiennes* (Paris: Etudes Augustiniennes, 1977), pp. 133-244.
24. *Moralia*, Epistle, 1 (= *Morals*, I, p. 4).
25. On Job 6.2-3 (*Moralia* 7.1.2 [= *Morals*, I, p. 366, incorrectly capitalizing the last 'he' in the quoted text]).

The spiritual life is therefore for Gregory a retreat from the external to the interior. How does the figure of Job sustain this position? Not very well, it must be said, and one misses in Gregory a close and systematic parallel of the history of the man Job with the spiritual experience. But in one respect Job plays out a key phase in the journey inwards and upwards: suffering, temptation, testing—which Job embodies—are the *flagella Dei*, which purify the soul and stimulate its desire to arise to God.[26] 'The soul [= "the interior man"] that lifts itself up toward Him He both lets loose to wars without, and endues with strength within.'[27] And 'the more the soul of the just suffers adversity in this world, the more thirst it has to contemplate the face of its Creator'.[28] Job as sufferer is thus the model of the believing soul who is driven by suffering towards the divine.[29]

A final note in the spirituality of Gregory is his extreme denigration of human worth. Confronted with Job's affirmation of his innocence, 'I know that I shall be found to be just' (13.18), and his apparent acknowledgment of sins (13.15, 26; 14.17),[30] Gregory concludes that 'in attributing to himself iniquity and to the omnipotent Lord his justification, he recognizes himself as a sinner on his own account (*ex se*) and acknowledges that it is as a divine gift that he has been made just'.[31] This severe disjunction of human sinfulness and divine merit takes rather

26. 'Les *flagella Dei*, les souffrances, les malheurs de tout genre sont donc destinés à opérer au coeur de l'homme une sorte de résurrection: la prosperité extérieure dissimule un effondrement intérieur; ce sont les épreuves qui, en troublant cette prosperité, inciteront l'homme à se ressaisir, en vue d'un redressement intérieur. Cette correspondance entre l'affaiblissement physique et le progrès spirituel est une des lois de la vie chrétienne: c'est ainsi que "par un grand principe d'équilibre, nous comprenons que nous recevons de Dieu à l'occasion de nos progrès intérieurs, et ce que nous sommes à l'occasion de nos défaillances extérieures"' (Dagens, *Grégoire le Grand*, p. 188, quoting *Moralia* 19.6.12).
27. On Job 10.10-11 (*Moralia* 9.53.80 [= *Morals*, I, p. 552]). The translation in the Parker edition misleadingly has 'the soul that is lifted up'; for the translation above, cf. Dagens, *Saint Grégoire*, p. 187.
28. *Moralia* 16.27.32.
29. Cf. Calvin, CO (see n. 79 below) 35.511: 'When we are struck down we are the better disposed to aspire to the heavenly life'.
30. Gregory takes *vias meas in conspectu eius arguam* in 13.15 as 'I will criticize my ways in his sight' (cf. *Moralia* 11.35.48) whereas the Vulgate may simply mean 'I will defend my ways'—which is what the Hebrew surely means.
31. *Moralia* 11.38.51.

unattractive form when he comments on Job's final confession of his ignorance:

> All human wisdom, no matter how great its acuity, is folly when compared with the divine wisdom. All things that are humanly just and beautiful, if they are compared with the justice and beauty of God, are neither just nor beautiful—nor are they anything at all (*nec omnino sunt*).[32]

Job becomes here a vehicle for a rather totalitarian impulse that is to be found also in some other forms of spirituality besides Gregory's.

Thomas Aquinas[33] set out, in his commentary on Job, on a path distinct from that of Gregory. 'Blessed Pope Gregory', he wrote, 'has already disclosed to us its mysteries [that is, its mystical senses] so subtly and clearly that there seems no need to add anything further to them'.[34] In fulfilling his own goal, however, to explain merely the literal sense of the book—the sense 'primarily intended by the words, whether they are used properly or figuratively'[35]—he does not fail to leave some hints of his estimation of Job and of the role Job played in his image of the spiritual life.

For Thomas, Job is a pious man; indeed, it is fundamental to his understanding of the book that Job is 'perfect in every virtue'. For the book of Job, being intended, as he believes, to show that 'human affairs are ruled by divine providence',[36] must deal satisfactorily with the problem of undeserved suffering, which 'most seems to exclude divine providence from human affairs'.[37] Job represents such a case. The only fault that can be ascribed to Job is that in speaking immoderately he

---

32. *Moralia* 35.2.3 (PL, LXXVI, 751).

33. T. Aquinas, *Expositio super Job ad litteram* (Sancti Thomae de Aquino, Opera Omnia, iussu Leonis XIII P.M. edita, 26; Rome: ad Sanctae Sabinae, 1965). The most recent English translation is: *Thomas Aquinas. The Literal Exposition of Job: A Scriptural Commentary concerning Providence* (ed. and trans. A. Damico [translator] and M.D. Yaffe [Interpretive Essays and Notes]; The American Academy of Religion, Classics in Religious Studies, 7; Atlanta: Scholars Press, 1989). I found useful some comments on Aquinas's treatment of Job by S.E. Schreiner, '"Through a Mirror Dimly": Calvin's Sermons on Job', *Calvin Theological Journal* 21 (1986), pp. 175-93 (178-79).

34. *Expositio*, Prologue, 99-102 (= Damico and Yaffe, *Aquinas...Job*, p. 69).

35. *Expositio*, 1.6.233 (= Damico and Yaffe, *Aquinas...Job*, p. 76).

36. *Expositio*, Prologue, 57 (= Damico and Yaffe, *Aquinas...Job*, p. 68).

37. *Expositio*, 1.1.6-8 (= Damico and Yaffe, *Aquinas...Job*, p. 71).

provokes scandal in the minds of his interlocutors,[38] and in speaking so strenuously of his own innocence he gives the impression of pride and of doubting the divine judgment.[39] Even Job's curse on the day of his birth (ch. 3) is nothing more than a natural 'sadness' proceeding from the 'lower part of the soul', the upper part of the soul being rationally convinced that some good must rightly be expected from his misfortunes.[40]

Job is then, for Thomas, an exemplar of the pious soul, afflicted by external troubles, including the intellectual challenges of his friends, but free of internal turmoil or doubt of God's benevolence. Even when the Hebrew text seems to have Job directly accusing God of injustice, Thomas interprets the sentence as a mere hypothetical, for it is not possible that a man of Job's piety could utter an accusation against God. Thus at 19.6, for instance, 'God has afflicted me with an inequitable judgment', Thomas's comment is that '[i]f adversities come about only in return for sins, God's judgment...is inequitable'[41]—but of course they do not, he means, and so God is by no means unjust. Other readers may of course find Thomas's reading too bland, and may discern a much sharper conflict within Job's own spiritual experience; Job, they may well feel, both believes, on the one hand, that adversities do only come about in return for sins and that God's judgment is inequitable, and on the other, maintains that he is a pious man nevertheless.

The Spirituality of the Late Middle Ages

The exegetical tradition that is exemplified by Gregory and Thomas and that was inherited by the Reformers is not the whole background to their readings of the figure of Job. Inasmuch as Job was for them a model of Christian spirituality, their construction of the figure of Job also has to be set against prevailing themes in late mediaeval piety in order to be best appreciated. In some respects, of course, their Job marks out new ground in a depiction of Christian holiness, but in others they are conforming their Job to the expectations of a Christian society with its own long history of spirituality. The old conundrum about the Reformation's periodization, whether it belongs best with the mediaeval

---

38. *Expositio*, 38.1.10-13 (= Damico and Yaffe, *Aquinas...Job*, p. 415).
39. *Expositio*, 42.1.1-5 (= Damico and Yaffe, *Aquinas...Job*, pp. 469-70).
40. *Expositio*, 3.4.98-99 (= Damico and Yaffe, *Aquinas...Job*, p. 101).
41. *Expositio*, 19.6.45-48 (= Damico and Yaffe, *Aquinas...Job*, p. 264).

period or with the modern,[42] though it is generally thought to have been satisfactorily disposed of in favour of linking together reformation, renaissance and enlightenment, comes back into play when we consider the Reformers' spirituality rather than their academic theology.

Among leading themes in the spirituality of the pre-Reformation period, François Vandenbroucke has identified pessimism, 'satanic fever' and popular piety.[43] There was a far-reaching pessimism, he suggests, about the state of the church, the morals of the clergy and the capacity of the church to meet the needs of the new nationalisms. The gloomiest manifestation of pessimism was to be found in the 'macabre sensibility' of the fifteenth century[44] that gave rise to numerous treatises on the art of dying and to the literature of the *danses macabres*. By 'satanic fever' he means the powerful fascination of the concept of the devil and his works that gripped the popular imagination from the fifteenth to the seventeenth centuries,[45] and that left a permanent mark in the art of Dürer, Bosch and Brueghel. To the repression of satanism the Inquisition turned its attention, while the treatise *Malleus maleficarum*, 'The Hammer of Witches' (c. 1487), sanctioned the persecution of suspected witches and cast women generally in the role of seductresses and potential agents of the devil. Popular piety gave an outlet for the 'subjective and psychological aspects of the Christian life',[46] which was losing touch with the formal Divine Office and developing instead, in the spirit of the *devotio moderna*, its own prayerbooks (*preces devotae*) and Books of Hours. The cult of the Virgin, the rosary and the angelus, together with the rise of charismatic preachers addressing the consciences of their listeners, contributed to what Vandenbroucke calls the

42. See E. Troeltsch, *Protestantism and Progress: A Historical Study of the Relation of Protestantism to the Modern World* (trans. W. Montgomery; London: Williams & Norgate, 1912). See further, George, *Theology of the Reformers*, pp. 15-16.

43. In J. Leclerq, F. Vandenbroucke and L. Bouyer, *The Spirituality of the Middle Ages* (A History of Christian Spirituality, 2; London: Burns & Oates, 1968 [French original, 1961]), Part 2, Chapter 9 ('Lay Spirituality from the Fourteenth to the Sixteenth Century'), pp. 481-505.

44. Vandenbroucke, *Spirituality*, p. 485.

45. Cf. H.A. Oberman, *Masters of the Reformation: The Emergence of a New Intellectual Climate in Europe* (trans. D. Martin; Cambridge: Cambridge University Press, 1981), pp. 158-83.

46. Vandenbroucke, *Spirituality*, p. 484.

'individualistic tendency' in spirituality.[47] Finally, he finds prominent a pietistic notion of the individual's relationship with God, 'an ear for the psychological overtones of the Christian mysteries' experienced as a 'source of lively emotions'.[48]

Such generalizations cannot of course encompass the whole of Christian spirituality of the period and other, detailed, studies indicate that the 'individualistic tendency' Vandenbroucke has isolated was only one strand. A.N. Galpern, for example, has graphically illustrated, admittedly for one small segment of the Christian world in the sixteenth century, more community-oriented forms of spirituality: the importance of prayer as a social activity, and of commitment to religious solidarity with other Christians in the developing system of confraternities under the aegis of a saint.[49] Marvin B. Becker has similarly analysed for early Renaissance Florence the importance of *caritas* in the sense of civic charity that created hospitals, hospices and orphanages, the role of the confraternities as embodying charity as a collective enterprise, and of a conception of human *dignitas* that did not reside 'in solitary experience or in strategic personal relationships' but in a sense of human solidarity.[50]

Against such a background, the present study shows that for both Luther and Calvin the figure of Job models the psychologically oriented, individualistic, pietistic tendencies in their contemporary spirituality. For both of them, Job is a lone hero of faith, valiantly wrestling with doubt, the devil and uncertainty. It is easy to see how their own psychological proclivities contributed to the fashioning of that image, but harder perhaps to admit that it was their tradition, their personalities and the spirit of their age, rather than the text of the book of Job, that determined his configuration. For the biblical Job could just as well have been read, for example, as the symbol of human solidarity, as the paterfamilias who gives meaning to his family, as the just magistrate who brings order and security to his society, as the man who himself is formed and

47. Vandenbroucke, *Spirituality*, p. 497.

48. Vandenbroucke, *Spirituality*, p. 498.

49. A.N. Galpern, 'The Legacy of Late Medieval Religion in Sixteenth Century Champagne', in *The Pursuit of Holiness in Late Medieval and Renaissance Religion* (ed. C. Trinkaus with H. A Oberman; Studies in Medieval and Renaissance Thought, 10; Leiden: E.J. Brill, 1974), pp. 141-76.

50. M.B. Becker, 'Aspects of Lay Piety in Early Renaissance Florence', in *The Pursuit of Holiness in Late Medieval and Renaissance Religion*, pp. 177-99 (196).

sustained by his familial and social relationships, as the representative of human dignity, as the suffering man who is restored not by having his intellectual problems solved or by experiencing a religious conversion—or even by having his medical condition healed—but by seeing his family renewed and all his acquaintances accepting of him.

Job in the Spirituality of Luther

Luther never wrote or lectured systematically on Job, and so his construction of the character of Job has to be gleaned piecemeal from the corpus of his writings.[51] But it is not difficult to discern the main outlines of his view of Job, for there are a few distinctive themes that are constantly recurring. Luther's exegesis in general may well have been, as Jaroslav Pelikan remarks,[52] little more than a product of the exegetical tradition that preceded him, but his Job is different: in many ways Luther's Job is a Luther clone, a model of the Reformer's own self-image.[53]

For Luther, Job is the site of an inner conflict: though he is a saint, he is also a sinner. Sometimes Luther expresses this conflict in objective, externalized language:

> God, who cannot lie, pronounces [Job] a righteous and innocent man in the first chapter (Job 1.8). Yet later on Job confesses in various passages that he is a sinner, especially in the ninth and seventh chapters...(9.20; 7.21). But Job must be speaking the truth, because if he were lying in the presence of God, then God would not pronounce him righteous. Accordingly, Job is both righteous and a sinner (*simul justus, simul peccator*).[54]

But more often Luther is himself identifying with the conflict that Job must feel, caught in this paradox of piety and guilt. How does Job handle this situation?, Luther is asking himself. It is of the utmost importance that Job does not repress the knowledge of the conflict;

51. See *Luther's Works* (54 vols.; ed. J. Pelikan; St Louis: Concordia Publishing House, 1957–76).

52. J. Pelikan, *Luther's Works.* Companion Volume. *Luther the Expositor: Introduction to the Reformer's Exegetical Writings* (St Louis: Concordia Publishing House, 1959), p. 38.

53. On the spirituality of Luther, see in general A. Skevington Wood, 'Spirit and Spirituality in Luther', *EvQ* 61 (1989), pp. 311-33.

54. On Gal. 2.18 (LW 27.230-31 = WA 2.497). The parallel with Gregory's language, quoted above (cf. n. 31) is striking.

indeed, his very saintliness consists, in some measure, in his recognition
of his own sinfulness and lack of self-worth:

> [N]o one blesses the Lord except the one who is displeased with himself
> and curses himself and to whom alone God is pleasing. So Job cursed the
> day of his birth (Job 3.1). He who regards himself as anything but
> completely detestable clearly has praise of himself in his mouth... [W]e
> never praise God correctly unless we first disparage ourselves.[55]

And he has no confidence in his own merits:

> [O]ur total concern must be to magnify and aggravate our sins and thus
> always to accuse them more and more... The more deeply a person has
> condemned himself and magnified his sins, the more he is fit for the mercy
> and grace of God... [W]e should above all and in all things be displeased
> [with ourselves] and thus with Job fear all our works (Job 9.28).[56]

This last text (Job 9.28) is an especially powerful one for Luther. The
Hebrew had read simply 'I fear all my pains', that is, no doubt, in the
context, pains yet to come;[57] but the Vulgate has *verebar omnia opera
mea*, 'I feared all my works'—which Luther evidently revelled in as an
expression of the dangers of works-righteousness, and quoted it over
and over again.[58]

Job reflects a deep strain in Luther of self-negation:

> Do not permit me to regard anything carnal as pleasing to Thee... Thus in
> Job 3.1f. the flesh is cursed, and Job prays that it may not be numbered
> with his senses, so that the spirit may be saved.[59]

55. On Psalm 34 (LW 10.162 = WA 3.191).
56. On Ps. 69.16 (LW 10.368 = WA 3.429).
57. I have translated 9.27-28 thus: 'If I say, I will forget my moaning, I will lay
aside my sadness and be cheerful, I become afraid of all I must suffer, for I know you
do not hold me innocent'.
58. For example: '[O]ut of a contrite and troubled heart...[Abimelech, the
Canaanite king of Gerar] is complaining in utmost humility about such a great
misfortune. He is one of those who say with Job (23.15): "I took fright at all my
deeds"' (on Gen. 20.9 [LW 3.348 = WA 43.125]); 'The godly, like Job, fear for all
their works. They trust in no righteousness of theirs and consider their sanctity as
dung' (on Ps. 1.1; LW 14.292 = WA 5.30-31). Gregory found Job's fear to be of
what his inner motives for his good works might have been (*Moralia* 9.34.53 [=
Morals, I, p. 535]). Another text Luther uses against works-righteousness is Job's
denial that he has 'kissed his hand' (31.27-28); that would be the act of a 'man who
trusts in his own works and glories in a righteousness that does not come from Christ
but is produced through his own strength' (on Ps. 2.12 [LW 14.348 = WA 5.73]).
59. On Ps. 69.27 (LW 10.381 = WA 3.439).

This self-negation goes much deeper than a conventional acknowledgment that no human being is perfect. Luther indeed refers to such statements in the book of Job: 'So Job says [it is Eliphaz and Bildad, actually], "The heavens are unclean in his sight" (Job 15.15) and "the stars are unclean before Him, and the moon does not shine", that is, the saints are not saints before Him (Job 25.5)'.[60] But these are no more than conventional statements of the perfect holiness of God, and Luther's exposition of the self-consciousness of the pious man derives not from such rhetorical generalizations but from the narrative itself. For Luther, Job is not someone who is almost perfect, or one who to some degree falls short of true piety; he is, through and through, a saint—who is at the same time also a sinner:

[E]veryone can be bewitched by Satan. None of us is so vigorous that he can resist Satan...Job was a blameless and upright man... But what could he do against the devil when God withdrew his hand? Did not that holy man fall horribly?[61]

Job suffers from the vices of his virtue; the conflict within himself is specific to his saintliness:

[J]ust as sexual desire is powerful in the body of the young man...so in the saintly man impatience, grumbling, hate, and blasphemy against God are powerful.[62]

Sometimes the inner conflict that Job, as the model of the godly man, endures has external causes—for example, the temptations of the devil:

[O]ne must be carefully fortified and strengthened against the displeasure of the flesh, which fights against faith and the spirit..., as that murmuring is described in the examples of two wives: the wife of Tobias and the wife of Job... These are the flaming darts of the devil with which he tries to overthrow us in order that we may despair and fall away from God.[63]

60. On Ps. 51.4 (LW 10.239 = WA 3.290).
61. On Gal. 3.1 (LW 26.193-94 = WA 40.318).
62. On Gal. 3.23 (LW 26.340-41 = WA 40.524).
63. On Gen. 28.10-11 (LW 5.203 = WA 43.568). Elsewhere, however, Job's wife, like Isaac's wife Rebekah, is a saintly woman, though 'not without trials' (on Gen. 26.1; LW 5.14 = WA 43.438). Similarly LW 5.30 = WA 43.449 on Gen. 26.8. On the ambivalence of Luther's attitude to women, see J.W. Zophy, 'We Must Have the Dear Ladies: Martin Luther and Women', in *Pietas et Societas: New Trends in Reformation Social History: Essays in Memory of Harold J. Grimm* (ed. K.C. Sessions and P.N. Bebb; Kirksville, MO: Sixteenth Century Journal Publishers, 1985), pp. 41-50.

There is indeed some uncertainty in Luther over the question of the cause of his sufferings. At times, it seems that they are simply to be ascribed directly to the devil—and not to God:

> God does not afflict the godly; he permits the devil to do this, as we see in the case of Job, whose children are killed by fire and his cattle by storms, not because God was angry with him, but because Satan was.[64]

But at other times, the devil is no more than an agent of the divine intentions:

> The devil at first takes all his property from him with his children and leaves him a peevish, irksome, and abusive wife... [E]xamples of this kind teach us that all the malice and vexation of the devil is only instruction and chastisement, by which we are aroused so that we do not snore and become listless.[65]

> The good God permits such small evils to befall us merely in order to arouse us snorers from our deep sleep and to make us recognize, on the other hand, the incomparable and innumerable benefits we still have. He wants us to consider what would happen if he were to withdraw His goodness from us completely. In that spirit Job said (2.10): 'Shall we receive good at the hand of God and shall we not receive evil?'... he did not simply look at the evil, as we would-be saints do; he kept in sight the goodness and grace of the Lord. With this he comforted himself and overcame evil with patience.[66]

The same adversity can then function both as an instance of satanic temptation to despair and loss of faith and as an example of divine testing:

> Sometimes God sends punishments, not because he finds in the man a sin that deserves such a punishment but because he wants to test his faith and patience. Job did not deserve such punishments... It tends to instruct and comfort us when we learn that God often causes even the innocent to experience the most serious misfortunes and punishments, merely in order to test them.[67]

But most often, in Luther's expositions, it is the devil with whom Job has to do—and, in so saying, we cannot help but observe how Luther is addressing a fundamental concern of the spirituality of his own time.

64. On Gen. 19.10-11 (LW 3.264 = WA 43.64).
65. On Gen. 32.3-5 (LW 6.95 = WA 14.70). For Job's sufferings as a trial by God pure and simple, see also LW 10.159 (= WA 3.189).
66. On Ps. 118.1 (LW 14.49-50 = WA 31.74).
67. On Gen. 12.18-19 (LW 2.319 = WA 42.490).

Luther's Job is at his most Luther-like when he experiences the assaults of the devil. Every protestation he makes against his trials is the language of the man of faith confronted by satanic persecution. What is more, the book of Job constitutes for Luther an unparalleled sourcebook for language about the devil, being pictured as Behemoth in ch. 40, and Leviathan in ch. 41.[68] Luther turned to the book of Job more often to read about the devil than about any other topic, it seems: one quarter of his citations from Job in the first volume of his First Lectures on the Psalms, for example, are to these chapters. Here Luther reads that

[T]he devil ridicules the preachers of the Word, as it is written in Job 41.20 [Vulgate, *Quasi stipulam aestimabit malleum, et deridebit vibrantem hastam*, 'He thinks a hammer a reed, and mocks at him who shakes the spear']. But if you take sword in hand, he will see that the matter is serious.[69]

'He (namely the devil or a stubborn Jew) will ridicule him who shakes the spear' [Job 41.20], that is, the threatening Word of God.[70]

Job embodies all the virtues of the pious person. His reaction to adversity is exemplary: 'Hope is easier in good times but more difficult in bad times. Therefore only a saint always hopes, always blesses, like Job.'[71] His suffering results from his identification with the sufferings of Christ, for which, incidentally, he is scorned by the Jews. The Christians are the

wounded of Christ...because they carry His cross. Tropologically, they have been wounded by the word of the Gospel and smitten by the Lord (as their head) according to the flesh. For they mortify themselves, they chastise and afflict themselves perpetually... The Jews, however, not only had no pity on such as were in this way the afflicted, humbled and wounded of Christ...but they persecuted them in addition, adding furthermore that God was persecuting them. So Job says: 'Have pity on me, at least you, my friends, because the hand of the Lord has touched me. Why do you, like God, persecute me...?' (Job 19.21-22).[72]

---

68. Aquinas had indeed seen in these chapters a description of the devil by analogy with Behemoth and Leviathan, but his primary interest was in the identifica-tion of them with the elephant and the whale, quoting Aristotle, Albertus Magnus, Pliny and Isidore on their natural history (*Expositio*, 40.10.221–41.25.457 [= Damico and Yaffe, *Aquinas...Job*, pp. 447-68); Luther has no interest in anything but their symbolic values.

69. On Ps. 40.2 (LW 10.189 = WA 3.228).

70. On Ps. 35.2 (LW 10.165 = WA 3.195). The reference is to Leviathan.

71. On Ps. 71.14 (LW 10.398 = WA 3.455).

72. On Ps. 69.26 (LW 10.380 = WA 3.437).

Job's piety is not simply that of the person who is justified by faith without works. For Job is an exemplar of the doer of good deeds. And 'those who are Jobs, that is, truly good and active people, who busy themselves with good works, are wiser than the devil. For works bear a true witness of the presence of the Holy Spirit.'[73] The prince of Tyre, who is the devil, may be wiser than Daniel (Ezek. 28.3), and he certainly 'knows all mysteries...and he is more brilliant than we'.[74] But he is not more wise than Job; for Job's wisdom consists in his good works.

And because Job is a saint, even expressions of his that we might regard as world-weary or bitter become models for the pious life. Thus Job's 'empty months' and 'wearisome nights', of which he complains in 7.3, are entirely appropriate for the pious man, for his days have not been fulfilling the lusts of the flesh and his nights have been wearisome because 'they have been occupied with the exercise of the spirit'.[75] Even Job's wish to be dead is, spiritually speaking, a yearning only to be free of earthly constraints. So when he says, 'My soul chooses hanging' (7.15), he is crying out for 'evangelical teaching' which 'does not rest on the earth or on human wisdom, but it arches overhead and takes every understanding captive to the obedience of Christ (2 Cor. 10.5)'.[76] 'Hanging' in fact means being lifted up from the earth and not resting on earthly things, that is to say, 'hanging' is the spiritual language for 'faith in Christ and contempt for visible things'.[77]

For Luther, then, Job is nothing other than a representative believer, justified in the sight of God while still conscious of his own ineradicable sinfulness, perpetually subject to onslaughts of the devil that nevertheless in some way serve the purposes of God, and prey to temptations of impatience and self-righteousness. As the site of inner conflict, Job models Luther's own experience of tension and paradox.

Job in the Spirituality of Calvin

Calvin has left a very much more considerable legacy of writing on Job than has Luther, namely his 159 sermons on Job preached in Geneva in

---

73. On Ps. 68.35 (LW 10.348 = WA 3.408).

74. On Ps. 68.35 (LW 10.347 = WA 3.408).

75. On Ps. 73.10 (LW 10.426-27 = WA 3.484-85).

76. On Ps. 42.7 (LW 10.201-202 = WA 3.240). This is the exegesis of Gregory, as has been noted above (n. 17).

77. On Ps. 36.5 (LW 10.170 = WA 3.201).

1554–1555,[78] and now to be found in their original French in the corpus of his works.[79] Only a selection has ever been translated into English.[80]

The difference in the personality—and so, to a large degree, in the spirituality—of Luther and Calvin is well illustrated in a pair of quotations Suzanne Selinger has illuminatingly set side by side.[81] Luther: 'It is by living—no, rather, by dying and being damned—that a theologian is made, not by understanding, reading, or speculating'.[82] Calvin: 'I count myself one of the number of those who write as they learn and learn as they write'.[83]

If for Luther the man Job is the site of conflict between Satan and God, between self-disgust and a consciousness of innocence, for Calvin Job seems rather to exemplify humanity in its 'perceptual agony', to use

78. For a vivid account of the transformation of the oral sermons into print, see T.H.L. Parker, *Calvin's Old Testament Commentaries* (Edinburgh: T. & T. Clark, 1986), pp. 9-12. The earliest publication of the sermons on Job was entitled *Sermons de M. Jean Calvin sur le livre de Job, recueillis fidelement de sa bouche selon qu'il les preschoit* (Geneva, 1563). See, on this edition, T.D. Smid, 'Some Bibliographical Observations on Calvin's Sermons sur le livre de Job', *Free University Quarterly* 7 (1960–61), pp. 51-56.

79. *Joannis Calvini opera quae supersunt omnia* (Corpus reformatorum, 61-63; eds. G. Baum, E. Cunitz and E. Reuss; Braunschweig: C.A. Schwetschke, 1887), XXXIII-XXXV (the translations are my own). On Calvin as an Old Testament commentator, see Parker, *Calvin's Old Testament Commentaries*; J. Walchenbach, 'John Calvin as Biblical Commentator: An Investigation into Calvin's Use of J. Chrysostom as an Exegetical Tutor' (PhD dissertation, Pittsburgh, 1974); A.G. Baxter, 'John Calvin's Use and Hermeneutics of the Old Testament' (PhD dissertation, University of Sheffield, 1987); J. Haroutunian, 'Calvin as Biblical Commentator', in *Calvin: Commentaries* (Library of Christian Classics, 23; trans. and ed. J. Haroutunian; London: SCM Press, 1958), pp. 15-50; H.-J. Kraus, 'Calvin's Exegetical Principles', *Int* 31 (1977), pp. 8-18.

80. But I have been unable to trace the volume edited by L. Nixon and entitled *Sermons from Job* (1952). Nor have I seen the volume, *Sermons upon the booke of Job, translated out of French* (trans. A. Golding; London, 1584), and so cannot tell if it was a complete translation.

81. S. Selinger, *Calvin against Himself: An Inquiry in Intellectual History* (Hamden, CT: Archon Books, 1984), p. 16. Cf. George, *Theology of the Reformers*, p. 204: 'If Luther was preoccupied with the anxiety of guilt…Calvin was haunted by the specter of the apparently haphazard and meaningless course of existence'.

82. WA 5.163.

83. J. Calvin, *Institutes of the Christian Religion* (Library of Christian Classics, 20; ed. J.T. McNeill and trans. F.L. Battles; Philadelphia: Westminster Press, 1960), p. 5. Calvin is citing Augustine, as it happens (*Letters* 143.2 [= PL, XXXIII, 585]).

Susan Schreiner's term, its incapacity to fathom the workings of providence and the pattern in human affairs.

> Central to [Calvin's] exegesis is the recognition of the noetic or perceptual limitations of the human mind trapped in the disorder of human history. Calvin's constant concern with the failure of the mind to know God, which dominates the first book of the *Institutes*, permeates his sermons on Job. Confronted with the disorder of history, the mind's eye squints and strains to see divine justice but cannot penetrate or transcend the present confusion which hides providence from its limited and fallen view. Calvin finds the heuristic key to the book of Job in 1 Cor. 13.12 ['Now we see in a mirror, dimly']. He repeatedly cites this verse to describe the difficulty of perceiving providence in the midst of history... Caught within the turmoil of earthly events, the believer now sees God's providence only as through a mirror dimly...[84]

For the spirituality of Calvin,[85] then, Job represents the believer's recognition of incapacity to comprehend the divine. The crisis of Calvin's Job is an intellectual crisis; experientially, the crisis is known as a sense of confusion and as a commitment to living in a state of uncertainty, with only a hope, and not an assurance, that the uncertainty will some day be dispelled. Knowing that God has his purposes, though they have not been disclosed, may prevent the experience being one of complete *anomie*. But the experience itself is of the provisionality of human existence, and of the recognition that humans are not in control of their universe. The crisis of knowing is a theme announced early in the *Sermons*:

> [Job] knows that God does not always afflict men according to the measure of their sins, but that he has his secret judgments, of which he gives no account to us, and, nevertheless, that we must wait until he reveals to us why he does this or that.[86]

True knowledge of God for Calvin is not simply an intellectual virtue; it is of the essence of piety itself: '[W]hoever have been endowed with this [true] piety dare not fashion out of their own rashness any God for

---

84. Schreiner, '"Through a Mirror Dimly"', p. 179.

85. See especially F.L. Battles (trans. and ed.), *The Piety of John Calvin: An Anthology Illustrative of the Spirituality of the Reformer* (Grand Rapids: Baker Book House, 1978), especially 'Introduction: True Piety according to Calvin', pp. 13-26, and 'Calvin on the Christian Life', pp. 51-89. Also R.S. Wallace, *Calvin's Doctrine of the Christian Life* (Edinburgh: Oliver & Boyd, 1959), and Richard, *The Spirituality of John Calvin*, esp. pp. 116-29 ('*Pietas* as the Essential Expression of Calvin's Spirituality').

86. On Job 1.1 (CO 33.23).

themselves. Rather, they seek from Him the knowledge of the true God, and conceive Him just as He shows and declares Himself to be.'[87]

There is another conflict in the person of Job: it is between the 'good cause' and the 'bad consequences'.[88] Job is essentially in the right; he does not deserve what is happening to him:

> Here is a cause that is good and true, though it is badly handled (*deduite*), for Job here loses his temper (*se iette ici hors des gonds*, lit. here throws himself off his hinges) and employs such excessive and terrible speeches that he shows himself in many places to be a man in despair. He even becomes so excited (*s'eschauffe*) that he seems to be wishing to resist God. So this is a good cause that is badly handled (*conduite*).[89]

The friends, on the other hand, are in the wrong about the reasons for Job's suffering, and so they have a 'bad cause', even though they speak in fine and holy sentences and 'there is nothing in their speeches that we may not receive as if the Holy Spirit had spoken it'.[90] Job is in the right, but his experience of righteousness is of an unsettling and anxiety-inducing state of being. His experience is thus a revealing expression of Calvin's own personal spirituality.

Job furthermore represents the tension between pious convictions and human weakness. For Calvin, the Old Testament in general serves as a mirror of Christian life and experience, and Job in particular mirrors 'how (good) men often act under severe trials. He desires to obey God but his emotions and sufferings get the better of him... Job, under Calvin's hand, becomes a mirror of our own weakness.'[91] When he curses the day of his birth, Calvin writes,

---

87. J. Calvin, *First Catechism* (ed. F.L. Battles; Pittsburgh: Pittsburgh Theological Seminary, 1972), p. 2; cf. Richard, *The Spirituality of John Calvin*, p. 119: 'The whole notion of *pietas* is dominated by the reality of the knowledge of God'.

88. Cf. D. Wright's characterization of Calvin's key distinction between 'laudable ends and reprehensible means' ('The Ethical Use of the Old Testament in Luther and Calvin: A Comparison', *SJT* 36 [1983], pp. 463-85 [466]).

89. On Job 1.1 (CO 33.23). Similar language is used on Job 32.1 (CO 35.7).

90. On Job 1.1 (CO 33.23).

91. Baxter, *Calvin's Use and Hermeneutics*, p. 42. On the image of the 'mirror', see Heinrich Bornkamm, *Luther and the Old Testament* (trans. E.W. and R.C. Gritsch; Philadelphia: Fortress Press, 1969). See also Schreiner on the contrast with the concept of nature as a mirror of the providence and control of God ('Calvin's Sermons on Job', esp. pp. 181-89).

There is a conflict here, in which on one side the weakness of the man is revealed, and on the other we see that he still has some strength to resist temptation...Job has no longer the same complete perfection as before... he has wished to obey God; but nevertheless he has not accomplished the good that he desired.[92]

Nevertheless, Job is also for Calvin, as for his exegetical predecessors *en masse*, the embodiment of piety, and not simply the believer under stress. Not surprisingly, therefore, we find in the *Sermons* some very conventional moral exhortations being drawn from the character of Job. For example, on Job 1.2:

We see here the praises that the Holy Spirit gives Job, not so much for his own sake as for our instruction, so that we may know how we are to govern our lives, that is, that we should walk in frankness (*rondeur*) of heart, that there should be no falseness (*fiction*) in us, but that our lives should give testimony of such simplicity.[93]

Or, on the wealth of Job reported in 1.3:

We see the character of Job's virtue in that riches have not blinded him with pride, and have not made him too much attached to the world or led him to abandon the service of God...By his example the rich of this world are admonished in their duty.[94]

Likewise, anger at suffering is bad: it shows lack of gratitude for God's mercies.[95] Praying for your enemies is good, as Job did in ch. 42.[96] And so on.

But the virtue of Job that strikes one most forcibly in Calvin is his obedience and acceptance of the divine will:

The history written here shows us how we are in the hands of God, and that it is for him to order our life, and to dispose of it according to his good pleasure, and that our duty is to make ourselves subject to him in all humility and obedience; that it is right that we are entirely his, whether to live or to die; and that, even when it pleases him to lift his hand against us, even when we do not understand for what reason he does so, nevertheless we should glorify him always, confessing that he is just and fair; and that

---

92. On Job 3.1-10 (CO 33.140, 142).

93. On Job 1.2 (CO 33.33).

94. On Job 1.2 (CO 33.34).

95. On Job 29.1-7 (CO 34.534): 'We are ungrateful to God, if the memory of his benefits does not soften all our angers (*fascheries*), when it pleases him to exercise us and to humble us'.

96. On Job 42.10 (CO 35.507).

we should not murmur against him, that we should not enter into dispute with him, knowing that we would always be overcome in any contest with him.[97]

Whether we like it or not, this is the expression, if not the encapsulation, of a comprehensive spirituality on Calvin's part; it is the spirituality of obedience, a mindless ('even when we do not understand') and a prudential ('knowing that we would always be overcome') obedience. It by no means does justice to the subtlety and intellectual force of Calvin's thought—nor to his humanity—and will seem to many nothing but naked 'Calvinism' of the least agreeable kind. The worry is that this is what the grand scope of the *Institutes* and the sweep of the Commentaries all boil down to; when the question becomes one of spirituality—no longer 'What shall I believe?' but 'How shall I live, as a believer?'—the book of Job appears, in Calvin's hands, to lead to nothing more inspiriting than recommendation to a quietism that does not doubt or struggle.

Conclusion

It is nothing surprising, and no criticism of the interpreters of Job, that they have made him to some degree or other in their own image. While characters in literature are inevitably paper-thin when compared even with the dullest of real-life humans, a characterization like that of Job has a huge potential for readers of different centuries to discern divergent and distinctive elements. The question that in most cases needs to be addressed to interpreters of the past, as well as to those of our own age, is not so much whether they have mistaken or misread their text, but how far their own creative engagement with the text has ignored or marginalized other elements or other readers.

So the question I would address to the Reformers and their forebears is not whether their depiction of Job as a pious man or as the site of spiritual conflict is in order, but what dimensions of the book are being ignored by the inherited framework within which they read the book. I identify two primary arenas in which a reader of today might take issue with them.

97. On Job 1.1 (CO 33.21). God, after all, is a patriarch: he 'knows what is proper for each one, and we should be willing to receive whatever portion he pleases to allot to us, just as a *paterfamilias* knows well what is useful for his household' (on Job 42.12 [CO 35.510]).

1. The first is the way in which the speeches of the friends are treated. The tendency, not only among the Reformers, but generally in the history of exegesis, has been to disregard the radical conflict between Job and the friends. True, the 'friends' are always seen as hostile to Job and as contributory to his suffering, as Thomas says; and Gregory finds in them a figure of the heretics, who 'mix good and evil'.[98] But their arguments and aphorisms are regularly treated as if they were on the same level of authority (religious or literary) as those of Job or of the narrator; and the book as a whole—not just the speeches of Job or of God—is for the Reformers a repository of wisdom. Luther, for example, not infrequently quotes sentences of the friends as sayings of Job.[99] The commentators occasionally show an awareness of how odd their own approach is, treating as wisdom both Job's words and his opponents' words; but Gregory, for example, argues that since Paul quotes Eliphaz[100] 'some things contained in their sayings were right', and 'many things that they say are admirable, were they not spoken against the afflicted condition of the holy man'.[101] Calvin, as we have seen, has recourse to the distinction between their 'bad cause' and their 'fine and holy sentences'—a doubtful one, for though 'fine' sentences may be used in a 'bad cause', could 'holy' ones be?[102]

As against the praxis of the reformed commentators, however, I would argue that the dynamics of the book require us to do more than read each sentence atomistically. For the book itself offers us several totalizing perspectives, and from each of them the friends' positions are in the wrong. If it is Job's perspective that we adopt, the friends' speeches are entirely misconceived. If it is the Lord's perspective in the final chapter that we adopt, the unambiguous judgment upon the friends' arguments is that they 'have not spoken of me what is right' (42.7).[103] And if it is the narrator's perspective that we adopt, then everyone is in the wrong, for Job as much as the friends has been labouring under the illusion that his sufferings must have something to

98. *Moralia* 5.11.28 (= *Morals*, I, p. 262).
99. See, for example, n. 60 above.
100. 1 Cor. 3.19, citing Job 5.13.
101. *Moralia* 5.11.27 (= *Morals*, I, p. 261).
102. See n. 89 above.
103. Gregory's explanation, that the following words, 'as my servant Job has', prove that some things they said were right but 'they are overcome by comparison with one who was better', will not convince (*Moralia* 5.11.27 [= *Morals*, I, p. 261]).

do with his sinfulness, real or alleged—whereas the prologue to the book has made it clear that it is solely for his piety, and not for any wrongdoing, that Job is suffering.

In short, the narrative of the book represents the friends as Job's enemies and wrongful accusers; but the Reformers, like most traditional commentators, were unable to jettison the speeches of the friends—as the narrative logic demands—because they found too much congenial and conventional 'wisdom' in them.

2. It has proved exceedingly hard for exegetes to take the ending of the book and therewith Job's restoration to wealth and influence, seriously—principally, I suppose, because the ending so evidently seems to undermine the thrust of all that precedes. According to the first 41 chapters, that is to say, wealth and poverty have nothing to do with innocence and piety, and according to ch. 42 they have.[104] In other words, in the bulk of the book the rich man, who is also the impoverished man, is consistently righteous; his wealth neither brings about nor sabotages his piety. And that has been the very point that the narrative has been set up to solve: 'Does Job serve God for nothing?' (1.9). And yet in the last chapter his restored wealth is evidently a reward for his piety, and the result of his maintaining his integrity.

Luther, not having written a commentary on Job, is under no obligation to deal with the ending of the book, and it is not surprising that he completely ignores it. Calvin, on the other hand, is under some compulsion to treat it—and treat it in conformity with his theology and his spirituality. His intention, it must be said, seems to be to deflect the implication of the final chapter—which can only be that suffering saints may expect to regain their wealth or health—by claiming (though not from the text) that the doubling of Job's goods does not always happen to saints, 'for God does not treat us with an equal measure; he knows what is proper to each one'.[105] And as for 'temporal blessings', by all means let us seize them if God sends them, but let us recognize that the main thing, and the real profit, is that we have been delivered and our faith has been strengthened.[106] Furthermore, material prosperity was the

104. On the 'deconstruction' of the book by its last chapter, cf. D.J.A. Clines, 'Deconstructing the Book of Job', in *What Does Eve Do to Help? and Other Readerly Questions to the Old Testament* (JSOTSup, 94; Sheffield: JSOT Press, 1990), pp. 106-23.
105, On Job 42.12 (CO 35.510).
106. On Job 42.12 (CO 35.510-11).

only way God could reward a saint of Old Testament times, for 'then there was no such revelation of the heavenly life as there is today in the Gospel'.[107] Job may have lived a long life, but longevity is a mixed blessing since there are many unbelievers who live long, and in any case the shorter life span today is more than compensated for by the afterlife. And what is more, God had to prolong the life of the ancients in order to give them more opportunity to experience his goodness; for us, three days in this world would be enough to experience the goodness of God.[108]

The very multiplicity of Calvin's arguments warns us that something is amiss. He needs to convince himself that the text does not carry the implications it seems to. It is especially revealing that throughout the *Sermons*, so long as Job has been suffering, he has been 'we'; the moment he is prosperous again he is not 'we'. Of his restoration Calvin says calmly, *Cela donc ne se verra tousiours*, 'But that will not always happen'.[109] There is something a little disingenuous here. And the issue is by no means a marginal one. For if Job in his restoration is not the image and model of the saint, by what reckoning is the suffering and maltreated Job a mirror of Christian spirituality? To view the Job of conflict as the model of Christian spirituality, but not the Job of success, is perhaps to cast spirituality in a too negative mode—or perhaps even to call into question the validity of the whole idea of Job as a model.

There are loose ends in the Reformers' readings of Job, loose ends perhaps that threaten to trip them up quite disastrously. But that is not the sum and substance of their engagement with the figure of Job, nor even its end result. Creatures of their time, and creating a Job in their own image, the Reformers nevertheless honoured the biblical Job by pressing him into the service of their own distinctive spirituality.

107. On Job 42.15 (CO 35.512).
108. On Job 42.16-17 (CO 35.512-13).
109. On Job 42.10 (CO 35.510). There may be a parallel to the exegetical move of Calvin that William McKane has commented upon, that 'Calvin has a general principle of interpretation that the content of weal or bliss in these [Davidic and Messianic] oracles can never be satisfied by referring them to historical kings of David's line or to any this-worldly polity' ('Calvin as an Old Testament Commentator', *Nederduitse Gereformeerde Theologiese Tydskrif* 25 [1984], pp. 250-259; I am grateful to Professor McKane for letting me have a copy of his paper).

SPIRIT, BIBLE AND PREACHING TODAY
WITH SPECIAL REFERENCE TO WILLIAM TYNDALE

Donald Coggan

The somewhat unwieldy title of this chapter reflects certain interests of
the writer which have been dominant in his mind during a ministry of
some sixty years. If, therefore, there is here an undercurrent of auto-
biography, the writer asks for understanding on the part of his readers.

Spirit

In the early part of this century emphasis on the work of the third
Person of the Blessed Trinity was, generally speaking, lacking in the field
of theological writing, of church worship and of religious experience. I
recall constantly praying and pleading for a new interest in and response
to the One whose nature and work are often described in Scripture in
terms of wind and fire. God often answers our prayers 'above all that
we ask or think' and in ways of which in our wildest moments we
should never have dreamed. The charismatic movement arrived and
spread throughout the world, showing an astonishing indifference to
denominational barriers.

When any great doctrine of the Church receives new emphasis, it
is almost always subject to misunderstanding and misinterpretation,
Corruptio optimi pessima. For example, as early as the time when Paul
wrote to the Romans, the doctrine of justification by grace through faith
had been abused. 'Shall we persist in sin, so that there may be all the
more grace?' Paul answered the question with an emphatic 'Certainly
not!' (Rom. 6.1-2). So it was a matter of no great surprise that the
rediscovery of the Holy Spirit in his manifold activity was mishandled by
some to the point of absurdity and mis-interpreted by others with
consequences which were grave.

In 1993 a book on 'Charismatic Renewal' by Tom Smail, Andrew Walker and Nigel Wright was produced by SPCK. Its sub-title 'The Search for a Theology' is significant. It should not, and does not necessarily, imply that the charismatic movement has not produced its theologians, but it does indicate the need for a more adequate, not to say a more available, theology to accompany the outward manifestations of the Spirit's activities within the Church and beyond it. The search for such a theology must be pursued further.

One would express the hope that such a search would issue in a renewed and deeper understanding of the *Trinity*. Good material is already available, but perhaps this is the next doctrine calling for *special* study by the theologians and consideration by the Church at large. Much attention during this century has been paid to the doctrine of the Fatherhood of God, the Sonship of Christ, and the person and work of the Holy Spirit. Now our attention might well be concentrated on the relationships of the Persons within the Trinity. Here we tread cautiously for the mystery is great. But it is a wonderful mystery which abundantly repays reverent and awe-full exploration. Here, in a 'communion' of Persons, of beings-in-relationship, of a fellowship of mutual love, is something which cannot be expressed merely in terms of the individual alone. It is relational. It is communal.

In a thoughtful chapter in *Liberating Sex: A Christian Sexual Theology* (SPCK, 1993), Adrian Thatcher laments the neglect of the Trinity in the West, and claims that it

> has profoundly impoverished Christian spirituality and led to the loss of the priceless insight that God in Godself is a community of love. God's Being *just is* the relationships of personal mutuality and sharing which together constitute the Divine Life (p. 55).

The relevance of that doctrine for life in society and for sexual relationships in particular can scarcely be exaggerated. Adrian Thatcher quotes with strong approval two sentences from Richard of St Victor (d. 1173): 'When I love another person and that love is reciprocated, I also want to share my love with a third person. The joy and the delight which I have in the Beloved has a tendency to overflow, so that I want to share my joy with a third person.'

The search for unity within the Body of Christ which was one of the marks of the Church during the middle years of this century seems to have run out into shallow waters. True, at the ordinary levels of Church life there is an understanding of people of different allegiances, and cooperation with them in social and community work, for which we can be truly thankful. But the failure of various 'schemes' for re-union has put a damper on the enthusiasm for Church unity, and we wonder what the next step should be. Could it be that we were too rigid in the drawing up of our favourite schemes? Did we rely overmuch on the correctness of formulae and allow too little of that 'untidiness' which wind always brings with it when it comes with refreshing power into stale situations?

Further submission to the Spirit, further research for a less inadequate pneumatology, further study of the doctrine of the Trinity, combined with a deep thankfulness for what we have recently learned in charismatic renewal—this may well be the way forward into the third millennium. If so, it will bring new life to the Church and new impetus in its mission to the world.

Bible

The last two centuries have been a period of great enrichment for biblical scholars. Knowledge has advanced by leaps and bounds in many fields which affect their work. To take but a few examples: The establishment of biblical texts of a greater degree of accuracy than was available, say, to Erasmus or Tyndale, is a forward step of great value. The discovery of ostraca and papyri, which reflect the language of the common folk and of the market place of first-century Palestine, has shed many rays of light on the meaning of biblical passages, as have the discoveries of the archaeologists at work in the Near East. The study of comparative religions has made its contribution, and continues to do so. The holding of international conferences of biblical scholars, facilitated by aerial travel, has made their contributions available to scholars in a way which was not possible in earlier times. A new approach to the problems of Old and New Testament study is now open to international scrutiny. The biblical scholars of the late twentieth century have been confronted by an *embarras de richesse*; they must run if they are to keep up to date with new discoveries, new 'schools of thought'. Some of these have withstood the test of time. Others have appeared, only to fade when further tested. They have been exciting years in our universities and theological faculties. We are grateful.

Outside such circles, however, even basic knowledge of the Bible on the part of the general public has slumped. Apart from a few Bible stories, and a few phrases which have become part of our common speech, the person in the street, even if possessing what is generally recognized as a good education, is almost totally ignorant of the main biblical themes, even of the characters which are behind the biblical narratives. People's whole outlook is focused elsewhere. The tiny world of—to cite them again—Erasmus or Tyndale is not their world. Theirs is the world of the galaxies, of infinite space, of the computer and of genetic engineering, yes, and of Bosnia, Iraq and AIDS. For them, there is no dimension beyond the dimension of the temporal—what is the meaning of 'eternal life' to such? 'Let us eat and drink, for tomorrow we die...'

The path of the theological teacher, and of the parish priest, is not an easy one at the end of the twentieth century. It is their task in some sense to function as *pontifex*—a bridge-builder—between two worlds in so many ways different the one from the other. They have the key to a treasure store with which they believe God has entrusted them, a treasure store immensely enriched by the discoveries of years gone by. To them that treasure is beyond all price, and they long that others should share it. Such people deal with matters of eternal significance, standing at the point where *that* world impinges on *this*, intersects with it, touches it to life. But how be God's bridgebuilders in a world like this? How deliver the burden which God has laid on our shoulders? 'Who is sufficient for these things?' Who indeed? We would want, at the end of the journey, to be able to say with Paul: 'I have kept back nothing that was for your good; I delivered the message to you, and taught you... I have disclosed to you the whole purpose of God' (Acts 20.20, 27). But how? It is at this point that we are thrown back on the present activity of the Holy Spirit, the Paraclete, the 'Animator', the Illuminator, whose task it is to take of the things of Christ and interpret them to us, and through us to others.

It is the experience of many theological students that, in the rightly rigorous treatment of Scripture in the lecture room, they are not shown the way from the analytical approach onwards to the point where truth becomes experiential and, moreover, begins insistently to demand to be received, expounded and taught. Somehow the light, if ever it has been kindled, goes dim or even goes out, and the student emerges with more questions than convictions. Let it be said with emphasis: This is not to denigrate the open and questioning mind. Far from it. But it is to affirm that analysis and criticism of the documents are only part of the work of theologians and students. They must press on in their prayer and study to the point where they dare to expect that, in those Scriptures, by the operation of the Holy Spirit, *they will be addressed by the living God*; that God will meet them there in demand and in grace.

It is at the meeting point of Spirit and Bible that scholarship and devotion converge in a holy alliance. At that point, mind and will unite in obedience. It is thus that individual discipleship is strengthened, and community is nourished. Thus God is seen to be 'most real when he ceases to be an object of enquiry, and becomes someone who beckons'.

Within the pages of Scripture the great questions of life are addressed: What is the nature of God? Of men and women? Of life lived in a community? Of human wrongness? Of divine intervention? What is the meaning of grace, forgiveness, glory, eternal life? Can a human being latch on to the purpose of God, be made after his likeness, share his beauty, be his agent?

If we are to allow ourselves to see the direction in which Scripture points in its wrestling with these questions, there will have to be an abandonment of *hubris* on our part. There will have to be a willingness not merely to pass judgment on the Scriptures but to be under their judgment as the Spirit does his life-giving work. As we shall see later, it was because William Tyndale knew in his own experience the power of the Spirit at work in him through the Scriptures that he was willing to devote his brief life to the letting loose of those Scriptures into the world; and for this he was content to die.

Preaching

Here I write with an ache in my heart. For many years I have pleaded, in books and addresses, for a recapturing of the concept of the glory of the pulpit. I find some response, but it is far from adequate. The writer of a recent leading article in *The Times* (27 March, 1993) regretted that 'in recent times, preaching has become a craft despised, and "sermon" a pejorative word in our debased lexicon'. The same article spoke of 'the forgotten potential of fine preaching' and noted that 'in the last decade, the evangelical revival has sparked the beginning of a return to preaching, which Anglicans of all theological hues should follow'. 'Sparked the beginning'—yes. I hope so. The article ended: 'If the Church wishes to be a force in a modern secular society, it must share its witness with... rhetorical passion'.

I know all the objections to a magnifying of the pulpit, some of them very real, some of them excuses to cover the nakedness of lazy or reluctant practitioners. I know, too, the difficulties which beset the path of the preacher—they are legion and often grievous. But if the man and woman in the pulpit have caught something of the thought in Thomas Carlyle's question, 'Who having been called to be a preacher would stoop to be a king?', if they refuse to insult their congregation by offering them platitudes or unprepared material, if they spurn the idea of talking down to them and thus inviting them to vote with their feet by absenting themselves from the church—in such a case, again and again they will come back for more, and the word will spread that the churches where such preachers serve are places where hungry people can find bread.

One more 'if'! 'If they believe that the main Operator in preaching is the Holy Spirit...' Here is the nexus in the title of this chapter—Spirit–Bible–Preaching. 'The Spirit breathes upon the word, and brings the truth to light.' As in the sacrament of the Eucharist the Spirit takes the elements of bread and wine and makes them the vehicle of his grace, so in the sacrament of the Word the Spirit takes the ordinary language of Scripture, and enlivens it, making it a means of new life to receptive minds and responsive wills.

Architects and church furnishers have not always been helpful to us in conveying to our congregations that balance of word and sacrament which is at the heart of healthy church life. A recent experience may serve to illustrate the point. I visited a church to preach at a service of Holy Communion. The excellent vicar was in process of rearranging the furniture of the church, and, very wisely, had brought the Holy Table down from its previous position in the far east end to a more central position nearer the congregation. That was good; one glance at the arrangement and one had no doubt that eucharistic worship mattered, was indeed central. Ample provision was made for its celebration.

The sacrament of the Word—how did that fare? I preached from a little shaky stand upon which, if a person were to lean some weight, disaster might well ensue. Let it be said at once that the re-arrangement had not been completed—and so, perhaps, there was hope for the future. But, on looking to a rather obscure place largely out of sight of the people, there was the old pulpit—a dignified and worthy piece of work. Originally, it had stood in some prominence in the building, as if to say to all who came, 'This *stands* for something. Here is a place where God is at work, wrestling with people for their welfare, offering them grace, enlightening minds, nerving wills, re-making characters after the pattern of his Son.'

I repeat, the new position of the old pulpit in the church to which I went may prove to be only temporary. But its present position could be a picture, in a wider context, of a de-throning of the word, a denigration of preaching, which could spell ruin for 'the church of the living God, the pillar and bulwark of the truth' (1 Tim. 3.15). It is greatly to be desired that those who are responsible for the building of new churches or for the refurnishing of older ones should, through their work, make clear for the eyes of the worshippers to see that there is a balance between Eucharist and preaching which is of fundamental importance. At the table of the Lord, we 'proclaim the death of the Lord, until he comes' (1 Cor. 11.26). The Eucharist is itself a proclamation; the breaking of the bread is there for all to *see*. It is a manifestation of the love of God, repeated and renewed. It is indeed a celebration of God's grace, and by it we are fed.

The sacrament of the word is also a proclamation, a manifestation, a celebration, there by God's appointment for all to *hear*. In those moments when the preacher goes into action, the church too goes into action. The sermon is a combined offering of worship to almighty God. On the part of the preacher, it is his or her offering of the work done, often at great cost, during the preceding week. On the part of the congregation, it is an act of cooperation of mind and imagination, of prayer and it may be hoped of will, with the one who preaches. And above them all hovers the Spirit, enlivening, enlightening, animating.

Hold together these two mighty acts—*verba visibilia* and *verba audibilia*—in a glorious balance of worship, and the power of the Lord will be present. Even 'some uninstructed persons or unbelievers', on entering, will find the secrets of their hearts laid bare, and 'will fall down and worship God, declaring, "God is certainly among you!"' (1 Cor. 14.23-25). Such worship in the power of the Spirit is a strong agency in the fulfilment of God's purpose for the salvation of his people.

Here again our theological colleges need to consider very carefully the content and quality of the training which they give to their students in the sphere of homiletics. The picture varies from college to college. There are no doubt some colleges where teaching on the theology of the Eucharist is deficient and direction on the conduct of eucharistic worship is inadequate. My guess would be that there are more colleges in which instruction in preaching is inadequate, sometimes woefully so. I refer not only to what we may call the mechanics of preaching—the use of voice, the avoidance of distracting habits and so forth. These matters are urgently important. But even more important is the theology of preaching—the idea of 'the word' in Hebrew thought, from the creative word of the Genesis story to the incarnate Word of St John; the idea of a human being as an agent of that word; the concept of 'burden' in the prophets; the trusteeship which is involved in receiving (digesting) a word from God and delivering it to others; the place of human frailty in impairing the power of that word in the course of its delivery, and so on. There are rich veins of treasure hidden in the rocks of Scripture which, surely, must be explored before a young man or woman can be launched upon a preaching career. Behind us is a long tradition of the teaching of the ministry of the word. We cannot afford to rest on our laurels. Each generation must tackle the matter afresh—with vigour and with imagination.

The year 1994 has been chosen as the year in which the quincentenary of the birth of William Tyndale shall be celebrated. (There is some difference of opinion as to the exact year of his birth, but most scholars think that 1494 is the most probable.) He has been called 'the forgotten father of the English Bible'. It is regrettable that when his name is mentioned in reasonably well-educated circles, the look on many people's faces today is blank. However, in preparation for this celebration, the William Tyndale Quincentenary Trust, under distinguished patronage, has been at work to ensure that the quincentenary does not go without due notice, and an excellent programme of lectures, radio programmes and conferences, in England, in Belgium, in the USA and elsewhere, has been arranged. We may confidently look for a renewal of interest in this great man. In his person he vividly illustrates the 'togetherness' of those words in the title of this chapter—Spirit, Bible, Preaching.

The barest outline of his life is all that is called for here. Twelve of his 42 years (the figures cannot be precise) were spent as an exile from his own country—on the run from people who would have had him hunted down and brought back to England if he had not escaped their clutches and so been enabled to continue his work. His years at Oxford (Magdalen Hall, now Hertford College—his portrait looks down on us at high table there and a window has recently been installed in the Chapel in his memory) and his time in Cambridge both proved formative in the making of young Tyndale's thought and character. These were heady years in which to come to manhood. Tyndale's alert mind responded to the stimulus of Renaissance thought and culture. The revival of the classics by men like William Grocyn and Thomas Linacre, Colet's lectures at Oxford on St Paul's epistles, the writings of Erasmus and especially his *Enchiridion Militis Christiani* (1504) and his *Novum Instrumentum* (1516), the fulminations of Martin Luther, founder of the German Reformation—all these things were grist to the mill provided by men who were roughly Tyndale's contemporaries. The cultural and religious world was in a ferment. Tyndale was content to be part of that ferment if, by so being, he could fulfil the one great passion of his life. To that we must come in a moment.

Tyndale's years at University were succeeded by a period at Little Sodbury Manor in Gloucestershire as tutor to the young sons of Sir John Walsh. That period may well have been formative in deciding the direction in which Tyndale's life should go and the cause in which his energies should be spent. The work as tutor cannot have been onerous. He had time in which to read and think. Among other things, he translated Erasmus's *Enchiridion* and gave a copy to his host and hostess. He was a priest and, though he did not have charge of the local church, he moved around the district and exercised his ministry faithfully. He was able to develop his skill in linguistic studies, though his knowledge of Hebrew seems to have been gained at a later stage in his life. Little Sodbury was no backwater; to the hospitable table of its Manor House came a stream of people whose conversation must have brought the wider world to the young tutor's attention.

As he came to understand the world into which he had been born, he grew more and more troubled about the Church which should have been its light. That light was dim. The ignorance of the clergy appalled him; many of them were unable to understand the meaning of the Latin words which they used when they celebrated the Mass. As for the leaders of the Church, they seemed to him to be wolves rather than shepherds. The more Tyndale saw of the condition of Church and people, the more clearly his life-work came to be defined: there was one thing needed above all others—it was access to the Scriptures in a tongue which priest and people could understand, and nothing must stand in the way of that access. To that he must give all his strength, his skill, his scholarship, even, if need be, his life.

Erasmus in his Greek New Testament of 1516 had written:

> I vehemently dissent from those who are unwilling that the sacred
> Scriptures, translated into the vulgar tongue, should be read by private
> citizens. I would wish even all women to read the Gospel and the Epistles
> of St Paul. I wish they were translated into all languages of the people. I
> wish that the husbandman may sing parts of them at his plough, that the
> weaver may warble them at his shuttle, that the traveller may with their
> narratives beguile the weariness of the way.

Tyndale was to echo these words. 'If God spare my life', he said to an
ignorant divine, 'ere many years I will cause a boy that driveth the
plough shall know more of the Scriptures than thou dost'.

His hopes of support from Church leaders such as Cuthbert Tunstall,
Bishop of London, were dashed. His translations were burnt at Paul's
Cross and he himself, after years of exile, was strangled and burnt at
Vilvorde in 1536—but not before he had prayed: 'Lord, open the King
of England's eyes'. His prayer was answered only a year later by the
royal recognition of the Coverdale Bible (the first *complete* English
Bible, which itself had made abundant use of Tyndale's work).

The influence of Tyndale on the English language has been formative.
Indeed, it has been claimed that he 'more than Shakespeare even or
Bunyan has moulded and enriched our language'. The main reason for
that claim is to be found in the part that his translation played in the so-
called Authorised Version, the King James Version of 1611. Some
ninety per cent of the New Testament in that version is Tyndale's. His
knowledge of the original languages was that of an expert. His
translation of the Pentateuch shows a mastery of the Hebrew language
lacking in all previous translations, and makes us regret that his early
death did not allow him to give us a complete translation of the Old
Testament into English. Spurning allegorical interpretations, he did his
best to cleave to the text, depending not on the Latin of the Vulgate nor
on other translations (though he consulted them) but on the best texts
then available in Hebrew and Greek. The immense care which he
devoted to his revision of the New Testament text showed his passion to
cleave to it and to render it into English which was clear, lively and
accurate. To take an example: his translation of *metanoeo* by *repent*
made clear the difference between that New Testament concept and the
Vulgate's translation of *do penance*. That one word brought him and his
readers close to the heart of what the Reformation was about.

If it is true that Tyndale's concern was that the ploughman should have access to the Bible, that it should be available, as we should say, to the person in the street, his concern was even greater for the preacher in the pulpit. What was being preached? Tyndale had little doubt about the triviality, the error, the heresy of much of that which ignorant priests gave to their people week by week. Behind his work—poring over his texts, fleeing from his persecutors, shipping his wares hidden in bales of cotton that they might be distributed in the land of his birth—was the longing for pulpits cleansed of superstition, for sermons which were based on the biblical revelation, for priests who were touched by the Spirit of truth. He knew that often his books would be burnt at the instigation and with the approval of men like Warham, Archbishop of Canterbury, of Tunstall, Bishop of London, of Cardinal Wolsey and Sir Thomas More. He was prepared to enter into controversy with any or all of them, controversy that was often sharp, caustic and even bitter. But he knew, and saw with a clarity of vision given by God himself, that when the essence of the Gospel is seen in its glory, when the Spirit lights up the basic doctrines of Scripture, the darkness is dispersed, the Church is revived, God is glorified. There is a wonderful unity in the three words of this chapter's title—Spirit, Bible, Preaching. It is because these matters have been—and still are—central to the life, thought and writing of James Atkinson that one has such pleasure in making a small contribution to the book now published in his honour.

THE COHERENCE OF THE TEXT: HOW IT HANGETH TOGETHER: THE BIBLE IN REFORMATION ENGLAND*

Patrick Collinson

I

The century or so which followed the Reformation in England (defined legally and constitutionally) or which *was* the Reformation, understood more generously as a profound and sustained religious and cultural revolution in a nation's life, was the age *par excellence* of Bible-reading; indeed, of something which transcended mere reading, as we nowadays read books, amounting to absorption not merely in the text but in a whole world of biblical thought, reflection, imagination and rhetoric.

Up to the fourth decade of the sixteenth century, the English, by contrast with some other western European peoples, had been protected against direct encounter with the Bible in the language which they themselves spoke, even if biblical elements met them indirectly and mimetically in the imagery and ritual of the traditional religious culture, so richly evoked by Eamon Duffy in *The Stripping of the Altars*.[1] To demonstrate, as Duffy does, that many religious texts and formulae were more familiar to the fifteenth-century laity in Latin than in English is to make the point about vernacular deprivation paradoxically.[2] To be sure, those vernacular versions of the Bible which were the work of the late fourteenth-century Wycliffite translators had begun to exercise a magnetic attraction towards a biblical mode of discourse and literary expression

---

* This essay began life as a lecture in the Faculty of Divinity of the University of Cambridge in November 1991, part of a special course of lectures, 'Holy Writ and How It's Read'.

1. E. Duffy, *The Stripping of the Altars: Traditional Religion in England 1400–1580* (New Haven and London, 1992).

2. Duffy, *Stripping*, pp. 213ff.

somewhat earlier than the early sixteenth century.[3] More copies of the Wycliffite text of the Bible survive than of any other late medieval English text: 250 (21 of them whole Bibles), compared with 64 of Chaucer. It was possible for a fifteenth-century shoemaker to express faith in 'the veray woordys of the gospels and the epistles, such as I had herd afore in our Englissh bookys'.[4] However, in England, unlike French, German and Netherlandish Europe, the medium of print had not hitherto fulfilled its destiny: the most potent of its uses in the first age of printing, which was the propagation on a liberal scale of the biblical text in its entirety, in the vernacular and in standard formats, a work of constant reference and cross-reference which dedicated Bible-readers had at their ready command, and by which their life was commanded.

So we may assume some demand for an English Bible in Tudor England, although, as so often with a new product, it is hard to say whether the product supplied a previously unsatisfied need, or whether it created its own market. William Tyndale, translator of the first printed English New Testament (1526), and consequently one of the greatest single influences on early modern, post-Reformation English culture, was an interested party, as the promoter of his own artefact. There was a conflict of motivation in Tyndale which is reminiscent of his guiding mentor, Luther, and was memorably stated when he wrote: 'This term, myself, is not in the Gospel'. There was an imperative to claim responsibility, even authorship, but it coexisted with a desire to disclaim it. Tyndale begged to be allowed not to exist if only the authorities could be persuaded to place in the hands of his fellow-countrymen what he called 'a bare text of the Scripture'. And yet he stamped the third edition of his Testament scandalously with the trademark of his own name, a warning in effect to 'Refuse All Imitations'[5] (Tyndale had nothing but contempt for the inferior talents of such rival translators as George Joy). This audacity provoked Thomas More beyond measure: 'That all

3.   J.M. Mueller, *The Native Tongue and the Word: Developments in English Prose Style, 1380–1580* (Chicago, 1984).

4.   A. Hudson, *The Premature Reformation: Wycliffite Texts and Lollard History* (Oxford, 1988), pp. 231-32, 275.

5.   *The newe Testament dyly gently compared with the Greke by Willyam Tindale: and fynesshed in the yere of oure Lorde God A.M.D. a. xxxiiii. in the moneth of November.*

Englande shold go to scoole wyth Tyndale to lerne Englysche' was 'a very frantyque foly'.[6]

And yet this is very nearly what happened. If Tyndale was at first speaking only of himself and for himself, he soon proved to be in resonance with the coming generations of English Bible-readers, which in a sense he brought forth, when he wrote: 'First, God gave the children of Israel a law by the hand of Moses in their mother tongue; and all the prophets wrote in their mother tongue, and all the psalms were in the mother tongue'. 'The sermons which thou readest in the Acts of the apostles, and all that the apostles preached, were no doubt preached in the mother tongue... Why may not we also?'[7] It was in Tyndale's preferred version of that mother tongue, direct, demotic, deceptively 'plain', in the sense that estate agents use the word 'deceptive' of houses, that sixteenth-century England found God, and itself, in the Bible. One of Tyndale's literary critics (an appreciative critic) has written: 'The truth is that Tindale hated literature. Next to a papist he hated a poet.'[8] Such a 'poet' was the Platonist, Thomas More. And yet Tyndale's translation was poetic in spite of itself, and a source of limitless inspiration to some of our greatest poets.

Most of the so-called Authorised Version of 1611 is Tyndale, perhaps 80% of the words his choice, and nearer to 100% of the nativity stories in Matthew or of the parable of the Prodigal Son in Luke. And yet in measure as the 'King James' version departed from Tyndale, its voice was less modern, more churchly, even less English than Tyndale's voice of almost a hundred years earlier. I know no-one in 1611 who qualified his utterances with 'verily verily'. Jesus does not say 'verily verily' in Tyndale's version. But it is his catchphrase in the Authorised Version, and it subtly qualifies his common humanity. Nor had Tyndale ballasted his text with the weighty, churchly device of 'doubling', which Archbishop Thomas Cranmer used so extensively in the Prayer Book,

6.   'The Confutation of Tyndale's Answer', in *The Complete Works of St Thomas More*, VIII, pt. 1 (ed. L.A. Schuster *et al.*; New Haven, 1973), p. 212. On the contradictions inherent in Tyndale's self-realization as he prepared 'by far the single most significant book in the language', see S. Greenblatt, 'The Word of God in the Age of Mechanical Reproduction', in his *Renaissance Self-Fashioning* (Chicago, 1980).

7.   *The Work of William Tyndale* (ed. G.E. Duffield; The Courtenay Library of Reformation Classics, 1; Appleford, 1964), pp. 324-26.

8.   G.D. Bone, 'Tindale and the English Language', in S.L. Greenslade, *The Work of William Tindale* (London, 1938), p. 67.

providing titles for modern novelists: sins and wickednesses, devices and desires. Bishop John Fisher had translated Rev. 14.13: 'Blessed are they which have made virtuous end and conclusion of their life in the Lord'. Tyndale renders the same text: 'Blessed are the dead which hereafter die in the Lord' (and it is typical of his enterprise that that was a theological as much as a stylistic alteration). The Authorised Version has 'blessed are the dead which die in the Lord from henceforth', which is close to Tyndale but mildly confusing. What about those who have already died in the Lord? When the AV translators departed from Tyndale in 1 Cor. 8.4, abandoning 'meat dedicated unto idols' for 'the eating of those things that are offered in sacrifice unto idols', our same friendly critic is moved to exclaim: 'I would not altogether trust the authors of that alteration to produce by themselves a simple translation of the Gospels'.[9] Almost one is tempted to ask: whom have we ever been able to trust apart from William Tyndale? Tyndale, thou shouldst be living at this hour.

In that pioneering work of social history, *A Short History of the English People*, J.R. Green pronounced, so famously that it has become a cliché, that between the middle years of Elizabeth and the meeting of the Long Parliament (1640) the English people became the people of a book, and that that book was the Bible. 'No greater moral change ever passed over a nation.'[10] That was no more (and no less) than an intuition, not subjected to any empirical test. But now another Green, Dr Ian Green of Belfast, has carried out an investigation which upholds J.R. Green so far as the statistics of production, sale and ownership are concerned. It begins to look as if the Bible really did enjoy a special if not unique ascendancy in the English church and nation, purchased as it was on a larger scale by more people than in any other protestant country, so far as such difficult comparative measurements can be made. The peak seems to have been reached in the mid-seventeenth century, ten times as many Bibles being printed and marketed in the 1630s as had been produced in the 1570s. Print-runs were larger, too, and pirated imports were an additional source of supply, hard to quantify. We may be talking about a quarter of a million Bibles and testaments offered for sale in a single decade to a population of perhaps four-and-a-half million, and that may be a conservative estimate.[11]

9. Bone, 'Tindale and the English Language', p. 64.
10. J.R. Green, *A Short History of the English People* (London, 1874), p. 447.
11. Information communicated by Dr Ian Green at a Reformation Studies

After that, Dr Green believes, the trade fell back. But we should not assume that the Bible was going out of use and fashion. Perhaps the statistics merely indicate that in a population which was no longer rapidly expanding, and in which literacy, too, was reaching a kind of plateau, families which had a use for a Bible already possessed one, whether in the very popular Geneva version or in formats of the Authorised Version designed for domestic and private use. There would be no further revisions of the text, such as might have created a new market, for two-and-a-half centuries. Bibles last longer than television sets. I possess a colour television in good working order which is now eighteen years old, which I am sure the manufacturers never intended. But I also own a copy of the Geneva Bible which was printed in 1602, when Queen Elizabeth I was still on the throne. My Geneva Bible was much used in the eighteenth century, if only for the purpose of trying out new pens on the fly-leaves. In 1994 I consult it almost daily, and not only for purposes of historical research. Until my wife gave me a modern edition of *Cruden's Concordance* at Christmas 1991, the concordance at the back of my 1602 Geneva Bible was the only one I had ready to hand, a useful if limited A to Z guide to a text with which I am probably much less familiar than were its seventeenth-century readers.

So the English people of the later sixteenth and seventeenth centuries were the people of the book, from the point of dissemination outwards and downwards, the question being, how far outwards and downwards? Did the Bible fail to penetrate beyond a certain social and cultural level, just as, according to Sir Keith Thomas, 'below a certain social level' not everyone went to church?[12] Was Bible ownership, Bible reading, Bible knowledge, one of those differentiating factors which made English society and culture a more complex and layered affair than it had been before the Reformation, when a different kind of scriptural knowledge was conveyed to 'everyone' by the mass media of biblical plays and pageants? Was more or less of the biblical story retained and stored in the memory, both individual and shared memory, in the mid-seventeenth century than had been planted there by other means in the early

Colloquium at the University of Sheffield, April 1990, and in correspondence; an unpublished paper by Dr Green, 'Développement et declin de la production des Bibles en Angleterre entre 1530 et 1740 environ': all foreshadowing a forthcoming work by Dr Green on Bible production and other related aspects of catechesis in post-Reformation England.

12. K. Thomas, *Religion and the Decline of Magic* (London, 1971), p. 159.

sixteenth century? The answers to such questions are no longer as self-evident as they may have seemed in the days of J.R. Green.

At the very top of the social heap, we can quote Queen Elizabeth I herself, assuring her parliament in 1585: 'I am supposed to have many studies... And yet, amidst my many volumes, I hope God's book hath not been my seldomest lectures...'[13] There is evidence too that King Charles I, while not a theologian of his father's standing, knew his Bible well enough to trust his memory of a familiar text against a written version.[14] Not only is the Shakespeare canon teeming with biblical resonances and refractions. It seems to be possible to detect in the earlier plays echoes of the version known as the Bishops' Bible which the young Shakespeare would have heard read in church and perhaps school; whereas in the later plays we can find the mark of the Geneva version which by then the dramatist probably owned and read, in common with many of his contemporaries.[15] He and I could have owned and read the same copy.

And lower down the social scale? The martyrologist and church historian John Foxe wrote of the Suffolk town of Hadleigh that, as early as the reign of Henry VIII,

> a great number of that parish became exceeding well learned in the holy Scriptures, as well women as men, so that a man might have found among them many, that had often read the whole Bible through, and that could have said a great sort of St. Paul's epistles by heart, and very well and readily have given a godly learned sentence in any matter of controversy.

'The whole town seemed rather a university of the learned, than a town of cloth-making or labouring people.'[16] A source-critical comment is called for. The historian, and especially the historian sympathetic to a protestant and progressive account of modern religious history, may conclude that if it was like that in precocious Hadleigh in the 1540s and 50s, how much advance there must have been in the world beyond Hadleigh by the 1640s and 50s! But Hadleigh was Hadleigh, and Foxe

13. J.E. Neale, *Elizabeth I and her Parliaments, 1584–1601* (London, 1957), p. 100.

14. *Nicholas Ferrar: Two Lives by his Brother John and by Doctor Jebb* (ed. J.E.B. Mayor; Cambridge, 1855), p. 117.

15. R. Noble, *Shakespeare's Biblical Knowledge and the Use of the Book of Common Prayer* (London, 1935).

16. *The Acts and Monuments of John Foxe* (ed. S.R. Cattley; London, 1838), VI, pp. 676-77.

was Foxe; and we can no longer be confident that Foxe's Hadleigh was the real, or at least the only Hadleigh. Its Bible-reading weavers were for Foxe only a supporting cast for the star, the massive figure of their pastor, the martyr Rowland Taylor—who turns out to have been rather rarely there.[17]

II

When 'revisionism' has done its worst, Foxe's famous Hadleigh passage remains useful for the light it sheds on how illiterate (in the technical sense, which is to say, non-Latinate) readers read, used and knew their Bibles. *How* books were read in the sixteenth and seventeenth centuries is now a far from minor academic industry, the subject of two academic conferences in Cambridge in a single year (1992). Suddenly we have been made aware of acoustic reading (which is to say, a reading aloud so that others can hear and are perhaps obliged to hear), readings which were anything but private—collaborative, shared readings, and readings which reconstructed and authorised the text anew.[18] To refer to the relevant volume of *The Cambridge History of the Bible*, published in 1963, is to encounter a total lack of curiosity about such matters: many pages on how Luther or Calvin *thought* the Bible should be read; no information about the practice of reading.

So let us, as academic denizens of the 1990s, notice that Foxe tells us three things about the deployment of the Bible in the town of Hadleigh. Many had 'often' read the whole Bible 'through'. They could have repeated a great deal of St Paul's epistles by heart. And they were ever ready with 'a godly learned sentence', which is to say, a 'text', especially in controversial situations.

I believe this to be an accurate description of the mental attributes,

17. Dr John Craig has found that Taylor, whom Foxe idealized, can rarely have been resident in the parish; and that the new religion met with more resistance in Hadleigh than Foxe allows (J.S. Craig, 'Reformation, Politics and Polemics in Sixteenth-Century East Anglian Market Towns' [PhD thesis, Cambridge, 1992], Chapter 5, 'Conflict: Hadleigh, 1530–1560').

18. M. Aston, 'Lollardy and Literacy', in her *Lollards and Reformers: Images and Literacy in Late Medieval Religion* (London, 1984), pp. 193-214; L. Jardine and A. Grafton, '"Studied for Action": How Gabriel Harvey Read his Livy', *Past and Present* 129 (1990), pp. 30-78; papers read at the Cambridge conferences on reading practices by Roger Chartier, Eamon Duffy, Adam Fox, William Sherman, Andrew Taylor and Helen Weinstein, with interventions by Professor Don McKenzie.

habits and skills of early modern Bible-readers. In the first place, the Bible was read 'throughly', quite literally from end to end. We read of a prominent Exeter citizen of the 1620s who had read the Bible 'above twenty times over', Foxe's 'Book of Martyr's (a much longer book) a mere 'seven times over'.[19] And in all probability this Bible student, Ignatius Jordan, read aloud, in and to his family. This in turn facilitated memorization, Foxe's second point. The Bible, or parts of it, especially, as Foxe reports, the epistles, but also the Psalms, were memorized, not only as a matter of simple necessity by the wholly illiterate (although the illiterate did trust to their memories, it being a mistake to suppose that religious ignorance was a necessary consequence of being unable to read for oneself) but as an essential component and reinforcement of religious education and conduct at all educational levels. Members of Pembroke College, Cambridge, are brought up on the story of Bishop Nicholas Ridley memorizing the New Testament (in Greek) as he walked up and down in the Fellows' Garden. Thomas Cromwell is said to have exercised himself in the same way, riding to and from Italy.

The case and example of Nicholas Ferrar, central figure in the curious 'nunnery' at Little Gidding in the reign of Charles I, is particularly instructive, since Ferrar is (and in his own time often was) thought to have diverged from the sturdy protestant bibliocentrism of his contemporaries; and since, as we shall see, Ferrar's particular brand of biblicism was a source of fascination for Charles I himself. The young Ferrar had memorized Foxe, especially the story of his namesake, the martyred Bishop Ferrar, which 'he had perfect'. It is a long story. (At Little Gidding, Foxe would be publicly read every Sunday.) In his own household and parish, Nicholas Ferrar regularly called what are described as 'the psalm-children' before him, rewarding each with a penny for the psalm learned in the preceding week, and then hearing all that had been previously memorized, 'which was the chief end of his design, that they should learn all, and keep perfectly all they had learned'. Ferrar encouraged the learning of the whole Psalter without book 'not only by the young people, but by the elder sort, and he would even hire the poorer sort, parents as well as children, to this easy task...'[20] My own Scottish mother retained to her dying day the rich resource of the entire

19. S. Clarke, *A Collection of the Lives of Ten Eminent Divines...and of some other Eminent Christians* (London, 1662), p. 453.

20. *Nicholas Ferrar: Two Lives*, pp. 3-4, 29-30, 284-86.

book of Psalms, memorized in childhood. This is a skill, like 'mental arithmetic', only recently lost.

Foxe's third point concerned the division of the text into 'texts', the most significant organizing feature of sixteenth-century English Bibles, and one which was consonant with mentalities which still highly valued the proverbial, the aphoristic, the sententious.[21] Biblical knowledge was commonly encapsulated in weighty and apparently conclusive gobbets and (as we say) sound-bites of authoritative scriptural doctrine which could then be deployed, as Foxe reports, 'in any matter of controversy', but also for the resolution of inner doubts and the confrontation of life's adversities. Familiar words quoted at a critical juncture may have no logical force as proof. But it is significant that they were (and are) widely considered to be conclusive.

What Foxe reports is consistent with the advice offered to the reader of my own copy of the Geneva Bible, in the form of a loosely logical argument organized in the shape of a Ramist diagram and bearing the name of 'T. Grashop'.[22] There should be a certain ordered discipline in the reading of Scripture: 'At the least, twise every daye this exercise to be kept'. The reader should mark and consider, amongst other things, the 'coherence of the text, how it hangeth together', the 'agreement that one place of Scripture hath with an other, whereby that which seemeth darke in one is made easie in an other'. Even by its visual impact this diagram suggests the constructive, coherent, non-problematical, if strenuous nature of Bible reading and absorption. There is, after all, such a thing as 'Scripture', and it is possible for the editor of this Bible to provide in a couple of pages what purports to be 'the summe of the whole Scripture', 'of the bookes of the old and new Testament'.

III

That Scripture is all of a seamless piece, without caesura or conflict, is implicit in the engraved title page of this same edition of the Geneva

21. A. Fox, 'Aspects of Oral Culture and its Development in Early Modern England' (PhD thesis, Cambridge, 1993).

22. C. Hill gives prominence to Grashop's editorial statements in the Preface to his *The English Bible and the Seventeenth-Century Revolution* (London, 1993). Both Dr Hill and I have attempted, without success, to identify Grashop. He may or may not have been connected with the Canterbury schoolmaster John Gresshop, whose remarkable library of 350 volumes (indicative of a 'godly' Calvinist) is inventoried in William Urry, *Christopher Marlowe and Canterbury* (London, 1988), pp. 112-22.

Bible. The Twelve Tribes of Israel and the Twelve Apostles, Old Testament and New, form a single continuous frame for the Four Evangelists, each engaged in the writing of his own distinct but harmonious version of the one Gospel. Two open books proclaim: '*Verbum Dei manet in aeternum*'. Similar claims are implicit in the concordance provided at the back of the Bible, to which the title page refers, 'for the ready finding out of anything'. For while a concordance is a handy searching device, like those serried ranks of computers in our modern university libraries (and how eagerly the promoters of the Geneva Bible would have been to appropriate Information Technology!), the word concordance implies more than index, and is interchangeable with the word 'harmony', in itself affirming what H.H. Rowley in the title of a once notable book called *The Unity of the Bible* (1953).

So much has by now been made of my own copy of the Geneva Bible, as a kind of 'prop', that it should be said that, in spite of the agency of such shadowy figures as 'T. Grashop', it should not be regarded, either as a text or as a vehicle for certain hermeneutical principles relating to the text, to be a sectarian production. Although the Authorised Version would eventually enjoy a kind of normative precedence as *the* English Bible, the Vulgate of Protestant England, the Geneva version occupied that position far into the seventeenth century. William Fulke, an Elizabethan master of Pembroke College, Cambridge, called it 'the text commonly used in the Church of England'.[23] When Archbishop Laud sponsored Bibles with 'popish' illustrations which caused ructions in Scotland and went on to the crime sheet which brought him to the scaffold in England, the captions to his scandalous Bible pictures were nevertheless drawn from the Geneva Bible.[24]

We shall return to the theme of 'the unity of the Bible' as perceived by its sixteenth- and seventeenth-century students. But first we may take account of a discordant polemic which insists either that the Bible has no single, coherent message, or that that message is unlikely to be consistently and reliably conveyed to the innocent and unadvised reader; a case of

> Both read the Bible day and night,
> But thou reads't black where I read white.[25]

23. Quoted by George Henderson, 'Bible Illustration in the Age of Laud', *Transactions of the Cambridge Bibliographical Society* 8.2 (1982), p. 183.

24. Henderson, 'Bible Illustration'.

25. W. Blake, *The Everlasting Gospel*, alpha.

John Locke was one who exposed conflict and contradiction as inherent in the modes of Bible reading and exposition which John Foxe, in his account of the men and women of Hadleigh, had found unproblematical and harmonious. In his 1707 *Essay for the Understanding of St Paul's Epistles. By Consulting St Paul himself*, Locke complained of the practice of dividing up all Scripture, and especially of St Paul's Epistles, into

> Chapters and Verses…whereby they are so chop'd and minc'd, and as they are now Printed, stand so broken and divided, that not only the Common People take the Verses usually for distinct Aphorisms, but even Men of more advanc'd Knowledge in reading them, lose very much of the strength and force of the Coherence, and the Light that depends on it.

Locke suggested that if the Bible were to be printed as it was written, 'in continued Discourses', and the implication was that it should be so *read*, its sense would be apparent and might even prove to be a consensual matter on which it would be impossible for reasonable men to disagree. But, as things were, Scripture, 'crumbled into Verses', quickly turned into free-standing aphorisms or proof-texts which tended to support this or that tendency in a divided religious scene.[26] By contrast, Foxe, and the editor of my Geneva Bible, had assumed that the knowledge and deployment of particular verses, what Locke called 'so many distinct fragments', was compatible with that over-arching scriptural knowledge which derived from reading the Bible 'throughly', always with the sense that there was such a thing as the over-all sense and 'sum' of Scripture.

It is not altogether clear whether Locke, a liberal eirenicist, albeit a polemical liberal eirenicist, believed that the sectarian potentiality of the Bible was in the nature of the Text itself, or whether it was brought to the text by the sectarian interests of its readers. But he does seem to be saying that the kind of useful information technology which we find in the apparatus of the Geneva Bible was an incitement to sectarianism, insofar as it encouraged the naturally aphoristic instinct which believes that to quote the proverb 'many hands make light work' settles the matter, whatever the matter may be, until countered with 'too many cooks spoil the broth'. And chapter and verse lent a greater authority than any proverb.

---

26. D.F. McKenzie, *Bibliography and the Sociology of Texts* (London, 1986), pp. 46-47; J. Drury, *Critics of the Bible 1724–1873* (Cambridge, 1989), pp. 16-19.

John Drury suggests that the kind of reading which Locke commended was most compatible with the solitary reader, absorbing the text with leisurely reflection in the study or 'cabinet': paradigmatically, Erasmus of Rotterdam and, behind Erasmus, his model, St Jerome.[27] And yet, as early as the late fifteenth century, John Colet had taken such a reading into the public setting of the Oxford schools. Locke himself would have approved of Colet's handling of the Epistle to the Romans:

> This Epistle to the Romans was written during the reign of Claudius, at the close of his reign, about the twentieth year of St Paul's ministry. At which time also, as I gather from the histories and from St Paul himself, both Epistles to the Corinthians were written, as well as that to the Galatians.[28]

Read the Bible like any other book, Benjamin Jowett would recommend in *Essays and Reviews* in 1860—meaning, like any other antique text— whereupon it will seem like no other book.

Who read, understood and expounded the Pauline corpus as Colet read, understood and expounded it, for a considerable time after Colet, and perhaps for centuries? That is to say, as texts located in space and time, comparable and cross-referential with such other texts as Suetonius and Tacitus? Was there anyone between Colet and Jowett? In this respect, Reformation and Counter-Reformation had much to answer for. For Colet, St Paul said what he said about obedience in Romans 13 because he wrote within particular political circumstances. 'This is the point of that expression of St Paul', 'hence the Apostle commands', 'I mention this that St Paul's great thoughtfulness and prudence may be remarked. For being aware that Claudius Caesar had succeeded to the throne: a man of changeable disposition...'[29] And so on. But for Colet's expository successors, what St Paul taught about obedience to the powers that be was simply the truth, the Holy Spirit speaking through him, and timeless truth to boot.

For the Reformation, it was either not the case or not a matter of

27. Drury, *Critics*, p. 9. Drury proposes as the model of the reflective scholar in his cabinet Erasmus, as depicted by Holbein. On the very deliberate fashioning of that image on the model of St Jerome, see L. Jardine, *Erasmus, Man of Letters* (Princeton, 1993).

28. *An Exposition of St Paul's Epistle to the Romans Delivered as Lectures in the University of Oxford about the Year 1497, by John Colet* (ed. J.H. Lupton; London, 1873), p. 94.

29. Colet, *Exposition*, pp. 95-97.

importance that St Paul was a human agent, limited by the contingencies
of the time and the space that be inhabited. The humanistic learning
which Colet commanded and exemplified was not jettisoned, but it was
restricted to the ancillary role of clarifying the biblical text verbally and
grammatically, not employed to historicize it. The motive of protestant
expositors and readers, at whatever level, was professedly anti-historicist,
making of 'Scripture' a text which was not only harmonious but of
timeless validity.

And, since there was presently no harmony of religious persuasion,
attacks were made on the culpability of autodidactic Bible reading which
were less eirenical than Locke's and as merciless as Dryden:

> And did not these by Gospel Texts alone
> Condemn our doctrine, and maintain their own?
> Have not all hereticks the same pretence
> To plead the Scriptures in their own defence?

In the Preface to Dryden's *Religio Laici* (1682) we find a reference to
'the many Heresies the first Translation of *Tyndale* produced in few
years', and in the poem itself these lines:

> The Book thus put in every vulgar hand,
> Which each presum'd he best cou'd understand,
> The *Common Rule* was made the *common Prey*;
> And at the mercy of the *Rabble* lay.
> The tender Page with horney Fists was gaul'd;
> And he was gifted most that loudest baul'd.[30]

In 1682, Dryden had professed to write in the interest of the Church of
England, whose articles gave the last say in matters of faith not to the
Church but to Scripture. His conversion to Rome in 1686 was not
unpredictable, or even unexpected. Now he put into the mouth of one of
the interlocutors in *The Hind and the Panther* (1687) these reflections.
You say 'the Word in needfull points is onely plain'. Yet

> the rule you lay
> Has led whole flocks, and leads them still astray
> In weighty points, and full damnation's way.

30. J. Dryden, *The Hind and the Panther*, pt. 2, ll. 152-55; *The Works of
John Dryden*. III. *Poems 1685–1692* (Berkeley, 1969), p. 144; J. Dryden, *Religio
Laici*, ll. 400-16, *The Works of John Dryden*. II. *Poems 1681–1684* (Berkeley, 1972),
p. 121.

The Council of Nicaea had been wise enough not to rest on the principle
of *sola scriptura*.

> The Council steer'd it seems a diff'rent course,
> They try'd the Scripture by tradition's force.

But the modern sectarian tried tradition by Scripture.

> I see tradition then is disallow'd
> When not evinc'd by Scripture to be true,
> And Scripture, as interpreted by you.

> Thus when you said tradition must be try'd
> By sacred Writ, whose sense your selves decide,
> You said no more, but that your selves must be
> The judges of the Scripture sense, not we.[31]

Dryden, and for that matter Locke, wrote in the context and under the
shadow of a fundamental challenge, Socinian, Arian, Deist, to what
earlier generations had professed to believe were unassailable truths,
whether primarily ecclesiastical or scriptural. Both Protestants and
Catholics had allowed themselves the luxury (as it were) of confessional
wars about matters which many in the later seventeenth century held to
be less than fundamental: soteriology, the sacraments, ecclesiology. Yet
the problem for the later seventeenth century, which was definitively
stated in Hobbes' *Behemoth*, was already confronted in the early
sixteenth century, as the consequence of Martin Luther's affirmations
and the enterprise of translation and propagation which Luther set in
motion. How could the universal availability of a text, which even in
principle 'authorised' could not be authorised in all its readings, be
reconciled with the claims of authority in a human and political sense?

  There was no straightforward answer. The problem was fudged by
Thomas More, who professed to believe, mistakenly, in the existence of
an orthodox version of the English Bible, distinct from the heretical
Wycliffite version; and by Bishop Stephen Gardiner, who favoured a
kind of macaronic text, half English, half Latin, its partial Latinity a
means of conserving ecclesiastical control: 'This is my dilect son, in
whom complacui'.[32] To restrict Bible reading to consenting adults under

31. Dryden, *Works*, III, pp. 144-45.
32. J.F. Mozley, *William Tyndale* (London, 1937), pp. 77-78; Richard Marius,
Thomas More: A Biography (London, 1984), pp. 347-49; J.F. Mozley, *Coverdale and
his Bibles* (London, 1953), pp. 273-75; B.F. Westcott, *History of the English Bible*
(London, 1868); A.G. Dickens, *The English Reformation* (2nd edn, London, 1989),
p. 158.

ecclesiastical surveillance (Henry VIII would presently add, 'adults of a certain social class') was a Canute-like defiance of the imperatives of print technology, as even More probably knew in his more realistic, or pessimistic moments.[33]

So the English Catholics, in their Elizabethan exile, physical and intellectual, published their own vernacular version of the Scriptures: the Rheims Testament, the Douai Bible. If you can't beat them, join them. And now the argument shifted from *whether* an English Bible to *what kind of* English Bible and to the partiality of translations, where More had pitched it when he first attacked Tyndale. In a voluminous and tedious controversy of the 1570s, the Catholic Gregory Martin in *A discoverie of the corruptions of the holy scriptures by the heretikes* (Rheims, 1582) and the protestant William Fulke in *A defense of the sincere and true translations of the holie Scriptures into the English tong* (1583) debated Martin's charge that the Protestants had perpetrated 'partial and false translations to the advantage of their heresies'. Martin claimed that Luther had called the Epistle of James, which weakened the doctrine of justification by faith, an 'epistle of straw', calling in question its canonical status. Fulke replied that Luther had retracted that statement, which nevertheless had a certain validity, the Epistle of James being not 'so excellent and necessary as the Gospels and other Epistles'. Martin said Luther had added a gratuitous and unjustified 'only' to St Paul's 'justified by faith'. Fulke answered again, Luther strictly speaking was at fault, and had admitted as much. But it was a virtuous fault, enhancing rather than altering the sense of the original text. 'Images' rather than 'idols' appeared in some English translations, applying the second commandment to all ecclesiastical imagery whatsoever. It took many pages to sort that one out, or rather not to sort it out.[34]

The underlying issue was always the same, in the hostile critique of Protestantism. The appeal to scriptural authority was spurious, since it

33. 'And yet, son Roper, I pray God…that some of us, as high as we seem to sit upon the mountains, treading heretics under our feet, live not the day that we gladly wish to be at a league and composition with them, to let them have their churches quietly to themselves, so that they would be content to let us have ours quietly to ourselves' (quoted by A.G. Dickens, *Reformation Studies* [London, 1982], p. 444).

34. W. Fulke, *A Defence of the Sincere and True Translations of the Holy Scriptures into the English Tongue* (1583) (ed. C.H. Hartshorne; Parker Society; Cambridge, 1843), pp. 14-18, 121-22, 154, 190-216.

concealed a reference to private judgment. For Luther to attribute to a single layman armed with Scripture an authority capable of prevailing over both popes and councils was anarchical, a dangerous nonsense which would deconstruct both church and civil society, there being in principle an infinitude of partial, prejudicial readings. Protestants, for their part, did not accuse their opponents of ignoring Scripture but rather of 'wresting' it. Tyndale wrote: 'They make it a nose of wax, and wrest it this way and that way, till it agree'. Catholics lobbed the same tennis ball back, the Dutch controversialist Albert Pighius complaining that among heretics 'the scripture is like a nose of wax, that easily suffereth itself to be drawn backward and forward, and to be moulded and fashioned this way and that way, and howsoever ye list'.[35]

IV

It is none of my concern to join in the 'nose of wax' debate, still less to stiffen the nose in the interest of either Protestantism or Catholicism. Let it stick out, like Cyrano de Bergerac's nose, and let it wobble. Both sides were in principle right, right in what they polemically affirmed, wrong in what they defensively denied, and the argument was won by the innocent or, in the case of Dryden, not-so-innocent onlooker. It is hard to disagree with W.B. Glover, who, in a book on *Evangelical Nonconformists and Higher Criticism in the Nineteenth Century* (1954), wrote that 'the traditional conception of the Bible did not so much support Christianity as depend for its support upon its alliance with a strong religious faith. The apparent foundation was in fact supported from above by the thing it was thought to support.'[36] Nor is it easy to dissent from Jowett's devastating verdict in *Essays and Reviews*: 'The uneducated, or imperfectly educated person who looks at the marginal references of the English Bible, imagining himself to gain a clearer insight into the Divine meaning, is really following the religious associations of his own mind'.[37] Similarly, when the late sixteenth-century theologian wrote of

35. Fulke, *Defence*, pp. 8, 539; H.C. Porter, 'The Nose of Wax: Scripture and the Spirit from Erasmus to Milton', *Transactions of the Royal Historical Society*, 5th ser. 14 (1964), pp. 155-74.

36. W.B. Glover, *Evangelical Nonconformists and Higher Criticism in the Nineteenth Century* (London, 1954), p. 18.

37. B. Jowett, 'On the Interpretation of Scripture', in *Essays and Reviews* (London, 1860), p. 383.

'the consent of all the parts of the Scripture', he was taking what Dr Harry Porter has called 'the Protestant leap in the dark'.[38]

Is there then nothing to be said for the great theme which Rowley handled in his *The Unity of the Bible*? Rowley surely protested too much when he wrote of 'a unity which lies in great diversity', 'a dynamic and not a static unity'. But for anyone reared in the protestant biblical tradition, Rowley's words about 'the continuing thread that runs through all and that makes this library also a Book' are seductive, if not actually persuasive. We too, like the young Dostoevsky within a different tradition, have wept in church, inwardly at least, as we have heard the story of Job, aware in spite of the disturbing theodicies of a unique text of affinity with other parts of the Bible, and with our own moral judgment. It may well be that, in the terms of Glover's image, all this is suspended from above rather than supported from below, but who can ultimately say, the Bible having itself contributed so much to that which is above and from which our conception of the Bible itself is suspended. This is what Frank Kermode has in mind when he writes of an 'occult plot' concealed in the Bible: a secondary plot, as it were, not arbitrarily read into the text by the reader, or even a collectivity of readers: a series of recapitulations and refractions, promises and fulfilments, operating intertextually and extratextually. The writers of Scripture were also the readers of Scripture, and very self-consciously so.[39]

It was in some such sense and by some such instinctive mental processes that the Bible was invested with coherence and a single meaning in protestant England. Counter-Reformation controversialists, Dryden and Locke, sceptical for very different polemical purposes about 'the coherence of the text', were not necessarily right and may have been (as it were) existentially wrong. It may be that their protestant opponents were not entitled to believe in the coherence of the text, how one place agreed with another. The fact is that they *did* so believe, in all sincerity, and it distorts our understanding of an entire intellectual and cultural epoch to read, for example, Dryden's polemic as an accurate and conclusive judgment upon their mentalities.

38. Porter, 'The Nose of Wax', p. 163.
39. H.H. Rowley, *The Unity of the Bible* (London, 1953), pp. 7, 27; F. Kermode, 'The Bible: Story and Plot' (The Ethel M. Wood Lecture 1984; c. 1984), pp. 7, 16. A particularly appealing and sophisticated plea for the unity of Scripture, couched in an exposition of sixteenth-century thought on the matter, is J.S. Coolidge, *The Pauline Renaissance in England: Puritanism and the Bible* (Oxford, 1970).

Much hangs on this. Turn Dryden upside down and make negative criticism positive, and what hangs on it is the modernization and secularization of the European mind, or, at the very least, the liberalization of thought.[40] Harry Porter pointed out that the nose of wax could turn into a twig from which the butterfly of free enquiry would take off, no longer constrained by either scripturalism or ecclesiasticism, the nose of wax irrevocably tweaked by the Enlightenment.[41] To insist on the reality and strength of a conservative scriptural consensuality, a consensuality grounded in a sense of the coherence of the text, may appear to glue the butterfly back on to the twig. The historian has no motive to wield the glue-pot, only to insist that the insect was pretty firmly so glued, for four or five generations after Tyndale.

The formal reasons for insisting on the inherent unity and consistency of Scripture were diverse and not necessarily mutually consistent. One reason, with deep medieval roots, concerned the replications of the Old Testament to be found in the New. Another concerned the harmony of the four Gospels. For the sixteenth and seventeenth centuries harmonization was an absorbing occupation, if less taxing than the intellectual labour of reconciling the conflicts between the biblical and classical or other non-biblical chronologies, an enterprise driven by a similar orthodox and conservative motive. John Calvin's *Commentary on the Harmony of the Four Evangelists* was translated by the Elizabethan Puritan divine, Eusebius Paget, apparently the occupation of long winters' evenings on the windswept promontory of Kilkhampton, on the borders of Devon and Cornwall.[42] As we shall see, such harmonies were

40. This is the hidden agenda of C. Hill's *The English Bible and the Seventeenth-Century Revolution*, becoming explicit in the final chapter, 'The Bible Dethroned'. The late Professor Perry Miller's interest in the ultimate legacy of protestant and puritan biblicism (in New England) was of a similar order. See the progressive intellectual history of early America contained in his *Orthodoxy in Massachusetts 1630–1650: A Genetic Study* (Cambridge, MA, 1933); *The New England Mind* (2 vols.; Cambridge, MA; 1939, 1953).

41. Porter, 'The Nose of Wax', pp. 155, 174.

42. J. Calvin, *A harmonie upon the three evangelists, Matthew, Mark and Luke... Whereunto is added a commentary upon S. John* (trans. E. Paget; London, 1584). Paget's translation was acknowledged but found 'unsuitable to modern taste' in W. Pringle's nineteenth-century translation of *Commentary on a Harmony of the Evangelists, Matthew, Mark and Luke by John Calvin* (Edinburgh: Calvin Translation Society, 1847); *Commentary on the Gospel according to John by John Calvin* (Edinburgh: Calvin Translation Society, 1847). In early French editions, the *Harmony*

almost an obsession with the Little Gidding community in the Huntingdonshire of the 1630s.

Yet another unifying principle was Pauline, the Bible read and understood from a standpoint in the Epistles, and especially in the light of the Epistle to the Romans. Tyndale, following Luther, called Romans 'the principle and most excellent part of the New Testament...a light and a way unto the whole Scripture'. Tyndale was not exercising a merely academic theological judgment. When he declared that we find in Romans 'plenteously, unto the uttermost, whatsoever a christian man or woman ought to know', 'the pith of all, that pertaineth to the christian faith', he had in mind what that text had to say to 'the bottom of the heart', in Luther's language, *Herzgrund*.[43] Bunyan's *Pilgrims Progress* opens with an emblem of the troubled *Herzgrund*, the dreamlike vision of a man 'cloathed with Raggs, standing in a certain place, with his face from his own House, a Book in his hand, and a great Burden upon his Back'; a man who, as he read, wept and trembled, 'and not being able longer to contain...brake out with a lamentable cry; saying *What shall I do to be saved*?' It would be hard to make too much of the centrality of this protestant salvific principle for seventeenth-century civilization. Professor Barbara Lewalski finds 'the classic Protestant paradigm of sin and salvation' the fundament of the protestant poetics of Donne, Herbert, Vaughan, and even of Traherne, the key to unlock the Psalms and much else in Scripture.[44] What Professor John Carey has written of Tyndale applies to Tyndale's posterity: 'Tyndale has only one thing to say, and the problem for the critic is how he manages to say it so often...yet still to conduct us forward, alert, through page after page'.[45]

Most fundamental of all was a perfectly circular argument, or position: Scripture its own interpreter, free of any external point of reference or validation, in Luther's words, proving, judging and illuminating everything. 'No man perceives one iota of what is in the Scriptures unless

---

was described as *La concordance qu'on appele harmonie* and *la concordance ou harmonie*.

43. W. Tyndale, 'A Prologue upon the Epistle of St Paul to the Romans', in *The Work of William Tyndale*, pp. 143, 121.

44. B. Lewalski, *Protestant Poetics and the Seventeenth-Century Religious Lyric* (Princeton, 1979), p. 8 and *passim*.

45. J. Carey, 'Prose Before Elizabeth', in *English Poetry and Prose 1540–1674* (ed. C. Ricks; London, 1986 edn), p. 336.

he has the Spirit of God', which is to say, abandons all normal, human(e) modes of perception.[46]

Such were some of the formal reasons for subscribing to the unity and coherence of Scripture. But the informal, existential reasons may have been more compelling. They are memorably stated in the official Homily of the Church of England 'On the Scriptures':

> And in reading of God's Word, he not alwayes most profiteth that is most ready in turning of the book, or in saying of it without the book, but he that is most turned into it, that is, most inspired with the Holy Ghost, most in his heart and life altered and changed into that which he readeth.

V

It was in some such fashion, a matter of cultural habits and rhythms as much as of mental capacities and disciplines, that sixteenth- and seventeenth-century English Protestants were altered and changed into what they read, and more or less regardless of divergent religious tendencies, 'Anglican' or 'Puritan', regardless too of social class and, within limits, of different levels of educational and cultural development. The principle of the coherence of the text, how it hangeth together, served to reconcile and unite not only actually or potentially discordant texts, but socially, intellectually and culturally diverse groups and strata.

Some of the most copious and eloquent evidence of lives turned into living patterns of the biblical text survives in the letters of the protestant martyrs of the 1550s, as collected and published by Miles Coverdale and Henry Bull from the manuscripts now preserved among the foundation deeds of Emmanuel College, Cambridge, sources given the widest ventilation in the immense prolixity of John Foxe's *Acts and Monuments*, the so-called 'Book of Martyrs'.[47] The trial narratives of the martyrs, composed by the victims themselves, are no less marinated in the language and imagery of Scripture. In these sources we find a new language, acquired with remarkable rapidity (for the Reformation was still young), deployed by minds saturated with Scripture and able to move around within it with the familiarity and ease of a blind man who knows the

---

46. *Luther and Erasmus: Free Will and Salvation* (ed. E.G. Rupp and B.D. Drewery; Library of Christian Classics, 17; London, 1969), p. 112.

47. S. Wabuda, 'Henry Bull, Miles Coverdale, and the Making of *Foxe's Book of Martyrs*', in *Martyrs and Martyrologies: Studies in Church History*, XXX (ed. D. Wood; Oxford, 1993), pp. 245-48.

position and feel of every stick of furniture in his own house.

Here is the martyr John Bradford, writing to a certain 'faithful woman in her heaviness and trouble':

> Therefore, my dearly beloved arise; and remember from whence you are fallen. You have a shepherd which never slumbereth nor sleepeth; no man nor devil can pull you out of his hands; night and day he commandeth his angels to keep you. Have you forgotten what I read to you out of the Psalm, 'The Lord is my shepherd, I can want nothing?' Do you not know that God sparred Noah in the ark on the outside, so that he could not get out? So hath he done to you, my good sister; so hath he done to you. Ten thousand shall fall on your right hand, and twenty thousand on your left hand; yet no evil shall touch you.[48]

Bradford was a learned man, yet there is no perceptible difference between his Bible talk and that of a more obscure martyr called Edmund Allin, a corn miller of Frittenden in the Kentish Weald, who defended his presumption in preaching and teaching though a simple lay man with these words:

> We are...as Peter writeth...lively stones to give light to others. For as out of flint stones cometh forth that which is able to set all the world on fire, so out of Christians should spring the beams of the gospel, which should inflame all the world.

Accused by his judges of too much familiarity with the Old Testament, the source of most of his precedents and proof-texts, Allin reminded them that while Old Testament ceremonial law was abolished in Christ, 'as St Paul proveth to the Hebrews; and to the Colossians', the judicial law still stood: Matthew 5 and St Paul in 1 Timothy 4. As text after text poured from the mouth of the miller of Frittenden, the tribunal exploded in exasperation. 'This rebel will believe nothing but Scripture.'[49]

Catholic authority, confronted with an unlearned heretic with his (and often her) head stuffed with the Bible, would soon be replaced by Anglican authority, and the reaction would be the same, Archbishop Bancroft sneering at Puritans 'learned in the margins of an English Bible'. But it would be a bad mistake to connect too closely the kind of biblicism routinely denounced by those for whom it was a nuisance to radical and deviant undercurrents. George Herbert, divine poet and exemplary pastor, advocated precisely the same Bible reading habits and

48. *Acts and Monuments of John Foxe*, VII (1838), p. 233.
49. *Acts and Monuments of John Foxe*, VIII (1839), pp. 323-24.

methods as I find prescribed in my Geneva Bible, which were the habits
of Foxe's Hadleigh weavers or of the Frittenden miller:

Oh that I knew how all thy lights combine,
And the configurations of their glorie!
Seeing not onely how each verse doth shine,
But all the constellations of the storie.
This verse marks that, and both do make a motion
Unto a third, that ten leaves off doth lie:
These three make up some Christians destinie.

In the prose of *The Country Parson*, Herbert commended 'an industrious
and judicious comparing of place with place', 'a diligent Collation of
Scripture with Scripture', not (or not only) for the miller and the weaver
but for the parson himself.[50]

In the unique quasi-monastic community formed at Little Gidding by
Herbert's friend Nicholas Ferrar, chapters of the Harmony of the Four
Gospels were read every day. And there was a room called the
Concordance Room, a serene place with shining green walls adorned
with scriptural texts and equipped with large tables. Here the women of
the family engaged in what has been called a 'sublimation of scissors and
paste'. Bibles were cut to pieces, verse by verse, only to be reassembled
into a continuous and harmonious textual confection by pasting them on
to large sheets of stiff white paper.[51] So skilfully was this done that it
was almost impossible to distinguish these up-market scrap books from
real printed books. Although they had no publisher, in the ordinary
sense, and derive entirely from other books, they have been allowed an
entry in the *Short-Title Catalogue* of books printed in England between
1475 and 1640. Every page was richly embellished with all kinds of cuts
and other pictures, taken from the collections which Ferrar had made
on his foreign travels.[52] Finally the Little Gidding harmonies were

50. *The Works of George Herbert* (ed. F.E. Hutchinson; Oxford, 1941), pp. 58,
229.
51. *Nicholas Ferrar: Two Lives*, pp. 111-34; C. Leslie Craig, 'The Earliest Little
Gidding Concordance', *Harvard Library Bulletin* 1 (1947), pp. 311-31; C. Davenport,
'Little Gidding Bindings', *Bibliographica* 2 (1896), pp. 129-49; Henderson, 'Bible
Illustration', pp. 173-204; T.A. Birrell, *English Monarchs and their Books from
Henry VII to Charles I* (London, 1987), pp. 52-54.
52. In addition to the pictures from Ferrar's collections which were utilized in the
harmonies, there are many others, preserved loose in the Pepysian Library of
Magdalene College, Cambridge. However, their provenance is not Pepysian, they

cased in bindings of unusual sumptuousness.

Charles I had occasion to borrow the first of these harmonies (now preserved in the Houghton Library at Harvard), and his notes in the margins suggest that it stirred more than a merely aesthetic sense. The Little Gidding people then presented the king with another of their productions for his own use, which Charles told Archbishop Laud and others present was 'a precious gem, and worthy of his cabinet'. So it was that several harmonies found their way into the royal collections and are today part of the British Library in Bloomsbury. They include several harmonies of the Gospels, but also of Kings and Chronicles, Acts and Revelation, 'reduced unto one complete Body of History', 'brought into one Narrative by way of Composition'. The king was fascinated by the harmonized conflation of Kings and Chronicles '*as if written*, said he, *by one man's pen*'.[53]

Essays are finite things, but we have touched only the outer edge of an almost infinite subject. We have not considered how a common sense of the coherence of the text may have been acquired and consolidated. There is an allusive and elusive hint of the religious culture out of which it came in the small lozenge-shaped picture which fills the bottom left-hand corner of the engraved title-page of Foxe's *Acts and Monuments*.

having arrived at the college by another route (Henderson, 'Bible Illustration', p. 187).

53. *Nicolas Ferrar: Two Lives*, pp. 115-22, 266-69; Craig, 'The Earliest Little Gidding Concordance', pp. 311-31. The elaborately decorated and highly self-conscious title-page of the Little Gidding Gospel Harmony of 1635 (British Library) expounds the principles and methods, as well as the underlying hermeneutical assumptions of the enterprise:

THE/ACTIONS &/DOCTRINE &/Other PASSAGES touching/Our Lord & Savior JESUS CHRIST, as they are Related by the/FOURE EVANGELISTS./Reduced unto one Complete Body of HISTORIE, wherein/That which is SEVERALLY Related by them is Digested into ORDER/And that which is JOINTLY Related by all or any two of them/is First expressed in their own Words by way of COMPARISON,/And secondly brought into one Narration by way of COMPOSITION./ And Thirdly extracted into one clear Context by way of COLLECTION./ Yet so as whatsoever is omitted in the Context/ is Inserted by way of SUPPLEMENT in/another Point In such manner as all the/FOURE EVANGELISTS may be read SEVERALLY from First to Last./ To which are added/Sundry PICTURES Exposing either the FACTS themselves/or those TYPES and Figures/ of other MATTERS appertaining thereto./AN MDCXXV.

(Birrell, *English Monarchs and their Books*, reproduced between pp. 52 and 54). The same title had been applied to the first harmony of 1630 (*Nicholas Ferrar: Two Lives*, p. 111).

A congregation, composed of both sexes and various ages, is clustered around the base of a pulpit from which a generously bearded preacher expounds, one hand on the pulpit Bible, the other using appropriate gestures to reinforce the message. The Bibles open on laps are illuminated by the sermon. It was often held, in puritan circles, that only the sermon, not the bare reading of the Bible, had saving and converting power.[54] And yet the open Bible on the lap, finger-nail underlining text, the leaf dog-eared for further reference,[55] was there to correct or confirm the words of the preacher. This is a picture of a complex, two-way traffic of minds, memories and texts, to be carried beyond the sermon into the highly valued seventeenth-century institution of sermon 'repetition', when the preacher might be present, or represented by the notes of his sermon carried away by the hearers. There was, as those same hearers were often reminded from the pulpit, an 'art of hearing' as well as of preaching.

'Take opportunitie', says Grashop in my Geneva Bible, to 'hear preaching and to prove by the Scriptures that which is taught'. John Drury has pointed out that the paradigm for this scene, it goes without saying a biblical paradigm, is to be found in Nehemiah ch. 8, where the people are gathered at the water gate to hear Ezra the prophet read the law upon a pulpit of wood, placed above them, with a whole corps of exegetes giving the sense, 'so that the people understood the reading'. As Drury observes, this was the very *mis-en-scène* of the Bible in the setting of English society two millennia later. 'The continuity is remarkable.'[56] And yet, thanks to Dryden and much else besides, this paradigm, indicative of the Bible as a totem of religious community, is less familiar than that other emblem: Bunyan's alienated but seeking man, guided by little other than the book in his hand.

Almost nothing has been said in this essay about the effect of the Bible in seventeenth-century England: about its hugely paradigmatic role in fostering a new sense of nationhood; about its radical political and

54. The forthcoming Cambridge PhD thesis by Arnold Hunt will include a definitive examination of this long-controverted issue.

55. In the 'character' of the She-Puritan in J. Earle's *Microcosmographie* (1628), we learn that 'her devotion at the Church is much in the turning up her ey, and turning downe the leaf in her book, when she heares named Chapter and Verse' (*John Earle: The Autograph Manuscript of Microcosmographie* [Leeds, 1966], p. 117).

56. Drury, *Critics of the Bible*, p. 3.

social potential, on which Christopher Hill has written a book of 466 pages.[57] (A larger book on the Bible as a conservative and conserving text can perhaps be taken as read.) And then there is the no small matter of the literary impact, on which Barbara Lewalski has written so magisterially in her *Protestant Poetics and the Seventeenth-Century Religious Lyric*, exploring the almost limitless poetic possibilities of those rich figures and tropes with which Scripture abounds and which were as accessible to Donne, Herbert or Traherne as to the miller of Frittenden: sin as sickness, Christ as physician, grace as balm; darkness and light, bondage and freedom; warfare, pilgrimage, chastisement and trial; sheep and shepherd; gardens of all kinds, from Eden to the Song of Songs, via the garden of cucumbers; branch and tree; marriage; the temple composed of lively stones; the heart. 'Such metaphors', observes Lewalski, 'provided a nexus between the biblical paradigms and the individual Christian life'.[58]

Professor Lily Campbell paused on the edge of a similar literary exploration with these words: 'If I were to undertake to trace the whole movement to make the Bible the guide to Christian living I should require more years than I can hope to live and more volumes than any printer would publish'.[59] I do not know if Professor Campbell was aware that even *that* sentence was a biblical resonance, an echo of Jn 21.25: 'Now there are also many other things which Jesus did, the which if they should bee written every one, I suppose the world could not containe the bookes that should be written, Amen' (Geneva version).

But it goes without saying that Professor James Atkinson, with his profound and humbling knowledge of both Holy Scripture and the religious thought-world of the Reformation, would not have failed to respond to such a resonance!

57. Hill, *The English Bible and the Seventeenth-Century Revolution*.
58. Lewalski, *Protestant Poetics*, pp. 86-103.
59. L.B. Campbell, *Divine Poetry and Drama in Sixteenth-Century England* (Cambridge, 1959), p. 3.

WAS LUTHER A HERETIC?

Benjamin Drewery

In 1966 our patristic *maestro*, Henry Chadwick, gave us his *Early Christian Thought and the Classical Tradition*, and we were treated in the final chapter to a masterly discussion of what he called 'the perennial issue'—was Origen orthodox or a heretic? He reminds us of Origen's own remark (*Comm. in Gen.* 24.296) that in advanced matters of theology, 'absolute confidence is possible only for two classes of people, saints and idiots'. In asking, then, whether or not Origen is orthodox, we are continually driven back to the prior question: what is the essence of orthodoxy? We turn the page eagerly to find from the Olympian Dr Chadwick what it is—and find instead that this *question* was the last sentence in his book. It is indeed ever thus. The definitive work of H.E.W. Turner, *The Pattern of Christian Truth* (1954), which more or less launched me on my own patristic studies, told us everything except what the pattern of Christian Truth really *is*. I fear to follow the example of these great scholars. Before I answer my own question 'Was Luther a heretic?', I feel bound to suggest what heresy *is*, and this means a search for *orthodoxy* itself, from which heresy is a deviation or whatever metaphor we choose to apply.

There is, of course, a strong tradition in modern theology, from Leonard Hodgson onwards, that denies the propriety of the categories of orthodoxy and heresy altogether. This thinking goes back to the seminal work of Walter Bauer in 1934, *Rechtgläubigkeit und Ketzerei im ältesten Christentum*. His thesis was ultimately simple: in the early centuries there was no clear-cut or fundamental distinction at all. 'Orthodoxy' and 'heresy' arose simultaneously: the former was merely one among many splinter-groups, but it had the advantage of episcopal leadership master-minded by the grand villain of the piece—the Bishop of Rome. Rome satisfied herself as to her own conscious 'orthodoxy' at an earlier period than the other churches, on whose leaders she proceeded to impose it. The West was easily dominated, and the East was subjugated by Corinth, Rome's own Greek agent. Hence 'orthodoxy', right down to Chalcedon (451), merely meant the Roman view: 'heresy' meant *other* views of the evidence. Historically and objectively they are on a level—so many 'possible options'. Search for the truth should divest itself of illegitimate preconceptions such as 'orthodoxy' and 'heresy'.

Now Bauer's thesis is, I think, spoiled by what I might call his Roman dimension. With one or two exceptions—above all, Tertullian, Hippolytus and Novation (all three schismatics, if not heretics!), the real Christian thinking in the early Church was not done by Rome or in the West at all, but in the Greek East. One has only to remember Clement, Origen, Athanasius, the Cappadocian trio of the two Gregories and Basil, the Great Antiochenes, Cyril of Alexandria. The influence of Rome in those centuries was almost always that of a *mediator*. In questions such as the rebaptism of heretics, Rome was understanding and moderate: in matters of doctrine (e.g. Montanism) Rome was anxious to keep doors open as long as possible. This is supremely the case with the Tome of Leo, in which that master of language sought to combine the Christologies of Antioch and Alexandria.

If we omit the Roman dimension, however, Bauer's claim remains formidable, and it is of the greatest interest that it was answered, in principle and in detail, by the 1954 work of H.E.W. Turner already mentioned. To those interested, I commend the 1971 translation of Bauer's work (SPCK) in which Georg Strecker brings the discussion up to date by two appendices, including the reaction of Turner and of such scholars as my Manchester predecessor, Arnold Ehrhardt. The heart of the whole matter seems to me to lie in Turner's own positive thesis, which is as follows.

The evidence points neither to the ultra-traditional theory that 'orthodoxy' sprang to fully developed maturity at a stroke, like Athene from the head of Zeus, nor to the ultra-modern theory of its being merely one among many options, but to '*the spiritual autonomy of a gradually evolving pattern of Christian truth*', culminating in Chalcedon but not however frozen and untouchable thereafter, as the Orthodox Greek Church would have it. In this formula every word is significant.

1. 'Orthodoxy' is the attempted apprehension of *truth*—ὀρθὴ δόξα 'right opinion' and the two cannot be sundered after the fashion of Bauer.

2. It is not a 'system' or even a 'creed' but a 'pattern'—a less cast-iron and finite word.

3. It is open to gradual 'unfolding' or 'evolution'.

4. It has its own 'spiritual autonomy'. This raises without solving the question of authority, but it suggests that the *truth* is its own self-witness, and the role of Popes, Councils, theologians is in the end not so much authentication as reception, recognition of what subsists as the truth in its own right.

Now the longer I read the early fathers, the more certain I am that something like Turner's view against the Bauer view must be the truth. I cannot make sense of their writings, confessions, creeds, anathemas, without the assumption that behind them all lay *something, someone*, which or who was the *truth*, objective, eternal, not to be bartered or spoiled at any price. The one query I would make about Turner's formula would be about the words 'gradually evolving'. I do not link my views with Darwin, and I do not see a steady, unvarying progress through the ages. There may be huge periods of recession and error—Martin Luther, *prima facie*, may for example symbolize one such. In any case, it is not so much the pattern that evolves, but its apprehension, exposition and application. *These* may well be (as I should say) varyingly but on the whole progressively perceptible throughout the Christian centuries.

But the pattern itself—the *something*, the *someone*—which lay at the heart of the Church's convictions, was *not* a visible standard to which the seeker for orthodoxy could be led. Look at the controversies of the second century—Marcion, Gnosticism, Montanism. The Church rejected them, as it were, *instinctively*. There were no Creeds or Confessions and there was as yet no canonical New Testament to which the Church could point. It was rather that *something, someone* against which the heresies offended. What then, *was* this something, someone? It is here that we look in vain to Turner himself. We must use his hints and insights to seek it for ourselves.

Of course, the prior authority must be Scripture—the Old Testament Law, Prophets, Writings, and the *events* to which the New Testament bears witness, even if the New Testament itself was not yet canonized in the form it has had since at least Athanasius in the fourth century. It will be useless to condemn Luther, for example, on the basis of *tradition*, however 'catholic' and sanctified that may be. The Council of Trent declared in 1546 that Scripture and tradition were to be received as of equal authority—*pari pietatis affectu ac reverentia*: this was the answer to the *sola scriptura* of the Protestants. But Vatican II, with all necessary diplomacy and delicacy of language, made it nevertheless clear that, as Roman Catholic scholars have increasingly held, all revelation is materially contained in the Scriptures.

Yet the New Testament, even when canonically complete, contained no Creed as such. Scholars speak of it as offering the *raw material* of developed belief, the *deposit* or *quantum* of later orthodoxy—all of which metaphors are objectionable as materialistic in the extreme. Here again Turner's metaphor of the *pattern* remains supreme. But what *is* this pattern? How do we describe it?

I confess that I have been helped here above all by the great scholar at whose feet I sat just after the War, and whose legacy remains unique— C.H. Dodd.

In 1936 Dodd published his *Apostolic Preaching*, in which he began by tracing what he calls the *primitive kerygma*: that is the original Christian message as it was apprehended before the superstructure of theological reflection was built upon it by Paul, John and the rest. This primitive kerygma he found in the sermons of Peter at Pentecost (Acts 2), in Solomon's porch (Acts 3), before Annas (Acts 4), before the Sanhedrin (Acts 5) and Cornelius at Caesarea (Acts 10). Alongside these Dodd set the words of Paul at Pisidian Antioch (Acts 13), and various passages where Paul speaks of the fundamental content of the Gospel he had received (1 Cor. 15 etc.). Dodd printed all this material in what became a famous end-paper to his book, and demonstrated a common *pattern* to it all, which was distinguished by five features. In reproducing these, I should make it clear that this pattern with these features is to be my criterion of Christian orthodoxy, against which I shall range the main thrust of the theology of Martin Luther. If I am wrong, I shall err with the first Christian preachers, not to mention C.H. Dodd himself!

The first feature of the pattern was that it was of *God*'s tracing,[1] that is, it was supernatural, 'objective', given. It was *not* an achievement of human construction or speculation. This seeming platitude is of prime significance. It is sufficient, for example, to rule out the whole work of so eminent a modern thinker as Don Cupitt of Cambridge, at any rate as

---

1.   C.H. Dodd, *Apostolic Preaching* (1936), p. 38.

Christian theology. Cupitt, you will recall, eschews objectivity *in toto*: theology is the critical investigation of our *subjective* emotions and the rest. If so, theology may be admirable as psychology, anthropology, sociology, what have you, but it is not the Gospel. More important, we are reminded by this first feature of the pattern of the true meaning, by contrast of *heretic, heresy*. The Greek *haireisthai* means to choose for oneself, and the heretic is one who selects and adopts what seems good to him, rather than what is *given* from without, from above, from God. The late John Robinson, who startled us over 30 years ago with his *Honest to God*, reduced it to an aphorism—'Religion is not revelation, but relation'—and much as some of us loved him, we could not but see that this fundamental feature of his own theology stamped it as heresy from the start.

The second feature of the pattern is that it is of *God's intervention in human history*[2]—the 'mighty acts of God', as we used to say—and *not*, for example, a pattern of value-judgements, or a metaphysical construction of the relative essence of divinity as contrasted with humanity. It is not only objective, it is historical.

The third feature of the pattern is that it is *Christocentric*.[3] The birth, ministry, death and resurrection form the key to the whole pattern.

Fourthly, the exalted Christ is head of *the new people* of God,[4] and this is witnessed by the presence of *the Holy Spirit* in the Church. The pattern is of a community in the communion of the Spirit: it is not a mystery-religion designed for individual salvation *only*.

Fifthly, the consummation of God's plan will be the *Second Coming of Christ*.[5] Hence the sharp edge of the Gospel—the demand for repentance and the offer of forgiveness.

Objective—historical—Christocentric—communal—eschatological. The pattern is traced, as I said, in the first offers of the Gospel to the world. Its presentation is, as Dr Nineham would insist, 'culturally conditioned', and it is not the presentation but the pattern itself which is determinative. It is that which, *pace* Nineham, persists throughout all subsequent change, if indeed the change is to be what Christians call 'orthodox'. Deviations from it, humanly-made alternative 'features', will be heresy proper—although, if indeed the pattern is of God's tracing,

2. Dodd, *Apostolic Preaching*, pp. 38-39.
3. Dodd, *Apostolic Preaching*, p. 39.
4. Dodd, *Apostolic Preaching*, pp. 41-42.
5. Dodd, *Apostolic Preaching*, pp. 43-44.

we shall not expect any Church or any theologian in any age to reproduce it in perfection.

The first feature of the pattern, that it is of God's tracing, is stamped on
Luther's theology from his conversion onwards—stamped so firmly
that it hardly needs demonstration. The very title of the book which did
much to herald the Lutheran revival in British theology after the Second
World War, was *Let God be God* (1947), and Philip Watson's
multitudinous learning proved his case to the hilt. Hear Luther:

> If man is to deal with God and receive anything from Him, it must happen
> in this wise, not that man begin and lay the first stone, but that God
> alone...must first come and give him a promise. This word of God is the
> beginning, the foundation, the rock, upon which afterwards all works,
> words and thoughts of man must build (*Treatise on the New Testament*).

Or again: 'If anything is to be ascertained, it must be through revelation
alone; that is, the Word of God, which was sent from heaven' (*Sermon,
Trinity Sunday*). Best of all would be to quote Luther's own account of
his conversion:

> I began to understand that the righteousness of God...is that by which the
> merciful God justifies us through faith.—There and then the whole face of
> Scripture was changed...*opus Dei*—that which God works in us; *virtus
> Dei*—that by which God makes us strong; *sapientia Dei*—that by which
> He makes us wise; and so the fortitude, salvation, glory of God.

Luther's matured theology is dominated by the category of *coram deo*
as contrasted with *coram hominibus*—'for what hast thou that thou hast
not been given?' Our whole theological enquiry is pursued in a divine
context. I like to illustrate this by Donald Tovey's reminder[6] that at the
first performance of *Elijah* at Birmingham, Mendelssohn had to submit
to the destruction of a vital musical motif because Victorian England
would have thought it blasphemous to change the Authorised Version
'but according to my Word' so as musically to fit the rhythm of
Luther's 'ich sage es denn', which 'looms ominously' (says Tovey)
throughout the following orchestral overture, and (he might have added)
at vital moments later in the oratorio. *Ich sage es denn...*The pattern is
of God's tracing.

The second feature of the pattern is that it is of God's mighty acts in

6.   D. Tovey, *Essays and Lectures on Music* (1949), p. 214.

history, rather than a complex of value-judgments or metaphysical diag-
noses of the divinity–humanity relationship. This again hardly needs
demonstration for Luther. 'Even as God in the beginning of creation
made the world out of nothing...so His manner of working continues
still the same, even now and unto the end of the world' (*The
Magnificat*). Luther's attacks on the rationalism, moralism and mysticism of Medieval Christianity are all focused on their attempting to
'climb up into the majesty of God'. 'God will not have thee thus ascend,
but He comes to thee.' The central 'intervention', as we shall see, is of
course the Cross of Christ—the false *theologia gloriae* is rejected for
the Christian *theologia crucis*. There is, however, a true realm for the
'theology of glory', which Luther expounds (above all in his *Bondage
of the Will*) as the culminating reflex of his well-known antithesis of
God hidden and revealed—*Deus absconditus* and *revelatus*. This
antithesis is not the simple one of God-apart-from-his-revelation-in-Christ
and God-thus-revealed. The Incarnation is both a 'veil' and a 'mirror';
there is in every self-disclosure of God a tension of hidden–revealed, of
mystery–revelation. The supreme self-disclosure is the Cross, where the
paradox is at its deepest. Our apprehension of it is on three levels, the
'light of nature', 'the light of grace', the 'light of glory'. To the first—
the wisdom of this world—there is no God, merely blind chance or fortune. To the second, such problems as unmerited suffering, which baffle
the first, are problems no longer. Yet a whole range of new problems
emerges, such as the rationale of the divine theodicy. These will only be
solved 'hereafter', when the light of glory will reveal those ultimate
secrets of God, implicit indeed in all the mighty acts of God and above
all in the Cross, but not to be truly apprehended until the veil of sin and
limitation is finally lifted from the redeemed in heaven. 'Now we see
through a glass, darkly, but then...'

The third feature of the pattern is that it is Christocentric—the focal-
point of the whole pattern. And so it is with Luther. He is of course
conventionally identified with 'Justification by Faith', and out come the
conventional criticisms of 'solifidianism', which on the face of it would
deny the first feature of the pattern—its God-centred objectivity. Here I
love to recall the insistence of my old tutor and subsequent colleague,
Gordon Rupp. *Sola fide* equals *sola gratia* equals *Christus*. Let Luther
speak, from his *Preface to Romans*: 'Faith is not that human notion and
dream that some hold for faith...Faith is a divine work in us.' It is the
way in which Christ gives himself to us, or alternatively 'the power

which takes hold of Christ'. Faith and grace are, as it were, correlatives, or rather twin poles, of that mysterious tension we call 'personal relationship', deepening to 'communion' and even 'mutual indwelling'—yet the integrity of the individual person remains unscathed. The communion is so close that faith, grace and Christ are one: yet there is no 'deification', after the fashion of the Greek fathers. 'When the soul', says Luther, 'is united with the Word, it becomes like the Word, just as iron becomes red like the fire in which it is heated.' Yet the iron is still iron and the fire is still fire. Through faith comes the free restoration of the sinful human being's lost standing by grace—by the personal indwelling of Christ in his or her heart.

Luther makes a well-known distinction between what he calls God's or Christ's 'strange work' and 'proper work', the former word suggested by Isa. 28.21: 'The Lord will rise up... He will be wrath...to do His deed—strange is His deed...and to work His work—alien is His work'. This is our condemnation by his Word as *Law*, bringing home our helplessness to redeem ourselves from our own sin—a condemnation which reaches its apex in the Cross. God's 'proper work'—to exalt us in his mercy and give us hope and salvation—is revealed in the Resurrection. Yet this is no mere succession in a series, whereby the latter begins when the former is ended. The Christian lives simultaneously in two spheres: 'in so far as he is flesh, he is under the Law; in so far as he is spirit, he is under the Gospel'—*simul iustus ac peccator*. 'Christ has freed us from the Law of sin and death, that is, from the *kingdom and tyranny* of sin and death, that sin indeed should be present, but with the tyranny taken away—and death present, but with the sting removed.' Luther gives a truer and more comprehensive presentation both of human nature with its tensions and inconsistencies *and* of the unfathomable resources of the grace of God in Christ, than any simplistic scheme of sin and salvation. To Luther Christ is truly central:

> The history of the Church Universal has confirmed in me the conviction that those who have had and maintained the central article in its integrity, that of Jesus Christ, have remained safely entrenched in their Christian faith... On the other hand..., all errors, heresies, idolatries, offences, abuses and ungodliness in the Church have arisen because this article...of the Christian faith concerning Jesus Christ has been either disregarded or abandoned.

The fourth feature of the pattern is its Holy Spirit-inspired communal nature—in other words the whole office and work of the Spirit himself:

Church, Sacraments, the Christian life with its distinctive ethical demands and opportunities. The sheer range and depth of Luther's thought in this vast sphere exempts us, in a way, from our present labours and responsibilities, for this feature of the pattern is so clearly present and powerful in Luther that detailed illustration is superfluous. A few quotations will suffice.

In the *Small Catechism* Luther really says it all.

> I believe that I cannot by my own reason or strength believe in Jesus Christ...or come to Him; but the Holy Spirit has called me by the Gospel, enlightened...sanctified...and preserved me in the true faith; even as he calls, gathers, enlightens and sanctifies the whole Christian Church...and preserves it in union with Jesus Christ in the one true faith. In which Church he daily...forgives me and all believers our sins, and at the last day will raise up me and all the dead and grant me and all believers in Christ everlasting life.

In Luther's *Table Talk*—'He is called a witness, because he bears witness only of Christ and of none other'. Or in a Pentecostal Sermon:

> It is a faithful saying that Christ has accomplished everything, has removed sin and overcome every enemy...But the treasure lies yet in one pile; it is not distributed or invested. If we are to possess it, the Holy Spirit must come and teach our hearts to believe...

In a multitude of passages Luther shows the Holy Spirit as the Lord and Giver of Life and Holiness—of the knowledge of God, strength and comfort against the attacks of sin, love, praise, thanks and honour to God—the *tres theologicae virtutes*, faith, hope and love.

In his *Brief Explanation of the Ten Commandments, the Creed and Lord's Prayer* Luther is unambiguous about the Church:

> I believe there is on earth...no more than one, holy, common Christian Church, which is nothing else than the congregation...of the saints... which is gathered, preserved and ruled by the Holy Ghost... I believe that no one can be saved who is not found in this congregation, holding with it to one faith, word and sacraments, hope and love... I believe that in this congregation, and nowhere else, there is forgiveness of sins... To this congregation Christ gives the keys, and says (Mt. 18) 'Whatsoever ye shall bind on earth shall be bound in heaven'. In like manner He says (Mt. 16) to...Peter, who stands as the representative of the one and only Church, 'Whatsoever thou shalt loose on earth shall be loosed in heaven'.

And Luther speaks of the Church as signifying in truth

> the holy Christian people...clear to the end of the world, in which Christ lives, works, and reigns *per redemptionem*—through grace and forgiveness of sins, the Holy Ghost *per vivificationem et sanctificationem*, through the daily purging out of sins and renewal of life (*Councils and Churches*).

And two of his well-known aphorisms bring out his distinction between the spiritual, inner Church and the bodily, external Church—not necessarily sundered, any more than a man's own soul and body: the body does not give the soul its life, and yet the soul lives in the body—although it cannot live without it. 'Thank God, a child of seven knows what the Church is—the holy believers and the lambs who hear their shepherd's voice' (*Schmalkaldic Articles*). 'Oh it is a high, deep, hidden thing is the Church which nobody may perceive or see, but only grasp by faith in baptism, Word and Sacrament' (*Wider Hans Worst*). One could add from the *Table-Talk*—'where God's word is purely taught, there is also the upright and true church: for the true church is supported by the Holy Ghost, not by succession of inheritance'.

I cannot here pursue further the enormous detail of definition with which Luther dilates on his doctrine of Church, ministry and sacraments. The 'Pattern of Christian Truth' demands that Holy Spirit and Church should be one of the prime features of orthodox belief. That they were so for Luther is clear beyond dispute.

Under the fifth heading of the Pattern—Eschatology—we look first at Luther's doctrine of eternal life. From the *Bondage of the Will*: 'There is a life after this life, in which will be punished and repaid, everything that is not punished and repaid here, for this life is nothing more than an entrance on...the life which is to come'. From a *Sermon*: 'Thus we need not be alarmed on account of death, as unbelief does; because in Christ it is indeed not death, but a fine, sweet and brief sleep...for a brief moment, as on a sofa, until He shall call and awaken us together with all His dear children to eternal glory and joy'. Luther in a way anticipates Dodd's 'realized' or 'anticipated' eschatology when he speaks, in another *Sermon*, of our spiritual resurrection previous to death, somewhat dubiously interpreting Rom. 8.11 ('But if the Spirit of him that raised up Christ Jesus from the dead dwelleth in you, he shall give life also to your mortal bodies') to mean that God, having saved you spiritually, will not forget the body. Hence Christians have the greatest blessings certainly awaiting them. But what of non-Christians? Strictly they would be excluded: but Luther is a kindly man, and more of a humanist than (say) Erasmus would grant. From the *Fourteen of Consolation*, we hear this:

> Those who are not Christians will find small comfort...since for them all is uncertain. Nevertheless God has not so utterly forsaken the sons of men that He will not grant them *some* measure of comfort in the hope of the passing of evil and the coming of good things... Not that He would have them lean on it, but that He would turn their attention to that firm hope which is in Him alone.

Luther will hear nothing of purgatory:

> Augustine, Ambrose and Jerome held nothing at all of purgatory— Gregory, being in the nighttime deceived by a vision, taught something of it... No place in Scripture mentions it, nor must we in any way allow it. The bounds of purgatory extend not beyond this world; for here in this life the upright, good and godly Christians are well and soundly scoured and purged (*Table Talk*).

As for prayers for the dead,

> we have no command from God to offer them, so no one sins by not praying for them. Yet as we cannot be certain that any such has received their final judgement, it is not sinful to pray for them—but let once or twice be sufficient, lest you tempt God and mistrust Him (*Sermon*).

When we pass to the Second Coming and the Last Day, we are, as always with eschatology, in acute difficulty. After all, the naive eschatology of the first Christian preachers, with their expectation of a speedy return of the bodily Jesus they knew, was the most obvious point for revision in the earliest presentation of the *kerygma*—witness Paul and John, revising by *deepening* the theology of the Second Coming. What really matters in eschatology is, first, the conviction that in his own way, God will achieve his final purpose in and beyond history, and that Christ in glory will bring the purpose of the Incarnation to fulfilment; secondly, that this coming of Christ in glory is a coming for *judgment*; thirdly, that as no one knows the secrets of the future, except God alone, so inevitably there is a *tension* running through all our living and being—a truly 'eschatological' tension, which cannot but look for signs and warnings of the Last Day in the events of the present.

All this is present throughout Luther's theology, even though no more than any other does he achieve a systematic and non-provisional presentation of it. I can only give a few quotations.

120   *The Bible, the Reformation and the Church*

> The prophet spoke…of the second coming of Christ as we do now; we know that the last day will come, yet we know not what and how it will be after this life, but only in general that we, who are true Christians, shall have everlasting joy, peace and salvation (*Table-Talk*).

This 'last day', according to Luther, is near at hand.

> The last day is already breaking, and the angels are preparing for the battle… The world will perish shortly…the last day is at the door, and…the world will not endure a hundred years. For the light of the gospel is now dawning (*Conversations*).

> I hope that the day is near at hand when the advent of the great God will appear, for all things everywhere are boiling, burning, moving, falling, sinking, groaning (*Correspondence*).

> All is done and fulfilled: The Roman Empire is at an end; the Turk has reached his highest point; the pomp of the papacy is falling away and the world is cracking on all sides (*ibid.*).

> The last day, after the present year of 1530, will free us from all evil and help us to everlasting joy (*ibid.*).

> Christ is at present not manifest in person, but on the day of judgement He will appear in refulgent splendour, in undimmed honour—a splendour and honour eternally manifest to all creatures. The last day will be an eternal day. Upon the instant of its appearing every heart and all things will stand revealed (*Sermons*).

So much for the five features of the Pattern of Christian Truth—stamped, as I hope I have demonstrated, on Luther's theology with no compromise. But (it might be objected), Luther's theology went much beyond all this. Like all Christian thinkers, he is endeavouring to express the *kerygma* in terms of his own historical and cultural conditioning, and one must look at the consequences—the outworkings, the elaborations, of Luther's own peculiar thought—and ask if in them he remained faithful to the pattern. After all, it was largely in consequence of Origen's outworkings or elaborations, such as the salvation of the devil, that he was condemned as a heretic in the sixth century—it must be sorrowfully added, with Luther's cordial approval: '*Origenem iam dudum diris devovi*'. What of Luther himself?

Here, contemplating Luther's vast output, I stand helpless before the mass of my material. All I can do is to suggest two matters—rather perhaps one only—in which Luther's characteristic elaboration tends to *blur* the sharp pattern of Christian truth. The first is his conception of *reason* as twofold—'natural' and 'regenerate'. The latter is when reason, illuminated by the Spirit, becomes the handmaid of faith. It is no longer an independent authority, as in the scholastic dichotomy, but the cognitive and intellectual aspects of faith itself, 'an excellent instrument of godliness'. So far so good: but there is a second level of reason— 'natural' or 'unregenerate'. 'Reason is the devil's whore', says Luther (with his usual delicacy of metaphor) 'and can do nothing but shame and disgrace everything which God says and does'. It is the task of faith to 'strike it dead', 'kill this beast which heaven and earth and all creatures cannot destroy'. The ostensible target of all this is scholasticism. But, as Luther acknowledges, in temporal affairs humanity *is* self-sufficient, guided by the light of reason. God does not teach us in the Scriptures how to build houses, make clothing, marry, wage war, navigate. Luther might well have gone further. After all, as Professor B.A. Gerrish has pointed out in his study of Grace and Reason in Luther, 'without the Humanists...there would have been no Reformation. The Biblical professor who won the admiration of Bucer, Melanchthon and Oecolampadius, the scholar who produced the massive Wittenberg Bible—surely this man was no stranger to the *bonae literae*' (or, one might add, the prevailing use of reason) 'of the Humanists'. No man has used his reason more persistently and remorselessly than Luther—either his 'natural reason' in the temporal realm or his 'regenerate reason' in the realm of faith. Is there not at least an *analogy* of scope and function between the two 'reasons', and are they not both God-given?

What is in principle the same question might be asked of Luther's famous doctrine of the *Zwei Regimente*—God's two spheres of kingly rule, Church and state. No doctrine of his has been subjected to such ill-informed criticism, culminating in William Temple's 1941 declaration that Luther prepared the way for Hitler, as Hitler's 'spiritual ancestor'. This is hopelessly unhistorical. Luther is in any case spanning the dying world of medievalism and the birthpangs of the modern era, and he should not be read solely in the terms of either. It is true, I think, that he makes insufficient provision for the *abuse* of its vocation by the temporal authority, although the problems from 1530 onwards of the forceful repression of the Anabaptists and the resistance of inferior magistrates to the Emperor brought from him a growing passion of conviction that Pope and Emperor alike were more like apocalyptic demons than genuine authorities. All this belongs to a historical rather than a theological enquiry, and in the latter field I should ask whether in the end Luther does not draw the lines of demarcation between the *zwei Regimente* much too sharply, as if in principle each excluded the other. If both are God's, this would be in any case surprising. Surely the Church—rulers, members, the community as a whole—has a legitimate work in the political sphere: the righteousness of the Law may well be a temporal expression of God's love. Luther accepts the 'intervention' of each *Regiment* on the other, but the intervention remains external and limited. The doctrine of the Incarnation—a prime element in the third feature of the Christian pattern—should have suggested an interpenetration in principle, at least, complete.

Here—almost at the end—I must pause. I have been asking, 'Was Luther a heretic?' I could have begun at the other end, so to speak, and taken the actual Bull *'Exsurge Domine'* of Pope Leo X (1520), with its listing of 40 of Luther's 'errors' which constituted him a 'heretic'. An examination of the 40 points would indeed be a matter of the most specialized Lutheran scholarship. It might well, as I should hold, be demonstrated that they fall into four categories.

First: where the issue is not so much theological as ecclestico-political. An example would be No. 28—'if the Pope...expresses this or that opinion...it is neither sin nor heresy to disagree'. This would imply that a view is heretical because the Pope condemns it, not that the Pope condemns it because it is heretical. I do not think that this view would win many adherents today, even Roman Catholic. Secondly: where the Pope simply misunderstands Luther. For an example, No. 32—'A good work perfectly executed is a venial sin'. Thirdly: where the Pope is clearly wrong and Luther right: take No. 33—'To burn heretics is contrary to the will of the Spirit'. Fourthly: where the Pope may well have struck home: No. 36—'Free Will after sin is a mere name'.

But the real point in all this is that any critical examination of the 40 points would end by demanding a prior demonstration of what orthodoxy and heresy *is*, and this I endeavoured to provide. And my last word would be a recognition that the terms themselves are to an undefined degree relative. If the pattern of Christian truth is of God's tracing, it is inevitable that any given theologian in any given age and culture who attempts to address the contemporary world with the Christian *kerygma, and* to apply to it questions that have not been asked before, *and* to elaborate his or her theology into a system which will hold its own against attacks both religious and secular, will be found on later examination to have intruded some 'self-choosing', or *hairesis*, onto the divine face of orthodoxy—to have blurred some feature of the pattern, while remaining, both in intent and execution, faithful to it as a whole. It would be instructive to show how true this is of the great 'orthodox' masters of the Church—of Athanasius, of Augustine, of Thomas, much later of the Protestant demigods Schleiermacher and even Karl Barth himself. It is certainly true of Luther.

Yet relativity is meaningless unless there is an absolute by which it can be judged. The orthodoxy of any given theologian will never be vindicated in its entirety, because no human devising can perfectly reproduce the pattern of divine revelation. But the intent, the achievement, can only be finally assessed against this divine background. Against it our verdict must be—*Luther was no heretic*. Through all his tumultuous torrent of sermons, commentaries, treatises, letters, conversations the pattern is clear. We can judge him at our leisure—doubting, denying, sometimes out of patience or in a fury with him. But in the end it is that same pattern of Christian truth which will judge us—and we may well hope that Luther will be one of the select company who will be our advocates.

THE GENEVAN VERSION OF THE ENGLISH BIBLE: ITS AIMS AND ACHIEVEMENTS

Basil Hall

The Hampton Court Conference

Among the generalized or particular discussions of the Genevan English version of 1560, certain matters seem to have escaped, or received too little, attention: the scholarship of its editors as well as of its text; their attitude to the Elizabethan Settlement of the Church; the nature of their debt to Calvin's French Bible; the interpretation of their 'Calvinism'; and the nature of their ecclesiology and piety. It may be well to say that 'The vitality of the Genevan Bible was wonderful...and it was a better translation than any of its rivals'; but it was far from being viewed with approval at the Hampton Court Conference in January 1604, where what was said in the discussion of this Bible is usually noted but not carefully examined.

Bishop Barlow, who published a full account of this Conference, stated that Reynolds as Puritan spokesman proposed a new translation of the Bible because of the inadequacy of the older ones. He gave three examples of corrupt translation: Gal. 4.25, Ps. 105.28 and Ps. 106.30, and showed, without mentioning the source, the correct version from the Geneva Bible. In these instances and in the examples of corrupted texts from the Apocrypha which he added at a later stage of the Conference, Reynolds was in effect challenging the Book of Common Prayer in which were contained these corrupt texts in its Epistles, Psalms and Old Testament Lessons.[1] The bishops were irritated by his

1. 'The Sum and Substance of the Conference...at Hampton Court, January 14, 1603 [1604], William Barlow, Dean of Chester', reprinted in E. Cardwell, *A History of Conferences* (1840), pp. 167-212. The criticism of the Geneva Bible at this

demonstration and it is reasonable to assume that they did not want a new translation since Barlow wrote that the bishop of London dismissed the proposal saying, 'if every man's humour should be followed there would be no end of translating', and was able to add that 'the worst of all his Majesty thought the Genevan to be'.

The bishops must have been even more relieved about the proposal when James also attacked the Geneva Bible because of its notes. He added a caveat, 'upon a word cast out by my lord of London', that 'no marginal notes should be added having found in them which are annexed to the Geneva translation (which he saw in a Bible given him by an English lady) some Notes very partiall, untrue, seditious and savouring too much of dangerous and traiterous conceits'. This is a strange statement reproduced, or manipulated by Barlow who may have omitted some other words made on the subject by James, since the implication that he was unaware of the Geneva notes before the lady's gift is indeed odd.[2] He had already said that it was the worst translation he had yet seen, for he certainly would have known this Bible well from boyhood. In fact he had been required to authorize it after it was proclaimed to be the Bible for public reading in Church, and for private study in the home, for the Scots nation by the General Assembly of their Church at least from 1568. It had not only been imported from England (whence would continue to come editions in small quarto and octavo sizes) but the second issue of 1562 was republished in Scotland in folio by Bassendyne and Arbuthnot in 1579 with a long dedication to James himself when he was still a boy.

The only English Bible his Presbyterian tutors, including the

Conference is almost unique, and deserves attention. Cardwell also included descriptions of the Conference by Patrick Galloway (a Scot present at the King's request), Archbishop Hutton, Bishop Matthews and James Montagu. These give a better balance than Barlow, but they are usually ignored as is *The Phenix* (1707), vol. I, pp. 178-80, which contains some possible material, especially in 'Another Copy'. In K. Fincham (ed.), *The Early Stuart Church* (1993), the authors use only Barlow and take him at his face value and selectively.

2.   T. Fuller, *The Church History of Britain* (1655), Century XVII, Book X, p. 21, ignores the lady in his account of the Conference. He wrote, '…[Puritans] complaine that this Conference is partially set forth onely by Dr Barlow, their professed adversary to the great disadvantage of their divines'. Barlow was far from being impartial: in his *To the Reader* he called Reynolds *Hercules Limbomastix* and Gnathonical, with two denigratory Greek tags, terms no doubt intended to please the royal pedant in this preface of embarrassingly distasteful flattery.

formidable George Buchanan, would have urged him to study would have been that of Geneva. In manhood he would have become hostile to some of the notes and the weight given to them by opponents of his vigorous endeavour to challenge and break the Hildebrandine claims of the Kirk. He wished to assert instead his claim that royal power is no more to be limited by the kirkmen of the General Assembly than by a contentious and, as he knew to his cost, dangerous nobility. The two passages he strangely implied that he saw for the first time through the lady's gift were, first, Exod., 1.19, where the note read, 'Their disobedience [that of Jewish midwives to the command of the king of Egypt] was lawfull but their dissembling evil'; James ignored the next verse of the text which reads, 'God therefore prospered the midwives'. The note is not necessarily justifying disobedience to kings but trying to modify the assumption which might arise from biblical approval of lawful Israelite disobedience to the king who ruled over them. Secondly, James referred to 2 Chron. 15.16, where the note criticized King Asa for only deposing his mother for idolatry instead of killing her. Again James is straining his point, the biblical text made it clear at v. 13 that Asa's mother should have been killed since this was required by Asa's covenant with God in v. 12. (There is a further dimension to the passage since it is referred to in the *Epistle to Queen Elizabeth* at the beginning of the Geneva Bible in 1560 admonishing her how to govern by utterly abolishing idolatry and advancing true religion.) This theme would have aroused understandably acute royal sensibility in James, during his Scottish experience of king and bishop baiting, because of the beheading of his mother—to kirkmen an idolater. It also seems to have led him, in these two biblical instances, to quarrel with Scripture itself and to blame the Genevan notes for supporting it. After his Scottish experience he rejoiced to escape from those ministers who rebuked him Bible in hand, and to find himself now at Hampton Court with bishops kneeling before him seeking for permission to speak, and flattering him for his admirable exegesis of Ben Sirach when Reynolds had challenged a translation in the Apocrypha.

Two points may be made about the Hampton Court Conference and the Geneva Bible. First, this version was the one that all those present knew well as a scholarly text: its considerable contribution to the making of the Bible of 1611 shows that it was the best, not the worst, translation available in 1604. Secondly, the bishops feared the association of the Geneva Bible with the religious stance of its originators at Geneva, as well as that of its later promoters under Elizabeth I, and also they were troubled by its popularity among lay readers including the gentry and the great earls. Moreover, in popular lay use and among the more Protestant-minded clergy it had thrust aside the challenge of the Bishops' Bible of 1568 and later.[3] Also it carried consistent theological implications, not only in its notes but also in its Arguments to the biblical books and the other accompanying helps to understand it, which gave comfort to Puritans and unease to the bishops, who were aware of their own lack of an equally consistent theological alternative and further hampered by the fact that they themselves agreed with many of the theological principles of that version—as Archbishop Whitgift had shown in his writings and as their Bishops' Bible had shown in its notes. Their defences of episcopacy, episcopal courts and their administration, the contents of the Prayer Book and clerical attire, lacked in themselves the doctrinal energy and edification required by the people of God in England, conforming as well as nonconforming. The Hampton Court Conference could not overcome the fact that, despite the time available, and their small number, the makers of the English Bible of Geneva in the years 1556–1559, including its immediate forerunners of the New Testament of 1557 and the prose Psalter of 1559, achieved a remarkably scholarly and readable version, clearly printed in Roman type in a convenient quarto size accompanied by a variety of annotations, maps, introductions to the biblical books, indices and other guides to study, and, also important, a metrical version of the Psalter.

The Scholarship of the Editors

It is difficult to establish the linguistic qualifications of the individual makers of this Bible—with two exceptions—since these have to be inferred from their university studies and the assertions of contemporaries. Claims have been made for Sampson, Coverdale, Baron, Kethe, Wood and, most improbably, Knox, for no other reason, apart from the

---

3.   G. Hammond, *The Making of the English Bible* (Manchester, 1982), p. 143, 'For the most part the Bishops' Bible is either a lazy and ill-informed collation of what had gone before, or, in its original parts, the work of third-rate scholars and second-rate writers. In no way could it hold comparison with the Geneva Bible'. In *The Seconde Parte of a Register* (ed. A. Peel; Cambridge, 1915), I, p. 176, there is a complaint, 'All the world knows that the [Bishops'] translation was patched together by men too little learned in the Hebrew, Sirian and Greke tongues' (1584).

scholarship of the first two, than that they were in Geneva for shorter or longer periods during the preparation of the Bible, and indeed some of them may have worked on it in some other capacity. William Kethe was in Geneva from 1556 to 1560 and possibly worked on the printing and proof-reading of the Bible, and certainly he contributed to the metrical Psalter.[4] Thomas Wood because of his close association with William Whittingham the chief editor at Geneva, may have worked on the project because we have his brief allusion to 'our Geneva Bibles' being 'called in' (by episcopal action?) in a letter to Whittingham in 1573.[5]

Above all William Whittingham (1524?–1579), a comparatively young but well-equipped scholar, was undoubtedly the central figure as editor and translator of this Bible. He was seven years at Oxford where he established his trilingual biblical learning at Brasenose and later as *socius* of Christ Church, and he studied for a time at the universities of Orléans and Lyon.[6] He left for Frankfurt in 1554 and after taking a prominent part in the 'Troubles' there he arrived in Geneva in September 1555. He was fluent in French as well as a German speaker trained in diplomacy, a man of standing well known to many highly placed persons in England as well as to leading scholars and Reformers abroad. He was married to a Frenchwoman of strong character from Orléans who left in her will at Durham, where Whittingham became Dean in 1563, her 'great French Bible' to her son. The French Bible of Olivétan, revised by Calvin, with its accompanying apparatus of notes, maps, indices and other aids to study, was fundamental to Whittingham's work in revising the Great Bible at Geneva. He also had available to him and to his helpers at Geneva all the scholarly equipment needed for the enterprise as well as the opportunity to consult with Calvin (though Calvin does not mention this) and especially with Théodore de Bèze (Beza) on biblical matters. At Geneva Whittingham would find the Complutensian Polyglot Bible. (Its text of the Apocrypha was used by the French

4.   The printing was funded by the wealthy Exeter merchant John Bodley, Kethe, who may have been concerned in the printing, was also a native of Exeter. Little is known of the printer Rowland Hall. The Cambridge University Library has a copy of the 1560 edition on magnificent paper using the type of the Genevan Italian Bible printed by Francesco Durone. The signature on the title page is that of G.H. Hastings who was the fourth Earl of Huntingdon, the protector of Gilby at Ashby-de-la-Zouch.

5.   P. Collinson, *Godly People* (1983), p. 90.

6.   M.A.E. Green (ed.), *The Life of William Whittingham* (1870), p. 2.

scholars for their version and was also to be the base of the English translation.) The New Testament in Greek edited by Estienne as well as Estienne's revised Latin Bible with annotations by Vatable, Beza and others, and the Latin translation of the New Testament with annotations by Beza; the literal Latin version by Pagninus, and the extensive annotations to the Hebrew Bible with a Latin translation by Sebastian Münster, both containing significant rabbinical material, were also available. To these should be added the Zürich Latin version of 1544, and the recent and admired Latin version of the Old Testament by Tremellius as well as the number of grammars and dictionaries for Hebrew, Aramaic and Greek. Further at Geneva there were several scholar-printers including Estienne and Eadius.

We can see Whittingham's ability in Greek, the felicity of his style and the careful annotations for explanation and edification, in his own revision of the New Testament issued at Geneva in 1557, but we do not know from any other source the extent of his ability in Hebrew and Aramaic, though this competence must have existed. From the beginning to the end of the biblical enterprise he was an essential figure. His New Testament of 1557 was a considerable improvement in Greek scholarship on Tyndale, because of its debt to the New Latin version with its effective annotations issued by Beza at Geneva in 1556, which showed this French scholar well set on the road to becoming the leading editor and interpreter of the Greek New Testament for over a century to come.[7]

In his address *To the Reader*, since the edition was his work, Whittingham used the first person: 'In this translation I chiefly had respect' for ordinary people of Christ's flock

> moved with zeale, conselled by the godly, and drawen by occasion, both of the place where God appointed me to dwell, and also of the store of heavenly learning and judgement, which so abundeth in this Citie of Geneva, that justely it may be called the patron and mirrour of true religion and godlynes.

He then explains carefully his procedure: the text was

> diligently revised by the moste approved Greke examples, and conference of translations in other tonges as the learned may easely judge, both by the

7.   I.D. Backus, *The Reformed Roots of the English New Testament: The Influence of Theodore Beza on the English New Testament* (Pittsburgh, PA, 1980). This also contains a useful appendix on Laurence Tomson.

55555555

faithful rendering of the sentence, and also by the proprietie of the wordes and perspicuitie of the phrase. Furthermore that the Reader might be by all meanes proffited, I have devided the text into verses and sections, according to the best editions in other langages, and also, as to this day the ancient Greke copies mencion, it was wont to be used. And because the Hebrewe and Greke phrases, which are strange to rendre in other tonges, and also short, shulde not be to harde, I have sometyme interpreted them without any whit diminishing the grace of the sense, as our langage doth use them, and sometyme have put to that worde, which lacking made the sentence obscure, but have set it in such letters as may easely be discerned from the common text. As concerning the Annotations…to my knollage I have omitted nothing unexpounded, whereby he that is anything exercised in the Scriptures of God, might justly complayn of hardenes…I have explicat all suche places by the best learned interpreters… Moreover the diverse reading according to diverse Greke copies, which stande but in one worde, may be known by this note", and if the bookes do alter in the sentence then is it noted with this starre *…

In fact the verse division, the italicizing of words not in the original text, the noting of different readings and the explanation in marginal notes, derive from the usage of the French Bible.

Those familiar with the problems of collating copies of the New Testament Greek text and of translating it, will recognize here how much work had to be done on readings, interpreting the Semitic background to the Greek text, and the problems of keeping close to the text while avoiding obscurity or running into undue paraphrase, and still retaining felicity of language. When we look at his version we cannot doubt the linguistic ability, the careful decision in choosing a reading from the available textual alternatives, his skill in using the manuscript collations of Estienne as well as his printed text of 1550, and his able analysis of the textual problems discussed in the annotations of Beza's New Testament of 1556.

Whittingham based his translation on the Tyndale English text revised a little by Richard Jugge in 1552. It was especially in the Epistles that he used Beza's Latin version and his annotations both for his own text and for its notes. This influence has been sufficiently shown in the examples of textual changes given by Westcott.[8] For instance, Eph. 2.12 'testamentes' changed to 'covenants' following Beza's *pactes* of 1556. The quality of Beza's scholarship can be seen in his improvement on

8.   B.F. Westcott, *A General View of the History of the English Bible* (revised by W.A. Wright, 2nd edn, 1905), p. 227.

Erasmus, for example, Lk. 11.17 where Erasmus gave *domus super domum cadit* followed by Tyndale as 'one house shall fall upon another', but Beza more correctly gave *domus adversus se partita cadit* which Whittingham followed as 'a house divided against itself falleth'. In Acts 27.9 Tyndale incorrectly wrote 'because also that we have over-long fasted'; following Beza Whittingham gave 'because also the time of the Fast was now passed'. In addition to Westcott's textual instances I myself have observed a number of Bezan influences in the 1557 notes, for example, 'this is ment in that the worde is made flesh, and that the holy Gost was powred on him without measure' is from Beza *verbum caro factum est, effusus in eum Spiritus sine mensura*. Again, Heb. 2.2, Whittingham, 'Which was the Lawe given to Moses by the hands of the Angels', Beza, *Legem intellegit...datam autem fuisse per ministeriam angelorum Legem et Mosi in manus traditam*. In following 'the singularly clear-sighted Beza' in 1557, and again in the 1560 revision, Whittingham was able to correct the renderings of his predecessors and provide well-informed interpretation in his notes. Beyond this, as Bruce Metzger has shown, Whittingham not only followed Beza's printed text but he was also using variant readings from both the Codex Bezae (as well as other Greek manuscripts) in 1557, and even more widely in 1560, which is of considerable interest since Beza did not obtain the Codex until 1562. Metzger showed that the marginal readings which Estienne had printed in his Greek New Testament and also the manuscript collations made by Estienne including the Codex which he had found in a French monastery, and which was eventually to find its way to Beza, must have been made accessible to Whittingham who would also be able to discuss readings with Beza himself.[9] It should be remembered that the Bishops' and Rheims and Authorized versions ignored the question of variant marginal readings, a fact which underlines the scholarly procedure of the Genevan editors, which was even further exemplified in those notes which gave the names of the pagan authors anonymously cited in Acts and by Paul, a matter ignored by later versions until this century.

From this evidence it can be claimed that we can reasonably infer the scholarship of Whittingham from his New Testament work. However, there was one other editor of this Bible whose scholarship can be seen in other writings than the Bible itself. This was Anthony Gilby, who was

9.   B.M. Metzger, 'The Influence of the Codex Bezae upon the Geneva Bible of 1560', *NTS* 8 (1961), pp. 72ff.

the only translator to leave some evidence of his ability in Hebrew. It has been overlooked hitherto that Gilby was not only a graduate of Christ's College, Cambridge, where trilingual learning could be obtained, and writer of several pamphlets in support of nonconforming principles— including inventive rebukes for conformists as 'upskips' and the nonce word for a conforming minister 'swingebreech'[10]—but he was also an Old Testament scholar of greater quality than his brief commentary on Micah (1551), suggests. This book is more concerned with fierce denunciation of the evils of contemporary England than with objective biblical commentary. He described London as being like Micah's Samaria, 'a puddle of all idolatry' and this phrase was to appear in the note to Mic. 1.5 in the Bible of 1560. He was scholarly, however, on the words 'the sin of Jacob' in that verse which he explained as a hebraism.

> Thys sentence can not stande as it is commonly translate, what is the sin?, because the interogative in Hebrewe is masculine gender, therefore [it] must be referred to the author of the synne... Here is to be noted for the variety of translacyon of thys text that it is a difectyve sentence and of sondry interpreters is diverseliy supplyed lyke as many more in the Old Testament. For in the Hebrue tonge in sentences of vehemency and also of great haste doth leave out certain words easye to be understande אתימי who wyth me? הֲשָׁלוֹם how peace? Such eclypsed phryases have we in the English tonge, as, howe now?[11]

Since the Bible of 1560 gave for this sentence '...what is the wickedness of Iaakob? Is not Samaria? and which are the hie places of Iudah? Is not Jerusalem?', we presumably can see Gilby's editorial hand at work. His pungent attack on the Edwardine clergy at Mic. 2.2 in his commentary was not a good starting point for a clerical career later in Elizabethan England, nor was it likely to endear the Genevan version when it was known or guessed that he was an editor:

    10. *A pleasant dialogue between a souldier of Barwicke and an English chaplaine...by Anthony Gilby* [Middleburgh?] (1581). The soldier responds to the conforming priest's [the 'Swingebreech'] criticism, '...al that you say agaynst the Genevians might be brought agaynst Christ and his disciples in the same wordes and sentences'; Acts 4.19, 'Whether it be right in the sight of God, to obey you rather than God, judge ye', was essential to these men: it had been a key text in Goodman's famous challenge to reigning Queens from Geneva. However, this text received no note in the 1560 Bible nor was there a note on it in the French Bible.

    11. *Commentary on Mycah* (1551). The hebraism, B 5 v. Idolatry, B 8 r.

The Bishops and priestes do look over as the divyll doth look over Lincoln...purchasyng other mens landes and houses to make their wifes ladies and theyr sons lordes... Will you yet be a church all alone, O English Bishops and priestes, will you neyther follow Christ nor his Apostles, neyther the Bishopp of Rome and his Bishoppes. Are you wyser than the one sort or wyl you be worse than the other?

Whittingham may have exercised editorial tact in seeing that no note of this nature appeared on Micah in 1560.

In an earlier work, *An Answer to the devilish detection of Stephen Gardiner Bishoppe of Wynchester...*[not to be seduced] *by his errours...*(1547), on folio clxxx, Gilby thrust more deeply than his words on 'eclypsed phrayses' were to do when he wrote in these pages against Gardiner that 'now labour you to have this name Missa or Masse derived of an Hebrue worde' (מִסָּה: Gardiner was using Deut. 16.10 on the 'voluntary offering of thy hand'), and Gilby quotes the *Thesaurus Linguae Sanctae* of the Italian Jewish convert Pagninus, 1529, about the use of the doubled *samech* (*Daghessatur samech*) and other rabbinical comments, where Pagninus continues 'Jerome writes here of a spontaneous oblation of thy hand', that is, a free will offering, 'so that some say that מִסָּה is an oblation made to God on account of something personal' (presumably Gardiner took his notion from Jerome), but Pagninus added firmly, 'I do not assent to this since none of the Hebrew doctors that I have read say this'. Gilby concluded 'which how wel it [מִסָּה] agreeth with our English word Masse, let the learned judge. It can not be tried hereby that it is a sacrifice for the quick and the dead: but rather clean contrairie by that which Pagninus affirmeth.' Gilby, it is reasonable to assume, simplified this verse in Deuteronomy in translating it in the 1560 Bible 'a free gift of thine hand...unto the Lord thy God'. Earlier on folio cxxvi Gilby accused Gardiner of using the old porteous (Breviary) Latin version of the Psalms which is 'very corrupt' and 'a confused barbarous stammeringe' since in Ps. 111.5, where the Hebrew reads, 'he did gyve a praye [prey] to them that feared him...yet do the papistes falsely corrupt thys text for they read in their porteous *Esca se dedit*' [he gave himself to be food]. Gilby rejected this attempt to bring in the eucharistic presence *carnaliter* and added,

As for the exposicion of Scripture (though you do accuse us therein) as we wyll answer before God at the great and dreadful day, we have brought them forth playnly in the same wordes and sens that they were spoken: neither bi craft wreasted nor bi ignorance adulterated as many of yours may sone be proved and that welmost thorowout the whole porteous and masse boke, where they be wholly disfygured.

Gilby was not exaggerating since the Old Testament of this Bible was a considerable advance on what had gone before and the majority of its notes are not exhortatory but much more frequently explanatory. Gerald Hammond makes the significant point that the division into verses instead of paragraphs showed fully for the first time the balancing and parallelism characteristic of Hebrew poetry. While verses held up the flow of historical narrative they considerably improved the method, clarity and force of prophetic poetry. Hammond demonstrated this improvement by focusing on Jeremiah 47 and its seven verses, 'in this chapter most of its vocabulary and perhaps more importantly virtually the whole of its syntax and word order goes directly into the Authorized Version'. There is not space to illustrate this matter in detail here, but it is clear that Hammond's close analysis of the Genevan treatment of Nahum 3, Isaiah 41 and Micah 7 provides for the first time a thorough account of the rendering of the Hebrew, even in its more obscure idioms, into an admirable English style: they kept the 'lively phrase of the Ebrue' as they claimed in their preface.[12]

Hammond rightly praises the stylistic quality of the Genevan rendering of Ecclesiastes, for example, Eccl. 1.2. Here the Great Bible was clumsy but Geneva gave the rhythm of 'Vanitie of vanities...' Hammond suggests that this came directly from the Vulgate replacing its Greek word by 'Preacher', but we should look to Calvin's French Bible which has, 'Vanité des vanités dit le Prescheur: tout n'est que vanité'. Hammond adds examples of their care in giving a clearer reading by interpretation rather than by adhering to an obscuring literalism while seeking to hold to the sometimes elliptical style of the original.[13] However, there is a note at Ruth 4.1, 'Ho such a one' which suggests to me Gilby's hand, 'The Ebrews here used two words which have no propre signification but serve to note a certaine persone, Ho syrray or Ho such a one.' In 1611 the Genevan wording was adopted. The Revised English Bible of 1989, however, evading the Hebrew, gives 'calling him by name' which is paraphrase not translation, since it is significant that Boaz ignores the man's name.

The Genevan editors had not only clarity to commend them but also felicity of style. There are phrases which echo in the mind of an older generation, 'He smote them hippe and thigh: Remember now thy

12. Hammond, *The Making*, pp. 116ff.
13. Hammond, *The Making*, pp. 131-32.

creator in the days of thy youth: Except a man be borne again: A cloud of witnesses: Even Solomon in all his glorie'—these are found for the first time in 1560. Yet there could be a curious reversion on rare occasions to the Wycliffite past. For example, Isa. 35.8, 'And there shall be a path and a way', and, memorably, Gen. 3.7, the word that gave a by-name to this Bible occurs, 'breeches', which goes back to the Wycliffite version 'brechis', although Hammond thought it to be a modernization.

The next stage of translation at Geneva was one in which Gilby, who was interested in the Psalms,[14] was almost certainly involved. This was the very small sized prose version of the Psalter issued also in 1557, 'translated according to the veritie and truth of the Ebrue [the Coverdale version, continued into the Book of Common Prayer was certainly weak here] wyth annotacions most profitable'.[15] It must have been closely associated with the metrical version, the preparation of which had been begun at Frankfurt for the use of that congregation. The vernacular metrical Psalter was a comparatively new concept in public worship, and was to prove to be one of the powerful influences attracting people to the Huguenots. Calvin wrote in the preface to the French Psalter in the metrical version begun by Clément Marot, 'Entre les choses qui sont propres pour recréer l'homme et luy donner volupté la musique est, ou la première, ou l'une des principales...la mélodie transperce beaucoup plus fort le coeur...' A beginning was made earlier

14. See his later book *The Psalmes of David opened and explained by Paraphrasis...set forth in Latine by that excellent learned man Theodore Beza, and faithfully translated into English by Anthony Gilby* (1581). The date of the Dedication to the Countess of Huntingdon is 1579; Beza had dedicated the Latin version to her husband. Gilby here wrote to her of 'mine old forworne rude simplicitie'. He considered that 'the Psalmes in English...in manie places read rather for taske...and for fashion sake than for good devotion and with understanding which the Spirit of God commandeth in al partes of divine service'.

15. J.D. Alexander, 'The Genevan Version of the English Bible: Its Origin, Translation and Influence' (DPhil. thesis, Oxford, 1957). Here for the first time that most rare work, the Psalms of 1557, a book of very small size with 450 pages of text and a long Confession of Faith before it, was described and discussed. Much of this useful study by Alexander is a close analysis of the making of the English text of 1560 through the revision of the earlier versions. He shows the use of Pagninus, Munster and other scholars, but, as previous writers did, he overlooks the fact that this material was widely used in the text and notes of the French Bible, a more readily available source.

at Strasbourg and then at Geneva in 1551 and was to be completed in 1562 with Beza contributing over thirty Psalms. It was, however, the musical quality of Louis Bourgeois, for twelve of these Psalms, and of Claude Goudimel for many of the others, which gave its powerful attraction to the French metrical Psalter. (Goudimel had taught music at Rome where Palestrina was one of his pupils; later he became a Hugenot musician and was killed in the St Bartholomew massacre.) A stranger attending a Huguenot service spoke of being ravished by the sound of men's and women's voices blending in the melody of the Psalms. At Frankfurt the English refugees would have brought with them the collection of a number of metrical Psalms made by Sternhold and Hopkins published in 1549 and several times reprinted. To this Whittingham added seven Psalms of his own and produced an edition at Geneva in 1556 with music. A further collection was made including more Psalms by the other Geneva men Kethe and Pullain.

Once again Whittingham's foresight here as in other ways led to one of the greatest influences in the religious life of Elizabethan England, the metrical Psalms, many accompanied by the music of two of the best musicians of the time for this work, and published with the majority of the editions of the Geneva Bible for use at home and in public worship. The English were to quicken their religious life not only from that Bible but also from singing the praises of God with a Genevan tone. We still sing the Old Hundredth in Kethe's words to the Genevan melody. It should be emphasized that all these metrical Psalms had exhortatory prefaces (mostly reprinted in the prose Psalter of 1557) showing their purpose and application. For example, Whittingham's setting of Psalm 119 has, 'The Prophet wonderfully commendeth God's law...adding notable complaints and consolations meete for the faithfull to have both in heart and voyce'. Again the Hildebrandine theme can be hinted in v. 46, where he wrote:

> Even before Kings I will them blaze [thy precepts]
> and shrink no whit for shame.

It is not surprising that James was 'much moved' at Hampton Court when the Puritan Knewstub raised the question of not being bound by an ordinance 'impeaching Christian liberty' for James compared this statement to the 'usage of a beardless boy' (one Mr John Black) 'at a conference with the ministers of the Kirk in 1602' where Black had 'blazed' the claims of the Kirk in relation to the royal power.

The collection of prose psalms of 1557 mentioned above begins with a short preface to Psalm 1 which is translated directly from the Argument for that psalm in Calvin's commentary on the Psalter published in August that year, and also Psalm 2 has the same preface as Calvin's Argument to it: other psalms have similar prefaces to Calvin's Arguments.[16] However, haste was driving its makers to complete the enterprise, for instead of continuing the revision they left Calvin behind after a time and followed Coverdale. Presumably they wanted to have a small pocket Psalter available as soon as possible (and also for other exile centres? or for England?). The second edition of the prose Psalter appeared in February 1559 as a new and thorough revision which was little changed in the Bible of 1560.

The Attitude to the Elizabethan Settlement

Its preface dedicated to Queen Elizabeth is significant for the dating of the work as well as for its pronounced admonitory style:

> ...your humble subjects...thoght it our duetie...to forther...your godly proceedings...and albeit we had begonne more than an yeare agone...to peruse the English translacion of the sacred Bible, and to bring it to the pure simplicitie and true meaning of the Spirit of God, as farre as we were able...by the knolledge of the Ebrewe tongue, the conference of moste perfect translacions in other langages, and by the judgement of the best learned in these parties...[since God] had...preserved you...from the furie of suche as soght your blood: with moste joyful mindes, and great diligence we indevored our selves to set forthe and dedicate this most excellent boke of the Psalmes unto your grace, as a special token of our service and good wil, til the rest of the Bible, which, praised be God, is in good readines, may be accomplished and presented...[she should avoid] false friends and also flatterers...the best remedy is, only to depend on God...[and] to be zealous of his glorie, obedient to his wil, careful and diligent to suppress all papistrie, vice and heresie, and to cause the light of God's worde spedely to shine throughout all your dominions. For if you honour God...he wil honour you... And finally, you shal learne [in this Psalter] to chuse you faithful counsellors, and knowe whome to admit into your friendship and whome to expulse your courts...[17]

16. *In Librum Psalmorum, Johannis Calvini commentarius* (Oliva Roberti Stephani, 1557). The French version was also published at Geneva by Conrad Badius, 1558.

17. I am grateful for permission to cite this rare text from the copy in the private collection of Mr Gervase Duffield of Appleford House, Appleford, Abingdon, Oxford.

It is significant that the editors could not resist telling the Queen what she should do. We can compare the monitions of these Genevan exiles with those in the sermon before the Queen of Thomas Cole, Archdeacon of Essex, a close supporter of Whittingham at Frankfurt and a signatory of the letter of the seceders there in August 1555. The text was from the Genevan version Deut. 12.32, 'Whatsoever I commaunde you take heede you doe it, thou shalt put nothing therto, nor take ought there-from'.[18] This was a favourite theme of the returned exiles in challenging the Elizabethan Settlement. Cole made clear to Elizabeth his intention,

> being called to thys place and purposing to speake only which God willeth to be spoken by my ministerie I hope our heavenly Father instead of feare arme me wyth godly boldnesse... Whatsoever we speake [those who preach] in the name of God it is the voice of God speaking by us, it is the pleasant raine of God, take you hede what earth you bee.

> The Church needs now as much aide, comfort and defence of her nourices as ever it had...[the duty of a godly nurse is] to maintain true Religion taught out of Goddes booke without addition or diminishing...to search their officers to see whether they have consenting hearts with them...[true religion must not have] any mingle mangle of their inventions.[19]

In the preface to this sermon Cole stated that many of those present had urged him to print it for its valuable content. His monitions have the assured and forceful tone of many of the returned exiles. What would Elizabeth make of such a sermon as this if she compared it with the address to her in the Bible of 1560, or if she leafed through this Bible with its marginal notes? There was a nest of notes in the books of Chronicles like the following from 2 Chron. 26.18, where the priests condemned King Uzziah for burning incense which was their preroga-tive, 'Though his zeale seemed to be good and also his intention, yet because they were not governed by the worde of God, he did wickedly, and was therefore bothe justely resisted and punished'. Again, in 2 Chron. 22.4, 'He sheweth that it must nedes followe that the rulers are

18. This text had been used by Jan Laski (John a Lasco) in the letter to Cranmer attacking the Book of Common Prayer for not being based on Scripture. A. Kuyper, *Joannis a Lasco opera tam edita quam inedita* (2 vols.; Amsterdam, 1860), II, p. 658.

19. *A Godly and Learned Sermon made this last Lent at Westminster before the Queenes Maiestie...March, 1564*, by Thomas Cole, Archdeacon of Essex (not to be confused, though he also was a former associate of Whittingham, with William Cole who had been at Geneva).

suche as their counsellors be and there can not be a good king that suffreth wicked counsellors'. When Cole addressed her with 'godly boldnesse' would she have seen 2 Chron. 18.7, 'True ministers of God oght not to cease to do their duetie thogh the wicked magistrates can not abide them to speake the trueth'? In all these instances Calvin's French Bible has no such notes.

Cole's style had already been made plain in the two prefaces of the Bible of 1560 which call for some examination. *The Epistle to the Queen* was, 'from your humble servants of the English Church at Geneva', but Elizabeth might well have pondered on the humility in subjects who addressed her as follows,

> The Lord who is the chefe governour of his Churche [not apparently Elizabeth] willeth that nothing be attempted before we have inquired therof at his mouth…we oght not…to do any thing without his worde…neither to prescribe any other ceremonies and lawes then such as the Lord had expressly commanded…by his worde… He hath…left an order in his Churche…some to be Apostles some Prophetes, others Evangelistes, some pastors and teachers [not bishops and priests].
>
> [She must] inquire of his ministres concerning the wil of the Lord, which is reveiled in his worde. For thei are, saieth Jeremiah, as the mouth of the Lord.

The threatening example of King Asa occurs here to urge her to 'the utter abolishing of idolatrie'. However, already by the summer of 1559 the Elizabethan Settlement of religion had been determined. Episcopacy was retained by *congé d'élire*. The Crown was to be supreme governor over things ecclesiastical and civil and this was to be enforced by an oath of acceptance required from all the clergy. The Prayer Book of 1559 was to be the only form of worship in law. An Act of Uniformity determined that no deviation from these principles was to be allowed. Manifestly the Queen's 'humble subjects' at Geneva had no use for these proceedings. For example, their only allusion to bishops was to 'ambicious prelates' who as Amariah and Diotrophes can abide none but themselves. For these Genevan Englishmen the Elizabethan Settlement on scriptural and therefore compelling grounds could only be seen as a temporary arrangement. Understandably this preface was to disappear in later editions of the Bible of 1560 when the style of Micah had become counterproductive.

The Indebtedness to the French Bible

The second preface of 1560 was addressed *To our Beloved in the Lord the Brethren of England, Scotland, Ireland etc*...which implied a more particular readership than the Church of England newly restored. This was later, without alteration to the text, to become *To the Christian Reader*. This Bible was authorized by neither the monarch nor the episcopate as were its future rivals. The editors gave the highest honour to Scripture,

> the worde of God which is the light to our paths, the keye of the kingdome of heaven, our comfort in affliction, our shielde and sworde against Satan, the schoole of all wisdome, the glasse wherein we beholde God's face, the testimonie of his favour and the onely foode and nourishment of our soules.

For these opening phrases the editors are indebted to Calvin since they translated them from his preface *Au Lecteur*,

> C'est l'Escriture saincte...ou lampe qui nous éclaire...c'est la clef qui nous ouvre le royaume de Dieu...c'est l'école de toute sagesse...c'est le miroir auquels nous contemplons la face de Dieu...c'est la tesmoignage de sa bonne volonté...c'est la pasture unique de nos âmes.

Instead of Calvin's 'le sceptre royal' of God and 'la houlette' of God as shepherd, and his ignoring of Satan, the English prepare for their war with shield and sword. The editors state that 'for the space of two yeres and more, day and night' they were occupied in this work and dated this preface 'From Geneva April 1560'. This when taken with the date given to the 1559 Psalter of February, and 'more than a yere agone', suggests that they began work on the Bible in November–December 1557 with the New Testament already in print and needing only moderate revision. The splendid range of materials in biblical texts, commentaries and the other trilingual aids for their work at Geneva has already been shown, and we must also remember that Whittingham and his fellows rightly referred to 'the great opportunitie and occasions which God presented to us in this Church, by reason of so many godly and learned men and such diversities of translations in diverse tongues'. They state that they have faithfully rendered the text, expounding all the hard places; provided alternative readings in the margin; tried to render the 'lively phrase of the Ebrewe'; italicized words absent in the original text but necessary to the English sense; spelled the Hebrew names nearer to the original; given the principal matters a paragraph mark (useful because the indenting of the verses broke up the flow of the thought) though this practice faded after Galatians showing perhaps the pressure of printing, to emerge again in Revelation. They added prefaces, 'Arguments', to each book with page headings describing the contents, also 'both by diligent reading of the best commentaries and also by conference with godly and learned brethren to gather brief annotations upon all the hard places' for understanding obscure words and for the application of the text to 'the edification of God's Churche'. They gave a continual flow of cross-references to form biblical teaching into a pattern as well as to illuminate, and they added maps as well as illustrations, for example, of the Temple and the Vision of Ezekiel, with Tables of the Hebrew names and the principal matters. Their 'brief annotations' were frequently translated from the French, and their Bible undoubtedly owed a considerable debt to the French Geneva Bible not least in following the French printing of clear Roman letter, and reprinting its maps and illustrations. Without that Bible the English Bible of 1560 would have lost much of its considerable effectiveness.

The most powerful influence of this English version came not only from the quality of its text but from its annotations, which while often borrowed from the French Bible, yet here, nevertheless, they could occasionally make some changes in both method and purpose. There was in Daniel a clear difference in the tone of the notes from that of the French, and these are the longest notes in this English Bible with the exception of those on the Psalms and Isaiah. In the French notes to Daniel there are over a hundred references to the Hebrew variants, sometimes with observations beginning 'aucuns', that is, 'some read thus or thus', whereas the English notes have approximately only ten and there is no comment on what scholars suggested. The English editors adopt a different method, they express no doubt about the right meaning of a word, and offer no balancing of opinions. Calvin published his commentary on Daniel nearly a year later in 1561 with a preface referring to the current persecution of French Protestants and to the help of this book in lightening 'the pressure of present calamities'. This was also the English aim, but Calvin's scholarly comments, such as 'I leave this point in doubt as nothing is said of it', or 'If some prefer [an interpretation] I will not object to it but it seems to me that...is the genuine sense', or his humanist scholar's interest in ancient history, and his comments such as 'this should be sufficient for us' (since he wished to avoid that apocalyptic speculation which was so attractive to the

English and reflected in their notes to Daniel), do not influence the English notes. The English identify themselves with the people of God in Daniel and treat the visions not so much as a historical record of scholarly interest in itself but as of immediate contemporary prophetic value since they repeatedly point to the need to obey God and his word before all in spite of emperors, kings and princes whose powers will melt away. Then and now, they assert, God punishes the wicked but succours his own who are obedient to him—Calvin prefers to point continually to Christ for the explanation of life's mysteries. (It must be assumed that the author of the English notes had attended Calvin's lectures on Daniel, the basis of his future commentary. For example, on Dan. 7.4 and Dan. 7.8 the English notes follow Calvin's later interpretation, which is different from the older notes in the French Bible, while they add their own application.)

The notes are not merely explanatory as in the French notes, but exhortatory as well as edifying, with an additional hint of self-righteousness. The English editors were trying to do more than to lighten 'the pressure of calamities', they wished to console returning exiles and confirm the Brethren in Britain—the French notes for Daniel did not go far enough for them. On Dan. 2.7 the French note offered a laconic alternative reading, but the English has,

> Herein appeareth their ignorance that notwithstanding their brags [a familiar word in Gilby's pamphlets later] yet were thei not able to tel the dreame except he entred them into the matter, and therefore they wolde pretende knowledge where was but mere ignorance and so as deluders of the people thei were worthy to die.

Here the astrologers of old are described as if they were contemporary priests. Dan. 3.2 has a note on the golden image set up by Nebuchadnezzar, 'This was sufficient with the wicked at all times to approve their religion, if the king's authoritie were alleged for the establishment thereof, not considering in the season what God's worde did permit'. Here there was no comment in the French Bible, whereas the English posed a question for those prepared to ask it, on the Queen's religious settlement at home. These notes are not isolated examples, others of a similar tone occur from time to time throughout Daniel which in this respect stands further apart from, for example, their Jeremiah. Nevertheless, these divergences from the French Bible are more occasional and are not to be found to this degree elsewhere where there is a consistent relationship to the French notes.

The considerable debt to the French Bible was not confined to prefaces and notes. Dissatisfied, as were the French, with the marked departure from the Hebrew original of the proper names, the English editors produced an index of those most used on the model of that in the French Bible, which was presumably based in turn on the earlier one of Pagninus. These include Shemuél, Iaakób, Sheth, Ieshaiáh, Shimson, Malchi-zéydek, accompanied by the accentuation, and with the meaning of the name provided for edification and for the understanding of Scripture. They also recommended the naming of children after these instead of the 'badge of idolatry' in the Catholic use of the names of non-biblical saints. This had been the subject of an ordinance for baptism by the Seigneury at Geneva. There was also a 'Table of Principal Things' in which again the influence of the French Bible occurred: 'Aaron et ses faits—Aaron and his doings; Le bastard n'entrera point en l'eglise du Seigneur—The bastard shall not enter into the congregation of the Lord; 'Le coeur bon parle bonnes choses—The good heart speaketh good things'. The French Bible was also accompanied by Calvin's extensive catechism expounding the Creed, the Commandments and the Lord's Prayer, and some editions of the English Geneva Bible contained a translation of this, for the Puritans had a long-standing complaint about the inadequacy of the Prayer Book catechism. Also published with the French Bible was *La Forme des Prières ecclésiastiques* which provided an example inadequately followed in *The Form of Prayers* published in 1556, for the English congregation at Geneva, containing also metrical Psalms and a translation of Calvin's catechism. Prayers from the French edition were printed with others in many editions of the Geneva Bible after the metrical Psalter. Knox, back in Scotland and soured after Frankfurt, used this Genevan book and called the Book of Common Prayer 'a mingle mangle', in Cole's words, preferring in the Puritan manner scriptural sanction for the framing of worship. In the event nonconforming Puritans were to be nearer theologically to Laski's sacramental services in London than to those of Calvin.

The 'Calvinism' of the Geneva Bible

From 1578 onwards many Black Letter editions of the Geneva version published *The Summe of the Whole Scripture* which is almost identical in content with *La somme de tout ce que enseigne la Saincte Escriture* of the French Bible. This retrograde step in printing in Black Letter was intended presumably to compete with the traditional type used in the Bishops' Bible. The next stage in the evolution of the Geneva Bible, apart from the updating of the spelling in later editions, was the issue of a slightly revised text of the New Testament in 1576 with many new notes, edited by Laurence Tomson.[20] Both the translation and notes were derived from Beza's second edition of his Latin version with some notes or commentary derived from other Reformed scholars. The influence of Beza in matters of doctrine is stronger than it was in 1560, and a more positive form of Bezan Calvinism now appears than the more moderate doctrines of 1560, especially on total depravity, the decrees of salvation and reprobation and predestination. Further, special attention was given to Revelation whereas Calvin had shown great caution on this book by confining the notes in the French Bible to the understanding of the Greek and in avoiding that apocalypticism which came to be so attractive to the English, from the time of John Bale onwards. They showed the Beast of Rev. 13.11-18 to be the papacy as Antichrist, whereas for Calvin the Beast is Antichrist, without comment save to describe it in a later chapter as the Roman Empire. The number of the Beast (666) was seen by the English in 1560 as the number of years following the vision on Patmos which resulted in papal supremacy over the church—Calvin ignored such speculation. After 1576 the next development on Revelation came in 1599 when lengthy extracts from the commentary on it by the Frenchman Francis Junius replaced the notes in Tomson's version. For Junius, for example, in a very long note, the Beast was Boniface VIII and his number represented the sixth book of the Papal Decretals; this was accompanied by further extensive denunciations of the papal Antichrist. This is a long remove from the comparative reticence of 1560 and further still from Calvin. Much of the distaste that some writers have shown for the Geneva Bible in more recent times is due to these notes which continued to appear in the thousands of copies of the supposedly 1599 edition published in Holland in several editions, with many misprints, in the seventeenth century.

Not only should Calvin not be blamed for the aggressive anti-papalism of the Junius notes, but the long-standing discussion of the 'Calvinist heresies' of the Geneva Bible should be challenged. It is a regrettable commonplace to assume that the doctrines of total depravity and the eternal decrees of election and reprobation, with their deterministic predestination, are essential to Bible study and preaching for Calvin.

20. Backus, *The Reformed Roots*, pp. 13ff.

(Calvin held that predestination should be believed as a mystery of faith but not analysed and prescribed in sermons and pamphlets addressed to the laity for edification.) That assumption implies that the French Bible, with its accompanying materials and notes, for which Calvin was largely responsible, contained these principles. However, in the three prefatory writings by Calvin to the French Bible there is no mention of any part of that nexus concerning predestination. In the French Table there are four passages listed on election which simply point to the Pauline words; on the other hand there are eleven listed in the English Table of 1560. Rom. 9.15 has no note in the French, but the English has a note which positively emphasizes election and reprobation. Ps. 147.20 has no French note, but the English note of 1560 emphasizes God's mercy to the elect and his judgment of the reprobate to eternal damnation. The French Table cites three Pauline passages which could concern predestination, two have no notes attached and the third (Rom. 8.29) is on 'une [rhetorical] figure...Gradation', where the English note draws attention to election. In his catechism added to the French Bible consisting of fourteen closely printed folio pages, Calvin never mentions election, reprobation, eternal decrees nor predestination. The doctrine of providence there, 'il dispose toutes choses par sa providence: et gouverne le monde par sa volonté', is biblical and Catholic orthodoxy; Augustine and others so defined it.

Calvin separated the doctrines of providence and predestination and related the latter to Christ; Beza, however, drew predestination back into providence on the pattern of the Scholastics. Beza wrote a number of short accounts of predestination in catechisms and brief treatises. John Stockwood, though aware later that Whittingham had made a translation of one of these by Beza on providence, thought he was justified in making another since Beza had made additions to it. He added a treatise by John Foxe on election, and another on election and reprobation by Anthony Gilby and published the collection in 1576. John Knox also wrote on predestination.[21] The Genevans in England

21. *The Treasure of Trueth...chiefest pointes of Christian Religion...with a briefe summe of the comfortable doctrine of God his providence...translated from Beza by John Stockwood* (1576). This was accompanied by the *treatise of the godly Father Maister I. Foxe* on the chief points of election *as the very simplest may easily understande it,* and by a *treatise of Maister Anthonie Gylbie on election and reprobation.* There were several English versions of short pieces by Beza on understanding predestination. Calvin had sought to avoid open discussion of this subject.

were obviously deeply committed to the subject and believed it necessary to edification and piety. Nevertheless, the notes in their Bible did
not follow the line they took with their proof texts in their treatises. It is
not until the Black Letter edition of this Bible of 1579 that the
'Calvinism' for which we should read 'Bezanism', was for the first time
emphasized in its demonstration of the predestinarian nexus; though this
had been somewhat adumbrated in notes to the 1576 New Testament
based on Beza by Tomson in, for example, the long thoroughly predestinarian note at Rom. 9.15. In the Bible of 1579 a brief catechism was
printed between the Testaments, *Certaine Questions touching the
doctrine of Predestination and the use of God's worde and Sacraments.*
After the blunt declaration that 'there are vessels of wrath ordained to
destruction and vessels of mercy prepared for glory', follow questions
on this subject leading to the most important one for the Puritans, 'How
do I know that I am ordained to eternal life?' Calvin had answered this
by his judgment that 'we cannot find the certainty of election in ourselves, we are ingrafted into Christ's body...we are in communion with
him, we have sufficiently clear proof: when Christ calls us we turn gladly
to him'. The answer given in 1579, however, points in another direction
by requiring 'feeling the motions of the spiritual life' described fully in
five further answers. Calvin's Church-oriented objectivity has been
replaced by the subjectivity of the group or society seeking
sanctification.

The Piety and Ecclesiology of this Bible

It was the Cambridge Puritan William Perkins who was to give academic
weight to an earlier growth in Puritan preaching on the need for feeling
this experience of sanctification. The 1579 catechism encouraged this by
'perceiving that nothing is more necessary than the word of
God...[and]...hearing of such as preach it' which is true, but to add that
by 'taste and feeling' of the sacraments our feelings that we are elect are
supported by them reduces word and sacraments from being means of
grace in their own right to being supports to feeling elect. This can
suggest a dubious subjectivism: Calvin preferred to emphasize life in the
Church rather than our feelings. The editors of this English Bible tended
here and elsewhere to emphasize the piety of the individual, rather than
to follow Calvin who saw piety as growing within the context of the
worshipping Church. The 1559 Psalter opened with a long Argument

indebted to Calvin's commentary, but its editors could take an independent line of exhortation in the notes of the slight revision of it in 1560. Their debt to the French version is seen in the note at Ps. 4.1, 'Thou that art the defender of my righteousness', where the French reads, 'Mon protecteur et celui qui maintient mon bon droict', but at Ps. 3.8 the English note states, 'Be the danger never so great or manie, yet God hath ever meanes to deliver his' and the French differs, 'Tu ne m'as point delivré ayant esgard particulièrement a moy, mais aussi en faveur de ton Église le salut de laquelle est fondée en mon regne'. For the English it is not the Church (a subject of considerable theological concern to Calvin) but the godly group or individual that is the focus of attention. In Psalm 23 the French heading assures of 'entière felicité en son Église et en la vie éternelle'. The English note here sees the individual as David who 'fully persuades himself that God will continue... goodness towards him for ever'. The first French note to this Psalm sees God as 'un fidèle pasteur envers ses brébis', but the English one reads, 'He hath care over me and ministreth unto me all things'. It is also plain that the French Bible sought an objective understanding of the Hebrew and used such phrases as 'some [commentators] say', but the English brushed this aside, wrote more subjectively and were more concerned for edification in a note than for the scholarly balancing of the best interpretation of the literal sense. They sought an accurate rendering but their eyes were firmly held on the goal of an informed piety. While they had Calvin's commentary on the Psalms before them, and used it, yet their notes were to encourage the practice of piety and the edification of the individual reader in the manner of the 'Gospellers' of Edward's brief reign. Calvin also aims at the promotion of piety, but the English were more individualistic on this same theme.

Accepting much from Beza, save his sacramental principles, the Presbyterianizing Puritans gained support from him in his declaration that Presbyterian polity was *De Jure divino* (that is, required by Scripture) and his assertion of the principle of resistance to tyrannous princes. This differed from Calvin who had not rejected episcopacy but prelacy, and who had advised obedience, martyrdom or flight not rebellion. These two themes are at times implicit, if not explicit, in some of the notes in 1560, and more so in the revisions of the New Testament with their additional notes. Because of their less patristic view of ecclesiology and their more subjective approach to the sacraments than Calvin's, the Puritans gave less emphasis to what they saw as these seals of a prior faith and were close to if not identified with Zürich here. Their people often communicated by sitting at the Lord's table and distributing the elements among themselves, as Knox did following the example of his former colleague Laski—this was not Calvin's procedure but it was that of Laski's 'Stranger Churches' in London under Edward.[22] Where the original heartland of Puritanism is to be found is still a matter of controversy, but it must surely lie not in Geneva but in the gravitational force of those pro-Zürich groups which emerged as 'Gospellers' in Edwardine England, admirers of Laski's worship as against Ridley's attempt to enforce the Prayer Book. The sermon by Thomas Sampson to his former parishioners, *A Letter to the trew Professors of Christes Gospell inhabiting in the Parishe of Allhallows...*, 1554, shows him holding the Swiss and not Calvin's view of the Lord's Supper (A iiii). Further, he points to the example of Dan. 3.2, which has a long note in the 1560 Bible cited above, disapproving of the royal authority for religion against God's word; challenges Nicodemitism; and refers frequently to 'the Gospell, Gospelling and Gospellers'. Sampson was at Geneva for several months during the making of the English version, though his working as a translator cannot be proven, but he represents the spirit and attitude of almost all of the Genevan exiles. They took what they wanted from Geneva but turned it into the context of the Edwardine Anglo-Zürich group of which Hooper had been the head. Their piety had its roots more in that group than elsewhere, since the range of Calvin's ecclesiology was not for them. (Knox's praise of Geneva focused on its practice of church discipline rather than on Calvin's full doctrine of the Church and sacraments.) Their pastors were preachers buoyed up with the sense of their own rightness, based on God's word which would be clear to his elect, and strongly convinced that they must obey God rather than man, as Cole had declared to Elizabeth on that

22. P. Ayris and D. Selwyn (eds.), *Thomas Cranmer, Churchman and Scholar* (1993); B. Hall, 'Cranmer, the Eucharist and the Foreign Divines', pp. 252ff. D.G. Danner, 'Anthony Gilby: Puritan in Exile', *Church History* (1971), pp. 412ff., provides a careful account of Gilby's career in which he states that Gilby was responsible for fostering a sacramentarian view of the eucharist in English Protestantism. This is a possibility, but his assertion that the editors of the 1560 Bible followed Oecolampadius and Martyr 'as sacramentarians' is erroneous since he bases it on the notes for Gen. 9.13 and Lk. 22.19 which are in fact translated from Calvin's commentary on Genesis and from Calvin's note in the French Bible respectively, and Calvin was not a sacramentarian.

text, Deut. 12.13, which Laski had truculently emphasized to Cranmer in his letter attacking the Prayer Book on the ground the Scripture alone must be the basis of all worship. In these circumstances it is remarkable how the notes to the 1560 Bible were so moderate, given the attitudes of the Geneva men Wood, Gilby, Samson and William Cole. Was this moderation due to Whittingham's scholarly principles and the influence of the restraint shown in the French Bible? Westcott was right to describe the marginal commentary as 'pure and vigorous in style...neither unjust nor illiberal'.[23] In brevity, cogency, religious insight and guidance in understanding the text, it was better than those in the Bishops' Bible and those that followed from the Westminster Assembly's Annotations onwards.

In spite of its later accretions in its Black Letter catechism and its Junius notes, it continued to instruct and edify thousands who had no stake in challenging bishops or promoting Presbyterianism or Separatism. It was the Bible used extensively by the poets Shakespeare, Spenser and Sidney,[24] as well as peasants and their squires, by merchants and burgesses, by the great earls and by the bishops themselves together with so many of their clergy.[25] For nearly one hundred and fifty years it was to be passed down in families as the heart of English religion with or without the Book of Common Prayer.[26]

23. Westcott, *A General View*, p. 93.

24. R. Noble, *Shakespeare's Biblical Knowledge*, (1935). N. Shaheen, *Biblical References in the Faerie Queen* (Memphis, TN, 1976).

25. R.T. Davidson, 'The Authorisation of the English Bible', *Macmillans Magazine* 44 (1881), pp. 441-43. Davidson, the future Archbishop, listed Stuart bishops and others who consistently used the Geneva version for years after the Authorized appeared.

26. L. Lupton, *A History of the Geneva Bible* (1966), contains six out of many volumes which alone relate to the editions of the Geneva Bible, 1557–1560. Those who have consulted these volumes, while acknowledging their range, will also know their weaknesses in scholarly procedure, and their particular religious viewpoint which, though it is assumed to be so, is not that of the original Genevan editors. This has precluded me from using these volumes, and neither Backus nor Hammond mentions them.

THEOLOGIAE PROPRIUM SUBIECTUM:
THEOLOGY AS THE CRITIC AND SERVANT OF THE CHURCH

Alister E. McGrath

> The proper subject of theology is humanity as a lost thing of sin and a
> justifying God and saviour of sinful humanity. Anything else which is
> considered or discussed in theology apart from this subject is an error and
> a poison (Martin Luther).

To honour James Atkinson is to do more than celebrate his enthusiasm
and scholarship for the Reformation, and above all Martin Luther. It is
to appreciate, with him, the abiding relevance of the Reformation for the
life and thought of the Christian church, whether catholic or evangelical
in its spiritual ethos, or Protestant or Roman Catholic in its denominational mindset. With the collapse of the Enlightenment, a whole series of
theological and spiritual options vetoed by its rationalist spirit have
become real possibilities once more for the western church. A 'theology
of retrieval' has been placed firmly on the western theological agenda,
as the church and academy seek to rediscover and reinstate theological
approaches which had been suppressed or apparently invalidated by the
rise of the Enlightenment. The Reformation makes available to the
modern church a series of options and approaches, until recently
regarded with disdain, but which are now coming back into favour. As
we seek to discover the relevance of the Reformation for our own situation, it is appropriate to salute those who were wise enough to plan for
this day—among whose ranks James Atkinson has a place of honour.

I remember how, as a small boy, one of my greatest pleasures was
rummaging through my grandparents' attic. For me, the room was
something of a treasure house, full of books, paintings and household
items dating back to the first decades of the twentieth century. Situated
at the top of a rambling Victorian house, this room had long served as a

repository for all kinds of items which, although old, nobody had the heart to throw away. 'They might come in useful sometime' was the homespun philosophy which lay beneath this reluctance to discard anything of potential value or use.

I have since come to discover that this same attitude underlies the best in Christian thinking. Responsible Christian theology and spirituality regard the ideas and values of the past, not as obsolete, but as items with a potential continued history of use. This is especially the case with the theology and the spirituality of the Reformation. The Reformation is a classic resource—a vital point of reference for modern Christianity, as it seeks to clarify its self-understanding, and a continuing resource for the modern church, as it seeks to bring every resource at its disposal to bear on the needs of its situation.[1]

The Reformation, like many other formative periods in Christian history, has much to offer us today. Works such as Jürgen Moltmann's *Crucified God* (which is a superb contemporary exposition of Luther's theology of the cross) have brought home to us the considerable potential of the theology of the Reformation period; that recognition has yet to be extended to its spirituality. Yet the Reformation did more than lay the foundations of classic evangelical theology and spirituality; it opened up new and invigorating approaches to the Christian life, like a breath of fresh air in a smoke-filled room. The Reformation offers us an invitation to return to consider our scriptural roots, in order that we may turn once more, refreshed, to our own situation.

The Reformation is a living option for the modern church, concerned on the one hand to remain faithful to Scripture, and on the other to engage with the realities of modern life. For example, the spirituality of the Reformation[2] represents more than a return to Scripture. It represents a systematic and coherent approach, by which the totality of the scriptural witness to the real and redemptive action of God through Christ could be focused upon and channeled into the everyday world. Scripture was not merely read and respected; it was recognized as possessing a relevance for every facet of Christian life. For the theologians of the Reformation did not develop their approaches to the spiritual life in the splendid isolation of monasteries or the ivory towers of the

---

1. For an introduction to the theology of the Reformation, see A.E. McGrath, *Reformation Thought: An Introduction* (Oxford: Basil Blackwell, 2nd edn, 1993).

2. On which see A.E. McGrath, *Roots that Refresh: A Celebration of Reformation Spirituality* (London: Hodder & Stoughton, 1992).

universities. These new approaches to the Christian life were forged and tested in the white heat of the crucibles of the great cities of early modern Europe.

To study the Reformation is not to luxuriate in romanticism. It is not to look back in nostalgia, like some old-timer hankering after the good old days when everything was better than it is now. It is not like the sentimental scrutiny of sepia-tinted photographs, nor the wistful recollection of days of lost innocence, a longing for a bygone period and its security. Rather, it is a hard-headed examination of past events, individuals and ideas, with a view to exploiting their present potential. It is to reach into our Christian past and recover some of its riches. It is a critical awareness that not everything in the Christian present is quite what it could be, linked with a willingness to consider alternative possibilities with a distinguished history of use within the Christian tradition.

The Reformation was fundamentally a quest for Christian identity and authenticity. It represents one of those great and rare moments in Christian history when the church was prepared to re-examine itself. It was prepared to face up to a series of deeply disturbing questions concerning its role and its relevance. The Christian church has always been prone to a form of inertia. By that, I do not mean that it stands still, immovable amidst the changing situations in which it finds itself. Rather, I mean that there is a certain inbuilt tendency to suppose that anything that happens in the life and thought of the church is invariably a good thing. There is an assumption that 'the way things are' is the same as 'the way things are meant to be'. It is a *laissez-faire* approach to Christianity. There is inertia, in the sense that there is a reluctance to adopt a *critical* attitude towards the ways things are, apparently on the basis of the assumption that what has happened is somehow *meant* to have happened. There is a reluctance to interrogate development, to challenge change.

And it is here that the Reformation has a fundamental contribution to make—a contribution which is continued in what has come to be known as 'the Protestant principle'. One of the deepest and most powerful wellheads which nourished the Reformation and its heritage is a spirit of creative protest, of prophetic criticism. This springs from the recognition of the sovereignty of God over his creation and his church, and of the living character of his revelation of himself in Jesus Christ and through Scripture. This creative and critical principle is grounded in a dynamic understanding of God's self-revelation, and his call to the Christian church to re-examine and renew itself in its light. Classical evangelical spirituality is aware of the need for the community of faith continually to examine itself—its ideas, its institutions and its actions—in the light of this revelation, leading to a characteristic pattern of Scripture-nourished recovery, renewal and reform. That pattern first appears definitively at the time of the Reformation itself.

There is much to be learned from the Reformation maxim *ecclesia reformata, ecclesia semper reformanda*—the reformed church must be a church which is always reforming itself. Reformation cannot be seen as a once-for-all event, now firmly located in the past. It must be a present and continuous process. (There is an interesting parallel here with Lenin's notion of a once-for-all revolution, and Trotsky's rival conception of a continuous revolution, always responsive to the needs and opportunities of the moment.) To study the spirituality of the Reformation is thus to be propelled into a new approach to the Christian faith, in which we continually ask what it means to be a Christian, and how this expresses itself at every level. The Christian churches need to undergo this self-imposed critique from time to time, to ensure that they remain in touch with their foundational visions. There is no sadder sight in Christendom than a church limping pathetically from one fad to the next, without the slightest idea what it is meant to be there for. The Reformation poses a challenge to modern churches which lack purpose, roots and a vision.

The Reformation represented an overdue, and hence traumatic, questioning of unquestioned developments in Christian life and thought during the Middle Ages. It posed a challenge to the notion of the irreversibility of history, by suggesting that certain developments in the life and thought of the church during the Middle Ages were improper and illegitimate—and more than that: that they could and should be undone. The Reformation was a quest for Christian authenticity, based on the belief that the medieval church had lost its way and its reason for existence. It represented a willingness to take a profound risk—that of assuming that the foundational resources of the Christian faith could be recovered and applied to the strange world of the sixteenth century and prove to be vital and relevant. Above all, the Reformation was a quest for Christian roots, grounded in the belief that a community which loses sight of its roots has lost sight of its reason for being in the world in the first place. So important is this theme to the contemporary relevance of the Reformation that we may explore it in more detail.

1. *Rediscovering Roots*

This history of European culture and of the Reformation has been deeply affected by the search for roots. Cultural stability and enrichment have often been seen as inextricably linked. This is perhaps most clearly seen in the case of the Italian Renaissance, rightly regarded as one of the most important and creative periods in European culture. The art galleries and museums of the world are packed full of exhibits showing the remarkable originality and imagination of the new culture which took hold of northern Italy during the period 1350–1550. By the end of the sixteenth century, virtually all of western Europe had been infected by this astonishing enthusiasm and vision. But what lay behind such a magnificent outburst of energy, of incredible artistic excitement, at the time?

The answer to this question is complex. However, a substantial part of that answer can be stated in two Latin words—*ad fontes*, 'back to the original sources'. Italian culture gained a new sense of purpose and dignity by seeing itself as the modern heir and champion of the long-dead culture of classical Rome. The Italian Renaissance could be said to be about bringing the culture of ancient Rome back to life in the modern period. The imaginations of artists, architects, poets, writers and theologians were seized by this vision. Imagine being able to allow the glory of the past to interact with the cultural void of fourteenth-century Italy! And as the process of recollection began, Italy began to gain a reputation as the cradle of a new civilization in Europe.

It is no accident that Italy was the birthplace and cradle of the Renaissance. The Italian writers of the period appear to have seen themselves as returning to their cultural roots in the world of classical Rome. A stream, they argued, was purest at its source; why not return to that source, instead of being satisfied with the muddy and stagnant waters of existing medieval culture? The past was seen as a resource, a foundational influence, whose greatness demanded that it should be allowed a voice in the present. The Italian Renaissance arose through a decision to allow the historic roots of Italian culture to impose upon the present, to inform it, to stimulate it—and to transform it. The explosion of creativity which resulted is an eloquent and powerful witness to the potential effects of returning to cultural roots, and allowing them to impact upon the present.

Many modern Christian movements, including evangelicalism, have been deeply affected by this concern for roots. One of the central insights here is a realization that the church of today needs to be constantly challenged and nourished by returning to its roots in the apostolic era. This is no historical romanticism, based on the belief that things were better in the past than they now are. Rather, it is the realization that the church needs to be reminded of its reason for being there in the first place, if it is ever to regain its sense of mission and purpose in the world. And just as the Italian Renaissance led to an enrichment of European culture by a return to its sources, so, in the same way, the life and witness of the modern church can be enriched and nourished by a constant return to its sources in the New Testament.

At first sight, this respect for roots might seem to be a recipe for a reactionary mindset, encouraging unoriginality and the stifling of creativity. That danger must be conceded. But there is another side to this story. Commitment to a tradition is not equivalent to an encrusted dogmatism, a denial of the freedom to think or of the importance of creativity.[3] To take tradition seriously is to allow the voices of the past to speak to us before turning, with a renewed and informed mind, to face the issues of the present.[4] Freedom to think without an accompanying commitment to a tradition can lead to little more than an unanchored chaos. The twentieth century has provided us with ample historical examples of what happens when a society breaks free from the restraining force of tradition. Nazi Germany and the Stalinist Soviet Union are excellent illustrations of the unacceptable consequences of a break with tradition. Walter Benjamin's 'Theses on the Philosophy of History' reflect his despair at the totalitarianism which results when a civilized society chooses to break with its traditional values.[5] It is very easy to break with one's roots; but, as the cultural history of the Soviet Union in recent years makes clear, it is very difficult to pick up those roots, once broken. David Tracy is one of many recent writers within a more liberal tradition to express concern over 'the wasteful and complacent obstruction of the rich resources of the tradition'.[6]

3. A point stressed by J. Pelikan, *The Vindication of Tradition* (New Haven: Yale University Press, 1984).
4. See the suggestive study of A. Nichols, 'T.S. Eliot and Yves Congar on the Nature of Tradition', *Angelicum* 61 (1984), pp. 473-85, which shows how 'tradition' and 'originality' are linked.
5. For analysis and comment, see A.E. McGrath, *The Genesis of Doctrine* (Oxford: Basil Blackwell, 1990), pp. 165-71.
6. D. Tracy, 'On Naming the Present', in P. Hillyer (ed.), *On the Threshold of the Third Millennium* (Concilium 1990–91; London: SCM Press, 1990), pp. 66-85 (75).

European cultural history emphasizes the need for continuity and responsibility. The suggestion that we should totally abandon the religious past in favour of some exciting new development (usually imported directly from California) is resisted, in the light of the European experience of the need to preserve the past as a check to the excesses of the present. It is perhaps only to be expected that the most bizarre recent religious cults, as well as innovative approaches to Christianity, generally have their origins in California, where a deep sense of rootlessness prevails. In his *Evolution of Human Consciousness*, John H. Crook comments as follows on the rise of the 'hippy' movement in California around the time of the Vietnam War:[7]

> It is no accident that the impetus came largely from the immigrant state of California where traditional cultural values are perhaps most fragmented and a need for new roots is most pronounced.

Churches with a strong sense of history lack this sense of rootlessness, and are thus resistant to many of the destabilizing developments especially associated with Christian churches in this fragmented and unstable region.

Roots are important for continuity and stability; they nurture the conditions under which growth and maturity may develop. Tradition encourages wariness, through exercising a restraining influence upon innovation. An enduring tradition, firmly located in history and taken seriously by those who claim to be its heirs, ensures caution and continuity within that community. Faithfulness to one's roots is not inconsistent with addressing contemporary needs and opportunities. In a world in which reality is widely regarded as self-created, the Reformation quest for roots reminds us that we are answerable to a heritage which stands over and above us.

2. *The Relevance of Theology*

Richard John Neuhaus, author of the highly-acclaimed volume *The Naked Public Square*,[8] puts his finger on one of the weak points of modern theology. Surveying the output of one leading North American religious publishing house, he remarks: 'most clergy, never mind lay

7.   J.H. Crook, *Evolution of Human Consciousness* (Oxford: Oxford University Press, 1980), p. 361.

8.   R.J. Neuhaus, *The Naked Public Square: Religion and Democracy in America* (Grand Rapids: Eerdmans, 2nd edn, 1986).

people, have given up reading theology'.[9] Why? Two reasons may easily be given:

1.   Much modern theology is written in a style and using a vocabulary which is alien to the vast majority of its potential reading public.
2.   Much modern theology addresses issues which bear little relation to the concerns of the Christian public.

Let me explore the second point further with reference to the novels of David Lodge. Lodge, formerly professor of English at the University of Birmingham, is a distinguished student of postmodern literature. His novel *Nice Work* explores two totally different worlds—that of a small business in Birmingham, specializing in the manufacture of machine parts, and that of a junior lecturer in the Department of English at the local university, who is deeply influenced by Jacques Derrida.[10] In a marvellously narrated section, Lodge describes the latter's gradual realization that the vital issues of her life—deconstruction, the arbitrariness of the relation between the signifier and signified—are an utter irrelevance to 99.9% of the human race. It is a painful realization, which alters her outlook upon the academic world.

It is a sad and simple fact of life, that much modern theology is perceived as totally pointless, not just by the general public, but even by educated lay Christians. Its vocabulary and concerns seem to belong to a different planet. Yet the Reformation offers us a vision of a time when theology was directed towards the issues which concerned the Christian public.

As a university teacher of theology at Oxford, I cannot help but notice the reaction of theology students to my lectures on Reformation thought. 'We can understand what these people are talking about!' is a typical response from students who have been bewildered by the verbal prolixity (often, it has to be said, masking a conceptual shallowness) of the writings of some recent theologians. 'They're dealing with real questions' is another response, grounded in a growing impatience with an academic theology which seems bent on pursuing questions of purely academic interest.

The issues which are today treated with what often approaches polite contempt by academic theologians were regarded as of vital importance

9.   R.J. Neuhaus, in *First Things* (October 1991), p. 71.
10.   D. Lodge, *Nice Work* (London: Penguin, 1989).

by sixteenth-century writers—issues such as the nature of the true church, the proper relation of the church and state, the grounds of Christian assurance, and a direct answer to the age-old question, 'What must I do to be saved?'

These issues are still debated today. But they are largely debated outside the academy, in local church study groups, in university Bible studies, and in many North American seminaries. The academy has become seriously isolated from the heartbeat of North American Christianity. Happily, this has happened to a far lesser extent in the United Kingdom. This anxiety is also reflected in the status of the theologian, to which we may now turn.

3. *The Status of the Theologian*

In the Middle Ages, theologians were often equally isolated from the community of faith. They were generally individuals, like the great Thomas Aquinas, who were based in the majestic monasteries of Europe. They were closeted within the confines of the monastic life, and wrote—when they wrote at all—for an audience of their fellow monks. It is rare—but happily, as the example of Thomas à Kempis reminds us, not totally unknown—to find a medieval theologian operating outside this context.

In our own day and age as well, theologians have become increasingly detached from the communities which they are meant to serve. They have become more and more professionalized, isolated within academic theological faculties, and becoming vulnerable to the charge of dwelling within ivory towers. Professionalization has tended to remove theologians from within the communities of faith, and placed them within the narrow confines of the universities. Secularization has led to a separation of personal faith and academic life; the professional academic theologian need not have any commitment to the faith or life of the church. These perceptions of a massive gap between church and academy are too easily reinforced by perusing the abstracts of the American Academy of Religion, where one encounters suggestions, such as the following, which seem to make depressingly little sense as English prose or as Christian theology:

Taylor's metaphorical 'body', then, is an (ex)tension of the phallocentric and phallocratic technology of modern theology, now confined to a two-dimensional wordplay indifferent to the cries and joys of a richly signed wor(l)d.[11]

Quite so. Surely, many ask, there must be a more satisfactory way of conceiving the task, calling and responsibilities of the theologian, than that offered by academic theology?

The Reformation bridges the gap between these two unsatisfactory approaches to the function of theology, and offers a working model to contemporary evangelicalism. The reformers, however diverse their origins may have been, were individuals who were based in the cities of Europe, living within the communities which they served, and sharing their faith. They were isolated by neither monastery nor university from the people who looked to them for guidance. Their task was to interpret and apply the gospel to the concrete situations in which they found themselves—above all, in relating to the lives of ordinary people.

Perhaps one of the most important moments of the Reformation may be traced to 1520, when Luther made the momentous and dramatic decision to cease being a purely academic reformer, addressing academic issues and audiences, and instead to make a direct and passionate appeal to the religious hopes and faith of the German people. Luther became both a preacher and a pastor—and his pastoral concern and experience shows up, time and time again, in his theology. Luther read and interpreted the New Testament as one who believed that it was of vital and continuing relevance to the life of the Christian community (another stark contrast between the theologians of the Reformation period and much modern academic discussion). His is a genuine pastoral theology, a theology which addresses the needs and concerns of ordinary believers and those who seek to minister to them.

Similarly, throughout Calvin's writings, we find a determination to engage with the real world of everyday life in the city of Geneva, along with all the problems and possibilities this brings with it. It seems that Calvin learned the lessons which Reinhold Niebuhr learned in downtown Detroit during the 1920s. In his *Leaves from the Notebook of a Tamed Cynic* (1929), Niebuhr wrote:[12]

11. See P.V. Mankowski SJ, 'Academic Religion', in *First Things* (May 1992), pp. 31-37 (34).

12. R. Niebuhr, *Leaves from the Notebook of a Tamed Critic* (New York: Meridian, 1957), p. 16.

> If a minister wants to be a man among men he need only stop creating a
> devotion to abstract ideals which everyone accepts in theory and denies in
> practice, and to agonize about their validity and practicability in the social
> issues which he and others face in our present civilization. That immedi-
> ately gives his ministry a touch of reality and potency.

Precisely this pattern stands out in Calvin's spiritual and homiletic
writings. Calvin addresses real and specific human situations—social,
political and economic—with all the risks that this entails. Here is no
abstract theorizing, conducted in the refined atmosphere of an ivory
tower. Rather, here is a theologian sharing the life of his people, and
attempting to interpret and apply the gospel in that situation. Calvin
wrote, worshipped and preached as a member of the community which
he addressed. He was not apart from them; he was not above them;
rather, he wrote from within his community, as part of it, sharing its life
and its problems. Here is no theology imposed from above or from outside, but a theology generated within a community, with the needs, possibilities and aspirations of that community in mind.

Is there not a model here which has relevance and appeal for today?
Again and again, ordinary Christians today comment on how irrelevant
they consider theologians to be. 'They seem so distant.' 'They don't
seem to understand the problems of everyday life.' 'They seem to have
a totally different agenda from ordinary believers.' 'We can't understand
what they are going on about.' While teaching as a visiting professor in
the United States in 1990, I even heard the following criticism of certain
theologians teaching at major North American seminaries: 'These people
don't even go to church—why should we listen to them?' 'There is no
way that these people present us with role models suitable for Christian
ministry.'

In brief, academic theology gets a very bad popular press. These
comments are deeply revealing, indicating the considerable gulf that has
opened up between the academy and the church. Surely, many ask,
there must be a more satisfactory way of conceiving the task, calling and
responsibilities of the theologian? It is thus vitally important to note that
the Reformation offers a very different model, with a distinguished history of application within the Christian tradition. The theologian is one
who is called to serve the community of faith from within. Part of that
service is criticism of its ideas and outlooks—but it is a loving and caring
criticism on the basis of shared Christian beliefs and commitments,
rather than the modern criticism of the Christian community by

academic 'theologians' on the basis of secular beliefs and values, often radically agnostic or atheistic, which that community feels no pressing reason to share.

This approach was developed by the Marxist writer Antonio Gramsci, who used the Reformation as a paradigm for his notion of the 'organic intellectual'. This idea, which originates at the time of the Reformation, is of considerable importance to contemporary evangelicalism. Gramsci argues that two distinct types of intellectuals can be discerned. In the first place, there are those who are imposed upon a community by an external authority. These 'institutional intellectuals' were not chosen by that community, and have influence only in so far as that authority is forced upon the community. In contrast to this, Gramsci notes—and commends—the idea of an 'organic intellectual'. The organic intellectual is one who arises within a community, and who gains authority on account of his or her being seen to represent the outlook of that community. Such people's authority emerges naturally, and reflects the esteem in which the community holds them.

This model of the theologian is enormously helpful. It resonates with the experience of many people within the western churches who have come to regard 'professional theologians' with intense skepticism as a result of the irresponsibility of the 1960s and 1970s. Theologians must now earn their spurs in the Christian constituency, gradually gaining respect and commanding authority on account of their observable fidelity and commitment to its ethos and norms, their ability to express themselves, and their concern for the well-being of the church and its members.[13] Turning to the evangelical wing of Anglicanism, John R.W. Stott is an excellent example of an 'organic intellectual'. He possesses no academic or institutional authority worth speaking of, but rightly enjoys enormous status within the world-wide Anglican community (and beyond) on account of his having *earned* that respect. Precisely the same could be said of Richard Holloway on the catholic wing of that same church; even before his appointment as Bishop of Edinburgh, he was regarded with considerable respect within world-wide Anglicanism. People regarded him as having authority because he had been accepted as being *worthy* of possessing authority. There was an organic and natural relationship between this person and the

13. For some perceptive observations on the dangers which the exercise of 'authority' can engender, see P. Avis, *Authority, Leadership and Conflict in the Church* (London: Geoffrey Chapman, 1992).

community for whom he spoke, and to whom he so clearly holds himself responsible. Precisely this same model applies to the great reformers, such as Luther or Calvin, who had authority because they were recognized to speak for and with their people.

Western Christianity has been prone to seduction by the reputation of the academy. If one wanted to know what Christians believed on some issue, one turned to a professor of theology at some respected university. Surrounded by an aura of academic respectability, this personage was deemed to be the most authoritative source available. But Gramsci encourages us to look instead towards the community of faith, to seek and find authority in individuals with a proven record of fidelity to the Christian tradition, a concern for the *consensus fidelium*, a love for the gospel, and a responsible and informed concern to relate it to the world—whether recognized by the academy or not. The best intellectuals may exist and operate outside the academy! This is not to suggest that being a Christian academic, or a professor of theology at a distinguished university, disqualifies someone from having authority within the community of faith. Nor is it to say that there is any place for anti-intellectualism inside the church. It is simply to make the point that such qualifications are not in themselves adequate grounds for the possession of such authority.

The notion of an 'organic intellectual' is also of importance in relation to the authority exercised by a church leader who seeks to impose his or her personal views upon a church, when these do not correspond to the 'mere Christianity' (C.S. Lewis) of ordinary believers. Organic authority is something which *emerges*, not something which is *imposed*. And it collapses if the individual in question proves to have lost support within the community, by failing to respect its beliefs and values. Individuals in a position of *institutional* authority can lose their *organic* authority, putting them in a position in which, having lost the latter, they could no longer meaningfully retain the former. Gramsci's approach allows us to draw a distinction between the institutional or traditional authority exercised by virtue of a church position, and the authority which arises from the esteem and trust in which an individual is held. A bishop who exercises authority *de jure* may have lost that authority *de facto*, in that the community may refuse to regard him or her as having any right to speak to them or for them. Such an individual would merely exercise ecclesiastical power without commanding spiritual authority.

In his famous reforming work of 1520, *An Appeal to the German*

Nobility, Luther argued forcefully that 'it is the duty of every Christian to espouse the cause of the faith, to understand and defend it, and to denounce every error.[14] Luther's doctrine of the priesthood of all believers, linked with that of the material sufficiency of Scripture, leads him to this challenging conclusion: precisely because all believers are priests, all are charged with the responsibility of maintaining the true faith, against the distortions of those who, claiming to be their leaders, ought to know and act better.

A modern interpreter of this doctrine is the famous Swiss theologian Karl Barth. For Barth, theology is far too important to be left to such people. It is a matter for everyone who believes, and thinks about his or her faith. It is a matter for anyone who wants to think responsibly about God, and the tasks and opportunities which faith in God brings.

> Theology is not a private subject for theologians only. Nor is it a private subject for professors. Fortunately, there have always been pastors who have understood more about theology than most professors. Nor is theology a private subject of study for pastors. Fortunately, there have repeatedly been congregation members, and often whole congregations, who have pursued theology energetically while their pastors were theological infants or barbarians. Theology is a matter for the Church.[15]

There is an urgent need to rediscover this close and organic relationship between theology and the church, a relationship which the reformers knew and cherished. As Luther put it, 'the proper subject of theology' is 'a God who justifies'.[16] We need to rediscover that theology does not

14. M. Luther, *Three Treatises* (Philadelphia: Fortress Press, 1970), pp. 21-22.

15. K. Barth, 'Theology', in *God in Action* (Edinburgh: T. & T. Clark, 1936), pp. 39-57 (56-57).

16. WA 40 II.328.17 'Theologiae proprium subiectum est homo peccati reus ac perditus et Deus iustificans ac salvator hominis peccatoris. Quicquid extra hoc subiectum in Theologia quaeritur aut disputatur, est error et venenum.' The issues which this quotation raises are enormous. See the classic study of E. Wolf, 'Die Rechtfertigungslehre als Mitte und Grenze reformatorischer Theologie', *Evangelische Theologie* 9 (1949–50), pp. 298-308. For further analysis, see A.E. McGrath, 'The Article by Which the Church Stands or Falls', *EvQ* 58 (1986), pp. 207-28; *idem*, 'Der articulus iustificationis als axiomatischer Grundsatz des christlichen Glaubens', *ZTK* 81 (1984) pp. 383-94; *idem*, 'Karl Barth and the *articulus iustificationis*. The Significance of his Critique of Ernst Wolf within the Context of his Theological Method', *TZ* 39 (1983) pp. 349-61; *idem*, 'Karl Barth als Aufklärer? Der Zusammenhang seiner Lehre vom Werke Christi mit der Erwählungslehre', *Kerygma und Dogma* 30 (1984) pp. 273-83. G. Ebeling, 'Karl Barth's Ringen mit Luther',

164   *The Bible, the Reformation and the Church*

mean 'the study of theologians' but 'the study of *God*'. The academy
has set a purely academic agenda for too long; it is time to redress that
balance. In his *Republic*, Plato argued that the world would only be a
better place when 'philosophers were kings, and kings philosophers'.
There is a sense in which the church would benefit considerably if
pastors were to be theologians, and theologians pastors.

The purely academic study of theology has forced an artificial division
between theology and spirituality. Karl Barth is rumoured to have been
in the habit of beginning his lectures with prayer, or even a hymn. This
practice would probably be outlawed in North American faculties of
religion today. Yet it points to the close link between theology and adoration, so central to the Reformation ethos, Lutheran and Reformed. In a
published lecture entitled 'An Introduction to Systematic Spirituality',
James I. Packer, a noted contemporary exponent of the Reformed tradition, stressed the utter impossibility of separating theology and
spirituality:

> I question the adequacy of conceptualizing the subject-matter of systematic
> theology as simply revealed truths about God, and I challenge the
> assumption that has usually accompanied this form of statement, that the
> material, like other scientific data, is best studied in cool and clinical
> detachment. Detachment from what, you ask? Why, from the relational
> activity of trusting, loving, worshipping, obeying, serving and glorifying
> God: the activity that results from realizing that one is actually in God's
> presence, actually being addressed by him, every time one opens the Bible
> or reflects on any divine truth whatsoever. This…proceeds as if doctrinal
> study would only be muddled by introducing devotional concerns; it drives
> a wedge between…knowing true notions about God and knowing the true
> God himself.[17]

Packer's point is that a genuine experience of God makes the detached
study of God an impossibility—a point appreciated by medieval mystical
writers, who often spoke in rapturous terms of their experience and
knowledge of God, and by Calvin, who stressed that true knowledge
of God led to both obedience and adoration. The demand for
'detachment' is like asking the lover to be neutral about the beloved.
Commitment is not merely a natural outcome of an authentically
Christian experience and knowledge of God; it is the substantiating

Lutherstudien, III (Tübingen: Siebeck, 1985), pp. 428-572.

17. J.I. Packer, 'An Introduction to Systematic Spirituality', *Crux* 26.1 (March
1990), pp. 2-8 (6).

hallmark of such experience and knowledge. This is an insight which the reformers knew and cherished; it is an insight which the modern church needs to recover.

Conclusion

The Reformation, as a historical event, lies in the past. Yet, as a model for the critical renewal of a church, it is very much a present reality. The Reformation issues a challenge to the churches to rediscover their sense of identity, distinctive vision, and sense of purpose in the world. The Reformation is all about a quest for identity, roots and authenticity. Christianity in the West needs to join in that quest. One of the greatest paradoxes of Christian history is that churches seem best prepared to move forwards when they first look backwards.[18] To study the Reformation is to look backwards with anticipation for the insights this will bring as we turn once more to face the future.

18. For an application of some of these insights to the situation of modern Anglicanism, see A.E. McGrath, *The Renewal of Anglicanism* (London: SPCK; Wilton, CT: Morehouse Publishing, 1993).

THE SPIRIT WITH THE WORD
THE REFORMATIONAL REVIVALISM OF GEORGE WHITEFIELD

J.I. Packer

I

If you ask an English Christian today who was the central figure of the mid-eighteenth-century revival, he or she will probably name John Wesley, the ex-Oxford don who for half a century led the network of societies which after his death became the Methodist Church, and whose Journal remains a classic of inspirational literature.[1] If you ask a modern American Christian to identify the central figure in New England's Great Awakening (1739–42), he or she is likely to point to Jonathan Edwards, still, perhaps, America's greatest theologian, whose *Narrative of a Surprising Work of God in the Conversion of Many Hundred Souls in Northampton and the Neighbouring Towns and Villages* (1735) became the model for all subsequent revival histories, and whose theology of the matter, set out in a series of masterful treatises published after the Awakening had subsided,[2] has commanded virtually unanimous evangelical assent from that day to this. But if these two questions had been put in Edwards's and Wesley's own lifetime to anyone with the least knowledge of either movement, it is as certain as

---

1. Wesley's Journal (actually, a sequence of 21 Journals) fills the first four volumes of his *Works* (ed. T. Jackson; 14 vols.; repr. Grand Rapids: Baker Book House, 1986). See also *The Journal of John Wesley* (ed. N. Curnock; 8 vols.; London: Epworth Press, 1938).

2. The writings in question are *A History of the Work of Redemption* (sermons preached in 1739; book published in 1744); *The Distinguishing Marks of a Work of the Spirit of God* (1741); *Thoughts on the Revival of Religion in New England in 1740* (1742); *A Treatise on the Religious Affections* (1746); all contained in *Works* (ed. E. Hickman; 2 vols.; repr. Edinburgh: Banner of Truth, 1974).

anything can be that the same name would have been given in reply to both, and it would not have been either of theirs; it would have been the name of George Whitefield, the 'Grand Itinerant', whose preaching sparked off and sustained revival religion of the Puritan type—reflective, assured, joyful, powerful, life-transforming—in tens of thousands of lives both sides of the Atlantic for more than thirty years, from the time of his ordination in 1736 to his death in 1770.

Preaching the grace of God in Christ was Whitefield's life, both metaphorically and literally. He kept a record of over 18,000 formal preaching occasions, and if the informal 'exhorting' (his term) which he regularly did in private homes be added in it is probably true to say that he preached twice that number of times. Three stated sermons a day was common; four was not unknown; and the 'exhorting' was done on top of that. 'Who would think it possible', wrote Henry Venn, vicar of Huddersfield, who knew Whitefield well,

> that a person...should speak in the compass of a single week (and that for years) in general forty hours, and in very many, sixty, and that to thousands; and after this labour, instead of taking any rest, should be offering up prayers and intercessions, with hymns and spiritual songs, as his manner was, in every house to which he was invited.[3]

Whitefield squandered himself unstintingly, and it is no wonder that in 1765, when he was fifty-one, John Wesley, eleven years his senior, should have noted after a breakfast meeting with him: 'Mr Whitefield...seemed to be an old, old man, being fairly worn out in his Master's service'.[4] The wonder is, rather, that Whitefield was able to maintain his non-stop preaching routine for nearly five more years, constantly testifying that the preaching which exhausted his body energized his heart.

To the last, a visit from Whitefield to any location was a major event, and he drew much larger crowds on his tours than did any other revival spokesman. Often over 10,000, sometimes more than 20,000, attended his open-air orations, and all heard his huge voice distinctly, even in the two-hour message he gave at Exeter, New Hampshire, the afternoon before the cardiac asthma attack that ended his life. It has been estimated

3. A. Dallimore, *George Whitefield* (2 vols.: I, London: Banner of Truth, 1970; II, Edinburgh: Banner of Truth, 1980), II, p. 521.

4. Wesley, *Works*, III, p. 238. Other similar comments: 'Humanly speaking, he is worn out' (133; May, 1763). 'His soul appeared to be vigorous still, but his body was sinking apace' (354; March, 1769). Whitefield died on Sept. 30, 1770.

that during his ministry he preached to combined audiences of over ten million, and that four-fifths of America's colonists, from Georgia to New Hampshire, heard him at least once—something that could be said of no other person. About eight years of his life were spent in America, where he died in the middle of his seventh tour; otherwise, apart from two months in Bermuda in 1748, the British Isles were his stamping-ground, and he criss-crossed them again and again as a messenger of the gospel of Christ. Cried John Wesley in his memorial sermon for Whitefield, which he preached in both the London centres (Moorfields Tabernacle and Tottenham Court Chapel) that had been put up as stations for Whitefield's ministry:

> Have we read or heard of any person since the Apostles, who testified the gospel of the grace of God...through so large a part of the habitable world? Have we read or heard of any person who called so many thousands, so many myriads, of sinners to repentance? Above all, have we read or heard of any who has been a blessed instrument in his [God's] hand of bringing so many sinners from 'darkness to light, and from the power of Satan unto God?'[5]

The expected answer, of course, was no; and the same answer would have had to be given through the next two centuries, right up to the glory days of electronically-boosted Billy Graham.

In Whitefield's own lifetime he had celebrity status as a preaching phenomenon, and was recognized as the pioneer of all the distinctives that marked the revival in Britain: use of the name 'Methodist';[6] evangelistic preaching in the open air as well as in churches, and on planned tours as well as in response to direct invitations; forming local Methodist societies and lining up lay circuit riders to provide them with regular evangelical instruction and exhortation;[7] publishing news of the ongoing revival in a weekly paper;[8] and printing his journals, a personal record of his life and ministry, as he did between 1737 and 1741. It is usual to credit Wesley with these procedural innovations, but in fact at each point Wesley did no more than follow the younger man's example.[9] Today,

5.   Wesley, *Works*, VI, p. 177.
6.   Dallimore, *George Whitefield*, I, pp. 381-83.
7.   Dallimore, *George Whitefield*, II, pp. 149-59.
8.   H.S. Stout, *The Divine Dramatist: George Whitefield and the Rise of Modern Evangelicalism* (Grand Rapids: Eerdmans, 1991), pp. 144-47. Whitefield's paper was called *The Weekly History; or, An Account of the Most Remarkable Particulars Relating to the Present Progress of the Gospel*.
9.   Dallimore, *George Whitefield*, II, p. 531.

however, Whitefield's pastoral pioneering, like so much else about him, is largely forgotten; which is, to say the least, an injustice and a pity.

When I became a Christian in 1944, Whitefield's role in the evangelical life of his day was unknown to those who nurtured me. But I knew his name, for I had attended his old school, the Crypt School, Gloucester,[10] and had seen him represented in a school pageant (not very accurately, as I later learned) hammering sabbath-breakers. Three months after my conversion, lying in bed with bronchitis, I read both volumes of Luke Tyerman's 1876 biography, and the career of the great Gloucestrian made a tremendous impression on me, securing him pride of place in my private heroes' gallery. I subsequently found that Whitefield had made a similar impact on C.H. Spurgeon, the nineteenth century's greatest pastoral evangelist,[11] and on Martyn Lloyd-Jones, Spurgeon's nearest twentieth-century counterpart.[12] Interest in Whitefield has grown in recent years, as witness the publishing of the first collected edition of his journals,[13] the facsimile reprint of his letters up to 1742 from the edition of 1771,[14] the big and painstaking 'filiopietistic' life of Whitefield by Arnold Dallimore, *George Whitefield: The Life and Times of the Great Evangelist of the Eighteenth-Century Revival*,[15] John Pollock's vivid and racy *George Whitefield and the Great Awakening*,[16] and Harry S. Stout's not-so-filiopietistic but shrewd biography, *The Divine Dramatist: George Whitefield and the Rise of*

10. Dallimore calls it 'St Mary's' (*George Whitefield*, I, p. 50) and 'the de Crypt School' (*George Whitefield*, II, p. 528), but is wrong both times. It was always 'the Crypt school' *simpliciter*. Stout, *The Divine Dramatist*, p. 2, moves the school, with the Bell Inn, Whitefield's home (almost next door), and Southgate Street, where both stood, from Gloucester to Bristol—a spectacular slip.

11. 'There is no end to the interest which attaches to such a man as Whitefield. Often as I have read his life, I am conscious of a distinct quickening whenever I turn to it. *He lived*. Other men seem to be only half alive; but Whitefield was all life, fire, wing, force. My own model, if I may have such a thing in due subordination to my Lord, is George Whitefield' (quoted from L. Drummond, *Spurgeon Prince of Preachers* [Grand Rapids: Kregel, 1992], p. 219).

12. See Lloyd-Jones's appreciation of Whitefield, 'John Calvin and George Whitefield', in *The Puritans: Their Origins and Successors* (Edinburgh: Banner of Truth, 1987), pp. 101-28. 'I could imagine no greater privilege, than to speak on George Whitefield', p. 102.

13. *George Whitefield's Journals* (London: Banner of Truth Trust, 1960).

14. *George Whitefield's Letters, 1734–42* (Edinburgh: Banner of Truth, 1976).

15. See n. 3 above. The adjective 'filiopietistic' comes from Stout.

16. (London: Hodder & Stoughton, 1973).

Modern Evangelicalism,[17] plus most recently the Spring 1993 number of the widely circulated journal of popular scholarship, *Christian History*.[18] Perhaps the recognition of greatness and significance that is Whitefield's due is coming to him at last. In any case, however, I am confident that my honoured friend James Atkinson, who is himself as much a preacher of the gospel as he is a historical scholar and theologian, will have some interest in the attempt of this essay to determine Whitefield's place in the Reformation succession for which he cares so deeply.

II

With his Oxford education, natural ease of manner, and slight West-country twang, which made him seem attractively human (his resonant speech was always somewhat nasal, and he pronounced 'Christ' as 'Chroist' all his life), Whitefield, having been ordained at twenty-one in 1736, shot quickly into prominence as a Bible-preaching pastoral evangelist on the grand scale. At a time when other Anglican clergy were writing and reading flat sermons of a mildly moralistic and apologetic sort, Whitefield preached extempore about heaven and hell, sin and salvation, the dying love of Christ, and the new birth, clothing his simple expository outlines with glowing dramatic conscience-challenging rhetoric, and reinforcing his vocal alternations of soothing and punching with a great deal of body movement and gesture, thereby adding great energy to the things he was saying. At a time when other Anglican clergy were watching their churches empty, Whitefield went out to preach in the open air, loved the experience, and saw vast crowds gather to hear him and many come to faith through his messages. To put his extraordinary ministry in perspective, we need to note that he was, first, a born orator; secondly, a natural actor; thirdly, an English Protestant pietist; fourthly, an Anglican Calvinist of the older Puritan type; fifthly, a disciplined, somewhat ascetic clergyman of inflexible single-mindedness and integrity, childlike in humility and passionately devoted to his Lord; sixthly, a transparently friendly, forthcoming, care-giving man, as far from standoffishness as could be, to whose spontaneous good will was added the evangelist's gift of making all the members of the crowd feel

17. See n. 8 above.
18. Published quarterly by Christianity Today, Inc., 465 Gundersen Drive, Carol Stream, IL 60188.

they were being addressed personally in what he said;[19] and seventhly, a Christian of catholic and ecumenical spirit whose vision of continuous revival throughout the English-speaking world led him to renounce all forms of institutional leadership and control, so that he might be entirely at the service of all. Each of these points calls for separate comment.

First, on Whitefield as an orator, the most insightful remarks come from a transcribed address by one who was himself a notable pulpit orator, and thus knew what he was talking about, Martyn Lloyd-Jones. I quote him at some length.

> A man is born an orator. You cannot make orators. You are either an orator or you are not. And this man was a born orator. He could not help it…and like all orators, he was characterized by the great freedom and appropriateness of his gestures. The pedantic John Wesley was not an orator, and he sometimes tended to be a bit critical of George Whitefield in this respect. I remember reading in Wesley's *Journal* of how once they both happened to be in Dublin at the same time and how John Wesley went to listen to Whitefield. In his account of the service, Wesley refers to his gestures, and says that it seemed to him that Whitefield was a little bit too much like a Frenchman in a box. He means that Whitefield tended to speak with his hands as much as with his lips and mouth. But that is oratory. One of the greatest orators of all time was Demosthenes. Somebody asked Demosthenes one day, 'What is the first great rule of oratory?' And Demosthenes answered, 'The first great rule of oratory is—action; and the second great rule of oratory is—action; and the third great rule of oratory is—action'…We are living in evil days; we know nothing about oratory. George Whitefield was a born orator. Have you heard what David Garrick is reported to have said? David Garrick was the leading actor in London in those times and whenever he had an opportunity he always went to listen to Whitefield. He was not so much interested in the gospel as in the speaking and the gestures…Garrick is reported to have said that he would give a hundred guineas if he could only say 'Oh!' as George Whitefield said it…[20]

19. 'He had a most peculiar art of speaking personally to you, in a congregation of four thousand people' (Cornelius Winter, who was Whitefield's factotum and travelling companion, 1767–70: in Dallimore, *George Whitefield*, II, p. 482).

20. Lloyd-Jones, 'John Calvin and George Whitefield', p. 117. I cannot track down Lloyd-Jones's reference to Wesley; but his Journal for February 1750 contains this equally condescending comment: 'Mr Whitefield preached… Even the little improprieties both of his language and manner were a means of profiting many, who would not have been touched by a more correct discourse, or a more calm and regular manner of speaking' (Wesley, *Works*, II, p. 172). And later that year: 'I have

Secondly, Whitefield was an actor—'a born actor', in Lloyd-Jones's phrase[21]—who, as his contemporaries sometimes observed, might have been equal or superior to Garrick had he gone on the stage. As a boy, he had excelled in school theatricals, where evidently he had mastered the actor's two arts, expression and projection. Stout underlines the significance of this actor's training. Acting manuals of Whitefield's day, he tells us, pinpointed

> ten dramatic passions to which appropriate actions and facial expressions were attached: joy, grief, fear, anger, pity, scorn, hatred, jealousy, wonder, and love. With these ten tools the actor could play any part, for they encompassed the sum and substance of the human condition. Of Whitefield's great contemporary David Garrick it was said that he could entertain guests by 'throwing his features into the representation of Love, Hatred, Terror, Pity, Jealousy, Desire and Joy in so rapid and striking a manner [as to] astound the whole country'... In place of thinking man the manuals substituted impassioned man...[22]

All this Whitefield absorbed in his youth, and as a result his public style was that of 'an actor-preacher, as opposed to a scholar-preacher'.[23]

As a born actor, now trained to wear his heart on his face and to pour it into his voice, Whitefield's instinct was for performance.[24] He lived to evangelize and nurture, and 'his private life shrank into a small and relatively insignificant interlude between the big performances'.[25] Stout,

---

sometimes thought Mr Whitefield's action was violent' (Wesley, *Works*, II, p. 195).

21. Lloyd-Jones, 'John Calvin and George Whitefield', p. 117.

22. Stout, *The Divine Dramatist*, pp. 9-10.

23. Stout, *The Divine Dramatist*, p. xix.

24. Compare Winter's observations, from the end of Whitefield's life: 'It was truly impressive to see him ascend the pulpit. My intimate knowledge of him admits of my acquitting him of the charge of affectation. He always appeared to enter the pulpit with a significance of countenance, that indicated he had something of importance which he wanted to divulge, and was anxious for the effect of the communication'. 'I hardly ever knew him go through a sermon without weeping, and I truly believe his tears were the tears of sincerity. His voice was often interrupted by his affection.' 'His freedom in the use of his passions often put my pride to the trial [i.e. embarrassed me]. I could hardly bear such unreserved use of tears, and the scope he gave to his feelings, for sometimes he exceedingly wept, stamped loudly and passionately, and was frequently so overcome, that for a few seconds, you would suspect he never could recover' (Dallimore, *George Whitefield*, II, pp. 482-83).

25. Stout, *The Divine Dramatist*, p. xxii.

with others, speaks of Whitefield's 'shameless' self-promotion,[26] but the adjective does not fit ('uninhibited' might do): no pride, self-aggrandizement or exploitation of others entered into what he did at any stage of his career to publicise his preaching of the gospel. As God's anointed barnstormer, he simply advertised coming performances, looking to God to cause each congregation to pull out of him fresh dramatic creativity in communicating the material he knew so well. It is in these terms that we should understand his statement, in a letter of 1750: 'The more we do, the more we may do; every act strengthens the habit; the best preparation for preaching on Sunday is to preach every day of the week'.[27] We need to remember that for an actor every performance is, among other things, a rehearsal for the next one.

Thirdly, Whitefield was a pietist, that is, one who saw practical personal devotion to the Father and the Son through the Spirit as always the Christian's top priority. Mark Noll types pietism in terms of

> (1) its experiential character—pietists are people of the heart for whom Christian living is the fundamental concern; (2) its biblical focus— pietists...take standards and goals from the pages of Scripture; (3) its perfectionist bent—pietists are serious about holy living and expend every effort to follow God's law, spread the gospel, and provide aid for the needy; (4) its reforming interest—pietists usually oppose what they regard as coldness and sterility in established church forms and practices.[28]

The pietism of Whitefield's day grew out of the devotional revival that broke surface in both Protestantism and Roman Catholicism in the seventeenth century, partly as a reaction against the hard-shell controversialist, imperialist and formalist mind-sets that the Reformation conflicts had left behind, partly as a renewed perception of biblical Christianity in its own terms. In Protestant England, this seventeenth-century movement was channelled mainly through Puritanism, where justification by faith and regeneration and assurance through the Holy Spirit were set in a clear and classic Augustinian frame of sovereign grace. The High Church devotional development, fed more by the Greek fathers, was at first less influential, just as it was doctrinally less clear. But it was High Church pietists who developed the religious

26. Stout, *The Divine Dramatist*, p. xxiii.
27. Dallimore, *George Whitefield*, II, p. 286.
28. *Evangelical Dictionary of Theology* (ed. W. Elwell; Grand Rapids: Baker Book House, 1984), *s.v.* 'Pietism', pp. 855-56.

societies (midweek gatherings for devotional exercises) in Restoration times, and it was as a participant in one of these, John Wesley's 'Holy Club', whose members were called 'Methodists' because of their methodical rule of life, that Whitefield first realized his need of the characteristic pietist experience, namely, the new birth.

Through a long and painful conversion process Whitefield finally found the new birth that he sought—assurance of sins forgiven and Christ's love set upon him, newness of heart, and an overflow of joy in God. One of his first acts then was to buy and devour Matthew Henry's commentary, a brilliant pietistic exposition of Scripture that draws on a century of Puritan theology, Bible study and homiletics. This classic became his lifelong companion,[29] and, reinforced by subsequent association with America's latter-day Puritans, Jonathan Edwards and the Tennents, it established his pietism in the Puritan mould. Thereafter all the marks of pietism as Noll profiles it—devotional ardour, Bible-centredness, holiness with evangelism and philanthropy, hostility to cold and formal religion—became marks of Whitefield's life and ministry. His printed sermons and pastoral letters, the latter numbering over 1400, show that he concentrated throughout his ministry on the basics of personal religion—new birth, faith, repentance, righteousness and good works, praise of God, and love to Christ. No breath of scandal ever touched his personal life; the lures of sex, shekels and empire-building never enmeshed him. The pietism of his outlook was given credibility by the piety of his life.

Fourthly, he was an Anglican Calvinist of the Puritan type. He embraced the sovereign-grace teaching of the Thirty-nine Articles with regard to personal salvation (see especially Articles 9–13 and 17), affirmed the developed federal theology of the seventeenth century, and insisted that sovereign-grace teaching, with its rejection of salvation by

---

29. See D. Crump, 'The Preaching of George Whitefield and his Use of Matthew Henry's Commentary', *Crux* 25.3 (September 1989), pp. 19-28. 'Usually, for an hour or two, before he entered the pulpit, he claimed retirement; and on a sabbath morning more particularly [when in London, where he had two pulpits to serve, and a new sermon was needed each Sunday], he was accustomed to have [Samuel] Clarke's Bible [a Puritan product, reprinted in 1759 with 'A Preface to the Serious Reader' by Whitefield: see *Works of George Whitefield* (ed. J. Gillies; London, 1771), IV, pp. 275ff.], Matthew Henry's Comment, and Cruden's Concordance within his reach' (Winter, in Dallimore, *George Whitefield*, II, p. 481).

self-effort in all its forms, bears directly on the purity or otherwise of the believer's devotion. Two extracts from his letters show this.

> This…is my comfort, 'Jesus Christ, the same yesterday, today, and for ever'. He saw me from all eternity; He gave me being; He called me in time; He has freely justified me through faith in his blood; He has in part sanctified me by His Spirit; He will preserve me underneath His everlasting arms till time shall be no more. Oh the blessedness of these evangelical truths! These are indeed Gospel; they are glad tidings of great joy to all that have ears to hear. These, bring the creature out of himself. These, make him hang upon the promise, and cause his obedience to flow from a principle of love.

> The doctrines of our election, and free justification in Christ Jesus are daily more and more pressed upon my heart. They fill my soul with a holy fire and afford me great confidence in God my Saviour.[30]

Whitefield constantly maintained these doctrines and the spirituality of dependent gratitude that flowed from them, declaring: 'I embrace the Calvinistic scheme, not because Calvin, but Jesus Christ has taught it to me',[31] and insisting that Anglicanism's historic formularies and best theologians were on his side at this point.

Whitefield's identification with the Puritan type of theology, both in and outside the Church of England, is apparent from his 'Recommendatory Preface' to the 1767 reprint of the works of the Baptist John Bunyan, which contained the following sentences:

> Ministers never write or preach so well as when under the cross: the spirit of CHRIST and of glory then rests upon them.
> It was this, no doubt, that made the *Puritans* of the last century such burning and shining lights. When cast out by the black *Bartholomew-act* [the 1662 Act of Uniformity, which triggered 2000 ejections from the ministry of the Church of England]…they in an especial manner preached and wrote as men having authority. Though dead, by their writings they yet speak: a peculiar unction attends them to this very hour; and for these thirty years past I have remarked, that the more, true and vital religion hath revived either at home or abroad, the more the good old puritanical writings, or the authors of a like stamp who lived and died in the communion of the church of *England*, have been called for.[32]

---

30. *George Whitefield's Letters, 1734–42*, pp. 98, 79.
31. *George Whitefield's Letters, 1734–42*, p. 442.
32. *Works*, IV, p. 306.

When in 1829 selections from Whitefield's works were published under the title *The Revived Puritan*, the phrase was uncannily apt.[33] That, precisely, is what Whitefield was.

Fifthly and *sixthly*, Whitefield displayed qualities of Christian character that added credibility to his public ministrations. He was no hypocrite, nor did those closest to him find great flaws and weaknesses in him. They found him, rather, to be a person of real genuineness, integrity, humility, poise and charm, affable and courteous in all company, with a genius for friendship, great practical wisdom, simple tastes, and much joy in living for God. To illustrate this properly would require virtually a retelling of his life story, which is not possible here,[34] but a few facts may be mentioned.

In 1738 Whitefield committed himself to fund Bethesda, Georgia's orphan house which he himself had founded. He carried this responsibility for the rest of his life, and nearly ruined himself in the process of discharging it.

In 1739 he and Benjamin Franklin became friends, though neither then nor thereafter did Franklin embrace his message of salvation from sin through new birth. But Franklin wrote of him in 1747: 'He is a good man and I love him',[35] and after his death: 'I knew him intimately upwards of 30 years. His Integrity, Disinterestedness and indefatigable Zeal in prosecuting every good Work, I have never seen equalled, I shall never see excelled.'[36]

In 1739 Whitefield also became friends with Howell Harris, the dynamic Welsh exhorter, and the friendship was lifelong, despite a period during which Harris' behavioural aberrations strained it to its limit.[37] In 1743 Whitefield was chosen as moderator for life of the Calvinistic Methodist Association of Wales, a body founded to regulate the evangelical religious societies that Harris and others had formed

33. *The Revived Puritan*. Select Works of the Rev George Whitefield, Containing a Memoir...Thirty Sermons...Fourty Seven Discourses...A Compendium of his Epistolary Correspondence...In One Volume (Lewes: Sussex Press, John Baxter, 1829).

34. See the biographies, especially those of Tyerman, Pollock and Dallimore. All the biographers are captivated, more or less, by Whitefield's personal qualities.

35. Dallimore, *George Whitefield*, II, p. 222.

36. Dallimore, *George Whitefield*, II, p. 453.

37. Dallimore, *George Whitefield*, II, pp. 295-303.

throughout the country, and Harris's praise for Whitefield's handling of his role was unstinting.[38]

In 1748, aged thirty-three, having reviewed the journals he published[39] at twenty-three, he wrote in a letter:

> Alas! alas! In how many things have I judged and acted wrong... I frequently wrote and spoke in my own spirit, when I thought I was writing and speaking by the assistance of the Spirit of God...I have likewise too much made inward impressions my rule of acting, and too soon and too explicitly published what had been better kept in longer, or told after my death. By these things I have given some wrong touches to God's ark, and hurt the blessed cause I would defend, and also stirred up needless opposition. This has humbled me much... I bless him [God] for ripening my judgment a little more, for giving me to see and confess, and I hope in some degree to correct and amend, some of my mistakes.[40]

Whitefield in maturity was able to see and eliminate the imprudences of his youthful zeal; they did not recur during the last twenty-two years of his life.

Finally, Whitefield distinguished himself as 'the peace-maker' (John Fletcher's description)[41] between John Wesley and himself, bending over backwards to heal the breach after Wesley and he had diverged in print over the meaning of predestination and 'free grace' (1740–41). Wesley's imperious single-mindedness and donnish didacticism, plus his eleven-year seniority to Whitefield and his fixed habit of treating Whitefield as his pupil and protégé, as he does most unbeautifully throughout his printed journals, made him a difficult man for

38. 'I was stunned to see his amazing wisdom, wherein he is taught to manage the Church, doing all calmly and wisely, following the Lord' (*Howell Harris, Reformer and Soldier* [ed. T. Beynon; Caernarvon: Calvinistic Methodist Bookroom, 1958], p. 41).

39. It should be noted that the publishing of Whitefield's Journals began without his consent. On his return to England from Georgia in 1738 he found that James Hutton, an ardent supporter, had at this point jumped the gun. 'Whitefield had sent his diary of the journey from London to Gibraltar, for private circulation. A printer called Cooper saw it, scented profits and put it in print; but as he could not always decipher Whitefield's handwriting the text was corrupt and Printer Hutton had decided the absent author would approve if he published an accurate version' (Pollock, *George Whitefield*, p. 69). Finding this Journal already a best-seller, Whitefield followed it up over the next three years with half a dozen more. For more details, see Iain Murray's introduction to *Whitefield's Journals*, pp. 13-19.

40. Dallimore, *George Whitefield*, II, p. 241.

41. Dallimore, *George Whitefield*, II, p. 352.

Whitefield to get back on terms with; but he managed it, at the cost of renouncing all his leadership roles in England and Wales in 1748 and operating thereafter from time to time as one of Wesley's assistants.[42] It was a triumph of humility on the part of the public celebrity who at the close of his life was signing his letters 'Less than the least of all, George Whitefield'.[43]

The *seventh* key fact about Whitefield, his passion for Christian unity as part of his vision of sustained spiritual vitality undergirding and transforming community life both sides of the Atlantic, is sufficiently illustrated by the foregoing paragraph, and need not be further displayed here.

III

We learn Whitefield's theology from his tracts and letters, and also from his seventy-five printed sermons.[44] These vary in style and provenance. They are all based on biblical texts, expounded, however sketchily, in context, but 46 of them were printed before Whitefield was twenty-five, and some were written out after being preached rather than before, and some were transcribed *viva voce* from Whitefield's lips as he orated and put in print sometimes with and sometimes without his approval. Such material needs to be handled with care, but theologically it is all homogeneous, and in no way innovative. We have already noted that, like all England's evangelical clergy then and since, Whitefield insisted that the religion he modelled and taught was a straightforward application of Anglican doctrine as defined in the Articles, the Homilies and the Prayer Book. We have seen that he took his interpretations of Scripture mainly if not entirely from the 'unparalleled', 'incomparable'[45] Matthew Henry. His developed understanding of justification by faith only through the imputed righteousness of Christ, and of the federal plan of salvation that five-point Calvinism spells out, came to him from Puritan and Scottish

---

42. Dallimore, *George Whitefield*, chs. 17, 23, II, pp. 247ff., 335ff.

43. To John Wesley, 12 Sept. 1769; to Robert Keen (Whitefield's last letter), 23 Sept. 1770; Dallimore, *George Whitefield*, II, pp. 475, 498.

44. Reprinted in one volume, *Sermons on Important Subjects* (London: Henry Fisher, Son, and P. Jackson, 1832).

45. *Works*, IV, pp. 307, 278.

sources.[46] But the things he took from the Reformed tradition came out in his own way, cast into meditations and messages that called for present response, and located every such response, or refusal of it, as part of the drama which the Puritans had already mapped with great skill, namely the personal drama of the soul's ongoing journey to heaven or to hell. 'Dramatize! Dramatize!' urged Henry James; plots and characters of novels should be full of 'felt life'. Whitefield's instinct for drama led him to preach sermon after sermon that dramatized the issues of eternity, and summoned his hearers to seek, in his phrase, a 'felt Christ'. We can sum up the substance of Whitefield's sermons in a series of imperatives, as follows.

First, Face God. People live thoughtlessly, drifting through their days, never thinking of eternity. But God the Creator, our lawgiver and holy judge, who made us for himself and holds us in his hands every moment, has revealed in Scripture that a day of judgment is coming when he will either welcome us into heaven's eternal joy or banish us for ever to hell's misery. So—*wake up! and reckon, here and now, with God!* Whitefield repeatedly shed tears of agonized compassion as he preached about the ruinous, suicidal, self-hating folly of those who would not do this.

Secondly, Know Yourself. We mortals all see in ourselves, and in our children, and in all our fellow-humans, self-centred, self-pleasing, worldly-minded, really vicious dispositions. These bespeak the universal corruption of nature called original sin. G.K. Chesterton called original sin the one Christian doctrine that admits of demonstrative proof, and that was how Whitefield presented it. From Genesis 3 and Romans 5 he analyzed it in the standard Reformed way: the sin of Adam, our

46. For details, see Dallimore, *George Whitefield*, I, p. 405. Dallimore corrects the mistake, traceable to Tyerman, of supposing that Whitefield learned his Calvinism from Jonathan Edwards, whom he first met in 1740. On the voyage to America, a year before, he recorded that he had been 'greatly strengthened by perusing some paragraphs out of a book called *The Preacher*, written by Dr [John] Edwards, of Cambridge, and extracted by Mr Jonathan Warn, in his books entitled, *The Church of England-Man turned Dissenter*, and *Arminianism the Backdoor to Popery*. There are such noble testimonies…of justification by faith only, the imputed righteousness of Christ, our having no free-will, &c., that they deserve to be written in letters of gold' (*Journals*, p. 335). Tyerman and others seem to have confused Jonathan with John Edwards.

progenitor and covenant head, was imputed to us, his posterity, in the sense that we all now share the penal deprivations that his sin incurred for himself—bodily decay and mortality, plus a morally twisted disposition that makes faith, love and obedience God-ward a natural impossibility, just as it flaws all the godliness of those whose hearts God supernaturally renews. The doctrine of original sin thus answers the question: why am I no better than I am? It does not excuse us by letting us shift the blame for our perversities on to Adam; it just confirms to us that we are all naturally lost, spiritually impotent and helpless, without hope of commending ourselves to God by anything we do. This is the bad news that we must accept and internalize before we can appreciate the good news of salvation.

Thirdly, See Jesus. Whitefield's preaching, like his personal faith, centred upon the person of 'the dear Jesus', the once-crucified, now glorified God-man, the gift of the Father's love and the embodiment of divine mercy. From Scripture Whitefield would set forth with rhapsodic rhetoric and arms-lifted, foot-stamping passion the incarnation, Jesus's friendship with sinners, his pity for the needy, his agonizing death for our sins, his bodily resurrection and ascension, his present heavenly reign and coming return to judgment, and then he would go to town, as we would say, on the invitations to faith, promises of justification, preservation and glorification, and guarantees of his own fidelity that comprise Jesus' word to the world. It was said of Charles Finney that in his evangelistic preaching he rode sinners down with a cavalry charge; Whitefield's way, however, was to sweep them off their feet with an overflow of compassionate affection, modelling his Master's good will towards the lost. Thus by word and action Whitefield enabled his hearers mentally and spiritually to see Jesus, with constantly overwhelming effect.

Fourthly, Understand Justification. Following the Restoration many Anglican minds, recoiling from all things Calvinistic, took up with a moralistic, indeed legalistic, recasting of justification by faith. Faith ceased to be thought of as self-despairing trust in the person, work, promises and love of Jesus Christ the Mediator, and became, in the words of the influential Bishop Bull, 'virtually the whole of evangelical obedience'—in other words, a moral life of good works lived in hope of acceptance for it at the last day, despite its actual shortcomings. The significance of the cross in the process of salvation was that, in Jeremy Taylor's grotesque phrase, Christ has 'brought down the market'—that is, made it possible to secure final salvation through a devotion that is far from flawless. The bottom-line effect of Christ's death was thus to rehabilitate self-righteousness. Works are the way to heaven, after all.[47]

This was in essence the theology of John Wesley during his Holy Club period, as it was of conventional Anglicanism all through Whitefield's life. It produced a religion of aspiration, perspiration, and, in sensitive souls, periodic desperation. Whitefield came to see it as blasphemous impiety, the religion of the natural man masquerading as Christianity, and he laboured constantly to wean people away from it. So he denounced self-righteousness, insisted that nothing we do is free from sin, and called on his hearers to come to Christ as guilty, helpless, hell-deserving offenders, and find righteousness and life in him.

Put your trust in Jesus Christ, said Whitefield, over and over again, and present justification (pardon and acceptance, both lasting for ever) will be yours—not because of what you are or have done, but because Christ's righteousness wrought out by his active and passive obedience, his law-keeping and sin-bearing, is now imputed to you. The Holy Spirit will help you to believe if you are willing to believe and show your willingness by asking to be helped to do so, and the Spirit will witness to your justification and God's fatherly love for you once a true change of heart has taken place. Keep seeking through prayer to turn fully to Christ till you know you have been enabled to do just that, so that the gift of righteousness is now yours, and then you will worship and obey your God and Saviour out of unending gratitude for being saved.

I quote at length the peroration of one of Whitefield's sermons, to give the flavour of this:

> Are any of you depending upon a righteousness of your own? Do any of you here think to save yourselves by your own doings? I say to you…your righteousness shall perish with you. Poor miserable creatures! What is there in your tears? What in your prayers? What in your performances, to appease the wrath of an angry God? Away from the trees of the garden; come, ye guilty wretches, come as poor, lost, undone, and wretched creatures, and accept of a better righteousness than your own. As I said before, so I tell you again, the righteousness of Jesus Christ is an everlasting righteousness; it is wrought out for the very chief of sinners. Ho, every one that thirsteth, let him come and drink of this water of life

47. See, on this, C.F. Allison, *The Rise of Moralism* (London: SPCK, 1966).

freely. Are any of you wounded by sin? Do any of you feel you have no righteousness of your own? Are any of you perishing for hunger? Are any of you afraid you will perish for ever? Come, dear souls, in all your rags; come, thou poor man; come, thou poor distressed woman; you, who think God will never forgive you, and that your sins are too great to be forgiven; come, thou doubting creature, who art afraid thou wilt never get comfort; arise, take comfort, the Lord Jesus Christ, the Lord of life, the Lord of glory, calls for thee… O let not one poor soul stand at a distance from the Saviour… O come, come! Now, since it is brought into the world by Christ, so, in the name, in the strength, and by the assistance of the great God, I bring it now to the pulpit; I now offer this righteousness, this free, this imputed, this everlasting righteousness, to all poor sinners who will accept of it… Think, I pray you, therefore, on these things; go home, go home, go home, pray over the text, and say, 'Lord God, thou hast brought an everlasting righteousness into the world by the Lord Jesus Christ; by the blessed Spirit bring it into my heart!' then, die when ye will, ye are safe; if it be tomorrow, ye shall be immediately translated into the presence of the everlasting God; that will be sweet! Happy they who have got this robe on; happy they that can say, 'My God hath loved me, and I shall be loved by him with an everlasting love!' That every one of you may be able to say so, may God grant, for the sake of Jesus Christ, the dear Redeemer; to whom be glory for ever… Amen.[48]

Fifthly, Welcome the Spirit. When Whitefield burst on the Anglican scene, very little was being said about the Holy Spirit, and it was commonly affirmed that the Spirit's activity in Christians' lives was something of which they would not be conscious. At the cost of being accused over and over of 'enthusiasm' (meaning, the fanaticism that thinks it receives direct revelations from God), Whitefield ridiculed this idea, and insisted that the Holy Spirit's presence in human lives would always be consciously felt, because of the change in experience that the Spirit would bring about. This change, which the Bible calls regeneration, new birth, new creation, sanctification, transition from death to life, and Christ being formed in us, and which expresses itself in a sense of one's sin, leading to self-despair, leading one out of oneself to look to Christ and trust him alone for salvation, as was described above, is wrought only by the Holy Spirit; therefore we should desire, seek, and be ready for the Spirit's ministry in our lives, bringing about and

48. 'The Righteousness of Christ, an Everlasting Righteousness' in *Sermons on Important Subjects*, pp. 207ff.

continually deepening the change itself. In a sermon on conversion, Whitefield expounds the matter as follows:

> They that are truly converted to Jesus, and are justified by faith in the Son of God, will take care to evidence their conversion, not only by the having grace implanted in their hearts, but by that grace diffusing itself through every faculty of the soul, and making a universal change in the whole man... The author of this conversion is the Holy Ghost... nothing short of the influence of the Spirit of the living God can effect this change in our hearts... and though there is and will be a contest between these two opposites, flesh and spirit, yet if we are truly converted, the spirit will get the ascendency... God grant we may all thus prove that we are converted. This conversion, however it begins at home, will soon walk abroad; as the Virgin Mary was soon found out to be with child, so it will be soon found out whether Christ is formed in the heart. There will be new principles, new ways, new company, new works; there will be a thorough change in the heart and life... first we are in bondage, afterwards we receive the Spirit of adoption to long and thirst for God, because he has been pleased to let us know that he will take us to heaven. Conversion means a being turned from hell to heaven... the heart once touched with the magnet of divine love, ever after turns to the pole...
>
> What say you to this change, my dear souls? is it not godlike, is it not divine, is it not heaven brought down to the soul? Have you felt it, have you experienced it?[49]

It will be observed that this teaching on conversion has an essentially Augustinian structure: God in grace gives us the faith and love that he requires of us. John Wesley focused on this Augustinianism, with which he claimed to identify, when he declared, in his memorial sermon for Whitefield:

> His fundamental point was, 'Give God all the glory of whatever is good in man'; and, 'In the business of salvation, set Christ as high and man as low as possible'. With this point he and his friends at Oxford, the original Methodists, so called, set out. Their grand principle was, There is *no power* (by nature) and *no merit* in man. They insisted, all power to think, speak, or act aright, is in and from the Spirit of Christ.[50]

Working with this perspective, Whitefield followed the Puritans in presenting the conversion process in a two-sided way, as Augustinians typically do. When speaking psychologically and evangelistically, he depicted the realizing of one's sin and need, the praying and seeking to which this

49. *Sermons on Important Subjects*, pp. 664-65.
50. *Works*, VI, p. 178.

must lead, and the decision-making that faith and repentance involve, as a person's own acts, which we must ask for the Holy Spirit's help to perform. When speaking theologically and doxologically, however, he interpreted the entire process as one which the Holy Spirit works from first to last, in which each of our steps Godward is taken only because the Holy Spirit is moving us forward by his secret action within us. God's irresistible prevenient grace (meaning, the Holy Spirit's work that dissolves resistance away) overcomes our natural inability, as slaves of sin, to turn ourselves to God: that is how we come to be born again and converted.

This, then, was the theological frame within which Whitefield admonished: 'See that you receive the Holy Ghost, before you go hence [i.e. die]: for otherwise, how can you escape the damnation of hell?'[51] Without the Holy Spirit there is no transformation through new birth; without this there is no salvation for anyone; and, though God has his own sovereign ways of breaking into people's lives, only those who seek the Spirit's influence, and open themselves deliberately to it, can expect to undergo it in a converting way.

The key principles of Whitefield's gospel message are now before us. On these themes his printed sermons ring endless changes, with remarkable rhetorical freshness and pungency, the impact of which, so we are told, was much intensified by his pulpit manner. 'The Lord gave him a manner of preaching, which was peculiarly his own', wrote John Newton.

> His familiar address, the power of his action, his marvellous talent in fixing the attention even of the most careless, I need not describe to those who have heard him, and to those who have not, the attempt would be in vain. Other ministers could, perhaps, preach the Gospel as clearly, and in general say the same things, but...no man living could say them in his way.[52]

All the evidence suggests that this was fair comment. Unmatched in his day for applying Reformed teaching about conversion and the converted life to the conscience, Whitefield was entirely free of doctrinal novelties. All he ever preached about, or desired to preach about, was personal salvation and godliness, and for that Puritan orthodoxy served him supremely well.

51. *Sermons on Important Subjects*, p. 489.
52. Dallimore, *George Whitefield*, II, p. 534.

IV

Revivals—that is, animatings and deepenings of the awareness of God, of the sense of sin, of the knowledge of Christ, and of the evangelical responses of faith, repentance, righteousness, prayer and praise—have from time to time characterized the inner life of Protestant communities ever since the Reformation.[53] The revival pattern of fresh outpourings of the Holy Spirit to reverse spiritual decline has recurred many times. The human lightning-rods through whose ministrations the power of God strikes in revival are naturally called revivalists, and the ministrations themselves are denominated revivalism. The title of this essay speaks of Whitefield's 'Reformational Revivalism'. We are now in a position to scrutinize this phrase, to justify the description, and to form an opinion about Whitefield's place in the history of Christian springtimes down the centuries.

But was Whitefield a revivalist? Here a distinction must be drawn, for the word 'revivalist' has a contemporary meaning that both dilutes the significance that it has when applied to Whitefield and distracts the attention from what Whitefield was actually doing—or perhaps we should say, was being used to do. Revivalism nowadays is a name for an American institutional development among conservative churches that directly reflects the populism, love of novelty and entertainment, fascination with technique, and consumerist orientation that have characterized America during the past two centuries. In terms of spiritual significance, this kind of revivalism has lost most of its links with revivals in the sense that Jonathan Edwards and George Whitefield and the Wesley brothers gave to that word. Revivalism in modern America means mounting what Charles Finney called 'protracted meetings', that is, a linked series of gatherings with a centrally evangelistic purpose, at which, in addition to forceful preaching that calls for decision and action, there is a programmed back-up of music (solos, choir items, and congregational songs, often with some twist of novelty), plus testimonies with an arresting human interest, plus ordinarily a modicum of hayseed humour from the emcee and the preacher, so that the entertainment dimension remains strong throughout. The purpose of the meetings is to

---

53. I have presented the morphology of revival in *Keep in Step with the Spirit* (Leicester: IVP, 1984), pp. 235-62, and in *God in our Midst* (Ann Arbor: Servant Books; Milton Keynes: Word Books, 1987).

renew Christian vision and commitment, and in particular to bring about on-the-spot entries into the reality of the new birth. By confronting people with one or two larger-than-life celebrities to admire and enjoy, and by grafting on to the vestigial remains of a church service something comparable to variety entertainment, these meetings are designed to stir up, warm up and open up the audience in the early stages so that they will be readier for decisive commitments later on. Such is modern revivalism, and today's revivalists are those who regularly minister within this kind of framework, whether in churches and meeting halls or on radio and television. Professor Stout sees Whitefield as their distant but direct progenitor, and so tends to describe Whitefield's ministry in a way that assimilates it to the modern development. But the differences between what Whitefield did and what revivalists nowadays do are at least as important as the similarities, and we shall misconceive Whitefield if we do not see this.

There is a watershed dividing the propagation of Christianity by Whitefield and his peers in the eighteenth-century awakening from the revivalism that has just been described. This parting of the ways is not always well plotted on our theological graphs. It does not concern the substance of our presentation of Jesus Christ as Saviour of sinners; nor does it relate to how we emphasize the importance of feeling and facing our need of him; nor does it touch the pietistic presupposition that our relationship with God is the most important issue for everyone; nor does it occur over the priority or otherwise of evangelism, for Whitefield went on record saying: 'God lets me see more and more, that I must evangelize';[54] nor does it have anything to do with the personal styles of different evangelists (Whitefield the dramatic actor, Wesley the paternalist martinet, Finney the prosecuting attorney, Billy Graham the giant-size man in the street, and so on). On all these matters the two sorts of revivalism see eye to eye at the level of principle, and are in full harmony with each other. The cleavage is over a single question: whether we approve of Whitefield and the other eighteenth-century leaders sending people away from the preaching to pray for a change of heart through new birth, and to keep praying and using the means of grace till they know they have been given what they sought, or whether with Finney and most moderns we opt for the so-called 'invitation method', 'drawing in the net' by calling for an immediate full-scale cognitive and volitional commitment to Christ in faith and repentance. The assumption

54. *Letters of George Whitefield, 1734–42*, p. 277.

that immediate conversion is within everyone's present power has far-reaching implications (it is semi-Pelagian at least, perhaps Pelagian), and the effect of making it is inevitably manipulative, for it turns the applicatory part of the sermon into a tussle of wills between preacher and people and radically obscures the sovereignty of the Holy Spirit in the bestowing of spiritual life.[55] I spoke of Whitefield's revivalism as 'Reformational' to make clear that on this issue he was in solidarity with more than two centuries of Reformed thought—not to mention Luther's theology as it was before Lutherans adjusted it[56]—and that he could not have countenanced the pragmatic anthropocentrism sponsored by Finney. Finney and his modern revivalist followers require people to find God; Whitefield, and those who have stood in the Whitefieldian succession, as did Spurgeon and Lloyd-Jones, required them to seek God. There is a difference.

Was Whitefield, then, in full accord with the Reformation and Puritan heritage to which he laid claim? In broad terms, the answer is yes; but on the surface, some differences appear.

We must certainly grant that no one with an itinerant ministry on Whitefield's pattern, and no one with comparable powers of rhetoric and projection, had ornamented British Christianity during the previous two centuries. Reformers like John Bradford, and Puritans like Richard Baxter and John Bunyan, excelled in evangelistic applications of gospel truth, but none of them could hold a candle to the torrential outpourings of compassionate persuasion that flowed from Whitefield's lips and heart every time he preached.

We must grant too that only in a culture where interest in playwriting, playgoing and playacting had blossomed, as it did in England in the early eighteenth century, could a sanctified barnstormer like Whitefield emerge. Whitefield, like the Puritans before him, opposed actual theatres as centres of vice,[57] but whereas the Puritans had been negative about acting too, with a negativism ranging from mild to furious, Whitefield, as we have seen, was deploying his actor's expertise in the pulpit all the time, and his dramatic way of conceiving life and its relationships, including the Christian's faith-relationship with 'the dear Jesus', went

55. See J.I. Packer, *Among God's Giants: The Puritan Vision of the Christian Life* (Eastbourne: Kingsway, 1991), ch. 18, 'Puritan Evangelism', pp. 383-407.

56. See M. Luther, *The Bondage of the Will* (trans. O.R. Johnston and J.I. Packer; London: James Clarke, 1957), pt. 7, pp. 273-318.

57. Stout, *The Divine Dramatist*, ch. 13, 'Dr. Squintum', pp. 234-48.

beyond anything that had been known in earlier times.

And finally, we should grant that by his regular preaching outside churchly contexts Whitefield, though himself an Anglican clergyman who took his office seriously and who saw himself as serving all the churches all the time, did in fact unwittingly encourage an individualistic piety of what we would call a parachurch type, a piety that gave its prime loyalty to transdenominational endeavours, that became impatient and restless in face of the relatively fixed forms of institutional church life, and that conceived evangelism as typically an extra-ecclesiastical activity. To foment tension between discipleship and churchmanship was the last thing Whitefield wanted to do, but involuntarily he did it. By contrast, the Puritans both sides of the Atlantic, and Protestants generally before Whitefield's time, were consistently churchly in outlook, and were always careful to set personal religion in a communal, ecclesiastical frame. Whitefield's own preaching about the fellowship aspect of discipleship seems not to have gone further, however, than to urge faithful participation in the life of the religious societies.[58] Thus in effect, as Mark Noll observes, 'Whitefield helped shift the theological emphasis on preaching. Up to the early 1700s, British Protestants preached on God's plans *for the church*. From the mid-1700s, however, evangelicals emphasized God's plans *for the individual*'.[59] So it has been among evangelicals ever since.

All these are significant moves beyond, or away from, the Puritan model, and should not be played down.

Basically, however, the assertion that Whitefield's mind and method as a revivalist were Reformational still stands. For, in the first place, the doctrinal solidarity is real and obvious. Whitefield's evangelistic message centred, as we saw, on what was central in the theology of the Reformers and Puritans, namely human fallenness and inability for spiritual good; the sufficiency, glory and accessibility of Jesus Christ; the law demonstrating the reality of our sin to our consciences, and the gospel promises leading us out of all forms of self-sufficiency and self-reliance to trust Christ alone for salvation; and finally, the sovereignty of the Holy Spirit, and of God through the Holy Spirit, in bringing sinners into newness of life. Regeneration, or new birth, had not been a central focus

---

58. *Sermons on Important Subjects*, no. 8, 'The Necessity and Benefits of Religious Society', pp. 107-18. This was actually Whitefield's first sermon.

59. M. Noll, 'Father of Modern Evangelicals?', *Christian History* (Spring, 1993), p. 44.

of thought for the Reformers, but pastoral Puritanism had developed the doctrine to the full dimensions that Whitefield's preaching gave it, and here, supremely, solidarity is seen. Then, in the second place, Puritanism in its pastoral aspect was essentially a movement of revival, as I have tried to show elsewhere;[60] and Whitefield's ministry was a true ministry of pastoral revival, blessed by God to the quickening of saints and the conversion of sinners in a most outstanding way. The Great Awakening of 1740, the Cambuslang revival of 1742 (the 'Cam'slang Wark', as Scottish locals called it), the Cheltenham visitation of 1757,[61] and many other exalted episodes that were put on record, bear ample witness to this.

The conclusions to which I believe this survey leads can be stated thus: (1) Whitefield was in essence very much a Reformational revivalist. (2) Though not everything he said and did was totally wise, and though there were weaknesses as well as strengths in his pattern of working, yet his pietistic priorities, according to which being alive to God is what most matters, were magnificently right. (3) The overall quality of his ministry as he sought to embody the compassion of Christ in pointing and directing lost souls to faith in Christ, was beyond praise. (4) A good dose of Whitefieldian revivalism, should God raise up a preacher capable of imparting it, would do today's churches more good than anything I can imagine. 'I speak to sensible people; judge for yourselves what I say' (1 Cor. 10.15).

60. *Among God's Giants*, ch. 3, pp. 41-63.
61. Dallimore, *George Whitefield*, II, pp. 392-93.

J.W. COLENSO'S CORRESPONDENCE WITH ABRAHAM KUENEN, 1863–1878

J.W. Rogerson

At the beginning of 1862 it was drawn to the attention of the bishop of Natal, John William Colenso, that the Dutch scholar Abraham Kuenen had published a critical study of the Pentateuch.[1] At that stage, Colenso had completed the first part of *The Pentateuch and Joshua*, which he would publish later that same year; but, characteristically, he obtained and read Kuenen's volume in Dutch, and referred to it in his own book. Meanwhile, in July 1862, Colenso returned to Britain, where he established contact with Kuenen by sending him volumes 1 to 3 of *The Pentateuch and Joshua*. Kuenen acknowledged their receipt in a letter dated 24 June 1863, to which Colenso replied the next day (the postal service was evidently speedier than today!). This inaugurated a correspondence which lasted, so far as our evidence allows, until 1878. Colenso died in 1883.

In the Kuenen archive in the University Library, Leiden, there are 30 letters written by Colenso to Kuenen between 1863 and 1878, plus a letter from Mrs Colenso written in 1884, and describing the tragedy in which the Colenso house and mission station were destroyed by a bush fire. They shed light not only on Colenso's personal struggles with Bishop Robert Gray of Capetown (who tried to depose Colenso from the see of Natal), as well as on conditions in the Church of England at the time; they indicate the astonishing range of Colenso's familiarity with

---

1. For further details see my article 'British Responses to Kuenen's Pentateuchal Studies', in P.B. Dirksen and A. van der Kooij (eds.), *Abraham Kuenen (1828–1891): His Major Contributions to the Study of the Old Testament* (Oudtestamentische Studiën, 29; Leiden: E.J. Brill, 1993), pp. 91-104.

the biblical criticism of the period, and demonstrate that, in comparison with him, his opponents were at best sincerely naive and at worst wilfully ignorant. The content of the letters will be set in their context in what follows. Before this is done, it is necessary to explain that the 30 letters amount to nearly 20,000 words, that a selection has had to be made, and that I have concentrated on those letters and parts of them that relate to Colenso's discussions with Kuenen on matters of biblical criticism. The letter from Mrs Colenso is also included, since it explains why the letters of Kuenen to Colenso (presumably among many others) are not extant.[2]

People who have a vague awareness of the history of biblical criticism have heard of the so-called Graf–Wellhausen hypothesis, and if they have slightly more detailed knowledge they will know that the hypothesis owes its name to a book published by Graf in 1866, and to Wellhausen's *Prolegomena* published in 1883.[3] What is not so well known is that Kuenen played an important part in making Graf modify the position argued in his 1866 book and that, in turn, it was Colenso who persuaded Kuenen to take a much more radical position compared with that adopted in 1862.[4] What these letters show, then, is what was going on in scholarly debate *before and contributing to* the emergence of the so-called Graf–Wellhausen hypothesis. In this debate, Colenso played an important part, and one all the more remarkable given that he was so far from the continent of Europe, and that he had great difficulty in obtaining the necessary scholarly material. This problem is adequately documented in the letters.

Reading Colenso's letters and reflecting on the condition of today's church, especially regarding its attitude to biblical scholarship, it is possible to wonder whether we have progressed very much in the hundred

---

2.   The *signatuur* of the Colenso letters in the Kuenen archive is BPL 3028. I am grateful to P.B. Dirksen for help with obtaining photocopies of the letters and permission to publish them, and to Georgia Litherland for doing an initial, and very accurate, transcription of all the letters.

3.   The matter is, of course, more complicated than this. K.H. Graf's *Die geschichtlichen Bücher des Alten Testaments: Zwei historisch-kritische Untersuchungen* (Leipzig, 1866) may mark the beginning, but Wellhausen published a series of detailed investigations of the Pentateuch in the *Jahrbuch für deutsche Theologie* in 1876–1877, and his *Prolegomena zur Geschichte Israels* (Berlin, 1883) was the second edition of his *Geschichte Israels* (Berlin, 1878).

4.   See further my article referred to in n. 1.

or more years since his death. It is, perhaps, understandable that his contemporaries regarded his views as dangerous and as potentially destructive of Christian belief. That critical scholarship should still be thus regarded is a tragedy; and it is an indication of the movement of the mainstream churches of Britain into a sectarianism that cuts them off from what shapes the outlook of the many thoughtful and sensitive people for whom the churches have become an irrelevance. Colenso expressed his own deepest convictions at the end of Part VI of *The Pentateuch and Joshua*, and they are the best way of introducing the man who is revealed in the letters that follow:

> There is no infallible Book for our guidance, as there is no infallible Church or infallible Man. The Father of spirits has not willed it thus, who knows best what is needed for the education of each individual soul, as well as that of the race. But He gives light enough along our path that we may do our work here faithfully and fear no evil. And the pure in heart will see God face to face in many a page of the Sacred Book—will recognise the Divine Revelation of all that is good and true throughout it—will hear God's voice, and feel His Living Word come home to the heart, and that it must be obeyed.[5]

23 Sussex Place
Kensington
London: W.

June 25. 1863

My dear Sir,

I have received with very great pleasure your kind letter, which has helped to cheer me not a little in the work in which I am now engaged, and in which I am obliged to labour almost alone at the present time, as far as the Bishops and Clergy of the English Church are concerned. Nevertheless, the truth, I am persuaded, is daily gaining ground among the clergy as well as the laity; and I share entirely in the confident hope expressed by yourself that I will ultimately prevail, and obtain a triumphant victory even over such long-established and deeply-rooted prejudices, as still (I am sorry to say) abound in England.

5. J.W. Colenso, *The Pentateuch and Joshua Critically Examined*, Part VI (London, 1872), p. 626.

I thank you very much for the promise of your Second Volume,[6] which will, no doubt, reach me in a day or two, and which I shall read, I am sure, with the same delight and profit, with which I read the first— every line of which, I can truly say, I have carefully pondered. I have never studied any work comparable to yours for clearness, complete- ness, and accuracy, in treating the great questions concerned. And, though you will see that I have not slavishly followed your judgment in all points, yet it is only with great hesitation and diffidence that I have even ventured to differ from your conclusions.

I shall anticipate with great interest the result of your examination of the Psalms. When you are about to enter upon the question, I should wish to lend to you the latest edition of my Part II , as I have already made some additions and amendments to the original matter—but none which affects the view which I have expressed about the later origin of the Name Jehovah. I feel all the weight of your own observations on this point, and have been very unwilling all along to give up the notion of the Mosaic origin of the Name. But I do not as yet feel myself at liberty to abandon the conclusion to which the facts before me seem to compel me; though I am quite prepared to do so, should you succeed in proving my position to be untenable.

Will you allow me to suggest one question for special consideration? Though starting originally from a totally different point of view, I am now more and more convinced that the Decalogue in its *earlier*, as well as its *later*, form is the work of the *Deuteronomist*. It appears to me that he at first intended merely to *revise* the then existing Tetrateuch and that, in so doing, he has inserted several passages, which can be easily distinguished by their style, and their moral and religious tone, corre- sponding to that of Deuteronomy itself, and also by their verbal forms of expression, which are also peculiar to the Deuteronomist. I believe, for instance, that Lev. xxvi is of this kind—the first *rough sketch*, as it were, of the whole book of Deuteronomy. Also it seems to me that Ex. xxxiv 1-20, Ex. xxiii 20-32, and other interpolations in Exodus, as in Ex. iii and vi, are his. Again, I can trace his hand distinctly in parts of Num. xii– xiv, and even in Genesis, as G. xxvi 5. In short, I cannot help thinking that he has spent a great deal of labour upon the older documents,

6.   Colenso is referring to Kuenen's *Historisch-kritisch onderzoek naar het ontstaan en de verzameling van de boeken des Ouden Verbonds, II Het ontstaan van de Profetische boeken des Ouden Verbonds* (Leiden, 1863).

which came into his hands,—much more than is commonly imagined—
intending, as I have said, at *first* only to revise and *perfect* that document, by introducing, here and there emphatic words, specially designed
to stir up the religious hopes and fears of the people of his own time.
Deut. xxxiii may have been written at this time as the close of the original story—*after* which he conceived the idea of composing the whole
book of Deuteronomy.

Among his interpolations, however, it seems to me Ex. xx 1-17 must
be reckoned. It is brought in abruptly as we know, and quite out of
keeping with the context. And it contains a number of pure
Deuteronomistic phrases, e.g. v. 3, 'other gods', see my Part III, p. 421,
V.b. *v.* 4 *pesel*, D. iv.16, 23, 25, v.8, vii.5, 25, xii.3, xxvii.15, *and
Lev.xxvi.1.*

pasal also is found only in *E. xxxiv.1, 4*, and in D. x.1, 3.

temunah, D. iv.12, 15, 16, 23, 25, v. 8, and *N. xii.8.*

v. 5, 'bow down and serve', D. iv.19, v. 9, viii.19, xi.16, xvii.3, xxix.26,
xxx.17, and *E. xxiii.24.*

etc. etc. etc.

I hope to work out this question fully in my Part IV. But I cannot help
thinking that this idea of the later composition of the Decalogue is not a
little confirmed by the fact that no reference is made to its existence in
the Psalms or Prophets, and also by the circumstance that the
Deuteronomist has so remarkably modified his 4th Commandment. He
might take such a liberty with *his own words*. But would he be likely to
have done the same with words believed to be ancient and Mosaic, even
if not regarded as Divine? Should you see no fatal objection to this sup-
position, it appears to me that the *strongest* of proofs to which you refer
(for this Mosaic origin of the Name Jehovah) would fall to the ground.

Shall you be at Leiden in the latter part of August or the beginning of
September? I purpose running over to the continent for a week or two,
and should be delighted to see you. I think that we might manage to
converse together, though my knowledge of your language is much like
yours of mine. Indeed, I learned Dutch *in order* to read your book, or *in
the reading* it.[7]

7.   Colenso visited Kuenen in Leiden at the end of August 1863, and some of the
letters not published here deal with that visit, and with Kuenen's visit to London to
see Colenso in July 1864.

Pray present my respects to your honoured colleague, Prof. Scholten,[8] whom I should also much wish to know personally. And believe me to be

Yours very sincerely

J.W. Natal

23 Sussex Place
Kensington
London.

Oct. 14 1863

My dear Professor Kuenen
We reached home safely a week or two ago, after taking a round by Dresden and Berlin. I was sorry not to find Prof. Hupfeld at home at Halle:[9] he was out upon his Summer tour—as I suppose you could have been, but for the happy event, which has disturbed the even tenor of your family life. I hope that baby is thriving, and that Mrs Kuenen and Miss Theodora are quite well. I can assure you that I have the most pleasant recollections of my short visit to Leiden, which the ladies helped to make most agreeable. Mrs Colenso begs me to send her kind regards to them, and her thanks for the care they took of us, and to say that she hopes to see one of them at least, when [you] run over to see us next year, if baby will not give leave of absence to *both* of them.

I am in the proofs with my Part IV. The storm is lulled just now in England: but I suspect it will break out in a final gush of fury upon the publication of this Part, which touches the vital questions of Calvinistic

8.   J.H. Scholten (1811–1885), Professor at Leiden 1843–1881, was a leader of the 'modernist' movement within Dutch Reformed theology. See S.J. de Vries, *Bible and Theology in the Netherlands* (New York: Peter Lang, 2nd edn, 1989), pp. 29-30.

9.   Hermann Hupfeld (1796–1866), Professor in Marburg 1825–1843 and Halle 1843–1866, was a major contributor to the so-called new Documentary Hypothesis given classical expression by Wellhausen, especially through his *Die Quellen der Genesis und die Art ihrer Zusammensetzung* (Berlin, 1853).

teaching, the Fall, the Evil Spirit, etc. I hope that it may be the last burst
of a gale which will bring us into port.

I send an appendix to my Part II, and should be glad if you would run
your eye over the matter along which I have drawn a line, in reference
to the 60th Psalm. Since leaving you, I have read Reuss's exhaustive
paper on the 60th Psalm[10]—and, I must say, it has rather helped to
confirm my conviction of the Davidic origin of that Psalm, though he
opposes it.

With very kind regards to Mrs Kuenen, and Miss Theodora, (in
which I am sure my friend David Buchanan would join, if he were at
hand), and hoping also to be remembered to Profrs Van Hengel,[11]
Scholten, and Rauenhoff,[12]

I am, Very truly Yours

J.W. Natal

23 Sussex Place
Kensington W

Nov. 17 1863

My dear Prof. Kuenen

Many thanks for your last kind letter. You shall hear how Mr Wilson's
case is decided, when the event takes place, which is expected towards
the end of this month.[13] The *conservative* party have been compelled to
show fight, as we say—that is, the Archbishops of Canterbury[14] and

10.   Edouard Reuss (1804–1891), Professor at the Protestant Theological Faculty
at Strasbourg, and an early anticipator of Wellhausen.

11.   W.A. van Hengel, New Testament Professor at Leiden.

12.   L.W.E. Rauenhoff, a 'modernist' Professor at Leiden.

13.   H.B. Wilson (1803–1888) who was convicted by the Court of Arches in 1862
for his contribution to *Essays and Reviews* and acquitted by the Judicial Committee
of the Privy Council in 1863.

14.   C.T. Longley (1794–1868), Bishop of Ripon, then of Durham, before
becoming Archbishop of York and then of Canterbury. In 1867 he convened the first
so-called Lambeth Conference of bishops of the Anglican Communion to deal,
among other things, with the controversy aroused by Colenso's work.

York,[15] upon the advice of no less a person than the Speaker of the House of Commons[16]—a *very* great layman in this country, as you may know—have formed a committee, to superintend a *critical* commentary of the whole Bible—the first which the English Church has been favoured with. The Pentateuch is assigned to Prf Harold Browne, of Cambridge[17]—the *best* man whom they could find—but they were greatly at a loss for Hebrew scholars—the difficulty having been to find men, who were at once, clergymen—good Hebrew scholars—well read in continental theology—and *strictly orthodox*. But Prof. Browne is about the best they cd. have found, being an *honest* man, I fully believe, though, of course, fully imbued with the traditional view, and, as I believe, knowing at present very little indeed about the subject which he has undertaken. However he will have to read, and will know a great deal more, perhaps, a twelvemonth hence—and I suspect will be rather astonished at what he does find. In short, I believe that the good cause is now in a fair way to a complete victory. My Part IV is nearly ready, and you shall have a copy forwarded to Leiden. Would you have any objection to my printing (if I see it good to do so) a few lines from your former letter to me, viz. these:-

I see, however, in your critical labour, more than a mere impatient episode of this Church-conflict of our days. It appears to me that through you already in Part I the attention has been fixed upon a series of facts, which, in the latest times, have been too much neglected, with great damage to the truth. You have entered upon the enquiry, as to the value and origin of the narratives about the Mosaic time, from a will to which by many scarcely any attention has been paid. This I say in the first instance with reference to myself. While writing my Introduction to the Pentateuch and to the Book of Joshua, I was, it is true, aware of the unhistorical character of many narratives: but I had not hitherto given to myself proper account of the extent of the difficulties. They could only be fully and plainly brought into the light through the method followed by you: and they now lie bare before everyone who is willing to see.

15. W. Thomson (1819–1890), a contributor to *Aids to Faith*, the 'orthodox' reply to *Essays and Reviews*.

16. J.E. Denison, Viscount Ossington (1800–1873), was Speaker of the House of Commons from 1857 to 1872, and the person after whom the *Speaker's Commentary* (1871–1881) was named.

17. E.H. Browne (1811–1891) Bishop of Ely (1864–1873) and Winchester (1873–1890).

When I take into consideration in how unsatisfactory a way even some of the very best writers indicate and clear out of the way these difficulties, I consider your endeavour to treat them entirely apart as equally opportune/ useful.

How is baby? With very kind regards to Mrs Kuenen, Yours sincerely

J.W.Natal

23 Sussex Place
Kensington

Sept. 2 1864

My dear Professor Kuenen

I duly received your most welcome letter, and am rejoiced, as we all were, to find that you reached home safely and pleasantly, and found the wife and the little-one well—I delayed my reply, wishing to be able to send to you a pamphlet which I have had in hand, in reply to Bishop Gray's last proceedings.[18] This work however, has expanded to a greater length than I intended, and has taken up a great deal of my time—since, you know, every word of mine requires to be carefully weighed at this particular crisis. The pamphlet is now complete, and will be published, I hope, next week—when copies will be sent to you and other friends in Leyden—and from this you will be able to gather better than from anything else how matters stand just now in England and at the Cape. Of course, my case is patiently waiting for the sitting of the Privy Council in November: but things are moving forward. And, if I do not mistake the signs of the times, we are rapidly tending towards a rupture between the High Church Party and the State. Very probably, my affair will help to precipitate this. But Mr. Pusey[19] has just published a violent attack upon the late judgment of the Privy Council[20]—which shows how uneasy that party feels under present circumstances. Should the Privy Council decide in my favour, they will be driven to fury.—The

---

18. R. Gray (1809–1872) was consecrated as Bishop of Capetown in 1847 and later became Metropolitan, in which office he 'deposed' Colenso.

19. E.B. Pusey (1800–1882), Regius Professor of Hebrew at Oxford from 1828.

20. See n. 13.

manuscript has been duly returned to W. Wright,[21] who conveyed it to Dr. Lee—with whom I have been staying for a few days.

I now wish to ask your leave for me to translate and publish that part of your Hist. Krit. Onderzoek which pertains to the Pentateuch and Book of Joshua. Indeed, I have translated the greater part of it already— and, if I get your permission, I shall send it to the press in two or three weeks from this—as I should like to bring it out before I leave England—which I *may* have to do soon after Christmas—and leave it as my parting present to the community. I cannot yet complete my own book: in fact, under present circumstances, it wd. be wisest for me not to publish any more of my own for a little while—and I would rather wish to take more time for the deliberate completion of the whole work before I publish Part [V]. But your views approximate on the whole suf- ficiently to my own—your criticism is so accurate and comprehensive— that I think it wd. greatly assist my own cause to show the English people a good continental work, which goes over pretty much the same ground.

It is impossible to judge beforehand what kind of sale it would be likely to have. I would propose, however, one of two plans, either of which will be agreeable, and both equally so, to me: (i) I would take all the responsibility of printing etc, as if the book were wholly my own— and *divide the profits*, whatever they may be, *equally with you*, for a certain time, say for three years after publication. But I must tell you that Messrs Longman do not begin to pay anything till more than 12 months after the publication of a book: e.g. if this book were published at the beginning of 1865, they will begin to pay on July 1, 1866—and then half yearly. On such a book, however, there would only be slow struggling sales, probably, *after* the first year—during which the principal sale would take place. I would, therefore, fix a limit—as three years—in order to avoid an account prolonged from year to year, about insignificant sums, which might be an annoyance to us, or to our fami- lies, in case of the death of either of us.

(ii) If you would prefer to receive a sum at once for the copyright, I shall be equally ready to agree to this. I would name Messrs Longman to settle the sum on my side, if you, through your agent, would name a man to discuss the matter on your side. I should propose that the two agents settle the matter between them, if they can, without our intervention.

21. Presumably William Wright (1830–1889), who later was Professor of Arabic at Cambridge from 1870 to 1889.

Let me know, please, what you say to this. And, if you consent to either proposal, please *not to make any more alterations in this edition*, than you feel to be *absolutely necessary* for your own credit. It suits my purposes so well in its present shape, that I am lothe[sic] to have any considerable alteration made in it—I would rather leave them for a 2nd Edn should such be wanted. Also please send me, as soon as you can, any corrections for the first 50 pages—that these, if I find it convenient, may go to the press.[22]

Mrs Colenso and my children send their very kind love to Mrs Kuenen and yourself, and some day or other we *do* hope to come and see you—but our future is still very uncertain. I hope you have thanked Prof. Scholten for his book on St John. I have really been too busy to write to him—but I have read a good bit of it, with great interest—and shall, you may be sure, in due time, study carefully the whole. Please also to convey my best acknowledgements to Prof. Van Hengel for the Whitsun Studies. And with my very kind regards Mrs Kuenen, and best wishes for the little one, I am

Yours very sincerely

J.W. Natal

23 Sussex Place
Kensington

Oct 1. 1864

My dear Friend

I duly received your first letter, and the corrections for p. 1-57—which I have introduced in the proper places, and sent the first sheets to the printers. I think that I shall refer throughout to the originals—not to any English translations—as these last are probably more or less defective and most of them are out of print. I presume that your references are correct.

---

22. The work appeared as A. Kuenen, *The Pentateuch and Book of Joshua critically examined*, translated from the Dutch and edited with notes by the Right Revd J.W. Colenso, D.D. Bishop of Natal (London, 1865).

I am fighting away here right and left—but on the whole the cause has gained ground considerably here of late. The grand 'Commentary' is promised to appear *next year*: it cannot be brought out *this* year because of McCaul's death.[23] To anyone who knows anything about the subject, it is perfectly ludicrous to suppose that a work of this nature— purporting to give full information on all the points of difficulty throughout the *whole Bible* can be completed in 10 months—by men who two or three years ago were in almost total ignorance upon the whole question of Biblical Criticism as regards the OT. However, we shall hail the appearance of these Volumes with great satisfaction—and I doubt not shall be able even to give a good account of them.

You received, I hope, and Profs Van Hengel, Scholten, etc. the copies of my 'Remarks'. They are producing, I think, considerable effect. We have just heard from the Cape that the Bp. of Capetown and Co have been duly served with my petition—so that we may now hope to have this case heard in November and I shall probably have to go out *for a time* at all events—soon after Christmas. I hope to bring out my *cheap* Edn and the translation first. Thank you very much for your kind words about pecuniary matters. It would, I think, upon the whole be best for both of us to settle affairs at once by an immediate payment—as that gets rid of all future possible perplexities. Will you please name any London Publisher, who could talk this matter over with mine, and decide for us in respect of the payment. Would 'Williams and Norgate' or 'Trübner' do? Or would you name W. Wright, or any other friend and a Publisher?

I forgot to tell you that Mr Fortescue mentioned to us that the gentleman to whose care he consigned you in the Ho of Commons was the Editor of the Times—Mr Delaine [sic].[24]

With kindest regards from me and mine to you and yours, I am truly yours sincerely

J.W. Natal

23. A. McCaul (1799–1863) was a missionary with the London Society for Promoting Christianity among the Jews from 1821 to 1832, and Professor of Hebrew at King's College, London from 1841. He contributed to *Aids to Faith*.

24. J.T. Delane (1817–1897), Editor of *The Times* from 1841 to 1877.

Bishopstowe
Natal

May 14. 1866

My dear Friend
I duly received your kind letter. And also one forwarded from
Mr. Neale about Mr Marriott's proposal. That, I suppose will fall to the
ground—at any rate, it must stand over till I return (if I ever do) to
England. Yet I should certainly like to be engaged even more in the field
of Biblical Criticism. Dean Stanley[25] has published another volume on
the Jewish Church, in which he has most generously referred to my
book three or four times as an authority. That is really a bold thing for
him to do, with his foot upon the footstool of a Bishopric. But in this
vol. he gives the history of the Kings of Judah and Israel—and throughout builds upon the Chronicles as if it were veracious history. I feel
strongly that we *shall* do nothing in England till the fictitious character
of very much of this writer's narrative especially where he touches on
Levitical matters—is thoroughly recognised and I am half inclined to
translate for my countrymen (as Hupfeld once suggested) De Wette's
little treatise on the Chronicles.[26] While I think of it, will you tell me
what you think of the argument of the *later* origin of N. x.33–36, in my
App.II to Oort's book on the Baalim.[27] If this perhaps is
Deuteronomistic, will it not affect the question of the age of Ps lxviii? and
also probably of Deborah's Song? Please also, if you are in correspondence with Dr. Oort to thank him for me for his kind letter, which I
have not yet answered for the same reason which has prevented hitherto
my writing to you—but I intend, please God, to write to him also before

25. A.P. Stanley had been Professor of Ecclesiastical History at Oxford (1856–
1863) and became Dean of Westminster in 1863. His Lectures on the *History of the
Jewish Church* (1863–1876) expressed a mildly critical attitude to the matter.

26. Colenso is referring to W.M.L. de Wette's *Beiträge zur Einleitung in das
Alte Testament*, I (1806), in which the historical reliability of Chronicles is attacked.
De Wette's uncoupling of the books of Samuel and Kings from the view of the history of Israelite religion presented in Chronicles opened the way to all subsequent
historical-critical study of the Old Testament.

27. H. Oort, *The Worship of Baalim in Israel*, translated from the Dutch, and
enlarged with notes and appendices by the Right Revd J.W. Colenso, D.D. Bishop of
Natal (London, 1865). Oort (1816–1907) was Professor of Hebrew at Leiden from
1875.

long. You will understand that having to write two sermons a week, every line of which (for they are printed at the request of the people) is scanned by friend and foe, is no light matter. I have now nearly finished the 2nd Series—and then shall stop the printing. I may fall back on old sermons a little, and on other help. Mrs Colenso and the children, thank God are quite well, and send their love to you and yours. Do let me have a line or two at your own convenience to say how you all are— and with my kindest remembrances to Mrs Kuenen, Prof Van Hengel, Scholten, and all my friends around you, Believe me to be

Ever yours sincerely

J.W. Natal

Bishopstowe
Natal: South Africa

Nov. 27 1866

My dear Friend

Of course, I have very little time for criticism—having two sermons to write for the Cathedral every week. I send you a few that you may see what sort of work I am about and I believe a volume is now published in England. I asked Mr Domville to send you a copy; but as it was some time ago I mentioned it, if you have not received it, please drop him a line some day, and ask for it.

I have, however, completed to my satisfaction the Analysis of *Joshua*, in the same way as I have treated Genesis—and believe that I have separated clearly the Deut. from the older matter; which appears to me to be entirely Jehovistic—at least, none of it Elohistic.

Many thanks for the notice of Graf's book, which I will order.[28] If any others of note are published in Germany or Holland which you may think it desirable that I should see, would you oblige me by writing to Mr Trübner
Paternoster Row London
and desiring him to send them to me.

We are all well, thank God! and Mrs Colenso and the children desire

28. See n. 3.

me to send their love to you and Mrs Kuenen, with best wishes for you and your little ones, numbering now, we hope, if it please God, three. Please remember me heartily to my good friends in Leyden—and believe me to be

Very sincerely Yours

J.W. Natal

Bishopstowe
Natal

Oct. 20 1870

My dear Friend,

Last evening the Mail brought me the Theol. Tijdschrift for July 1, and I read with the greatest satisfaction your article—'Critische bijdragen etc'. The result is that I must write and ask you to do me a great kindness by ordering some *Leyden* bookseller to send me *as soon as possible* certain books, which I will name below. I might ask you to send the list to Trübner: but that would lose time, as he would have again to send to the continent for them: and I have thought that your bookseller would probably be willing to send them on your authority, and I have requested my brother-in-law to pay any sum which may be due upon him on his forwarding the enclosed order.

The fact is that I am just on the point of sending my 6th volume to England for the printer, and hope to do so, indeed, by the next mail, having been occupied of late in revising and retouching it. I have already—within the last two years *printed* the *whole* remaining portion of my work by means of my native boys for my private use, and 1100 pages of it lie before me including the Appendices, which will be increased to 1200 by an additional chapter and preface, etc. This is too large for one volume, and I have decided to print half of it first, which will take me through the whole of the criticism of the Pent. and Joshua, and also through the books of Judges, Samuel, and Kings, which I have been obliged to include (as Graf has done) in the consideration of the Pentateuch. In the 7th and final volume, I shall print the chapters in which I have examined all the other books of the OT, with reference especially to the subject of this Criticism—in preparing which I have been greatly indebted to your work.

To return, however, to part VI, which I hope may come as a bomb-shell upon our sleek English dignitaries, who suppose that they have silenced and in fact crushed me—I may as well enclose a copy of my results, which will show how entirely I agree with your views in the above article as to much of the history as well as to the laws belonging to the L.L. (*Later* or *Levitical Legislation*), having been written after the captivity. As you feel, there is *absolute certainty* now to be attained as to the general question of the manner in which the whole Pentateuch has been formed. My only remaining doubt of any importance is as to the 'Elohistic' matter in *Genesis*. I fully admit—and to a greater extent than Graf does—the resemblance in *phraseology* between this matter and the L.L.: but yet there are many phrases of the latter, if I mistake not (I shall have to spend a little more time on this point), which do *not* occur in the former, and might support the conjecture that the later writer was only imitating the style of the *oldest* writer in the work that lay before him, and I would draw your attention particularly to D. iv.32 which seems to be a reminiscence of the E passages, Gen. i.1, 27, ii.3, v. 1, 2, vi.7, more especially cf, *v.* 1 observe that D does not use *bara'* elsewhere, but see Jer. xxxi.22, ff., and that the J story in Gen. ii.4b *which alone* we must suppose him to have had in his mind, if the Elohistic in Gen. i–ii.4a was not in existence, uses a different phraseol-ogy, then again the Decalogue in Ex. xx is undoubtedly the *oldest* of the two forms, and thus refers unmistakably to Gen. ii.2. Is not this last point decisive against the idea of Gen. i–ii 4b, forming part of the L.L.?

However, I am very anxious to receive as soon as possible the follow-ing works if you will kindly order them to be sent to me—I suppose through some London firm who would despatch them by the first Mail Steamer to Natal. They are almost all those referred to by yourself in your article—all of them, in fact, *what you think worth my reading*, Knobel, Graf, Oort, except Popper, which I have long ago read, and Schrader which (from your remarks) does not seem to be worth much.[29] I have the Theol. Tijdsch., and perhaps you may have sent me part II of your work Godsdienst van Israel, which you so kindly promised and which I am most anxious to see.

Oct. 21. On further consideration I will not trouble you about these books but write to Trübner: only please send me immediately by post

29. A. Knobel was Professor at Giessen from 1838 to 1862 and published a series of studies on the Pentateuch from 1852 to 1860. The work by Julius Popper is presumably his *Der biblische Bericht über die Stiftshütte* (Leipzig, 1862).

your own Part II of 'Godsdienst', if you have not already sent it.[30] With kindest regards to Mrs Kuenen and to yourself from Mrs Colenso and the girls—the boys are in England, one at Cambridge and the other at Oxford. I am Ever Yours sincerely

J. W. Natal

[There follows a list of passages from the Pentateuch and Joshua which Colenso assigns to the Later Legislation.]

Bishopstowe
Natal

Sept. 14 1871

My dear Friend

By this Mail I have written to England to request Mssrs Longman and Co. to forward to your address 12 copies of Part [VI] of my work on the Pentateuch and 2 copies of a reply which I have written to the long-expected 'Bishops' Commentary' on the Pentateuch, which in this pamphlet I have handled so far as regards Bp. Browne's work upon Genesis. I have also completed a similar examination of the Commentary on *Exodus*, which I hope to send to England by the next monthly mail. And by keeping up a dropping fire in this way, at intervals of about three months, I am inclined to hope that a good deal may be done to keep alive the attention of the English public to these questions—This Commentary, however, and its friends and opponents, will not be likely to interest much a foreign reader—as it is utterly beneath the attention of any well-informed Biblical Scholar, being merely a feeble repetition of Hengstenberg and Keil,[31] with such information on matters of Geography, etc. as may be drawn from any good 'Dictionary of the Bible'.

30. Colenso is referring to Kuenen's *De godsdienst van Israël tot den ondergang van den Joodschen staat* (2 vols.; Haarlem, 1869–1870).

31. E.W. Hengstenberg (1802–1869) became Professor in Berlin in 1828 and opposed biblical criticism from a neo-orthodox Lutheran standpoint. C.F. Keil also defended traditional views of biblical interpretation. He was Professor at Dorpat (1833–1858) and Leipzig (1859–1888). Many works by Hengstenberg and Keil were translated into English in order to show that biblical criticism had been routed in Germany.

I am going to ask you to be so kind as to distribute these books for me at your convenience and in any way you think best among scholars in Holland and Germany. Of course, they will be already acquainted with the main results maintained in this volume—especially those who have adopted your views as to the later origin of the Levitical Legislation. Still I think it possible that they may find one or two suggestions worthy of consideration, and at any rate the Appendices, which have cost me a good deal of labour, will I hope be of use to spare the same toil to others. You will see that I maintain with you the Post Captivity origin of the Lev. Legislation and have thoroughly examined Nöldeke's work, and compared his results with my own.[32] On the other hand, I feel compelled at present to maintain that the Elohistic matter in Genesis does not belong to the L.L., and is the oldest portion of the whole story of the Exodus. You will see that I have given fully my reasons for this conclusion, and it is, I assure you, a real source of regret to me that I cannot wholly adopt your view, not only because I do not like to differ from you, but because there is still room left by this doubt as to the earlier or later date of the Elohistic Narrative, for the triumphal sneers of our adversaries at our want of agreement.

Now I must ask you, in looking at my book, to do one thing more—and that is, not be appalled or offended by its *size*. You know, it is perfectly useless for me, writing for Englishmen, to start with assuming what with you would be a matter of course. I am obliged to put everything fully before my readers, as if for the first time—having scarcely a single English writing on the liberal side to refer to, except my former volumes, so as to save labour. Then again, I have had to write and print the book under such difficulties—not only harassed by perpetual warfare and the necessity for going from home on visitation tours, perhaps for weeks together, without writing a line—but also deprived of the benefit of studying such books as have appeared since I left England except the few which you yourself have so kindly sent or recommended, as well as of the benefit of discussing critical questions, mouth to mouth, with friends who know something about them—there not being a single individual here, who is in the least degree acquainted with Modern Criticism, except one of the clergy in opposition, living 120 miles away,

32. Colenso is referring to T. Nöldeke's very important 'Die s.g. Grundschrift des Pentateuchs', which was part 1 of his *Untersuchungen zur Kritik des Alten Testaments* (Kiel, 1869). Nöldeke was Professor of Oriental Languages at Kiel from 1864 to 1872 and at Strasbourg from 1873 to 1906.

and as self conceited and opinionated, as he is ignorant, though proud of the little smattering of knowledge which he possesses, and which enables him to be (as we say in England) 'a Triton among the minnows (little fishes)'. Then, lastly, I have had to print it in England, and was 8,000 miles away, and to leave the correction and adjustment of the matter to friends, who have done their best, but have left much which might have been omitted, so as to condense and reduce the book in size, if I had been on the spot.

However, having said all this, I still hope that I may be of use to smoothe [sic] the path for others. And as it is out of the question that foreign professors should trouble themselves to procure copies of such a book from England, and I am very desirous that some portions of it should come under their notice, I will ask you, as I have said, to be so kind as to circulate these volumes, when they reach you, in such a manner as shall seem to you best. A few names come to me at once, such as Kuenen, Nöldeke, Kosters,[33] and, of course, the '*Maatschappij der Nederlandsche Letterkunde*'—to which please add such others as you know to be the names of men really interested in these studies—and perhaps your Leiden Bookseller would kindly forward them. I imagine that Johann Bleek, who edited his father's posthumous work, is dead: if not, please include him for a copy, or any *critical* representative of the family.[34]

Hoping that Mrs Kuenen and the children—how many?—are all well, as thank God! we are in Natal, only bothered with the diamonds on our border, which drag away our population—and with kindest regards from all here to you and yours, and my best remembrances to friends in Leyden, no longer alas! including Prof. Van Hengel, I am

Ever sincerely yours

J.W. Natal

33. W.H. Kosters succeeded to Kuenen's chair in Leiden after the latter's death in 1891.

34. Colenso is referring to F. Bleek's *Einleitung in das Alte Testament*, which was edited posthumously by his son Johannes Bleek and A. Kamphausen in 1860. Another son of F. Bleek, W. Bleek was curator of the museum and library in Capetown, and had helped Colenso to obtain German books.

Is there any representative of Graf, to whom a copy might be sent, as a token of my respectful admiration of his critical works?

I expect that Part VI will be published in November and the Reply, perhaps, in December of this year.

The two copies of the 'Reply' are for yourself and The Maatschappij.

Bishopstowe
Natal

Dec. 24. 1871

My dear Friend

Before this reaches you, you will have received, I hope, copies of my Part VI and will hold up your hands, I am sure, at the bulk of the book. But that cannot be helped, as I explained in my last. *This* is the first evening that I have really had a leisure hour for many months past, having been hard at work in demolishing Mr Speaker's Commentary. I have now finished my work upon it, and sent most of it to England for publication—and Deuteronomy is in a friend's hands for revision. Longman's will send you a copy of this also. I consider its publication under the circumstances of the time a positive disgrace to the Church of England. I am afraid from what you say in your letter to me that you will speak too gently of their performance. The best of them are mostly copied, I believe, from Smith's Dictionary of the Bible, which is really a work of some value, especially in respect of its *geographical* articles, and also it contains some more liberal articles by Stanley, Perowne,[35] etc.—who, however, almost all swear by Ewald[36] and have not got beyond his point of view. But this Commentary, except what is derived from that source, is merely Keil done into English. I know this well: because I have just been studying Keil throughout, as the type of the

35. J.J.S. Perowne (1823–1904) edited the *Cambridge Bible Commentary* from 1872. As opposed to the *Speaker's Commentary*, it was more sympathetic to critical scholarship.

36. Heinrich Ewald (1803–1875) was a thoroughly critical scholar who nonetheless opposed, on critical grounds, the views first advanced by de Wette which culminated in the work of Wellhausen. Because Ewald's position, though critical, was closer to traditional views, he was enthusiastically embraced by liberal scholars in Britain such as A.P. Stanley.

conservative school, and have answered him in Part VI, and now I find all his arguments pretentiously put forth again by these Commentators. There are, to be sure, Canon Cook's Egyptological researches which look very learned:[37] but I know the writer well—once knew him intimately—and I have not the best confidence in any of his criticisms. You would have, I fancy, a very poor opinion of him, if you had dredged deliberately through his Commentary on Exodus i–xix, as I have done, and marked the dishonest evasions and subterfuges to which he has recourse in maintaining his traditionary [sic] views. I remember that in the Dict. of the Bible his great argument to prove that Job was the oldest book in the Bible was based upon the fact that it makes no allusion to the Pentateuch. He is just a good natured, easygoing, comfortable fellow, who is perfectly content with the material useful for orthodoxy, but shows himself lamentably ignorant of the very elements of modern Biblical Criticism. Then one long note on the style of Exodus which has a very imposing appearance to the uninitiated, turns out upon examination to be full of errors, and, when these are corrected, is worthless for his purposes; and this is the only note of the kind in his contribution to this 'great work'.

Thus I think the publication most opportune for me. It enables me to load another revolver of five barrels, or rather five metrailleurs—for each of my Parts (upon the Commentary) discharges a whole volley of destructive missiles against the foe: for such of course I must consider this work to be, it having been started expressly to answer my work, and give the deathblow to the spread of intelligent Biblical Criticism in England.

Now I want to ask you to do me a real service. Part VI is published, and about 250 pages of Part VII, which completes my work, have also been printed in England, having formed part originally of Part VI. In those pages I have gone through Judges–2 Kings, comparing them with my previous results; and I have here on my table the rest of the volume (privately printed in Natal) in which I have done the same for the remaining books of the OT. In fixing the dates of the Prophets I have been guided chiefly by your work: but I see that you appear to have modified your views about the age of Joel, and De Goeje somewhere says that Oort has put his age in Zedekiah's time[38]—I believe in the

---

37. F.C. Cook (1810–1899) was Canon of Exeter from 1864, and editor of the *Speaker's Commentary*.

38. M.J. de Goeje was a Leiden scholar who published a series of articles on the Pentateuch in scholarly journals in the 1860s.

Godg. Bijdr. Ned., finding references in your work to De Gids,[39] I sent to England for the number in question, and of course they have sent me out the whole series for some years past, in which I find very little of any service to me in my present work, though my excellent Dutch friend (Mr Stuart) enjoys reading the literary and other articles. If I were in England, all the foreign periodicals wd be accessible to me at the Atheneum Club in London or the University Library at Cambridge: here, of course, I cannot get any of them, unless I order them, and then I am saddled with the expense of the whole series—and that I really cannot afford. I want to ask you if it is possible for you to arrange for me with your bookseller at Leiden to send me copies of any number of any foreign periodicals (Dutch, German, etc) in which there are articles which you think might be of use to me—without sending the whole series—though, if necessary, of course I must go to the expense of that. Possibly some friend might *lend* me such numbers through the bookseller, sending them by post, and I would return them when read, and send an order at once or anually (if any expenses occurred in postage etc) upon my agents in London. I take regularly the Theolog. Tijdschr., but I see no other foreign periodical—It will be a great act of kindness, if you can help me by any suggestion in this matter—as I am certain that many valuable papers must miss my eye altogether.

With kindest regards to Mrs Kuenen, and friendly greetings from my wife and children, I am Ever yours sincerely

J.W. Natal.

I take for granted that there is a Book Post from Leiden to Natal: if not, the expense of postage would be too great for my purposes. But, if there is, I should be obliged if you wd from time to time order your bookseller to send to me any important work which may be published in Germany or Holland on the subject of the OT Criticism, and which you think I ought to see—I believe there is a book by Merx,[40] but do not know its value—I have Graf, Kosters, Schrader and Nöldeke.

39. *Godgeleerde Bijdragen* and *De Gids* were scholarly journals.

40. Adalbert Merx was Professor at Giessen (1873–1875) and Heidelberg (1875–1909). E. Schrader published *Studien zur Kritik und Erklärung der biblischen Urgeschichte* in 1863. He was Professor in Giessen (1869–1873), Jena (1873–1875) and Berlin (1875–1889).

Bishopstowe
Natal

April 1st 1872

My dear Friend

Many thanks for your last kind letter of Jan. 20, and for the trouble you have taken in distributing my books. You have done exactly what I wished with them. Only I think there may be some other critics of mark to whom it might be well to send copies—for, of course, the price will put it out of reach of most German students. If you know of any such, I wish you would be so good as to fill up the enclosed blank form and forward it to Messrs Longman who will send you the copies. *Do not be sparing of them*—for it is far better that they should get into the hands of persons who will really appreciate what is good or ill in them, than they should lie idle upon my publisher's shelves. I shall have to pay for them all the same: and it would be a real satisfaction to know that even one or two dozen had a chance of being read by worthy readers, who might correct any of my errors or be able to benefit by any of my labours—especially the Analyses which might save some time to some zealous enquirer.

I see that on p. 120 of the Appendix my printers and revisors in England let pass an awkward misprint, which very probably your eye will have rectified. After *land of Canaan* in line 19, should be placed a comma, and the sentence is continued with the paragraph a few lines lower down beginning xii. 5. *Is it conceivable*

Another argument in support of the greater antiquity of the Elohistic Narrative in Genesis has occured to me, and that is the existence of passages using *only* or *chiefly* Elohim in other parts of Genesis, which I regard as possibly due to the same writer at an earlier state of his literary activity, but which you will at any rate (I suppose) admit to be more ancient than the same decidedly *Jehovistic* passages. As far as I can see, there is no difference whatever in point of style between these pseudo-Elohistic and the Jehovistic passages—though *fancy* might suggest they had perhaps a more antiquated air, and were not so fluent. But, however this may be, I assume that they *are* more ancient than the more thoroughly Jehovistic passages—and if so how can we account for the use of Elohim? If they existed only in Genesis, *I* might say—from my point of view that some disciple of Samuel was merely following the lead of his master, and suppressing Yahveh until the revelation of the name in E vi. But then such passages occur in Exodus also after the revelation of the name. Thus I make no doubt that you will agree with me that Ex. xix.14-19, xx.18-21, were consecutive passages in the Original Story. But why have we here 'Elohim' five times and 'Yahveh' once—if the use of 'Yahveh' was as *familiar* to the writer as that of 'Elohim'? And this must have been one of the *oldest* passages— fundamental perhaps—of the Original Story. Compare also N. xxii-xxiv, which is strongly Elohistic, as are G. xx 1-17, xxi.6-23, xxii.1-13, as is also the main part of the story of Joseph, ch. xxxix [sic] being a later interpolation, and so is also E. iii.1-15.

My comment on the Speaker's Commentary, Genesis–Deuteronomy, has long ago been sent to England for publication. But I do not know when Exodus will be sent to press; my friends are waiting until Genesis has paid its expenses or nearly so. It is absolutely necessary, in the state of feeling in England, to follow up these writers step by step, note by note: a formal contradiction, new instances here and there, wd avail nothing. Remember that you are backed by an immense weight of critical authority—and the large amount of knowledge on such subjects possessed by the ordinary students in Holland and Germany. *We* have nothing of the kind, and what is not contradicted will be supposed to be established.

Ever yours sincerely

J.W. Natal

May 13 1872[41]

Since the above was written, no mail has left Natal for England, but one has just arrived bringing your kind letter of March 4, and the two books you were so good as to send, and also the packet of articles from Dr Oort. Let me thank you, first, for the trouble you have so kindly taken with reference to my request. I do see the Academy: and, probably, the notices in that journal will answer my purposes, if you will kindly forward it to me to the care of 'Messrs Longman, Paternoster Row, London' for me any papers or books which you may deem of

41. This is a postscript to a brief letter dated 22 April 1872.

special importance. Please write 'Immediate' on the address, if you advise their being sent by Post: otherwise they will reach me inexpensively by a sailing vessel with some little delay.

2. I thank you also for Gelbe's little work, which I shall peruse with interest, as it covers the ground of my own criticisms.

3. Please thank for me Dr Oort for his kindness in forwarding the articles of the Godg. Beidr., two of which I gladly accept, and the other two (on Joel and Zephaniah) I will be careful to return when done with.

4. Lastly, my thanks are due to Dr. Oort, Dr Hookyaas and yourself for the first part of the Bybel voor Jongelingen, the idea of which is excellent, and I doubt not, the execution first rate, though I have not yet had time to study it. I have long had the wish and the purpose to prepare some such a little book for English Educational Purposes, as soon as I had acquired the right to do so by having completed my Criticisms on the Pentateuch.[42] If I ever seriously undertake such a work, this book of yours will be of the greatest service.

I beg you to forward my most sincere congratulations to Dr and Mrs Pyzel on their marriage, which I hope has ere this taken place, in accordance with the notification of their purpose which duly reached me. May they be blessed abundantly.

I am going to send to the Press at once my Comment on the Speaker's Commentary, Part II (Exodus).

May 16. I have read the papers of Land[43] and Oort on N. xvi, xvii, and I confess that my own view in Part VI seems much more simple and satisfactory.

But I am disposed to adopt Oort's view on Joel.

42. In fact, the work by Oort and Hookyas was translated into English by P. Wicksteed, who was also the translator of the 2nd edition of Kuenen's *Historisch-kritisch Onderzoek*. See H. Oort and I. Hookyas, with the assistance of A. Kuenen, *The Bible for Young People*, I (trans. P.H. Wicksteed; Manchester, 1873). The work was used in Unitarian Sunday Schools, and presented, for the times, a radical view of the history of Israelite religion. See further my article cited in n. 1.

43. J.P.N. Land, a Leiden scholar who taught Philosophy but who researched and published on the Old Testament. Colenso is probably referring to Land's article 'De wording van staat en godsdienst in het oude Israel', in *De Gids* 35 (1871), pp. 1-39, 243-74.

Bishopstowe: Natal

Feb. 24. 1873

My dear Friend

I have been reading with much interest your article on 'De Stam Levi' in the Theol. Tijdschr. for November, 1872, which has just reached me. With your general conclusions in that paper I entirely agree. But there are one or two statements made in the course of your argument with which (from my own point of view) I venture at present to differ. And, as is so desirable that at a time, when with many eminent critics of the day the fact of the post-captivity origin of the Levitical Legislation of the Pentateuch has attained the mark of a positive certainty, there should be as little difference as possible in respect of the details of that Legislation, I should wish to lay before you the points in question, and request your consideration of them, whether the result may be to correct or to confirm my own opinions.

I. You say, p. 640, that in the older narrative of the Exodus—or what I have called the Original Story (O.S.)—'Aaron is known as one of the leaders of Israel at the march out of Egypt, as the helper and brother of Moses, and *even as a priest with the ark of Jahveh during the meandering through the wilderness*'. I venture to doubt the correctness of the statement above italicised. On p. 669 you speak of 'Aaron the Levite, the brother and colleague of Moses the prophet (N. xii), who was *probably* in fact, the presiding person at the national sacrifices in the wilderness'. With the last sentence I should agree if you would write 'perhaps' instead of 'probably'. But, as far as I can see, there is not a shadow of ground for suggesting that Aaron was recognised anywhere in the O.S. as a priest: rather, as it seems to me, the story in E. xxxii indicates the contrary, as well as the manner in which he is mentioned in Mic. vi.4, N. xii, together with Moses and Miriam as co-leaders of the host, or together with Moses alone in I S. xii.6, 8, Jos. xxiv.5, comp. also 'Moses, Aaron, and Hur' in Ex. xvii.10, xxiv.14, 'Aaron and all the elders of Israel' in Ex. xviii.12, 'Moses and Aaron, Nadab and Abihu, and seventy of the elders of Israel' in E.[xxiv.1, 9]—without the least reference to the priesthood, which we might surely have expected in E. xxiv.5. Nor does D. ix.20 help to make him out a priest, nor D. x.6, in its original form, which contained merely the notice of Aaron's death, 'there Aaron died and there he was buried', precisely similar in form to the notice of the death of Miriam in N. xx.1 and in substance to that of Moses in D. xxxiv.5, 6. It is certain that the additional clause in D. x.6, 'and Eleazar his son acted—as—priest in his stead', is due to the L.L., which alone knows anything about Eleazar and Phinehas, and, as it seems to me, about Aaron's priesthood. I would venture to refer you to my Part VI.137-145 on this point, where I have made one or two suggestions which as far as I know are new and appear to me worthy of considera-tion. The only other passage quoted by you, which connects Aaron with the priesthood is E. xix.24: but I think you will agree with me (VI.216, *App.* 106) that *v.* 20-25 is an insertion in the L.L., and in its present position utterly out of place and unmeaning. I have very little doubt that in the O.S. the Levites were set apart as a priestly tribe in connection with their act and the promise held out to them in E. xxxii.26-29 (VI.152-162). But it does not follow that *Aaron*, though a Levite, was made a priest on this occasion, any more than his brother Moses. All that can be said is that it may *possibly* have been intended that Aaron should preside over the priestly body: but, as far as I can see there is no trace of this in the story, unless it be found in the fact of his having two sons, Nadab and Abihu, who are named in E. xxiv.1, 9, and who are replaced in the L.L by Eleazar and Ithamar L. x. But then comes the question, were Nadab and Abihu *regarded* as 'Sons of Aaron' at all in the O.S.? There is no sign of it in E. xxiv.1, 9.

[II.] On p. 659-60 you say that the setting up of the Tent of Meeting at Shiloh, Ju. xviii.1, 8, 9, xix.51, xxi.2, xxii.19, 21, is due to the L.L.— that the O.S. in Joshua mentions the Ark, but without the corresponding Tent, but does not tell us what became of the Ark after the settlement of the Israelites in Canaan.

To the above statement I must also demur, as it appears to me clear that Jo. xviii.1, 8, 9, belongs to the O.S. (VI.183, App. 67), see especially Jo. xviii.7, where the expression 'for there is no portion to the *Levites* among you for the priesthood of Jehovah is their inheritance', does not agree with the language of the L.L., but does agree with that of the O.S. (App. 64.VI). I see that Nöldeke also gives *v.* 1 to the O.S. Hence in Ju. xxi.12, as you observe, a very old passage, the camp at Shiloh is men-tioned. Of course, the 'Tent of Meeting' set up at Shiloh was (on my view) the Tent of the O.S. in E. xxxiii.7, and the Tent implies the Ark. If this be admitted, may there not be some truth in my explanation of the allusion to Shiloh in G. xlix.10, viz. that Joshua is regarded in some sense the Counterpart of David, and as Joshua set up the Tent of Meeting

when he had 'come to Shiloh=rest' so David set up *his* Tabernacle at
Jerusalem when he had 'come to Shiloh' that is, had 'come to rest', as it
was supposed, from his conflicts—though the rest, it is true, was afterwards broken.

I should much wish to know what you think also of my suggestion in
(VI.53, 87-90), to which I attach some importance, as throwing light on
the form of the O.S. Unfortunately, there are very few in England who
take sufficient interest in these studies to care to read a book of labori-
ous criticism, much less to review it with sufficient care and previous
knowledge of the subject. My excellent friend, the Rev. G.W. Cox,
reviewed Part VI in the Theological Review with the best intentions:[44]
but it was quite superficial, and did nothing whatever to point out the
real merits or defects of the work, and had moreover the result of pre-
venting a really appreciative review being written for that Journal by
Prof. R. Martineau,[45] who offered to write for it, but was told that the
ground was preoccupied by Mr. Cox. D[r]. Davidson also has written
the most kindly meant review in the Atheneum and Westminster, in
both of which his well known style can be easily detected.[46] But even he
deals in generalities—commends or condemns with equal positiveness,
but without giving any other than subjective reasons for his assertion
that the notion of the post-Captivity origin of the L.L. is not likely to be
accepted—and altogether disappoints one's hope for a searching examn.
of the contents of the book. How much I wish that I could run over to
Leyden and have a talk with you and Dr Oort on some points on which
my views still differ materially from yours as I gather them from Part III
of the 'Bible for young persons' which has just reached me through
Mr. Wicksteed, and for which I am very much obliged to you.
Unfortunately he has sent me by mistake *two* copies of Part III, and,
instead of sending me at once my copy of Part II, he merely writes to
tell me of his mistake, and ask if he shall send me one or two copies of

44. G.W. Cox was Colenso's first, and, so far, main biographer, as well as the
author of books on mythology.

45. R. Martineau (1831–1898), Lecturer at Manchester New College from 1857
to 1866, and Professor from 1866 to 1874. His unpublished lecture notes indicate
that he was closely in touch with critical scholarship, while erring on the side of
caution. See my article cited in n. 1.

46. Samuel Davidson (1806–1898) was dismissed from his post at the Lancashire
Independent College in 1857 for his allegedly critical views. From 1862 he was
Scripture Examiner for the University of London. He remained in close touch with
continental scholarship.

Part II. Hence I shall probably not get Part II for nearly six months, which I regret, as it evidently contains some passages that would be of great interest to me e.g. the Ten Commandments, the origin of the name Yahveh; etc. I have also completed my little book of 'Lectures', and send you a rough copy by this Mail, printed in Natal: it will be reprinted in a better form in England. I wish very much that I could have approximated more closely to your views and Dr Oort's on some points—e.g. it seems to me with the evidence before me which I have produced in Part VI, improbable to maintain that Moses gave the Israelites the Ten Commandments in a shorter form, as Ewald holds, and as I gather from Part III of 'Bible for Young Persons' you also hold, or at least Dr Oort does. There is absolutely no room for the Decalogue in the Original Story.

We are all delighted with the tidings which you give us of Mrs Kuenen and your family. We are all well at present—our three girls here, our two boys at Oxford and Cambridge. In Church matters we are very quiet—especially as the Cape people are in great perplexity about electing a new Bishop. I don't know how it will end. With kindest regards to Mrs Kuenen, Ever yours sincerely

J.W. Natal

Bishopstowe
Natal

July 25. 1873

My dear Friend

And now for the Pentateuch. I have sent for Riehm's paper in the Theol. Stud. u. Kritiken, and hope to receive it shortly, and give due attention to its contents.[47] Many thanks also for your kindness in distributing copies of Part VI. I come now to your remarks on some points.

[1.] It appears to me that 1S. ii.27. etc. does not refer at all to the House of *Aaron*, but merely to the House of *Levi*, to which Yhvh 'appeared in *Egypt*', when he appeared to Moses and Aaron the heads of that House, E. iv.27-31. That House was 'chosen out of all the tribes

---

47.   E. Riehm (1830–1888) succeeded to Hupfeld's chair in Halle in 1866, where he worked until his death.

of Israel to be the priests of Yhvh'—not in Egypt, this is not stated in the text—but at Sinai, as I suppose, after E. xxxii, in a passage which perhaps followed E. xxxiv.29-32 (see VI.159): and so in *v.* 30, 31, 'the House of thy father' = the House of Levi. I enclose a section from my Part VII, now in the press, which will explain my views on this point more fully.

[...2.] I still adhere to my view about J. xviii.1 etc. being Jehovistic notwithstanding your objections: *v.* 7 is entirely in the style of the Jehovist, not of L.L., who would not have said that 'the priesthood of Yhvh' was the inheritance of the Levites: and the fact that Joshua alone directs the whole proceeding, and Eleazar is not even named, strongly confirms this view: nor I confess do I see any force in the mention of dividing the land by *lot*, on which you seem to lay a special stress, as indicating the L.L. Of course, xix.51 is due to L.L. *havu v.* 4, is never used by L.L, nor *havah*, which are common with J.; and there are other signs of J authorship, as it seems to me, while there is certainly nothing characteristic of L.L. In my mind *hishkin* is really needed here to express the *permanent* setting up of the tent of worship—its being 'made to dwell' at Shiloh. If the *cloud* dwelt in the Tabernacle, why should not the tent be said to dwell? *comp.* also Prov. VII [.2], G. iii.24. I see that you are right about Nöldeke.

If my view of J xviii.1, etc. be correct, the interpretation which I have give[sic], of G. xlix.10 will become more probable. It seems to me in fact that in the Pentateuch *Moses* shadows forth the work of Samuel, and Joshua that of David.

[3.] I shall rejoice to see what conclusion you come too [sic] finally about the 'Ten Words'. I am convinced that Ewald's notion of them having been ten brief commands in the O.S., is a baseless imagination—and I rather think that Graf disputed this also.

You called me once a 'great sceptic' because I wd not believe in the historic reality of Joshua. I am afraid that you will think me a greater one when I say that I see no ground whatever for believing the historical existence of Moses. But so it is. Doubtless they had a local leader or leaders as of right whose tribe were the Levites, but apart from this no priesthood... But we heard nothing about the real doings from the Pentateuch. Ever yours sincerely,

J.W. Natal

Bishopstowe
Maritzburg
Natal

Dec. 26. 1876

I need not say that I always read with the greatest interest whatever you write in the Theol. Tijdsch., and in the Theol. Review. I have carefully perused your article on the name Yahveh. But I am not convinced by it, that the Israelites did not adopt the name from the Canaanites, while to my mind it is *clear* that the idea of *Moses* having introduced it in the supposed shorter form of the 1st Commandment is contradicted by the fact that there is no room for the Ten Commandments in any form in the narrative of Exodus, the original story going on without interruption from Ex. xix.19 to Ex. xx.18. I have never met with any reply from you to this point, or to some others which I have advanced in my Parts V and VI, and which still appear to me of importance—e.g. the fact that the *Second Elohist* uses only Elohim, and yet preceded the Jehovist in writing, as (I suppose) is universally admitted. *I wish I could bring myself more to your view on this point*: I have tried my best to do so, but I cannot with a clear conscience give up the arguments which I have advanced without seeing them disproved. I am now (very slowly) preparing my final Vol. Part VII for the Press, and should very much like to see what can be said in answer to the above points and others before I send it to the Publishers, which may be a year hence, for I have very little time at my disposal for such work, and I don't feel as strong for my work of any kind as in former days. I am beginning (at 63) to look for rest. How I should like to look in upon you and yours for an hour or two! Your children must now be fast growing up around you. Three of mine are now in England, two sons and our youngest daughter: but we expect the latter to return with one of her brothers very soon, when he will be called to the English Bar and will, I expect, practise in Natal.

Pray remember me most kindly to Prof. Scholten, and any who may still remember me in Leyden—and with kindest regards to Mrs Kuenen and her sister, when you write to her, as well as to yourself from Mrs Colenso and our two eldest daughters who are here,

I am Ever yours sincerely

J.W. Natal

Bishopstowe
Maritzburg

March 30 1877

My dear Friend
I have sent for Wellhausen's papers, and shall read them, I have no doubt, with great interest. And I need hardly say that I shall very much desire to see how you are able to make room for the Ten Commandments in any form in Exodus. To me, at present, it seems impossible that the Original Story can have contained them. I have just published in Zulu Genesis with a Commentary (after modern ideas) which I imagine will give other missionaries some trouble. But the time is past when ignorant natives should be crammed with falsehoods, now known to be such. I have also prepared in manuscript a similar edition of Exodus with Commentary. Of course, I am obliged to adopt for these my own present views as to the authorship of different portions: but I have said that difference of opinion may exist still on these points, but not on the *great* questions, as to the Non-Mosaic origin and composite character of the whole Pentateuch, and the Post-Captivity date of the L.L.

Bishopstowe
Natal

March 21 1878

My dear Friend
I send you by this mail another copy of my treatise on Wellhausen (with two or three for distribution) which I have amended considerably after a careful study of the essays by Klostermann, Hollenberg, and Kayser[48] which last I have translated, and compared throughout with

---

48. A. Klostermann was Professor at Kiel (1868–1913). A. Kayser's *Das vorexilische Buch der Urgeschichte Israels und seine Erweiterungen* (Strasbourg, 1874) played an important part in establishing the so-called Graf–Wellhausen hypothesis. See my *Old Testament Criticism in the Nineteenth Century: England and Germany* (London: SPCK, 1984), p. 159. I have not been able to trace Hollenberg.

my own results, and sent to Dr Muir for the Theological Translation Fund, if they will accept it. In the corrections in this pamphlet I have assumed some conclusions for which I could not here give full proof— but I give it in my translation of Kayser.

In this pamphlet the most important amendments are on p. 60, 61, 62, and p. 74, 75 and p. 77, 78, which I commend to your consideration.

My Part VII, completing my work on the Pentateuch, is in the Press, and will be published, I hope, during this year.

I dare say that other articles or books have been published in Europe, which I ought to have read, besides those above named. But there is no library here, and it is only through some friend like yourself, or else by mere accident, that I hear of such publications. I have now, however, sent for Schader's De Wette, by which I expect to be benefited [sic].

With kindest regards to Mrs Kuenen,

Ever yours sincerely,

J.W. Natal

Bishopstowe,

Oct 3, 1884

My dear Dr Kuenen

We are very grateful to you for bearing your testimony to the value of my dear husband's critical work. We have had your tract translated in to English and are sending it home to my son F.E. Colenso who is settled at Norwich.

I had written so far about month ago when a great calamity befell us!—The wind being very high and strong and the face of the country parched with long drought a grass fire lit some miles off came down upon us with irresistable fury and in less than an hour burnt our house, which was a large one and covered a great deal of ground in ashes, also our chapel, our stables and various outhouses, the printing office with its press and stores of type and tents in the native village and the house of the schoolmaster etc. etc. Yet, thank God—no life was lost even our horses and cattle were saved. Many beautiful trees are destroyed which he took such pleasure in having planted, some however seem as if they might recover especially the oaks and the weeping willows. It was a beautiful site and as a home much endeared to us of course tho' for the last year and 1/4 it has been but the shell of its former self. We are housekeeping for a time in a little farm house at the bottom of the hill which is crowned now by the Ruins.

I wish to send you a photo of my dear Husband taken when he was at Capetown some years before the Zulu war. The 1st vol of my daughter's book 'The Ruins of Zululand' which I have written to my son to send you contains the last photo which was taken of him. I shall want to know what you think of them. I am, my dear Dr Kuenen,

Yours very sincerely

S J Colenso

ZWINGLI AND THE SALVATION OF THE GENTILES[1]

W.P. Stephens

The controversy between Luther and Zwingli did not end with Zwingli's death in 1531. Five years later, in 1536, Bullinger published Zwingli's *Exposition of the Faith*,[2] which he described as a 'kind of complete defence of true faith and religion'.[3] This work provoked Luther to write *Brief Confession concerning the Holy Sacrament*,[4] in which he charged Zwingli with repudiating the articles which they had agreed at Marburg, and accused him of being a heathen.[5]

The passage which particularly outraged Luther was in the chapter on Eternal Life. In it Zwingli promises the King of France, to whom the work was dedicated, that if he governed well he could hope in heaven to see first God himself and after that 'the whole company and assemblage of all the saints, the wise, faithful, brave, and good who have lived since the world began'. Then Zwingli enumerates the company:

1. I have used the word 'Gentiles' rather than the words 'Heathen' or 'Pagans', since it reflects better the various words which Zwingli used. In *Commentary on True and False Religion*, for example, we have 'gentiles' (Z III.641.21; cf. V.379.14), 'gentes' (641.36), 'prophanis scriptoribus' (646.31), and 'ethnico autore' (662.31).

2. The text of *Christianae fidei brevis et clara expositio ad regem Chistianum* is given in Z VI/V.50-162. An English translation, *A Short and Clear Exposition of the Christian Faith...* (abbreviated as *Exposition of the Faith*), is published in W.J. Hinke, *The Latin Works of Huldreich Zwingli*, II (Philadelphia: Heidelberg Press, 1922). It is abbreviated as *Works* II—and was reprinted as *Zwingli on Providence and other Essays* (Durham, NC: Labyrinth Press, 1983).

3. Z VI/V.162.15-18 (*Works* II.236).

4. The text of *Kurzes Bekenntnis vom heiligen Sakrament* is given in WA 54.119-67. An English translation, *Brief Confession concerning the Holy Sacrament*, edited by M.E. Lehmann, is published in *Luther's Works* (Philadelphia: Fortress Press, 1971), vol. 38, *Word and Sacrament* IV 279-319.

5. WA 54.143.15–144.15 (LW 38.289-91).

Here you will see the two Adams, the redeemed and the redeemer, Abel, Enoch, Noah, Abraham, Isaac, Jacob, Judah, Moses, Joshua, Gideon, Samuel, Phineas, Elijah, Elisha, Isaiah, and the Virgin Mother of God of whom he prophesied, David, Hezekiah, Josiah, the Baptist, Peter, Paul; here too, Hercules, Theseus, Socrates, Aristides, Antigonus, Numa, Camillus, the Catos and Scipios, here Louis the Pious, and your predecessors, the Louis, Philips, Pepins, and all your ancestors, who have gone hence in faith. In short there had not been a good man and will not be a holy heart or faithful soul from the beginning of the world to the end thereof that you will not see in heaven with God. And what can be imagined more glad, what more delightful, what, finally, more honorable than such a sight?[6]

It is not surprising that Luther's response to this passage was vigorous. It lays bare, moreover, some of the points where Zwingli's theology and his differ: God, Christ, Scripture, word, sacrament and faith.

Tell me, any one of you who wants to be a Christian, what need is there of baptism, the sacrament, Christ, the gospel, or the prophets and Holy Scripture, if such godless heathen, Socrates, Aristides, yes, the cruel Numa, who was the first to instigate every kind of idolatry at Rome by the devil's revelation, as St Augustine writes in the *City of God*, and Scipio the Epicurean, are saved and sanctified along with the patriarchs, prophets, and apostles in heaven, even though they knew nothing about God, Scripture, the gospel, Christ, baptism, the sacrament, or the Christian faith? What can such an author, preacher, and teacher believe about the Christian faith except that it is no better than any other faith and that everyone can be saved by his own faith, even an idolater and an Epicurean like Numa and Scipio?[7]

The reference to the Gentiles or heathen in heaven could be seen as associating Zwingli with pagan elements in renaissance thought, of which perhaps Erasmus's 'Holy Socrates, pray for us' is the best-known example. Zwingli's vision, with its enumeration of biblical and non-biblical figures, is surprising for several reasons. First, it has no necessary role in the argument, for the chapter is an affirmation of life after death for 'saints and believers' and an attack on the Anabaptist view that 'the soul sleeps with the body until the day of judgment'. Moreover the promise to the king that he will enjoy that life, with its vision of God and the saints, does not need any examples outside the Bible or the history of the church. Secondly, there has been no discussion of the Gentiles or

6. Z VI/V.131.13–132.11 (*Works* II.271-72).
7. WA 54.143.15–144.6 (LW 38.289-91).

heathen in this work, so that the reference comes out of the blue. Thirdly, the elements in Zwingli's theology which relate to the Gentiles are less evident in *Exposition of the Faith* than in many of his other writings. Fourthly, the Gentiles or pagan leaders were hardly the best examples to use to stimulate the king to engage in reform, which was Zwingli's hope in dedicating this work to him. (In the next chapter he makes such an appeal.) Fifthly, the names of the king's ancestors, which could have been held before him as an example, were qualified by the words 'who have gone hence in faith', yet this or a similar phrase was not applied specifically to the Gentiles.

This passage must be understood initially in its context in *Exposition of the Faith*, even though that work offers only a few clues. A further context is the other work dedicated to the King of France, *Commentary on True and False Religion*.[8] It is the most systematic presentation of Zwingli's theology, and therefore, of all his works, offers the context least likely to distort an understanding of this passage. It needs to be supplemented by the works which follow it, in particular where they discuss the issue.[9]

First, it must be recognized that Zwingli's reference to the salvation of Gentiles in *Exposition of the Faith* cannot be understood as implying that they have achieved salvation by their life or works, or by some faith of their own. In the previous chapter on Faith and Works Zwingli relates salvation to God's goodness, not ours, and to Christ's atoning work, not our works. He states that everlasting happiness comes 'only by the grace and bounty of God, which He pours out upon us abundantly through Christ' and that 'if our works merited blessedness, there would have been no need of the death of Christ to satisfy the divine righteousness'.[10] He argues, moreover, that works are acceptable to God, only if they

8. The text of *De vera et falsa religione commentarius* is given in Z III.590–912. An English translation, *A Commentary on True and False Religion*, is published in C.N. Heller, *The Latin Works of Huldreich Zwingli*, III (Philadelphia: Heidelberg Press, 1929). It is abbreviated as *Works* III—and was reprinted as *Commentary on True and False Religion* (Durham, NC: Labyrinth Press, 1981).

9. There are many discussions of this passage and the issues it raises. The most important is R. Pfister, *Die Seligkeit erwählter Heiden bei Zwingli* (Zürich: Evangelischer Verlag Zürich, 1952). See also P. Eppler, 'Die Gedanken der Reformatoren über die Frömmigkeit und Seligkeit der Heiden', *Evangelisches Missions-Magazin* 62 NF (1918), pp. 43-52, 6-15.

10. Z VI/V.121.2-10 (*Works* II.266). Zwingli discusses the person and work of Christ in ch. 2.

spring from faith. If not, they are an abomination to God. Faith, more-over, does not come from us, but 'from the Spirit of God alone'.[11] Zwingli is not discussing Gentiles or pagans here, though the idea—which he expresses on the basis of Jn 14.12 and Mt. 17.20—that the greater one's faith the greater one's works could perhaps be used to indicate that the works of the Gentiles imply a measure, however small, of faith.[12]

Secondly, election, which is the most important support in Zwingli's case for the salvation of the Gentiles, is not prominent in *Exposition of the Faith*. However, at two interesting points Zwingli moves almost imperceptibly from arguing from faith to arguing from election. In the chapter on Faith and Works in response to his opponents' quotation of Mk 9.41 to prove that works have merit, because they are rewarded, he turns from the doctrine of faith, without which no work is acceptable to God, to that of election. This, he says, is 'free and by grace' and cannot be related to our works because our election took place 'before the foundation of the world'.[13] In the chapter on the The Remission of Sins there is a similar switch from faith to election. Zwingli relates remission of sins—and with it everlasting life—to faith, but then at the end of the exposition, without any previous mention of election, he places election alongside faith, saying 'yet none obtains this remission except the believer and the elect', while adding that 'the election and faith of other men are hidden from us'.[14]

The references in *Exposition of the Faith* to election and to the role of Christ and his death are few and brief. They are, however, significant, and reflect a theology expressed at greater length in earlier works. In this work faith is in some ways more prominent than election. Indeed references to election are fewer and its role less important here than the most obviously parallel work, *Account of the Faith*, written in 1530.[15]

There is a third clue, in the chapter on Christ, which throws (or may throw) light on the salvation of Gentiles. There Zwingli refers briefly to Christ's descent into hell. He states that the reference to this in the creed shows that Christ really died and also that 'the efficacy of His

11. Z VI/V.119.10-18 (*Works* II.265).

12. Z VI/V.123.3-10.

13. Z VI/V.120.19–121.16 (*Works* II.267).

14. Z VI/V.116.1–118.4 (*Works* II.264).

15. For example, it defines the church in terms of election, whereas *Exposition of the Faith* defines it in terms of faith.

redemption extended even to those below'. Peter, Zwingli says, hinted at this when he spoke of Christ preaching to the dead, 'that is, to those below who following the example of Noah from the foundation of the world, believed the warnings of God, when the wicked were scornful'.[16] This reference would seem most naturally to include Gentiles as well as Jews. It refers to faith ('believed the warnings of God'), but not to faith in Christ and the gospel. Such faith itself might indeed come with Christ's preaching of the gospel to them, although that is not something which Zwingli says here.

This reference could include the Gentiles. However, that is not the way Zwingli seems to interpret the phrase in a sermon which he preached on the creed in Bern on 19 January 1528. In the sermon he applies it to 'those alone who had departed this life in true faith and had trusted in the promised saviour'. This would seem to refer to those in the Old Testament, whom Zwingli, as Augustine, describes as believing in the Christ who is to come. It is these whom Christ delights with the news of his coming and whom he leads to heaven.[17] Only his earlier discussion of Mal. 1.11 could perhaps be interpreted as suggesting that the sacrifices of the Gentiles, like those of the Jews, pointed forward to Christ. Bucer develops this idea in his commentary on Romans in 1536, but Zwingli does not.[18]

In the chapter on Eternal Life there are only two significant phrases which might be held to qualify the references to the Gentiles. First, there is the opening sentence which speaks of life after death as for 'saints or

16. Z VI/V.70.3-10 (*Works* II.245).

17. Z VI/I.466.24–467.11. Zwingli interprets the descent into hell to show that only with the death, resurrection and ascension of Christ did those who died in faith—before Christ's coming—enter heaven.

18. In a discussion of the mass in 1524 Zwingli deals with Mal. 1.11, a text cited by his opponents. He argues from it that the Gentiles before Christ sacrificed to the one true God. He also mentions Josephus's reference to Alexander the Great and Pompey, as sacrificing to the true God, and quotes the Old Testament examples of the Queen of Sheba and Melchizedek. (Z III.195.28–206.14)

The interpretation of Mal. 1.11 as a reference to the sacrifices of the Gentiles, pointing forward to the sacrifice of Christ, is not developed by Zwingli. For Bucer's use of it and related ideas, see W.P. Stephens, *The Holy Spirit in the Theology of Martin Bucer* (Cambridge: Cambridge University Press, 1970), pp. 121-28. For a critical examination of Bucer, see W. Holsten, 'Christentum und nichtchristliche Religion nach der Auffassung Bucers', *Theologische Studien und Kritiken* 107 NF (1936) pp. 105-94.

believers', terms which are repeated in the context of the vision which speaks of 'the souls of the faithful' as flying to heaven, and describes those in heaven as 'all the saints...the faithful...and good' or as good men, holy minds, and faithful souls.[19] However, though the Gentiles mentioned may be described as brave and bravery may be linked by Zwingli with goodness, yet they are not all people obviously described as 'saints or believers'. Moreover, the phrase is a description of the people enumerated rather than a limitation or qualification of them. It intensifies the problem, since it is not clear what faith they had, nor that they were good and holy.

The other qualifying phrase is more significant. It is the reference to 'the two Adams, the redeemed and the redeemer'.[20] The comparison and contrast between the two Adams is an important one in Zwingli. He uses it to argue, as we shall see, that what was lost in Adam is restored in Christ, for the redeeming work of Christ cannot be less than the effect of Adam's fall. Moreover, the placing—before all the names—of the names of Adam, as the human origin of sin, and of Christ, as the saviour from sin, could be intended to set all the names which follow in the context of humanity's fall in Adam and its redemption in Christ. However Zwingli does not make this clear to the reader, and Luther is certainly not alone in being shocked by the passage, which seems to have more in common with humanist ideas than reformation theology.

Commentary on True and False Religion provides something of the wider context within this passage can be more fully understood. Since it was written for the French court with its humanist leanings, it is not surprising that the humanist elements in Zwingli's theology are expressed. He is himself aware of this and of the extensive way in which he draws on non-Christian writers.

The book begins with a discussion of Religion (based on a quotation from Cicero) and Between Whom Religion Subsists (God and Man), before expounding first The Christian Religion and then The Gospel. The theocentric emphasis in Zwingli's theology is evident in his insistence at the end of the section on God that 'the knowledge and worship of God' come from God alone and in his statement in the section on Religion, that 'True religion, or piety, is that which clings to the one and only

19. Z VI/V.126.9-12, 130.1-2, 131.10-13, 132.7-9. For Zwingli, 'saints or believers' are elect, yet he does not describe them here in terms of election.
20. Z VI/V.131.13.

God'.[21] But Zwingli is sensitive to the criticism which could be made
that he had up to that point discussed religion without reference to
Christ and salvation through Christ.[22]

Zwingli makes a threefold defence of his approach. Besides stating
that he 'cannot say everything at once and in the same place', he argues
that all that he has said 'of the marriage of the soul to God applies to
Christ just as much as to God (for Christ is God and man)' and 'because
knowledge of God in the nature of the case precedes knowledge of
Christ'.[23] Zwingli's defence is thus in part a trinitarian one. It is a
response to two groups of opponents: those who accuse him of attributing too much to Christ and those who charge him with attributing too
much to the Father. For him whether the reference is to the Father, the
Son or the Holy Spirit, it is a reference to God, and in speaking of one
you understand all three.[24] However the third of his arguments (that
knowledge of God precedes knowledge of Christ) is in apparent conflict
with this, unless it is understood historically as a reference to the life,
death and resurrection of Christ, for Zwingli has clearly affirmed knowledge of God prior to and independent of that.

Zwingli clearly does not see any need to elaborate his case, perhaps
because in the discussion which follows he stresses that our salvation is
through Christ alone and through his death. After citing a range of biblical references in support of this he concludes, 'I think it is now
sufficiently clear that through Christ alone we are given salvation,
blessedness, grace, pardon, and all that makes us in any way worthy in
the sight of a righteous God'. This is related to the fact that Christ
'made atonement for the sins not only of all who had been, but of all
who were yet to come'.[25]

A second point which throws light on *Exposition of the Faith* is the
detailed ten point comparison between the two Adams. It is a consideration of 'all the things done by the two Adams, that is, our parent in the
flesh and Christ...how Christ by means of the proper antidotes restored

21. Z III.654.16-18, 669.17-18 (*Works* III.75, 92). The 'chief and essential point
of the Christian religion' is seen as cleaving to the creator rather than the creature. Z
III.723.14-18 (*Works* III.156).
    22. Z III.675.27-29.
    23. Z III.675.29-34 (*Works* III.99).
    24. Z III.675.3-27. In the same passage Zwingli can relate becoming a new
person both to trusting in Christ and to knowing God and hoping in him alone
(Z III.717.5-17).
    25. Z III.700.16-18, 686.22-33 (*Works* III.129, 112).

man by satisfying the divine justice'. At the end of the comparison he affirms, 'To become ours, therefore, He, great God that He is, just, holy, merciful, Creator, became man, that we through His fellowship might be raised to gods'.[26] The argument from Christ as the second Adam, making good what Adam lost, features in the works which follow, and should almost certainly be taken as explaining why the names of those in heaven begin with the two Adams.

The third point which may be related to the salvation of the Gentiles in *Exposition of the Faith* is Zwingli's stress on the freedom of the Spirit. This is evident in the discussion of the sacraments, where he insists that the sacraments do not automatically give what they signify. Rather, for Zwingli, the Spirit gives when and where he wills, and to whom he wills. He affirms this, moreover, not as an abstract theological principle but as a judgment based on the Bible, in cases such as that of Cornelius, where the Spirit was sometimes given before baptism and sometimes afterwards.[27]

These arguments, which we may describe as trinitarian and christological in the first case, and as soteriological and pneumatological in the second and third, are both characteristic of Zwingli's theology and directly relevant to the issue posed by the vision in *Exposition of the Faith*.

At the beginning of 1526 Urbanus Rhegius expressed doubts about Zwingli's understanding of original sin. In response to his concern Zwingli dedicated to him an extended treatment of original sin in August 1526.[28] This work was followed by an exchange of letters.[29]

It is in this work that the doctrine of election begins to have a significant role in Zwingli's theology. There are references to election before this, but the doctrine to which Zwingli appealed in discussion, for example, of merit or free will, was that of providence, not election. Now, however, as soon as he deals with the question whether 'this disease

26. Z III.683.31-35; 685.5-7 (*Works* III.109, 111 [amended]).

27. Z III.761.1-15.

28. The text of *De peccato originali declaratio ad Urbanum Rhegium* is given in Z V 359–96. An English translation, *Declaration of Huldreich Zwingli Regarding Original Sin, Addressed to Urbanus Rhegius* (abbreviated as *Original Sin*), is published in *Works* II.1-32. In it he discusses original sin as a disease, shows how and whom it damns, and argues that it can be cured only by the death of Christ, not by baptism (370.21-29).

29. Z VIII.726-27 and 737-40.

[original sin] condemns all mortals to the woes of everlasting death', his immediate response is,

> The bliss (*salus*) of everlasting life and the pain of everlasting death are altogether matters of free election or rejection by the divine will. Therefore, all who have ever discussed this question seem to have drawn the lines rather incautiously in damning all infants or grown persons who have not been circumcised or washed with the water of baptism.[30]

It is significant that the appeal to election is in the context of circumcision and baptism, for Zwingli is concerned to overthrow the view that makes everlasting life dependent on circumcision or baptism, and that those not circumcised or baptised will be consigned to the nether regions.[31] This leads to the discussion of the unbaptised children of Christians and Gentiles. For Zwingli the tying of salvation to the sacraments, as he argued in *Commentary on True and False Religion*, denies that salvation is from God. (Zwingli constantly insists, referring to Mk 16.16, that Christ did not say, 'He that is not baptised, shall not be saved'.) The stress on election secures this. Moreover it enforces the argument against our part in salvation, since election takes place before people are born.

An important further argument in this reference to election is the one which Zwingli draws from Romans 2, where Paul compares a circumcised Jew unfavourably with an uncircumcised Gentile who does what the law requires.[32] This passage is also used against the view that salvation comes from circumcision or baptism. Zwingli argues that when Gentiles who have not been circumcised do what the law teaches, then we should recognize the tree by its fruit. Since it is God who has engraved the works of the law on their hearts, we should not damn

30. Z V.377.28–378.2 (*Works* II.10-11). Compare 'blessedness [*beatitudo*] and grace are from election', Z V.385.29 (*Works* II.20).

31. Z V.379.5-8.

32. 'For it is not the hearers of the law who are righteous before God, but the doers of the law who will be justified. When Gentiles who have not the law do by nature what the law requires, they are a law to themselves... They show that what the law requires is written on their hearts, while their conscience also bears witness and their conflicting thoughts accuse or perhaps excuse them on that day when, according to my gospel, God judges the hearts of men by Christ Jesus' (Rom. 2.12-16). 'So, if a man who is uncircumcised keeps the precepts of the law, will not his uncircumcision be counted as circumcision?... For he is not a real Jew who is one outwardly... He is a Jew who is one inwardly, and real circumcision is a matter of the heart, spiritual not literal. His praise is not from men but from God' (Rom. 2.26, 28-29).

them simply because they have not been circumcised or baptised.[33]

Zwingli acknowledges that his position, which he sees as Paul's, could be open to the objection that he is teaching salvation by works and therefore rejecting the role of Christ and the'place of faith in salvation. He deals with both of these, though the arguments are—perhaps inevitably—intertwined and not clearly distinguished. After criticising those—however great or ancient—who consign 'the Gentiles' to everlasting damnation, he asks, 'For what do we know of the faith each one has written in his heart by the hand of God?' He proceeds to quote a passage from Seneca which he sees as evoking admiration for 'the faith of that holy man Seneca', and poses the question, 'Who wrote this faith in the heart of this man?' He admits that some accuse him of 'taking away Christ's office', but he argues that the things which he has said 'magnify His glory', insisting that all who come to God must come through Christ, who is 'the way, the truth, and the life'.[34]

Zwingli meets the challenge of the text, 'He that does not believe will be condemned' (Mk 16.16), by arguing that this saying is to be understood only of those who hear the gospel and refuse to believe it. For adults who have not heard the gospel, 'the point is whether the law of God is written on the hearts or not'. On the basis of Christ's words, 'If I had not come and spoken to them, they would not have sin' (Jn 15.22), Zwingli says, 'Let their ignorance, therefore, not be counted against them to whom none hath come to preach the mystery of Christ'.[35]

His statements, such as the reference to Seneca's faith, seem to imply that Gentiles doing the works of the law have faith, although not presumably faith in the gospel. Joining the argument from election with that from Romans 2, he concludes, 'In a word, election is unshaken and the law written on the heart of men, but so that those who are elect and do the works of the law in accordance with the law written on their hearts come to God through Christ alone'.[36] At this point, however, Zwingli does not explain what he means when he says that they come through Christ alone. What he does later is to argue that salvation comes through the atoning death of Christ. He does this both in the context of Christ's death as undoing Adam's sin and in the context of salvation being

33. Z V.378.10-25.
34. Z V.379.5-29 (*Works* II.12-13).
35. Z V.379.29–380.15 (*Works* II.13).
36. Z V.380.15-18 (*Works* II.13).

through Christ's death and not through baptism.[37] This is the way God had resolved to reconcile the world, says Zwingli, and it is sacrilege to ask whether he could have done it by another means or person.[38]

Zwingli's affirmation of those who do the works of the law is not an appeal to their works as the basis for salvation, but is rather an appeal to the action of God who has given them faith. He makes it clear that he is not referring to Gentiles who are hypocrites, but is arguing that where people do works worthy of God the fear of God is present, as in the case of Jethro and Cornelius. He points out that before Cornelius heard the gospel, God had regard for his prayers and alms.[39]

Zwingli recognizes that the charge could be made against him that faith is being replaced by works. He states that Paul in Romans 2 presupposes faith and that both Paul and James are arguing that people do not have faith if they do not do the works of faith. He says that if they do the works required by the law (from faith and not hypocrisy), then that shows that the fear of God is written on their heart. Once more at a crucial point in the argument Zwingli is elusive. He says, in effect, that the works are done from faith, if they are not done from hypocrisy, whereas there could be other possibilities. Then he states that if they are done from faith, they show that the person concerned has the fear of God, although strictly speaking the question concerns not fear but faith. (Of course faith and fear are, in a sense, interchangeable, because Zwingli says that fear, as faith, is a sign of election—yet fear cannot without more ado be identified with faith.) However, Zwingli immediately asserts that faith is demanded above all things and that it comes from God and not from signs, such as circumcision or baptism.[40] The nature of faith is not explored.

Besides the arguments from election and from the Gentiles who do

---

37. Z V.382.9–383.15; 390.21–392.9.
38. Z V.391.20-22.
39. Z V.389.4-12. There is an interesting though undeveloped reference to Cornelius as early as 1523 in *Exposition of the Articles*. It comes in a section in which Zwingli uses the doctrine of providence to deny merit to our works, for we are simply instruments of God. All good works come from him and are therefore his works. Since we are evil, there is nothing we can do of ourselves to please God. Zwingli uses the example of Cornelius to show that it is what God moved him to do which pleased God. But—in contrast to his later use of Cornelius—he adds that Cornelius was moved by God 'so that he might see that his idols were nothing and might desire to come to knowledge of the true God'. (Z II.186.16–187.17)
40. Z V.389.27–390.4.

the works of the law (Rom. 2), Zwingli uses a further argument against the damnation of the Gentiles through original sin. It is in terms of Adam and Christ, especially in Romans 5. The comparison and contrast of Adam and Christ is expressed primarily in terms of Christ's death as a sacrifice which undoes Adam's sin. Without God's intervention in Christ, the human race would have been damned. But however great the effect of Adam's fall, the effect of Christ's redemption is greater. It is effective for Adam and for those within the covenant before Christ, including their children, so that they are not damned because of original sin. It is on this basis (together with the examples of God's election of Jacob and Jeremiah before their birth) that he argues that the same applies also to Christians and their children.[41]

Zwingli admits that there is no explicit biblical support for applying this to the children of Gentiles, but he affirms that if someone says that 'it is more probable that the children of the heathen are saved through Christ than that they are damned, certainly he will diminish the work of Christ less than those who damn those born within the Church, if they die without the washing of baptism, and he will have more basis and authority for his view in the Scriptures than those who deny this'. By contrast, if it is only the church which is restored, and not Gentile children and Gentiles keeping the law, then the salvation brought by Christ would not extend as widely as the disease brought by Adam.[42]

On 28 September 1526 Urbanus Rhegius wrote to Zwingli. In his letter he expressed concern about universalism and stressed the necessity of faith for salvation. Quoting the words, 'Without faith it is impossible to please God' (Heb. 11.6), he states, 'We know that no one can be saved, unless he is in Christ. We judge that no one can be grafted in Christ without faith. To anyone who does not receive Christ, power is not given, by which he becomes a son of God and heir.'[43] In relating faith to Christ and to incorporation in Christ, he sees the weak point in Zwingli's presentation and one which he does not seriously examine.

Zwingli replied on 16 October. In his letter he emphasizes election and the role of Christ, but defends his view that Mk 16.16 and Heb. 11.6 are not to be understood absolutely, but only of those who hear the word. In 1523, in the context of a discussion of purgatory, Zwingli used these texts to state that those who die without faith are condemned. Now,

41. Z V.381.27–388.14.
42. Z V.388.15–389.26 (*Works* II.23).
43. Z VIII.727.18-20.

however, he relates salvation to election rather than to faith. It is election which is fundamental, though faith or love or the fear of God are a sign of it in adults. He insists that Christians have great advantages in comparison with the Gentiles, such as the preaching of the gospel and the role of Christ as advocate, but also that they are saved who do the works of the law which God has written in the heart.[44]

The stress on God's freedom or sovereignty is expressed in the later Zwingli primarily in terms of election. Indeed, in his final work on baptism in 1530 the propositions, which he saw as cutting all the knots in religion, largely concerned election.[45] It is also the major argument used in the third part of *A Refutation of Anabaptist Tricks* in July 1527.[46]

When he deals there with the covenant, he argues that God's will and his election are free. God is not bound to any outward sign, and equally his election or choice of Israel does not mean that no one would be saved who was not in that people.[47] The same freedom is manifest in God's speaking through Sibyl prophetesses, although Israel was his priestly people.[48] When he turns to election he points out that it is superior not only to baptism but also to preaching and faith. It is superior to preaching in the sense that it is the inward not the outward calling which leads to salvation. It is superior to faith in that those who are elect are already sons of God before they respond in faith.[49] However, he insists that election is in Christ (Eph. 1.4) and he repudiates the anabaptist view that all will be saved.[50]

Zwingli continues to affirm the necessity of Christ and his death for the salvation of all, but without relating this necessarily to the proclamation of Christ in word and sacrament. God's freedom to elect whom he will is not limited to or by word and sacrament, any more than it was limited historically to Israel. In a letter in May 1528 he relates God's acting in this way to the fact that the Spirit created not only Palestine, but also the whole world. He therefore produces piety in those he elects, wherever they are. In that sense a Gentile 'is a Christian even if he does not know Christ'. In asserting this, Zwingli draws on the analogy of the

---

44. Z VIII.737.7–738.20.
45. Z VI/IV.29.1-3.
46. The text of *In catabaptistarum strophas elenchus* is given in Z VI/I.1-196.
47. Z VI/I.160.4-12.
48. Z VI/I.162.4-6.
49. Z VI/I.172.9-11; 176.4-20.
50. Z VI/I.181.19-22; 192.13-17.

person in Rom. 2.28-29 who is a Jew, not because of outward circumcision, but because of circumcision of the heart.[51]

God's freedom to save without the outward preaching of the gospel is expressed also in the commentaries, but with the insistence that people, including the Gentiles, are saved through Christ and not saved without faith.[52] He draws on Augustine to support the view that Gentiles who do what the law requires do so 'by grace, by faith, by the Spirit of God, and are to be counted among those justified by the grace of Christ'. He regularly uses the examples of Jethro and Cornelius in this context.[53]

The Providence of God, based on the sermon preached at the Marburg Colloquy in 1529 and published in 1530, is undoubtedly the most philosophical of Zwingli's works.[54] It draws freely on Greek and Roman writers, adduces Plato and Seneca as witnesses alongside Moses and Paul, and in quoting them can speak of them as tasting and drinking from the same source (God), from which he derives all he is saying.[55] However Zwingli does not say much directly relevant to the salvation of the Gentiles, except in the excursus on Faith.

---

51. Z IX.458.5–459.7.

52. 'Salus et vita aeterna electione constat, neque enim manus eius clausa est aut abbreviata, ut inter gentes neminem servet. Potest enim deus infundere fidem in cor gentium, quam deinde operibus comprobant et ostendunt, qualiter non temere de Socrate, Seneca, aliisque multis sentio. Dicat quis: Sed non crediderunt. Respondeo: Si non credunt, non servantur. Debent ergo verba Christi hoc sensu accipi, ut dicta sint de illis quibus praedicatum est evangelium, qui si praedicato evangelio non credunt, damnantur. Dicit enim Christus: Si non venissem, et loquutus eis fuissem, peccatum non haberent. Is ergo locus: Qui non crediderit condemnabitur, nihil ad eos pertinet, quibus evangelium nunquam praedicatur. Nam etsi illis evangelium externum de Christo non praedicatur, per Christum tamen potest eos servare deus. Quicunque enim servantur, per Christum servantur, hoc est, per misericordiam dei quam mundo in Christo obtulit. Nemo enim tam iustus tamque innocens esse potest, qui coram iustitia dei consistere possit. Omnibus ergo ad misericordiam dei per Christum confugiendum'. (S VI/II.69.21-36)

53. S VI/I.242.6–243.1.

54. The text of *Ad illustrissimum Cattorum principem Philippum sermonis de providentia dei anamnema* is given in Z VI/III.1-230. An English translation, *Reproduction from Memory of a Sermon on the Providence of God, Dedicated to His Highness Philip of Hesse* (abbreviated as *The Providence of God*), is published in *Works* II.128-234.

55. Z VI/III.83.15-16; 106.5–107.1; 110.12-20.

In discussing the relation of faith to salvation, he argues that it is not 'a universal rule that he who has not faith is damned', by citing the biblical examples of those who were elect as infants, before they had faith, and of the Gentiles who do the works of the law, as in Romans 2. After quoting Rom. 2.14-15, Zwingli makes the statement, 'For nothing prevents God from choosing from among the heathen men to serve Him, to honor Him, and after death to be united to Him. For his election is free.' This is followed immediately by a striking reference to Socrates and Seneca. He asserts that he would

> prefer to choose the lot of Socrates or Seneca, who though they knew not the one Deity, yet busied themselves with serving Him in purity of heart than that of the Roman pontiff who would offer himself as God if there were only a bidder at hand... For though those heathen knew not religion in the letter of it and in what pertains to the sacraments, yet as far as the real thing is concerned, I say, they were holier and more religious than all the little Dominicans and Franciscans that ever lived.

In particular, he criticises the hypocrisy of the latter and their failure, unlike the former, to give glory to God.[56] The meaning of and the issues involved in Gentile knowledge of God and faith in him are not examined.

Zwingli does not develop his argument for the salvation of the Gentiles in this work. What it shows is the increasing emphasis on the freedom of God's election, which is used to explain the absence of faith, and the continued use of Romans 2 to describe the Gentiles who are saved. There is here a contrast not only between their holiness and the hypocrisy of some Christians (an interpretation or application to his own day of Romans 2) but also between their sense of dependence on God and their giving of glory to God and the pride and self-glory of some Christians. The implication of Romans 2 is that the way the Gentiles live is the fruit of God's work in them. It is notable that the sacramental controversy continues to be the context in which these views are expressed. (Underlying this controversy is the fundamental opposition in Zwingli's theology to idolatry, that is putting one's trust in the creature rather than the creator.) Zwingli sees the case of his opponents, Roman Catholic as well as Lutheran, as similar to that of Paul's opponents in Romans 2.

56. Z VI/III.180.29–183.13 (*Works* II.200, 201). He has earlier referred to the Gentile poets as recognising that they depended on God alone (Z VI/III.164.11-19).

Account of the Faith,[57] which Zwingli presented to the Diet of Augsburg in 1530, adds nothing new, though it has a stronger emphasis on election than *Exposition of the Faith*. Articles 2 to 5 stress the atoning death of Christ, God's election in Christ, the death of Christ as the second Adam, redeeming the whole human race from the calamity inflicted on it by the first Adam, with a reference to 1 Cor. 15.22. The issue of the salvation of the Gentiles is not discussed, but the contrast between the two Adams is the basis on which Zwingli says it is rash to condemn the children of Gentiles. He then reinforces this point with the argument from election, which is one of the two main arguments normally used in support of the salvation of the Gentiles.[58]

In *Questions concerning Baptism*,[59] with its strong emphasis on election, there is a revealing reference to the Gentiles. Zwingli states that some are in the visible church who are rejected in the sight of God. Some, however, are judged strangers to it who are in the church of the first-born. Examples of these are those to whom the apostles were later to go, when they saw that Gentiles could belong to the church and consequently went beyond Judaea to preach to them.

> According to human judgement they were rejected and outside the church, but in the sight of God they were elect and had a place in that church which has neither spot nor wrinkle, though they did not have faith. But at length, when the time ordained of God was at hand, they obtained the blessing of faith from God, and knew that they were elect of God, as indeed they had been before, but did not know it.[60]

This proposition, the ninth of the twenty which Zwingli advances, seems to confirm what he has said on one problem raised by the salvation of the Gentiles. It is that the Gentiles may have faith, but not faith in the gospel until it is preached to them. They would, presumably, be doing the works of the law before that, as Cornelius did, and be pleasing to God, but are nevertheless without the faith in God's mercy and assurance

57. The text of *Fidei ratio* is given in Z VI/II.753-817. An English translation, *An Account of the Faith of Huldreich Zwingli Submitted to the German Emperor Charles V, at the Diet of Augsburg* (abbreviated as *Account of the Faith*), is published in *Works* II.33-61.

58. Z VI/II.794.31–800.15, especially 799.4-21. The sixth article concerns the church. It is defined primarily in terms of election.

59. The text of *Ad Leonhardum Fontanum contra Suenckfeldium [Huldrici Zuinglii ad questiones de sacramento baptismi responsio]* is given in Z VI/IV.1-74.

60. Z VI/IV.31.19–32.16.

of salvation which the Christian has. This fits what Zwingli says about the advantage of the Christian in his letter to Urbanus Rhegius.[61]

When Zwingli's earlier works are read in conjunction with *Exposition of the Faith*, certain important elements in his understanding of the salvation of the Gentiles become clear. He sees it as based on the Bible and supported by the fathers. He roots it in God's freedom in election; relates it to Christ, especially his death; and links it with faith.

For Zwingli what is fundamental in his statements about the salvation of the Gentiles is God's election. God's election is free and is not limited in time or place. It is not limited in place to Israel, for the Bible relates God's salvation to all nations and not just to Israel; and it is not limited in time to those living after the coming of Christ, for there were those in the Old Testament who believed in the Christ who is to come as we believe in the Christ who has come. God's election is also free in the sense that he is not limited to word and sacrament, so that he cannot act apart from them.

Zwingli draws his conviction about God's freedom to elect the Gentiles from the Bible, both directly and indirectly. He refers by name to various Gentiles in Scripture, especially Jethro and Cornelius. He expounds Romans 2, arguing from its reference to Gentiles in whose hearts the law has been written by God and from its calling such Gentiles Jews, inwardly though not outwardly, in that they were not circumcised. By analogy with this, you might call such Gentiles Christians, although they have not been baptized.

Zwingli does not regard the salvation of such Gentiles as happening apart from Christ. Rather he constantly insists that election is in Christ. Moreover, Christ's death is necessary as a sacrifice for sin, and only with his death, resurrection and ascension is heaven open to those who believed before Christ's coming. Furthermore, without faith in Christ no one is saved, although Zwingli does not make it clear what faith in Christ means for the Gentiles in whose hearts God has written the law. Salvation is related to Christ in a further sense, in that the salvation brought through Christ's death must be at least as extensive as the disease brought by Adam's fall, which affects the whole human race.

61. 'Si dicas: Quid ergo magis est Christiano, quam impio? Multum per omnem modum; primum, quod Christianis exponitur euangelium, praedicatur innocentia; dein, quod, dum non peccamus, habemus qui pro nobis advocet, quo monente ac castigante perpetuam agimus poenitentiam' (Z VIII.738.12-17).

Although left to itself that disease would lead to damnation, yet it does not do so in the case of those who die as infants and who have not come to the knowledge of the law.

Only two pages after the vision of heaven in *Exposition of the Faith*, Zwingli affirms that 'there is not one jot of my teaching that I have not learned from the divine Scriptures, and I advance no doctrine for which I have not the authority of the leading doctors of the church...'[62] For Zwingli, that conviction would apply to his other doctrines, but also to this one which he sees as scriptural and supported by the fathers, not least, by Augustine.

There are, however, even on Zwingli's terms difficulties with his identifying by name the Gentiles whom the King of France will see in heaven. He states at the end of the chapter on The Remission of Sins that 'the election and the faith of other men are hidden from us'.[63] He ought therefore not to affirm of individuals that they were 'elect or believers', unless Scripture had said so. Moreover, he recognizes in many places that we can be taken in by hypocrites, just as people in the Old and New Testament were taken in. What is said of faith as 'hidden from us' must apply equally to the fear and love of God which he says are signs of election. Ultimately the truth is hidden from us, and we can be taken in by people's hypocrisy. The fact that the moral character of some of the Gentiles referred to could be challenged would not, however, be a decisive argument against their election, as a similar charge could be made about others in the list, such as David and Peter. There is, however, the significant difference is that what is said about them is based on Scripture, which for Zwingli is authoritative.

There are three related areas where Zwingli is far from clear: knowledge of God, faith, and the relationship with Christ. He speaks of the Gentiles both as having and not having knowledge of God, but he does not examine the problems involved in this. For example, he writes that 'the law of nature is nothing other than true religion, to wit, the knowledge, worship, and fear of the supreme deity', but also of Socrates and Seneca as those who 'though they knew not the one Deity, yet busied themselves with serving Him in purity of heart...'[64]

He ascribes faith to the Gentiles in some contexts and denies it, at least implicitly, in others. When he is considering Mk 16.16 and Heb. 11.6, he

62. Z VI/V.137.1-7 (*Works* II.274).
63. Z VI/V.117.18-19 (*Works* II.264).
64. S VI/I 244.22-27; Z VI/III 182.18–183.1.

states or implies that they do not have faith, for he argues that the passages do not apply to those who have not heard the gospel preached. Yet he speaks of Gentiles, such as Seneca, as having faith. Moreover, while he states that without faith in Christ no one can be saved, yet he does not indicate in what sense the Gentiles had faith in Christ. It is not clear that he intended Christ's preaching to those in prison, mentioned in 1 Peter, to apply to the Gentiles.

The text which Zwingli uses most often about faith is Heb. 11.1. Indeed he uses it in the preface to *Exposition of the Faith*, where it means trusting 'unwaveringly in the unseen God'.[65] The reference is to God rather than to Christ, though Zwingli would resist an opposition between the two, since Christ is God. Clearly one can speak, as he does, of the Gentiles as trusting in God and attributing glory to him and not to themselves, but that is not the same as trusting in Christ. It is interesting that Urbanus Rhegius in his letter to Zwingli relates faith to incorporation in Christ, but Zwingli in his reply does not; indeed incorporation in Christ is not really a feature of his theology.

Luther regarded Zwingli as departing from the Marburg Agreement. This is understandable because Luther wrote the articles and knew what he meant by them—in the light, of course, of his own theology. Zwingli, however, interpreted them differently from Luther—in the light, of course, of *his* theology. Luther would naturally think that Zwingli's vision was in conflict with articles 5 to 9.

> Fifth, we believe that we are saved from such sin and all other sins as well as from eternal death, if we believe in the same Son of God who died for us etc...
> Sixth, that such faith is a gift of God which we cannot earn...or achieve..., but the Holy Spirit gives and creates this faith in our hearts as it pleases him, when we hear the gospel or the word of Christ.
> Seventh, that such faith is our righteousness before God, for the sake of which God reckons and regards us as righteous, godly, and holy...
> Eighth, that the Holy Spirit, ordinarily, gives such faith or his gift to no one without preaching or the oral word or the gospel of Christ preceding...
> Ninth, that holy baptism is a sacrament which has been instituted by God as an aid to such a faith...[66]

For Luther these articles relate salvation to faith in Christ and his death for us. They speak of it as given to us by the Holy Spirit through

65. Z VI/V.53.1-3 (*Works* II.237).
66. Z VI/II.521.25–522.24 (LW 38.86-87).

the preaching of the word and as strengthened in us by the sacraments. His interpretation of them differs from Zwingli's, a difference which is manifested in their approach to the salvation of the Gentiles. Thus there is no evidence that the Gentiles mentioned by Zwingli had faith in Christ, that they heard the gospel or the word of Christ through which they might receive faith, or that they had been strengthened in faith by baptism or holy communion. Moreover, as we have seen, Zwingli does not present a case for their salvation in *Exposition of the Faith*, nor does this work include in other contexts some of the arguments which he uses elsewhere. It would be natural for Luther to hold that if the Gentiles were saved by faith, then it could not have been by Christian faith.

These articles can, of course, be interpreted in a Zwinglian way, for example, to stress the freedom of the Spirit to use or not to use the word. There is, moreover, a case that Zwingli could have made, as we have seen, in terms of Christ and Scripture for the salvation of the Gentiles. However, the reference to faith in Christ is one where what Zwingli says about the faith of the Gentiles does not correspond straightforwardly with the Marburg Articles.

It is not surprising that Luther raised the question what Zwingli's Gentiles knew about Christ, the gospel, Scripture, and the means of grace, and therefore what need there was of these for salvation. Luther's understanding of Christ and of the means of grace underlies his difference from Zwingli in his attitude to the Gentiles. However, Luther's attitude is perhaps less absolute than it appears here.[67]

Zwingli was not engaged in a general discussion of the salvation of the Gentiles. His discussion was of Gentiles before Christ, both inside and outside the Bible. Indeed, he made some strongly critical passing comments about Islam. However, the case he made to support the salvation of the Gentiles would seem capable of use in the wider context of Gentiles living after Christ as well as before him, not least because of the sentence which follows Zwingli's enumeration of the Gentiles whom the king will see in heaven: 'In short there has not been a good man and will not be a holy heart or faithful soul from the beginning of the world to the end thereof that you will not see in heaven with God'. It is therefore

67. For Luther, see, for example, W. Holsten, *Christentum und nichtchristliche Religion nach der Auffassung Luthers* (Gütersloh: Bertelsmann, 1932) and P. Eppler 'Die Gedanken der Reformatoren' (see n. 9).

legitimate to ask what a Zwinglian case for the salvation of the Gentiles might be today.

It is clear that it would not be a typically humanist or semi-Pelagian (let alone Pelagian) one. It would not be based on the good lives people live or on the view that all religions are more or less the same. Rather, it would be rooted in Zwingli's strongly theocentric theology. It would be expressed in terms of God's election in Christ, of God's effecting in the elect who have not heard the gospel works in accordance with his law, and of God's saving them through the death of Christ as a sacrifice for their sin. The fear or love of God would be signs of election, though no one can tell whether another person is elect, since one can be taken in by a hypocrite. The salvation of such Gentiles would not derive from their search for God, their choosing of God, or their serving him, but from his choosing of them, his seeking after them, and his effecting in them a life of love in accordance with his law.[68]

68. For example, religion 'took its rise when God called runaway man back to Him'. Z III.667.30-32 (*Works* III.90).

LUTHER'S ITIO SPIRITUALIS*

Robert Stupperich

I

Luther's point of departure was always determined by godliness. It was godliness that led him to interpret the thunder and lightning he experienced in the year 1505 near the village of Stotternheim (10 km north of Erfurt) as *fulmen Dei* and which he understood to be the voice of God. It was a crystal-clear message directed at him, compelling him on pain of death to take the oath as a monk. Later too when doubts came along and his friends tried to stop him, he stood firm. The voice of God leading him to the monastic life had to be obeyed.[1]

Luther's inner development, guiding him through all the peaks and troughs of the devotional life, had this event as its point of departure. When two years later, on 2 May 1507, he conducted his first Mass as an ordained priest and met his father again for the first time, he talked with his father of the event which had filled him with such fear and trembling, and to which he still firmly clung. In the preface to the work *De votis monasticis*[2] which he wrote at the Wartburg in 1521 and dedicated to his father, he reminded him of that same conversation which had increased his doubts about the reality of what had happened. Indications are already to be found in it of the inner struggles beginning. They lead on to that time when he first became able to find a meaning for his life.

---

* Translated from the German by Hamish Ritchie, Department of German, University of Aberdeen.

1. On his monastic life, see K. Benrath, *Luther im Kloster*; C. Augustijn, *Luthers intreden in het kloster* (Kampen, 1968); H. Beintker, *Phase domini* (FS R. Herrmann; Berlin, 1957); O. Scheel, *Martin Luther*, I (Tübingen, 1921), pp. 241-65; E. Hirsch, 'Luthers Eintritt ins Kloster', *TSK* 92 (1919), pp. 307-14; and *idem*, 'Noch einmal Luthers Eintritt ins Kloster', *TSK* 95 (1923/24), pp. 155ff.

2. WA 8.578ff.

This dedicatory preface is one of the few sources to give some insight into the 'monastic struggles' of the Erfurt monastery. Only gradually did he arrive at a full awareness of what he had experienced.[3]

Not until Luther began to preach in the monastery, at the same time giving his first lectures, did it become apparent that meditation and inner experience had prepared him. When he spoke of experiences of God, he did not use scholastic language. He spoke of elemental experiences, suggestive of something deep-seated. Fundamental and powerful words came from his lips: 'God tears and compels, I am no longer master of myself'.[4]

When Luther read Holy Scripture he had a certain basic understanding, one which has reminders of Erasmus of Rotterdam. But cool comprehension, the *intelligentia frigida*, was not sufficient for him. It is true that he too saw Scripture as a historical document, but for him it was more: it was God's living voice. The images he used in his first lecture on the Psalms already pointed to the heart of the matter.[5] In it he spoke of the field that has to be worked before the treasure in the field can be found. The point of comparison is with the rigour of the work, before the word of life is reached. In his later *Table Talk* the same image recurs: *Laborent exponendo scripturas, educere panem verbi Dei.*[6] Work is necessary in order to find in Scripture the bread of life. And yet it is not within our might or in the power of our spirit (*scriptura non est in potestate nostra nec in facultate ingenii nostri*).[7] But contact with Scripture produces something essential—*compunctio*.[8] Then the reader truly possesses those things of which Scripture speaks.

Even many years later Luther would recount at table how his inner path had run. He had certainly not learned everything at once; on the contrary, by his own account, he had had to make his way slowly and gradually into God's secrets.[9] In this connection he used the word *Grübeln*.[10] But he did not want this word to be understood in the sense of speculative thinking or analysing the meaning. What he had in mind

3.   Cf. O. Scheel, *Martin Luther*, I, p. 258.
4.   WA Br 1.344.8 (20.2.1519).
5.   His wish was for *oculos spirituales* to read the law.
6.   WA Tr. 1.143.
7.   WA 3.517ff.
8.   Cf. WA 56.431.19.
9.   WA Tr 1.146.
10.   WA Tr 1.146.13.

was an inner process of comprehension. *Grübeln*, 'digging deeper and deeper', should indicate something in the nature of penetrating from outside in. And yet this should not come about through the power of one's own thought, but through intuitive understanding. It is not thought which leads onwards on the inward path, but experiences taken by many people to be obstacles, which however are essentially steps forward.

Luther rates highly those experiences which are connected with a transformation of the inner life (*transmutatio mentis*).[11] These bring with them practical changes, without which no-one can progress. Luther here speaks of the encounter with God, who addresses him through his 'improbable' word. The meaning of this is, *ut audiamus, quid loquitur in me*.[12] Much of what Luther experienced in his early years reappears in his lectures. What previously tormented him now brings him to a state of peace with God. Aristotelian thought-processes hold no sway when God speaks with him. Now he has a new goal: *Volo esse quietus*, even if the torments he has experienced still reverberate within him.

Basically, the *transmutatio mentis* is an improbable process: Scripture changes a person in the direction of its creator. Even if the believer continues to be aware of personal inadequacy, weakness and poverty, even if sin has not been discarded, the hand of God still lies over him or her.

Very early on Luther links the experience (*experientia*)[13] of which he speaks here with tribulations.[14] This is for him a deciding factor. In his early years especially, he had often experienced situations of distress which he described as tribulations. Because of this he stressed that for him religion was not something acquired by study, but through experience. *Experientia* is the practical test.

In a letter to Gerhard Wilskamp, the rector of the 'Brethren of the Common Life' at Herford,[15] to whom he had become closely attached, Luther writes that from his earliest years (*ab adulescentia*) he had experienced temptations of every kind. He does not complain that he has occasionally had doubts and severe misgivings. In the life of the individual every truth has first to prove itself, to stand up to second thoughts and have overcome doubts, otherwise it remains uncertain.

11. WA 3.397.
12. WA 3.153.20.
13. Cf. WA 30.III.672.
14. See also the inner witness WA 30.III.688.
15. WA Br 4.319; cf. H. Hering, *Luther und die Mystik* (1879), pp. 116-17.

Accordingly the worst temptation is to be without temptations: *maxima tentatio est, nullam habere tentationem.*[16] In the matter of religion everything does not go smoothly. Understanding the truth is mostly born out of greatest need. Luther stresses that this is his own experience (*experientia teste*). Experience teaches that the path to God leads through pain and suffering.

But experience and temptation alone are not enough. It is true that he acknowledged that through them he advanced in his inner life. In hours of inner oppression he felt himself being carried further. In his inner development some advance was being made. Then there came answers to many questions. Putting the final touch to a question long since cleared up was precisely what Rom. 1.17 was all about.[17]

II

External impulses are hard to trace in the early life of Luther. It is known that he observed the rules of his Order. But whether he had read Augustine, the Saint of his Order, before 1509 cannot be proved. This whole area has been researched by H.U. Delius.[18] In 1509 Luther had the edition of the *Opuscula* in his hands.[19] As his marginal comments indicate, this gave him much cause for thought.[20] He was moved by Augustine's concept of grace, namely that God does not force his grace upon anyone.[21] It is in his first *Lectures on the Psalms* that he really gets down to quoting Augustine repeatedly. His lectures on the Epistle to the Romans consist mostly of remarks by the Father of the Church in his work *De spiritu et littera.*[22] On the inner questions he was pursuing he never wavered from his path. Augustine occupied him greatly. And yet at table he remarked: *Augustinus non recte intellexit articulum iustificationis.*[23] If by that he meant inner emotion, then Augustine did not help him much.

16. WA 3.420.17.

17. WA 56.171.18.

18. H.U. Delius, *Augustin als Quelle Luthers* (Berlin, 1984); R. Staats, 'Augustins "De spiritu et littera"', in *Luthers reformatorischer Erkenntnis: Der Durchbruch* (ed. B. Lohse; Wiesbaden, 1985), pp. 384ff.

19. WA 9.1-27.

20. WA 9.72.

21. WA 9.62.25.

22. Cf. K. Bauer, *Die Wittenberger Univ. Theologie* (Tübingen, 1928), p. 31.

23. WA Tr 2.138.

But was his inner perception influenced by impulses from the circle of the Brethren of the Common Life? From the time of his Magdeburg school days he reports: 'In my 14th year, I went to the Null Brothers' school (in Magdeburg) with Hans Reinecke at that time'. He lived with a clergyman from Mansfeld, Dr Paul Messhauer, and not as a resident. The Brothers were there not for school instruction, but were responsible for the general upbringing of the pupils. Things were no different in the Schalbe College in Eisenach. About his inner development at this time no further details are known, but it is possible that at this early stage Luther had access to writings from the tradition of *Devotio moderna*. In his first lectures he names Gerhard Zerbolt von Zutphen's *De spiritualibus Ascensionibus*.[24] This is someone who must have made a strong impression on him. Of other writings there is no mention, though F. Lau thought the Waldensians could have been an influence.

In those years Luther experienced a decisive change. In 1512 when he became an academic in Wittenberg and received official permission to teach biblical theology and exegesis he interpreted the Psalms as was the academic custom. But then he went on to take up the Epistle to the Romans which had concerned him for some time. In Rom. 12.2 the word *reformari*[25] occurred. But what did it mean? Paul admonishes his brothers not to conform to the world, to uproot any personal obstinacy: the *sensus proprius* belongs to the world. Luther sought a way forward: *Hoc pro profectu dicitur*. But does *profectus* mean the same as *processus*? Luther understands it to mean 'to start to move', 'not to be at rest', to strive to move from what is good to what is better. The image of the Good Samaritan is often there before his eyes. In his care the *homo semivivus* is to get well again. Luther calls what is happening here the *transformatio grandissima*.[26] In all of the Epistle to the Romans he sees the *itio spiritualis* marked out. He knows the natural man and knows that he moves in the opposite direction (*contrario motu*). And always he sees before him the man lying there covered in blood. He is the one who must first be made well, that is, he must become a different person, not by his own efforts, for he is not capable of that, but through God, the sole justifier. Legalistic thinking must be eliminated (*in hac re nullus iurista utilis est*).[27] Under all circumstances

24. WA 56.313.14ff. and WA 3.645.
25. WA 56.441.
26. WA 56.442.
27. WA 56.448.4 and WA Tr 1.148.

backsliding must be avoided. But *recidivatio*[28] is a great danger. For the natural man considers himself just and good, even when he is not. This is something he must first become. Here Luther is manipulating not dogmatic thoughts, but his own experience.

As vicar of his Order he had to comfort Brothers afflicted with grief and depression. In one of his pastoral letters he mentions Staupitz, who had helped him in this situation. By reason of his own personal experience (*experientia doctus*) he was enabled to pass on his words of advice. To Georg Spenlein, a member of his monastic order, he writes, 'Get to know Christ, the crucified Christ, and learn to sing to him: "Lord Jesus, you are my righteousness, but I am your sin. You have taken what was mine and given me what was yours"'.[29] This is the concept of the 'joyful exchange'.[30] Luther never expanded on how he imagined this. To want to achieve everything by one's own efforts renders Christ unnecessary. What then has he died for? In this epistle Luther also uses the image from the Song of Solomon (2.2), saying, 'The change in you comes about amid thorns, if you want to become a rose of Christ. See to it that by impatience, boldness and hidden pride you do not turn into a thorn.'[31] In another of his consolatory epistles, to Georg Leiffer from Erfurt, Luther employs another image for the Christian's innermost path: Christ's cross is spread throughout the whole world. Every Christian shares in it. 'Do not throw it away! If sacred relics are cast in gold, then you too should take the cross into your heart filled with love.'[32] This thought, however, does not point in the direction of mystical concepts: it binds to the faith.

The monastic sermon he preached on Jn 1.1 at Christmas 1514 in Wittenberg is particularly revealing as regards Luther's inner standpoint.[33] Its contents suggest the Black Monastery rather than the city church. In this sermon, which is so important for Luther's development, he says among other things the following: God and His Word are one.[34] God's divinity consists in the Word (*Ipsa divinitas est verbum*). If in the

28. WA 56.276.12.
29. WA Br 1.35.24.
30. T. Beer, *Der fröhliche Wechsel* (Einsiedeln, 1980), pp. 382ff.
31. WA Br 1.36.49.
32. WA Br 1.37.5 to 38.1ff.
33. W. Löwenich, *Die Eigenart von Luthers Auslegung des Johannes-Prologs* (Bayr. Akad. d. Wiss. Philos.-Histor. Klasse, 1960, 4), p. 32.
34. WA 1.21, 7ff. and 26ff.

Gospel we are told, 'the Word was with God', then it is differentiated from God: *et aeternus est et distinctus*. With these words Luther rejects the Arian concept that God and his Word are in the same relationship to each other as sun and sunbeam. He is firmly convinced that in the Word the complete Godhead is contained (*totus deus in verbo*). Fourth-century thoughts about the relationship of Father and Son are not important as far as he is concerned. More important is the paradox: *distinctus a patre filius, qui tamen cum ipso deus*.[35]

After all, here belief and thought belong together. Even when he differentiates between inner and outer word, then it is the inner word which speaks to the heart, in greater degree and more strongly than the outer, audible word. In this Luther is appealing once again to the individual's experience. Everyone can sense what he is expounding here. With the outer word alone nobody could move the heart of another: *nulli potes per verbum oris cor movere*.[36] And yet this is what the Word become visible is capable of, the *verbum visibile*, with which God lets us look into his heart (*nos introducit in cor suum*).[37]

God drives like a raging rain-storm over the earth. This is a 'proprium' of the Word. Without our doing anything, Christ takes possession of us through preaching. For Luther this experience was of decisive importance. Not through what he is, but through what he does, is God the Mover.

Not that we ourselves find the truth, but by accepting the Word we become divine and true (*divini et veraces*). This is what Luther understands by 'being born of God' (Jn 3.4).[38] He can also express the same thus: with the Word we don his clothing, that is his righteousness and glory.

When Luther in 1512 composed a synodal sermon for the Prior of Leitzkau, he chose as his text Jn 1.12. His theme was: *Voluntarie genuit nos verbo veritatis*.[39] The word of truth gives birth to the true person. Luther is here speaking of heavenly birth, which is far from all earthly things. This new person must shed everything false. Everything belonging to the worldly realm must remain far from the reborn, who must not

---

35. WA 1.21.14-15.
36. WA 1.23.28.
37. WA 1.24.10 and 15.
38. WA 1.29.6.
39. WA 1.11.8 and 17.

pursue the obligations of this world. Luther also knows from personal experience how difficult it is for the confessor to judge external matters.[40] The examples he quotes are forgetting to pray or false interpretation of the word. And yet this is practically the only sin in which he is truly and horribly sinful (*horribiliter*). If Pope and priest sin as regards the Word, then they must be counted among the wolves. The priest serves his office only as God's messenger. All other aspects of his service are to be taken lightly (*levicula!*).[41] Whoever teaches what is false and tells false tales has performed all good acts in vain. *Nam hic rerum cardo est, hic legitima reformationis summa, hic totius pietatis substantia.*[42]

What did Luther experience as the 'world'? Essentially only evil inclinations (*mali affectus*). When he considers his path, then he proceeds from outside in. *Mox cum hoc ipso mundo nobis oritur.*[43] What he experienced others also experience. They too should look not to *quid extra nos*, but to what is going on inside us. *Cum fides substantia est rerum non apparentium,*[44] then it is not only reason which should be questioned. Only where faith lives in the heart are all uncertainties overcome. That is the *Christus praesens!*

On 9 May 1518 Luther wrote to his old Erfurt teacher Jodocus Trutfetter[45] that he did not believe the Church could be reformed as long as canons and decretals, scholastic theology and philosophy as understood at that time were not ripped out by the root to make room for other values. The Word, buried under the growth of legalism, should return to its rightful place. The basis of the theses he set up about this time was his piety. Trutfetter responded to him with severe reproaches, saying: he was bound by the law. His letters have not survived. Luther was expecting opposition when he stepped into the public arena with his inner position. His fundamental position was simply this: *Biblia et sanctorum patrum purissima studia.* To a certain extent it is true that Erasmus had quoted a similar position in his *Enchiridion militis*

40. WA 1.12.37.
41. WA 1.13.19.
42. WA 1.13.34.
43. WA 1.14.17.
44. WA 1.16.23.
45. WA Br 1.170.33.

christiani, even in the revised edition of 1518, but Luther meant something rather different.[46]

III

What concerned Luther again and again was the conviction that the person who accepts the Word does not remain the same. We are shaped into that which we have accepted. That is the experience of the interpretation of the Psalms: *et ita portat dominus in hac vita omnes verbo virtutis suae*. This certainty he also presents in his early sermons, imbued with the truth of what he has experienced. He repeats it in various ways, regardless of which text he chooses. Through his Word Christ shares himself. That is his *impletio*.[47] Here he uses the image of the hen, protecting its chicks under its wings (Mt. 23.24). Luther here means man after his encounter with the word alone, the *verbum nudum*. In the form of the nobleman (Jn 4.46-54) he sees him surrendered totally to the word. At thy Word! Now he is capable of what he could not do before. He lets himself be led by another, and this through the Word alone (*solo verbo*).[48] In the third Christmas sermon of 1514 Luther already speaks of the *Simul*,[49] sinful and just, sick and healthy, at one and the same time. This is his great theme in the later lectures. Here he speaks of conflicting powers like fear and hope, vanity and humility, and all the other such opposites. The believer can be called just, though he is not but is to become so (*iustus vocatur, non qui est, sed qui fit*). Because he believes this he does not engage in speculation about it, but keeps to God-given reality. Because he has experienced it all himself, he can look to God: *dicimus iusti credendo et sperando in deum*.[50]

On 21 December 1516 Luther preached on the Cross, God's 'alien work'.[51] His starting point was Psalm 19. First of all he expands on what is for God an *opus proprium*, namely the kind of immediate creation appropriate to him alone. For Luther *iustificatio* is an integral part of this. But he also employs a alien work (*opus alienum*). This is the

---

46. Cf. R. Stupperich, 'Das Enchiridion militis christiani', *ARG* 69 (1978), pp. 345ff.
47. WA 1.35.30.
48. WA 1.38.4; cf. also WA 1.88.4.
49. WA 1.42.33; cf. also WA 56.272.17
50. WA 1.84.20.
51. WA 1.112.33.

Cross. In it human beings must see themselves as God sees them. In their blindness they think they are pure, instead of praying for a pure heart. Aristotelian logic left to one side, he extracts what is decisive from God's works, which can only be grasped as paradox. What he has learned from Augustine comes into play here. Only the person who has encountered mercy can escape dire necessity and fear in his or her own life. Now he knows: *misericordia nobis gratis data et merita Christi nobis imputata.*[52]

As can be seen, for the young Luther certain concepts are already attached to God's word. One of the most important is the idea of being directly addressed by God. He arrives at this conviction not only in his early stages but also later. One must see it as the decisive 'moment' in the life of the believer. In the first Lectures on the Psalms he says that he considers it an especial act of God's grace and wondrous recognition that he lets people read and hear the words of Scripture as if he were himself speaking with them.[53]

This is a remarkable experience: to be addressed by God through his 'invisible, incredible Word'. Such direct address imparts an internal gift. Now, says Luther, I can hear inside for myself what God wishes, what he wants to say to me (*quid loquitur in me*).[54] Hence Luther understands the word of Scripture as personally addressed to him. Not an 'inner voice': God himself speaks with him. He stands by this experience. It is not a passing experience, but an enduring one. And it holds him, of that he can be sure. It is no fleeting feeling, it is a hard fact. And this word is a force which proves to be effective.[55]

To this inner understanding Luther gave the name *intus sentire*. When God speaks to the heart (*Deus ad cor loquitur*) then what is spoken of in Scripture becomes a presence. What the psalter says now becomes our own. *Intus sentire* leads on out of all uncertainty. What is understood can be made understandable to others. Now it is true, as Karl Holl says, that this is a *circulus*, but no *circulus vitiosus*: rather a circular process in which all intellectual understanding inevitably moves.[56] Luther was perfectly clear in his own mind about this process. This is, after all, the inner certainty imparted to him, of which Scripture and

52. WA 1.140.30.
53. WA 3.157.
54. WA 4.2.11.
55. WA 1.24.11.
56. K. Holl, *Gesammelte Aufsätze* (Tübingen, 7th edn, 1948 [1943]), I, p. 549.

experience speak. This certainty he arrives at from the *medulla scripturae*, the kernel and core of Scripture. This is the real turning-point (*hic rerum cardo est, hic legitima reformationis summa, hic totius pietatis substantia!*).[57]

In deep isolation Luther had come to this awareness. His godliness was not bound to liturgical customs, even if he called it 'worldly' and possessing full powers.

Luther often repeats that it was not only in his early years that he had the experience of standing in immediate relationship to God. In the first Lectures on the Psalms[58] he makes the irrevocable statement: through the invisible Word something miraculous happens, he receives lasting inner comfort. This is not something imaginary, but something factual, the awareness of its reality. No-one can contest this fact: here God himself is and acts.[59]

Luther's *itio spiritualis* started long before any of his statements in writing. That is why it is so difficult for him to record it. His development can best be extracted from his letters. A problem of a particular nature is presented by the *Table Talk* in which Luther reflects on earlier events and which are then written down by somebody else. Luther grasped his *itio spiritualis* not in the event itself, but generally only when he reflected upon it. It therefore lies a long way back. In addition his observations from his earlier years are mostly fragmentary. Despite this, the *itio spiritualis* is an inner progression and does not merely register fleeting moments. The turbulent years of 1516 and 1517 can be regarded as the final stage in the path he started to take a long time before. His position committed him to preaching, saying mass, and pastoral care, combined with the communication of inner experiences. Later on external events made the inner experience fade more rapidly. Theological reflections took the place of meditation. This kind of activity, it is true, is also bound up with the *itio spiritualis*; but theological considerations are not always helpful for the inner person. In fact, thinking about inner experience raises doubts. Earlier on he could not give these up.

Encounters with people or impressions from older writings gradually faded into the background. The age of mediaeval mysticism was dead

57. WA 1.13.34-35.

58. Cf. H. Junghans, 'Das Wort Gottes bei Luther in der ersten Psalmenvorlesung', *TLZ* 100 (1975), pp. 101-104.

59. WA 3.342.27.

and gone. Luther still hearkened to related echoes from it, but he himself chose a different path. His *itio spiritualis* is characterized by obedience to the Word. He follows him who calls him. He looks to the future and expects something significant. 'Something dreadful is at the door', he writes in a letter. 'Only God knows what is to come. I shall be swept along and carried away by these flood waters.'[60]

What has he really experienced, to cause such utterances? What was going on inside him? He noted that he was under pressure, to which he had to give way. He would have much preferred to hide away in a corner. Instead he had to declare openly what was the truth. He was quite well aware of the sin around him. And yet he could still hear God's deep and secret Yes. For he does not see God in visible reality, but in inner suffering. Whoever concludes from the visible to the invisible makes sight impossible and is not on the right path.

When Luther preached on the seven penitential psalms[61]—which he also did in the period after the first Lectures on the Psalms—he showed that he could stand firm under attack and suffering. If God were to take his hand away from him, then he would really suffer, that is to say, in his conscience. The desperate times of which he here speaks are the worst experiences from his time in the monastery. It was these experiences that made him look out for the 'New Man'. What he thought of these experiences his own words show: 'The world does not feel what I have felt'.[62] Actually what he read in the Psalter proved to be true for him. It was his own life. Luther is here going back to the description of the state of affairs of which he says: tribulations drive him away from God into the distance, where God threatens finally to disappear completely. This, then, is a 'foretaste of the sufferings of hell'.[63] This state he describes in the words: *Infernum in se habet.* In later years he described these experiences differently. Then he spoke of the fear of being forsaken by God.[64] But he does not spend too much time on the tumult or uproar within himself. He calls it *tumultus mordacis conscientiae.* God knows what he is doing when he lets us fall into temptation. There we find out what we are and what God is. Humankind does not arrive at real godliness by speculation, but through suffering and dying. And Luther

60. WA Br 1.344 (20.2.1519 to Staupitz).
61. WA 1.158ff.
62. Cf.WA 1.163.7.
63. WA 1.161.5.
64. Cf. WA 1.183.20 and 36.

concludes: those who have not trodden this path know nothing of faith and love. The *salutaris desperatio*[65] is really necessary. The hearts of those who suffer it are directed to God.

Later, too, when Luther came to speak of tribulations, he took the opportunity to speak of his *itio spiritualis*, for in this he saw the *via domini*.

65. Cf. WA 1.161.24-25.

LUTHER AND BARTH ON 1 CORINTHIANS 15:
SIX THESES FOR THEOLOGY IN RELATION TO RECENT
INTERPRETATION

Anthony C. Thiselton

I

This study consciously draws together the three elements which form
the title of this volume. Attention to *the Bible* finds expression in an
exegetical discussion of 1 Corinthians 15. Further, this work explores
the hermeneutical claim made explicitly by the early Barth that
1 Corinthians 15 provides the most appropriate vantage-point from
which to understand the argument and theology of the first fourteen
chapters of the epistle. This claim might also be said to be implicit,
though not openly stated, in the approaches of Luther and of Calvin to
the resurrection chapter.

Our discussion focuses also on issues fundamental to *the Reformation*.
In the first place, and most obviously, from among the many interpretations of this chapter in 1 Corinthians which have been offered I have
chosen to enter into dialogue primarily with that of Luther. I have also
selected for special consideration Karl Barth's exposition of this chapter,
since Barth represents a voice, if not the voice, of Reformation theology
in our own century. The whole of Barth's exposition centres in the proposal that throughout 1 Corinthians, when Paul makes such a declaration as 'Everyone shall receive praise of God' (1 Cor. 4.5), then, in
Barth's words: 'This "of God" is clearly the secret nerve of this whole
(and perhaps not only this) section'.[1] This becomes evident most clearly

---

1. K. Barth, *The Resurrection of the Dead* (ET; London: Hodder & Stoughton,
1933), p. 18; German: *Die Auferstehung der Toten* (Munich: Kaiser Verlag, 1924),
p. 4.

in the resurrection chapter. Life after death is *not an innate capacity of human nature* or of 'the soul' but a *sovereign, gracious, transforming act of God*. Hence Gaston Deluz observes: 'Like many modern Christians, they confused this pagan doctrine of immortality with Christian teaching on the resurrection'.[2] But this contrast between the initiative and all-sufficiency of God's grace in Christ as pure *gift* and the notion of some *human capacity* as a contribution which 'the dead' who have been brought to nothing can supposedly provide, constitutes a recurring theme which coheres with Reformation theology.

The third theme of the title, namely *the Church*, stands as an inescapable theme in 1 Corinthians. The epistle raises issues about unity and groups or factions; about ministry and charismatic enthusiasm; about order, freedom and ethics; and about gifts and worship. But the very prominence of ecclesiology in the agenda serves only to reveal the unqualified contrast between the ecclesial self-importance and obtrusiveness which shapes the agenda at Corinth and Paul's own counter-agenda: 'What do you have that you have not received? If, then, you have received it, why do you boast as if it were not a gift?' (4.6). The church, or certain groups within the church, might lay claim to possess *gnosis*, but 'our knowledge is imperfect...now we see in a mirror dimly' (13.9, 12). Prior to the resurrection of the dead, Corinthian triumphalism and their enthusiasm of the Spirit is to be held in check by *theologia crucis*: in Luther's sense of the term. Paul proclaims the implications of the cross (1.18–3.4). If the Corinthians think that they are 'already filled', why do the apostles suffer as 'offscourings' (περίψημα) and are treated like 'dirt' (περικάθαρμα 4.13)?

The resurrection chapter offers an answer. Only when the whole person (σῶμα) comes fully under the unhindered transforming agency of the Holy Spirit at the last day (ἐγείρεται σῶμα πνευμάτικον 15.44) do claims made by the Corinthians to be 'people of the Spirit' at last become properly timely. For what was 'sown in weakness' (15.43) will at the last be raised by God to be transformed fully into the image and likeness of Christ, the last Adam, the Man from Heaven (15.48, 49). Although in the present it has already begun, transformation into the image of Christ reaches full completion only in the post-resurrection mode of existence to which Paul points the Corinthian community in ch. 15. The future orientation of 1 Corinthians 15, then, says much about

2. G. Deluz, *A Companion to 1 Corinthians* (London: Darton, Longman & Todd, 1963), p. 225.

the nature of the church in the present, including its fallibility, its need of correction and continuous reform, and the impropriety of any unqualified spiritual 'enthusiasm', which despises order.

II

The interweaving of these three themes of the Bible, the Reformation and the Church constitutes a pre-understanding which informs the exegesis of 1 Corinthians 15. This, in turn, leads us to propose six specific theses which may be tabled for discussion. After we state the theses we shall compare them with modern exegesis and with recent reconstructions of theologies at Corinth. The following represents a preliminary formulation of these six theses.

1. 1 Corinthians 15, in the view of Karl Barth, 'forms not only the close and crown of the whole Epistle, but also provides the clue to its meaning, from which place light is shed onto the whole, and it becomes intelligible...as a unity'.[3] Luther's exposition of this chapter also presupposes that its argument takes up threads already apparent in various other chapters. For example, he recognizes, anticipating certain modern arguments, that a variety of grounds for denials of the resurrection may reflect outlooks of different groups or factions at Corinth, to which Paul alludes from the first chapter onwards (1.10-13). If a person does not believe in the resurrection, Luther declares, 'he must deny in a lump the Gospel and everything that is proclaimed of Christ and of God. For all of this is linked together like a chain... Whoever denies this article must simultaneously deny far more...: in brief, that God is God'.[4] If these approaches are valid, it may be necessary to revaluate the partition theories of J. Weiss, W. Schmithals, R. Jewett and others, as an analysis

---

3.   Barth, *Resurrection*, p. 11.

4.   M. Luther, *Luther's Works*. XXVIII. *Commentaries on 1 Corinthians 7, 1 Corinthians 15, Lectures on 1 Timothy* (ed. H.C. Oswald; Saint Louis: Concordia Publishing House, 1973), pp. 94 and 95; on denials of the resurrection and their multiple reasons see p. 59. In *Martin Luthers Werke*, Weimar edn (hereafter abbreviated as WA), the *Commentary on 1 Corinthians 15* appears in vol. 36, pp. 482-696; cf. here pp. 525 and 526, and p. 482. In a very recent study no less than five possible reasons are traced for the denial of the resurrection, out of which the author selects one as the most probable: G. Barth, 'Zur Frage nach der 1 Korinther 15 bekämpften Auferstehungsleugnung' *ZNW* 83 (1992), pp. 187-201. For a historical survey see B. Spörlein, *Die Leugnung der Auferstehung: Eine historisch-kritische Untersuchung zu 1 Kor. 15* (Regensburg: F. Pustet, 1971).

of 1 Corinthians, or at least to consider their possible implications.

2. The resurrection chapter places the central weight of its argument on the 'of God' which Barth identifies as the 'secret nerve' behind most of the epistle. H.A.A. Kennedy rightly argues that if there is any 'organic link' between the 'bare grain' (γυμνὸς κόκκος) of the corpse which rots away (15.37) and the future 'whole person' (σῶμα 15.38), Paul answers with 'the only one we can expect him to give...."the sovereign power of God". "He giveth it a body according as he willed" [v. 38] (ἠθέλησεν) "the aorist denotes the final act of God's will, determining the constitution of nature"...illustrated by Gen. 1.11, "And God said...and it was so"'.[5] Karl Barth rightly singles out as the key to whether resurrection belief is intelligible, or whether its denial renders the effects of the gospel 'void', 'vain' or 'empty' (15.14.17) the issue: 'Some have no knowledge *of God*' (15.34).[6]

Martin Luther expresses this principle with the words: 'Be content to hear what God will do. Then *leave it to Him* what will become of it.'[7] Everything rests, not on a doctrine of human capacities, but on a recognition of the inexhaustible and infinitely resourceful creative power of God already evidenced in creation, to bring about that mode of existence which is appropriate and glorious for its *new role*. Luther makes precisely this point. He writes: 'Since He once before *created us from nothing*, He can also again give us life from the grave and *give the body a new form*...Each will have its *own peculiar glory*.'[8]

3. A dead person cannot contribute anything to a new process of life, at least in the sense of initiating life or rendering it possible as an 'achievement'. A creative and transforming act of God brings this new life into being. As Jeremias rightly pointed out in a well-known research article, there is more to Paul's words 'flesh and blood cannot inherit the kingdom of God' (15.50) than the dualistic problem of how a physical mode of existence can enter into a trans-physical realm.[9] Luther, in fact, anticipates Jeremias' line of approach by citing this very verse with the explanatory gloss: 'Christ also says (John 3.3, 6) "Unless one is born

5.   H.A.A. Kennedy, *St Paul's Conceptions of the Last Things* (London: Hodder & Stoughton, 1904), p. 243.

6.   Barth, *Resurrection*, p. 139; see equally pp. 17-18, 189-91, and elsewhere.

7.   LW 28.180 (my italics; WA 36.647).

8.   LW 28.182 and 183 (my italics; WA 36.649, 651).

9.   J. Jeremias, '"Flesh and Blood Cannot Inherit the Kingdom of God" (1 Cor. XV.50)' *NTS* 2 (1955), pp. 151-59.

anew, he cannot see the kingdom of God", for "that which is born of the flesh is flesh"'.[10] This is why resurrection, as Deluz asserts, invites a different focus and a different logic of belief from that of notions of immortality.

Luther therefore insists that belief in the resurrection 'is surely not man's competence and power... When reason approaches this article of faith and reflects on it, it is entirely at a loss.'[11] In a five-hundred page study of resurrection published in 1984 Pheme Perkins makes this same point. Philosophically it may be possible, she argues, to conceive of personal identity in ways which do not limit it to a physical body. Thus the *Vedanta Sutra* presupposes continuing threads of consciousness, and Socrates and Plato argue that the human soul belongs to the indestructible realm of forms or of trans-empirical reality. But, Pheme Perkins concludes, 'Resurrection cannot be made philosophically coherent without distorting some of its fundamental commitments... In the end the two [notions of immortality and resurrection] must part company.'[12]

4. If resurrection entails an act of new creation which lies entirely beyond the capacities of the human self to achieve, there emerges a clear and a close parallel between the grace of God which bestows new life out of nothing, and the grace of God which bestows a new relationship or 'putting to rights in righteousness' which transcends all human capacity or competency to achieve. Paul alludes to this parallel explicitly in Romans 4, where he expounds the nature of Abraham's faith as trust in the God 'who *gives life to the dead* and calls into existence the things *that do not exist*' (Rom. 4.17). This 'believing against hope' (v. 18) entails Abraham's self-perception that it did not lie within his own capacities or competence to actualize God's promise, since he 'was as good as *dead*' (v. 19). But 'fully convinced that *God was able* to do what he had promised...his faith was "reckoned to him as *righteousness*"... It will be reckoned to us who believe in him that *raised from the dead* Jesus our Lord' (Rom. 4.21, 22, 24). Luther sums up the point in his *Lectures on Romans*: 'Let him cease to believe *in himself* and believe *in God*'.[13] This is closely parallel, however, to Barth's comment on the issue which

10. LW 28.198 (WA 36.672).
11. LW 28.59 (WA 36.492-93).
12. P. Perkins, *Resurrection: New Testament Witness and Contemporary Reflection* (London: Chapman, 1984), p. 438.
13. M. Luther, *Luther's Works*. XXV. *Lectures on Romans* (Saint Louis: Concordia, 1972), p. 284 (= LW 28.284, my italics; WA 56.296).

shaped the entire argument of 1 Corinthians: 'They believe not in *God* but in *their own belief* in God and in particular leaders... They confuse belief with specific human experiences, conviction...'[14]

To accept that one is justified by grace is part of the same logic as trust in the promise of the God of resurrection. Resurrection transforms the believer into the image and likeness of Christ as the last Adam, from whose character and righteousness the nature of the resurrection mode of existence is drawn. Hence Luther urges that the event of resurrection entails 'divesting' the nature of the prototype who was the first Adam to 'become like the celestial Man, Christ... We shall divest ourselves of that image and essence and receive another's, namely the celestial Christ's.'[15] But language about clothing draws together the discourse of justification and the discourse of resurrection. Without such 're-clothing', Luther observes, Paul declares that 'you are still in your sins' (15.17). On this turns whether, in Luther's words, the reader is 'justified by His resurrection'.[16] Christ's resurrection completes what Luther perceives to be a substitutionary work of Christ: 'Christ brought it about that the venom...[was] deadened and completely swallowed up by Him... "Death, where is your sting?"'.[17] Among twentieth century writers Oscar Cullman most notably calls attention to this christological basis of a 'stingless' death. Paul's joyous exclamation: 'Death, where is your sting?' (15.55) belongs together with his trustful assurance: 'Whether we live or die, we are the Lord's' (Rom. 14.8).[18]

5. If this close relation between resurrection and justification, each on the basis of divine grace alone, genuinely reflects the arguments of Romans and of 1 Corinthians, this now invites a radical reappraisal of the particular line of argument associated with A. Schweitzer and others to the effect that justification occurs in Romans and Galatians only as a polemic imposed by force of the circumstances of controversy. Schweitzer rejects the Reformation principle which ascribes to justification by grace the status of a central hermeneutical principle in Pauline theology. This conceptual scheme, Schweitzer argues, arises only when Paul is confronted with Jewish–Gentile controversy in Galatians and

14. Barth, *Resurrection*, p. 17 (my italics).
15. LW 28.196 (WA 36.670 and 671).
16. LW 28.102 (WA 36.536).
17. LW 28.204 (WA 36.681).
18. O. Cullmann, *Immortality of the Soul or Resurrection of the Dead* (London: Epworth Press, 1958), p. 55.

Romans. Schweitzer's heavy metaphor about justification as a mere 'subsidiary crater which is formed within the rim of the main crater' in Pauline thought is known to all students of Pauline theology.[19] If, however, the concept remains implicit in, or very closely related to, Paul's theology of grace in 1 Corinthians, and is focused especially in the event of resurrection, Schweitzer's arguments become seriously problematic. The theme becomes more than the product of circumstantial factors; it lies at the heart of Pauline theology. 1 Corinthians, no less than Romans and Galatians, stresses the priority and exclusivity of grace, and the event of the resurrection of the dead provides a paradigm case.

This principle receives added confirmation in the light of Schweitzer's own ready admission that justification by grace through faith 'belongs strictly speaking' to the future in Paul's thought. For it belongs to the conceptual scheme in which 'believers possess in advance the state of existence proper to the Messianic kingdom'.[20] This calls into question the claim which Schweitzer inherits from Lipsius and from Lüdemann that justification belongs to a conceptual frame which is incompatible with, or at least radically different from, a participatory notion of Christ-union. Both conceptual schemes, if they differ, derive this currency from eschatological promise. Thus J. Weiss, who stands close to Schweitzer in this context, views justification in Pauline thought as a 'pre-dating of what is really an eschatological act'.[21] P. Stuhlmacher develops further the apocalyptic context presupposed by Ernst Käsemann, in which justification operates as both gift and power. For Stuhlmacher it is equally a creative and a forensic act of God, in which God actualizes an eschatological promise of freedom and righteousness. In the present there remains an 'eschatological reservation', a 'now-and-not-yet', a 'hiddenness', prior to the apocalyptic manifestation of judgment and resurrection as declarative and promissory speech-acts by the Creator.[22]

Karl Barth likewise associates justification by grace in his *Church Dogmatics* with 'the right of God' as vested in the eschatological judgment of God and the resurrection. He observes: 'The event of the

19. A. Schweitzer, *The Mysticism of Paul the Apostle* (London: A. & C. Black, 1931), p. 225; cf. pp. 219-26 and also pp. 294-97.

20. Schweitzer, *Mysticism*, p. 205.

21. J. Weiss, *Earliest Christianity* (New York: Harper & Row, 1959), II, p. 502.

22. P. Stuhlmacher, *Gerechtigkeit Gottes bei Paulus* (Göttingen: Vandenhoeck & Ruprecht, 1965), pp. 217-36.

resurrection is the revelation of the sentence of God which is executed in this judgment; of the free resolve of his love...the righteousness which has come to man...'[23] He rightly criticises Schweitzer and Wrede at this point for allowing themselves to be misled by subordinating Christology to an eschatological programme. In 1 Corinthians, no less than in Galatians or in Romans, '"Christ Jesus is made unto us wisdom, righteousness, sanctification and redemption" (1 Cor. 1.30)'.[24] Strikingly, R. Bultmann entirely endorses Barth's view here, in his essay of 1926. Bultmann agrees: 'The contending parties in Corinth rob God of what is his, of his right of judgment...his freedom'.[25] He accepts Barth's 'masterly exegesis' which identifies this 'of God' as 'the secret nerve' of 1 Corinthians: '"Let no man glory in men" (iii.21), or expressed in positive form: "He that glorieth, let him glory in the Lord" (i.31)'.[26] Bultmann endorses Barth's view of the importance of the resurrection chapter for the rest of the epistle. Paul attacks 'a spiritualistic belief in immortality'. But this belongs to the logic of grace and divine promise. 'Death is not overcome by us by means of a pious frame of mind'; faith is 'a waiting for...what is promised'.[27] In Galatians this is how Paul formulates the nature of justification by grace: 'By faith we wait for the hope of righteousness' (Gal. 5.5).

Luther, as we may expect, perceives this dimension in 1 Corinthians 15. God, he writes, 'will create a new and eternal life... We must judge contrary to our feeling and in accordance with what God says, as convinced as though this had already come to pass...trusting in it...I on my part contribute nothing...I merely accept this, or receive it by faith.'[28]

6. Our sixth thesis concerns the relation between the future promissory focus of the fifteenth chapter and claims among groups in the church at Corinth to have direct possession already of a fulness of experience of the Holy Spirit which, in Paul's judgment, will become a reality only when the entire person (σῶμα) will be transformed into a σῶμα πνευματικόν at the last resurrection (15.44). The term 'spiritual body'

23. K. Barth, *Church Dogmatics* (5 vols.; Edinburgh: T. & T. Clark, 1956–1977), IV.1, p. 514 (hereafter cited as *CD*).

24. Barth, *CD*, IV.1, p. 524.

25. R. Bultmann, 'Karl Barth, *The Resurrection of the Dead in Faith*', in *Faith and Understanding*, I (London: SCM Press, 1969), p. 68; cf. pp. 66-94.

26. Barth, *Resurrection*, p. 17, cited with approval by Bultmann.

27. Bultmann, 'Karl Barth', p. 85.

28. LW 28.99 and 121; (WA 36.530 and 564).

denotes the openness of the whole person to the unhindered transforming agency of the Holy Spirit, who will change the hitherto flawed character into the image of Christ (15.49).

If Luther and Barth are correct in seeing the epistle as a unity which
receives light from the fifteenth chapter, here is the climax of a sustained
argument in earlier chapters to redefine the Corinthians' notions of
'spiritual' and 'spirituality' in accordance with what it is to be like
Christ, to 'bear the image of the Man from heaven'. The first explicit
appearance of this theme comes in 3.1: 'I could not address you as
"spiritual" people (οὐκ...ὡς πνευματικοῖς ἀλλ' ὡς σαρκίνοις). The
reason for this which Paul offers lies in their being characterized by the
unChristlike qualities of jealousy and quarrelsomeness (3.3). However,
even the passage from 1.18 to 2.5 contains an allusive or implicit overture for those with eyes to see. For if the message is, in Luther's sense, a
theologia crucis, not a *theologia gloriae*, it is telling that Paul recalls his
own 'weakness, fear, and trembling' when he preached the cross. God's
choice of the socially and intellectually lowly stands in contrast to the
church's pre-occupation with wisdom and the Spirit. As we shall note,
some argue that 'weakness' includes a social dimension in 1 Corinthians.

Spiritual 'enthusiasm' leaves little room for a sense of need: the
eye says to the hand, 'I have no need of you' (1 Cor. 12.21). It seems
that all wish to be apostles, prophets, teachers, or miracle-workers
(12.29). The charismatic 'spiritual people' have become like kings
(ἐβασιλεύσατε 4.8); the apostles are treated like dirt (περικάθαρμα
4.13). To be so far above the law that they can welcome a believer
whose life-style is incestuous is a cause of inflated self-congratulation
(πεφυσιωμένοι 5.2). Every single one has 'knowledge' (γνῶσις 8.1).
Unlike Paul, they claim certain 'rights' (ἐξουσία 9.13 as against 9.15).
As long as they can make their presence felt at worship as 'spiritual'
people (14.27) it does not matter if 'lesser' believers feel like strangers in
their own home community (βάρβαρος 14.11; ἐν ἑτερογλώσσοις
14.21; μαίνεσθε 14.23).

In contrast to all this, the resurrection chapter reminds the readers the
whole person is not yet fully under the unhindered control of the Holy
Spirit. The test of this, moreover, turns on whether transformation has
yet re-shaped them fully into the image of Christ, 'the Man from
heaven'. Luther makes this clear. The one who will receive the σῶμα
πνευματικόν will be like 'the spiritual Adam...completely new and

spiritual and lives solely of and by the Spirit'.[29] Luther anticipates the
supposedly 'modern' view (which in fact can be traced to Chrysostom
and which I have advocated elsewhere) that there were some at Corinth
'who tried to be clever and subtle and alleged that the resurrection had
taken place a long time ago'.[30] This provides one reason among others
for their denial of the resurrection.

Karl Barth points out in this connexion that ch. 13 on love and 15 on
the resurrection radically relativize chs. 12 and 14 on spiritual gifts. Love
and resurrection constitute permanent eschatological realities which
cannot become obsolete. 'Spiritual gifts' will pass on and will pass away
because they are circumstantial. Thus ch. 13 indicates 'a great passing
away of all those things that are not love'.[31] Thus whether the *phenomenon* of spiritual gifts can offer parallels in pagan religion remains
for Barth neither here nor there. He writes, 'What we are really concerned with is not *phenomena* in themselves, but with their *whence*? and
whither? to what do they point?'[32] If they are reduced to instrumental
tools for mere self-affirmation or for self-fulfilment, they do not correspond with the eschatological and christological realities to which the
chapters on love and on the resurrection bear witness. It becomes a different matter if their basis is authentically 'of God' and their use and
purpose genuinely for 'mutual edification'.[33] But 1 Corinthians 11 and
1 Corinthians 15 speak of 'order': God, Christ and Spirit relate to one
another in ordered, purposive, structured ways, in which even the Son
hands back ultimate dominion to God (15.26-28; cf 11.3). The resurrection of Christ and of believers proceeds 'each in his own order' (15.21).
Barth comments that if someone is a 'real' prophet or pneumatic, such a
person 'will understand that'.[34] The result will not be 'the troubled sea
of spiritualistic and theosophical illumination...the bliss and terror of hys-
terical hallucination and intuition which should be more the concern of
the nerve specialist than of us theologians'.[35]

Luther was compelled to address such claims in some of the effects of

29. LW 28.192 (WA 36.665).
30. LW 28.59, and A.C. Thiselton, 'Realized Eschatology at Corinth', *NTS* 24
(1978), pp. 510-26.
31. Barth, *Resurrection*, p. 76.
32. Barth, *Resurrection*, p. 80 (my italics).
33. Barth, *Resurrection*, p. 94; cf. p. 96.
34. Barth, *Resurrection*, p. 99.
35. Barth, *Resurrection*, p. 75.

the work of Carlstadt and of Thomas Müntzer. Luther urged by contrast that a 'full' experience of the Spirit would be perfected only at the resurrection. In his Sermon on *The Creed* of 1528 he declares: 'The Holy Spirit...begins to sanctify now; when we have died, he will complete this sanctification through both "the resurrection of the body" and "the life everlasting"...Then we will be...raised "in glory."'[36] Luther and Barth both stress, however, that the issue of 'spiritual phenomena' does not turn only on such manifestation as the contrast between triumphalism and suffering. Even 'the fanatics' (as Luther calls the followers of Müntzer) may 'select their own cross...make their suffering meritorious' as if it were a kind of 'achievement'. All 'spirituality', for Paul, for Luther, and for Barth, depends for its validity on whether it reflects the character of Christ. In such circumstances, Luther continues, 'you suffer willingly...because Christ and his suffering is being bestowed upon you and made your own'.[37] This is the kind of experience to which Paul alludes in 1 Cor. 4.9-13, and especially in several passages of 2 Corinthians also.

III

Luther's exegesis of 1 Corinthians 15 has a far more 'modern' ring about it, in the sense that it seriously engages with historical questions about the Corinthian community, than might be suggested by those who often view him as the last medieval exegete prior to the 'modern' era of Calvin. To be sure, the vast range of Luther's commentaries written over a long period of development allows for a variation of assessments of his different exegetical material. But here Luther writes sometimes ahead of his times. Our next task is to compare the exegetical work of Luther and of Barth on this chapter which has contributed to the formulation of our six specific theses with issues discussed in recent specialist biblical scholarship. This will both clarify the significance of our theses and assist in evaluating certain exegetical conclusions. We begin with the extensive modern literature which has been produced on reasons for the denial of the resurrection at Corinth.

Luther rightly perceived that denials of the resurrection may well

36. LW 51.168.
37. M. Luther, 'Sermon at Coburg on Cross and Suffering' (1530), in LW 51.99 (WA 32.30).

have emerged on a different basis within different groups at Corinth.[38] The recent discussion by Gerhard Barth (1992) together with the historical exegetical surveys of Bernhard Spörlein (1971) and Christian Wolff (1982) seem to bear this out.[39] A.J.M. Wedderburn insists that whatever the fine-print details concerning Paul's understanding of the theologies of the groups at Corinth, there is a general scholarly consensus that 'he quotes them accurately' when Paul observes: '*Some*' (τινες) say 'there is no resurrection of the dead'.[40] But within this general recognition about 'some', five explanatory hypotheses have been offered in detail.

1. Some writers have held that the church at Corinth in general denied the possibility of life after death as such. W.M.L. de Wette argued that these believers had been over-influenced by Epicurean philosophy; hence Paul seems to cite an Epicurean slogan 'let us eat and drink, for tomorrow we die' (15.32) in order to reject it.[41] Conzelmann (1969, Eng. 1979) and others reject this view, but Gerhard Barth (1992) urges that we should not underestimate the importance of pagan influences. Paul's allusion to his willingness to sacrifice his life (1 Cor 15.19, 30-32), G. Barth argues, utilizes a recognized topos in these circles for hope beyond the grave. H.A.W. Meyer follows Michaelis in construing the denial of the resurrection also as a denial of survival after death as such; but now he does this not on the basis of *pagan* influence, but through the effect of *Sadducean Jewish* influence.[42] Wedderburn (1981) attacks the plausibility of such a diagnosis on the ground that if they did not believe in life after death in any form, why should the Corinthians practise 'baptism for the dead' (15.29)? But quite apart from the multiple interpretations of this verse, Wedderburn concedes that the group identified by de Wette or by Meyer may not be the same group as that to which Paul alludes in 15.29. This, in turn, contributes to the

---

38. LW 18.59 (WA 36.482).

39. G. Barth, 'Zur Frage nach der in 1 Corinther 15 bekämpften Auferstehungsleugnung', *ZNW* 83 (1992), pp. 187-201; cf. B. Spörlein, *Die Leugnung der Auferstehung*; and C. Wolff, *Der erste Brief des Paulus an die Korinther (Zweiter Teil)* (THKNT; Berlin: Evangelische Verlagsanstalt, 2nd edn, 1982).

40. A.J.M. Wedderburn, The Problem of the Denial of the Resurrection in 1 Corinthians XV', *NovT* 23 (1981), p. 229; cf. pp. 229-41.

41. Spörlein, *Die Leugnung*, p. 7.

42. H.A.W. Meyer, *Critical and Exegetical Handbook to the Epistles to the Corinthians*, II (Edinburgh: T. & T. Clark, 1884), p. 36.

plausibility of Luther's claim that because of factions or differences in outlook at Corinth, more than one basis for the denial of the resurrection may be involved.

2. Luther also cites the possibility that denials of the resurrection might come from those who 'alleged that the resurrection had taken place a long time ago'.[43] A number of modern scholars express sympathy with this view, including J. Schniewind (1952), J. Munck (1954, Eng. 1959), U. Wilckens (1959), R.M. Grant (1963), E. Käsemann (1965), H.M. Shires (1966), J.H. Wilson (1968), C.K. Barrett (1968), F.F. Bruce (1971), my own analysis (1978) and that of C.H. Talbert (1992).[44] Although in my study I suggested certain counter-replies, this view has also been attacked and rejected (at least as a major or comprehensive explanation) by H. Conzelmann (1969), W. Schmithals (1971), E. Earle Ellis (1974), R.A. Horsley (1978), in part A.J.M. Wedderburn (1981) and G. Barth (1992).[45] In the end, however, all that these critiques appear to establish is that hints of different problems may apply to different groups, as Luther rightly implied.

This situation of confusion was perceived as long ago as in Chrysostom's Homily 38 on this chapter, where he considers the

43. LW 28.59; WA 36.482.

44. J. Munck, *Paul and the Salvation of Mankind* (London: SCM Press, 1959), p. 165; U. Wilckens, *Weisheit und Torheit: Eine exegetische-religionsgeschichtliche Untersuchung zu 1 Kor. 1 und 2* (Tübingen: Mohr, 1959), p. 11; R.M. Grant, *An Historical Introduction to the NT* (London: Collins, 1963), p. 204; H.M. Shires, *The Eschatology of Paul in the Light of Modern Scholarship* (Philadelphia: Westminster Press, 1966), pp. 53-54; J.H. Wilson, 'The Corinthians Who Say There is No Resurrection of the Dead', *ZNW* 59 (1968), pp. 90-107; C.K. Barrett, *A Commentary on the First Epistle to the Corinthians* (London: A. & C. Black, 1968), p. 109; F.F. Bruce, *1 and 2 Corinthians* (London: Oliphants, 1971), pp. 49-50; E. Käsemann, *New Testament Questions of Today* (London: SCM Press, 1969), pp. 125-26; A.C. Thiselton, 'Realized Eschatology at Corinth', *NTS* 24 (1978), pp. 510-26; C.H. Talbert, *Reading Corinthians: A Literary and Theological Commentary on 1 and 2 Corinthians* (New York: Crossroad, 1987 and 1992), p. 98.

45. E. Earle Ellis, 'Christ Crucified', in R. Banks (ed.), *Reconciliation and Hope* (Exeter: Paternoster Press, 1974), pp. 73-74; H. Conzelmann, *A Commentary on the First Epistle to the Corinthians* (Philadelphia: Fortress Press, 1975), p. 262; R.A. Horsley, '"How Can some of you Say that there is no Resurrection of the Dead?" Spiritual Elitism at Corinth', *NovT* 20 (1978), pp. 203-31, esp. pp. 203-205; Wedderburn, 'Problem of the Denial', pp. 231-33; and W. Schmithals, *Gnosticism in Corinth* (Nashville: Abingdon, 1971), pp. 157-59.

hypothesis that some of the Corinthians anticipated the problem that
'the resurrection is past already' (citing Hymenaeus and Philetus in
2 Tim. 2.17, 18). However, he then adds: 'At one time they said thus,
but at another that the body rises not again but the purification of the
soul is the resurrection'.[46] This entirely coheres with the most
appropriate translation of εἰκῆ in 15.2. Paul would be less likely to
suggest that as a whole the church had 'believed in vain' (15.2 RSV)
even as a hypothesis in a *reductio ad absurdum*; more probably they
believed 'in a *confused, haphazard* way'. This offers a perfectly
acceptable lexicographical meaning.

3. Chrysostom's alternative suggestion that the readers also confused
the resurrection of the body with the immortality of the soul finds sympathy among many modern scholars. However, this view may be held in
two distinct versions. Both cohere with our six theses. The first version
strengthens our second, third and fourth theses; the second version
coheres especially with our sixth thesis. We have already noted the
comments of G. Deluz (1963) and P. Perkins (1984) that whereas the
notion of the survival of the self as threads of continuing consciousness
beyond the boundaries of the body may find a home within philosophical exploration of pagan religion, the notion of resurrection as a
sovereign act of divine gift belongs to a distinctively Christian theology.[47] In this sense, confusion between immortality of the soul and
resurrection of the whole person distinguishes faith in God's sovereign
power to create from nothing, and faith in innate human capacities to
survive. This represents the first of the two versions under discussion
and is central to my argument.

Hans Lietzmann (1949), Paul Hoffmann (1966), R.J. Sider (1977),
Jerome Murphy O'Connor (1979), G. Sellin (1986) and A. Strobel
(1989) follow W. Bousset (1907) and J. Weiss (1910) in seeing behind
the denial of the resurrection a confusion with a notion of a state of
immortality which was achieved when the soul was released from the
physical body.[48] Such a view not only rests on a dualistic anthropology,

46. J. Chrysostom, *Homilies on the Epistles of Paul to the Corinthians* (Nicene
and Post-Nicene Fathers; Edinburgh: T. & T. Clark; rpr. Grand Rapids: Eerdmans,
1989), Homily 38, p. 226.

47. G. Deluz, *Companion to 1 Corinthians*, p. 226; P. Perkins, *Resurrection*,
pp. 293-308 and 431-40.

48. J. Weiss, *Der erste Korintherbrief* (Göttingen: Vandenhoeck & Ruprecht,
1910) p. 344; H. Leitzmann, *An die Korinther I/II* (Tübingen: Mohr, 1949), p. 79;

but also presupposes in the strongest form that life after death continues as natural human capacity. If such a view was current among a group at Corinth, this alone is sufficient to explain Paul's appeal to an apocalyptic framework of thought (whatever the current criticism about the 'loose fit' of this term), since all apocalyptic looks for a divine sovereign act of providing, or of setting to rights, that which human persons cannot provide or set to rights through their own natural capacities and resources. Martinus de Boer (1988) is correct to conclude that 'what he [Paul] says about death in 1 Corinthians 15...is to be understood in the light of Paul's christological apocalyptic eschatology'.[49] Indeed his valid coupling of 1 Corinthians with Romans 5 in this context strengthens our third and fourth theses, about the relation between resurrection and justification by grace, as well as our second thesis about resurrection as a sovereign act and gift of God.

4. A second specific version of this more general explanatory hypothesis relates to the phenomenon of spiritual enthusiasm at Corinth. Since at least 1908, with the proposals of Wilhelm Lütgert, a steady stream of modern writers have identified Paul's main opponents at Corinth as 'spiritualistic enthusiasts' of a libertine or triumphalist outlook. R. Reitzenstein attempted to argue that this was compounded by influences from Hellenistic mystery religions; while U. Wickens (1959) and most especially W. Schmithals (1956, Eng. 1971) argue for a gnostic or proto-gnostic influence. Certainly, as *De resurrectione epistula ad Rheginum* demonstrates, gnostic sources later than Paul re-contextualised and thus re-conceptualised 'resurrection' in a sense other than that used by Paul.[50] Birger A. Pearson correctly asserts: 'We can see at work a conflict of dualisms. The opponents were operating on a

P. Hoffmann, *Die Toten in Christus: Eine religionsgeschichtliche Untersuchung zur paulinischen Eschatologie* (Münster: Aschendorff, 1966), pp. 241-43; R.J. Sider, 'St Paul's Understanding of the Nature and Significance of the Resurrection in 1 Cor. 15.1-19', *NovT* 19 (1977), p. 137; J. Murphy O'Connor, *1 Corinthians* (Wilmington: Michael Glazier, 1979), p. 137; and G. Sellin, *Der Streit um die Auferstehung der Toten* (Göttingen: Vandenhoeck & Ruprecht, 1986), p. 290.

49. M.C. de Boer, *The Defeat of Death: Apocalyptic Eschatology in 1 Corinthians 15 and Romans 5* (JSNTSup, 22; Sheffield: JSOT Press, 1988), p. 181.

50. M.L. Peel (ed.), *The Epistle to Rheginos* (London: SCM Press, 1969), pp. 143-49 on 'spiritual resurrection' in *De resurrectione ep. ad. Rheg* 45.32-30, and more broadly S. Laeuchli, *The Language of Faith: An Introduction to the Semantic Dilemma of the Early Church* (London: Epworth Press, 1965).

non-eschatological plane in dividing man's present existence into a duality of heavenly-earthly, spiritual-psychic, incorruptible-corruptible, immortal-mortal, levels. Paul can use the *same* terminology, but employs it in a completely eschatological fashion, in which a dualism of "the present age" and "the age to come" are the principle factors'.[51]

A consensus has emerged to the effect that Schmithals overstated his case concerning a developed and explicit 'gnosticism' at Corinth. A convincing attack was launched by R. McL. Wilson, and by 1980 R.A. Horsley is able to comment: 'Scholars are gradually relinquishing the belief that the Corinthians were Gnostics'.[52] But this does not invalidate the claims of Pearson and Cullmann that a temporal or eschatological conceptual contrast was in danger of being replaced by a spatial 'elitist' or quasi-ecclesial one. Further, it does not call into question Horsley's contention about a 'hellenistic Jewish religiosity focused on *sophia* and *gnosis*'.[53] John Painter makes this point explicitly. He comments, 'There is no evidence of a Corinthian gnostic redeemer myth. Paul was opposed to their understanding of man and "spirituality."'[54] In particular Paul attacks their notion of 'those who boasted in their "natural abilities"...the privileged elite...Theirs is not true wisdom.'[55]

James A. Davis in *Wisdom and Spirit* (1984, based on a Nottingham PhD thesis supervised by J.D.G. Dunn) presses further the role of this influence of Jewish wisdom traditions on notions of 'spirituality' at Corinth.[56] These encouraged an achievement-orientated enthusiasm, he argues, which stood in sharp contrast to Paul's 'spirituality' of the cross. 1 Corinthians 1–3 revealed distorted attitudes towards the cross, towards 'wisdom', and towards the ministry. Davis concedes, however, that this

51. B.A. Pearson, *The Pneumatikos–Psychikos Terminology in 1 Corinthians: A Study in the Theology of the Corinthians Opponents of Paul and its Relation to Gnosticism* (SBLDS, 12; Missoula: University of Montana Press, 1973), p. 26.

52. R.A. Horsley, 'Gnosis in Corinth: 1 Corinthians 8.1-6', *NTS* 27 (1980), p. 32; cf. pp. 32-51, and R. McL. Wilson, 'How Gnostic were the Corinthians?', *NTS* 19 (1972), pp. 65-74.

53. Horsley, 'Gnosis', p. 32.

54. J. Painter, 'Paul and the Pneumatikoi at Corinth', in M.D. Hooker and S.G. Wilson (eds.), *Paul and Paulinism: Essays in Honour of C.K. Barrett* (London: SPCK, 1982), p. 245; cf. pp. 237-50.

55. Painter, 'The Pneumatikoi', pp. 240 and 241.

56. J.A. Davis, *Wisdom and Spirit: An Investigation of 1 Corinthians 1.18–3.20 against the Background of Jewish Sapiential Traditions in the Graeco-Roman Period* (Lanham, MD: University Press of America, 1984).

may characterise a segment rather than the whole, of the Corinthian community. C.K. Barrett's essay 'Christianity and Corinth' also relates the Corinthian claims about 'wisdom' and 'knowledge' to a 'spiritualistic' background, just as R.A. Horsley also associates 'the language of exalted religious status and spiritual perfection provided by Sophia' with 'spiritual elitism in Corinth'.[57] This 'spiritual elitism', Horsley concludes, manifests itself in such varied forms as ecstatic prophecy, including glossolalia, a sense of being 'ethically pure and incapable of sin (implications of viii 7ff.; x 1-13, 14-22)'. He adds: 'In so far as they possessed the divine Sophia they possessed all things...they belonged to the type of heavenly "anthropos", as opposed to that of the "anthropos" who is still too much attached to earthly and bodily matters...expressed in terms of *perfect vs. children*...The true self (soul or mind) is secure in its incorruptible spiritual nature...Accordingly the Corinthian *teleioi* denied "the resurrection of the dead" (the body)...a threat to their immortality.'[58] Even if Horsley's complex and wide-ranging explanation may perhaps over-paint the picture, there remain key elements of validity which cohere well with the six theses proposed above.

5. Finally, two sub-categories of explanation may be grouped together. Both propose that the problem rested on a misunderstanding between the Corinthians and Paul. Both are too implausible, however, to invite equal consideration with the other four, each of which contains some element of truth with respect to some specific group at Corinth. A. Schweitzer speculated that an 'ultra-conservative eschatology' of imminent expectation overtook the hope of the resurrection, because it rendered it unnecessary except for the few who, surprisingly, had died before the Parousia (11.30). W. Schmithals attempts to argue that Paul misread the problem 'in his ignorance of the actual situation'.[59] But both of these writers are swept along by the logic of the very distinctive approach which each wishes to advocate, and neither now commands a wide following. The other four explanations, however, especially the second, third and fourth, add weight to the six theses formulated above to which the approaches of Luther and of Barth gave firm encouragement.

57. C.K. Barrett, 'Christianity at Corinth', rpr. in his *Essays on Paul* (London: SPCK, 1982), pp. 1-27, esp. pp. 8-10; and Horsley, 'Spiritual Elitism', pp. 215 and 229-31.

58. Horsley, 'Spiritual Elitism', p. 231.

59. Schmithals, *Gnosticism*, p. 157.

IV

Before I offer some concluding comments about the theology of the resurrection chapter with particular reference to Luther and to Barth, I need first to note the state of recent discussions about the unity of 1 Corinthians. Barth concedes that superficially the variety of topics raised in 1 Corinthians 1–14 may seem 'haphazard' since Paul responds to a series of different controversies. Nevertheless, deeper reflection reveals 'a thread...which binds them internally into a whole'.[60] Further, the disclosure of this single thread occurs primarily in the light of 1 Corinthians 15.[61] In my study of 1978, I argued that in this epistle 'Paul builds up a systematic and coherent set of replies to a varied range of issues, all of which have arisen from the same two basic causes'.[62] These two causes concerned distorted views of eschatology and of the Holy Spirit, for which Paul achieves a positive and proper focus in 1 Corinthians 15.

Luther's exposition of ch. 15 regularly picks up allusions to issues in chs. 1–14 which receive in this resurrection chapter a due focus. These include, for example, in Luther's words, the issue of 'factions' (1.10-17; 3.3; 10.23-30; 11.21-22; 12.25; 15.12); of claims to be 'excellent teachers' (3.18; 8.1; 12.29); of over-confidence that 'spiritual' people 'cannot fall' (10.12); of irresponsible pastors (3.17) who 'spoil and undo' what Paul 'planted' (3.6); of the scope of 'reason and human competence' (1.18–2.5).[63] This is to cite only allusions which occur in the first ten pages of 155 pages of Luther's exposition. Calvin likewise insists that 1 Corinthians 15 constitutes the crown of the whole epistle, since without the resurrection 'the whole Gospel collapses', and this subject 'takes precedence over everything else.[64]

An utterly different view of the relation between this chapter and the rest of the epistle is adopted by Hans Conzelmann. He asserts: 'Chapter 15 is a self-contained treatise on the resurrection of the dead'.[65] But in his commentary his comment is brief and virtually assumed

60. Barth, *Resurrection*, p. 12.
61. Barth, *Resurrection*, p. 13.
62. Thiselton, 'Realized Eschatology', p. 256.
63. LW 28.59-60, 61, 65-66 and 69 (WA 36.482-93).
64. J. Calvin, *The First Epistle of Paul to the Corinthians* (Edinburgh: St Andrews Press, 1960), pp. 14 and 312.
65. Conzelmann, *1 Corinthians*, p. 249.

rather than argued, and in his introduction to his commentary he contents himself with observing that 'differences of situation' at Corinth cause 'breaks' in the material which suggest the kind of partition advocated by Weiss and by Schmithals.[66] The most serious difficulty of these partition theories, however, is identified by Gordon Fee (1987). Although he gives surprisingly little space to a discussion of this major issue in a commentary of over 800 pages, Fee puts his finger on the central point when he observes, 'The very fact that there is so little agreement in the theories suggest that the various reconstructions are not as viable as their proponents would lead us to believe'.[67]

We need not delay on these theories in detail, except to substantiate this point about their diversity. J. Weiss (1910) posits a first letter (letter A), 10.1-23; 6.12-20; 11.2-24, with 2 Cor. 6.14–7.1; a second (letter B) 7-9; 10.24–11.1; and 12-15; and a third letter (letter C) 1.1–6.11.[68] Maurice Goguel (1926) also postulates three letters, but assigns different blocks to each. Although he follows Weiss broadly in his view of letter A, his 'letter B' contains 5.1–6.11; 7.1–8.13; 10.23–14.40; 15; and 16.1-9, 12; and 'letter C' includes 1.10–4.21; 9.1-27; and 16.10, 11.[69] J. Héring (1948) carefully assesses these proposals, as entailing contradictions, but concludes that two separate letters exist within 1 Corinthians: 'letter A' contains 1–8, 10.23–11.1, and 16.1-4 and 10-14; 'letter B' contains the rest, including ch. 15.[70] W. Schmithals (1973) proposes that Paul wrote *nine* letters to Corinth, the first four of which contain no less than *thirteen or fourteen fragments from our 1 Corinthians*.[71] Robert Jewett (1978) distinguishes six letters, five of which contain sections from 1 Corinthians. 1 Corinthians 15 comes in letter B, together with 6.12-20; 9.24–10.22; 16.13-22 and 2 Cor. 6.14–7.1; while letter C, 'the main frame' contains eight separate blocks; letter

66. Conzelmann, *1 Corinthians*, p. 3.

67. G.D. Fee, *The First Epistle to the Corinthians* (Grand Rapids: Eerdmans, 1987), p. 15.

68. Weiss, *Der erste Korintherbrief*, pp. xxxix-xliii; also *Earliest Christianity*, I, pp. 323-41.

69. M. Goguel, *Introduction au Nouveau Testament*, IV.2 (Paris: Leroux, 1926), p. 86.

70. J. Héring, *The First Epistle of St Paul to the Corinthians* (London: Epworth Press, 1962), pp. xii-xiv.

71. W. Schmithals, 'Die Korintherbriefe als Briefsammlung', *ZNW* 64 (1973), pp. 263-88; cf. his *Gnosticism*, pp. 87-113.

D, various fragments; and letter E, 1 Cor. 9.1-18 and 2 Cor. 10–13.[72] W.O. Walker and Gerhard Sellin both write in 1987. Their schemes are simpler, but Sellin still proposes a complex series of blocks for more than one letter, which derive from 1 Corinthians.[73] Allusions to other approaches are catalogued by W.G. Kümmel and by J.C. Hurd.[74]

Three distinct responses may be offered. The first is to note the insuperable difficulty identified by Gordon Fee, mentioned above, concerning the very striking lack of consensus in such theories. The second is to recall that writers such as Schmithals are easily carried along by the logic of the distinctive thesis they make. The third point is that, even if partition theories could be established, all of the material at issue remains part of a sustained and extended dialogue between Paul and the groups at Corinth. Hence it does not become incoherent to argue that 1 Corinthians 15 remains a key hermeneutical vantage-point in the light of which these other specific issues can best be understood, even if they are articulated on more than one occasion. Moreover, Karl Barth believes that the theological significance and role of 1 Corinthians 15 *crosses the boundaries of this epistle to shed light on the whole Pauline corpus*, or even beyond, into *other parts of the New Testament.* Barth declares, 'What is disclosed here is *Paul's key position.* The resurrection of the dead *is the point from which Paul is speaking* and to which he points. From this standpoint, not only the death of those now living, but above all their life *this side* [Barth's italics] of the threshold of death is...seen, understood.'[75] Barth adds: 'The ideas developed in 1 Corinthians 15 could better be described as the *methodology of the apostle's preaching* [Barth's italics]...It is really concerned *not with this or that special thing, but with the meaning and nerve of its whole.*'[76]

In positive terms a number of writers have consciously argued for the

72. R. Jewett, 'The Redaction of 1 Corinthians and the Trajectory of the Pauline School', *JAAR, Suppl.* 46 (1978), pp. 398-444.

73. G. Sellin, 'Hauptprobleme des ersten Korintherbriefes', *Aufstieg und Niedergang der römischischen Welt* II.25.4 (1987), pp. 2964-86. cf. W.O. Walker, 'The Burden of Proof in Identifying Interpretations in the Pauline Letters', *NTS* 33 (1987), pp. 610-18.

74. W.G. Kümmel, *Introduction to the New Testament* (London: SCM Press, 1966), pp. 203-205, and J.C. Hurd, Jr, *The Origin of 1 Corinthians* (London: SPCK, 1965), pp. 43-47.

75. Barth, *Resurrection*, p. 107 (first two italics mine; last italics, Barth's as indicated).

76. Barth, *Resurrection*, p. 115. (first italics, Barth's; second italics mine).

278   *The Bible, the Reformation and the Church*

integrity of the epistle in full awareness of the analyses offered by those who dispute it. I entirely endorse the view of E.-B. Allo, who, having carefully examined the theories of Weiss and Goguel, concludes: 'We do not hesitate to endorse the judgment of Godet, who sees an intellectual edifice admirably conceived and executed, in spite of the diversity of the material'.[77] Allo offers some tart comments about the methods and aims, and limited perspectives of Weiss, Goguel, and others. Lest it might be thought that Allo has become outdated (imprimatur apparently 1934; publication 1956), we may note that recent study by Margaret M. Mitchell (1991) equally stresses the logical (or, to use her term, 'rhetorical') coherence of the epistle as a rhetorical unity. She traces a 'rhetoric of reconciliation' through from a focus of the issue in 1.10 to ch. 15.[78] Although from a different angle, her work nevertheless coheres with Barth's firm and valid assertion: 'the discourse of the whole epistle proceeds from a single point and harks back again to this same point'.[79]

V

We may now return to review the six theses which I formulated in section II. For the sake of brevity I shall consider them as three pairs of claims, although sequential attention will be given to theses 5 and 6.

1. and 2. The key, the 'secret nerve', of the epistle remains the '*of God*' which Barth has identified in such passages as 'everyone shall have praise [or whatever verdict] of God' (4.5); 'Sober up! Some have no knowledge of God' (15.34); '*God* gives it a body as *he has chosen*' (15.38). Barth rightly observes that in 15.34-44 one might well speak of the issue of the 'conceivability' of the resurrection. But, he urges, Paul is not conceptualizing, as if he were a philosopher, the nature of the new σῶμα as such; rather, its 'conceivability' depends on how and whether we can *conceive of God* who as inexhaustibly resourceful and versatile creator has the power to create the kind of σῶμα which he decrees as appropriate for its mode of existence in his presence. This surpasses 'the

77. E.-B. Allo, *Saint Paul: Première Epitre aux Corinthiens* (Paris: Gabalda, 1956), p. lxxxv.

78. M. Mitchell, *Paul and the Rhetoric of Reconciliation: An Exegetical Interpretation of the Language and Composition of 1 Corinthians* (Tübingen: Mohr, 1991).

79. Barth, *Resurrection*, p. 113.

limitations of human knowledge'.[80] Luther urges a parallel point. We may need to judge 'contrary to our feelings' and 'contrary to our experience', because the focus of confidence lies not in the boundaries of human thought, but in the promise of God concerning that which transcends what 'can be believed humanly' because it derives purely from 'God's own power and might'.[81] This invites four comments by way of elaboration.

a. This theme becomes so transparent when it applies to the resurrection that it substantiates Barth's claim to view ch. 15 as the hermeneutical key to all the previous chapters. In 1.18 the 'folly' and the word of the cross reflects the limitation of working within a previously determined frame of reference in contrast to which 'the power of God' opens new horizons. Hence in 1.19 'I will destroy the wisdom of the wise'; for this sets us on the wrong track. 'God chose what is foolish...that no human being might boast in the presence of God' (1.27, 29). This is because the only ground on which to boast is 'to glory in the Lord' (1.31). Thus, as we saw in section III, wisdom traditions may minister, even if unwittingly, to notions of spiritual or pietistic 'achievement', which misses the point which emerges transparently from ch. 15 that everything depends on the creative power and gift of God.

b. This invites attention to what M. de Boer calls 'the pneumatic triumphalism' of certain groups at Corinth.[82] As Luther notes, Paul's allusion in 1 Corinthians 15 to the apostolic experience of struggle and conflict ('Why am I in peril every hour?' 15.30) looks back theologically to the principle which is also expressed in 4.8-13: 'you have become kings...we hunger and thirst...we have become, and are now, the refuse of the world' (4.8, 10, 13). By contrast, Luther writes, only in the post-resurrection mode of existence for which all believers still wait 'we shall have all spiritual gifts'.[83]

---

80. Barth, *Resurrection*, pp. 194 and 195; cf. A. Robertson and A. Plummer, *A Critical and Exegetical Commentary on the First Epistle of St Paul to the Corinthians* (Edinburgh: T. & T. Clark, 1914), p. 368.

81. LW 28.99 (WA 36.530).

82. De Boer, *The Defeat of Death*, p. 103.

83. LW 28.142; cf. pp. 105-106 (WA 36.594, 540-41).

280	*The Bible, the Reformation and the Church*

c.	This represents precisely the broad significance of resurrection which has been exemplified in theological terms by such writers as W. Künneth. Künneth declares: 'The resurrection witness itself produces a crisis for every philosophical optimism which imagines it can command life and immortality'; it speaks of 'a life which does not lie within the power of men'.[84] This latter concept of life, he insists, would distort the uniqueness of the resurrection of Christ as the basis of resurrection for believers. But resurrection, he continues, '*is a primal miracle, like the creation of the world*...the assault of life upon the spatio-temporal reality of death'.[85] As such, it delivers those from bondage to decay and chaos into the glorious liberty of new life in Christ. This theme reverberates throughout 1 Corinthians as a hope of glory which underlines the *theologia crucis* of the present period and reflects part of the doctrine of sovereign grace and new creation which may also be formulated as a theology of justification by grace.

d.	These observations also will match the concept of faith shared by Paul and Luther, which many at Corinth had misinterpreted. To quote the sentences of the writer in whose honour this volume has been prepared, James Atkinson declares: 'Luther emphasises faith as *the work of God* and not man's own... He removes it *out of the realm of psychological subjectivising altogether* and sets it in its happy, healthful, sphere, of *divine* activity and *initiation*' [my italics].[86] M.E. Dahl stresses the important point that in the Pauline writings 'God' always remains the *active, initiating subject* or agent, even when Paul refers to the resurrection of Christ. The heart of Paul's logic is: 'He who raised Christ Jesus from the dead will give life to your mortal bodies also through his Spirit who dwells in you' (Rom. 8.11). Dahl comments: 'For the whole eschatological plan of creation demands that all Powers hostile to God shall be forced into his service... Death is such a power...God does not suffer his Holy One to "see

84. W. Künneth, *The Theology of the Resurrection* (London: SCM Press, 1965), p. 39.
85. Künneth, *Theology*, pp. 75 and 76.
86. J. Atkinson (ed.), *Luther: Early Theological Works* (London: SCM Press, 1962), p. 25 (my italics).

corruption."'[87] Resurrection is the sovereign act of God which, like creation, calls being into existence out of the Void, out of chaotic non-being. Through solidarity with Christ, the New Creation can never slip back into the Void again, for 'The last Adam became a life-giving Spirit... Death is swallowed up in victory' (1 Cor. 15.45, 54). This contrast between God's creative life in Christ and 'subjective' notions of faith runs through the whole of 1 Corinthians, but can be fully grasped in all its implications only in the light of the resurrection as creative act and gift.

3. and 4. I have begun already, in effect, to expound my third and fourth theses. Each of the four observations which I have just made also constitutes an exposition of the theological ground on which justification by grace through faith alone depends. Luther writes concerning the resurrection: 'Be content to hear what God will do. Then leave it to Him what will become of it'.[88] But is this not equally an invitation to accept the grace of acceptance through promise, which is justification? The resurrection shares with any concept of justification that it is, in Luther's words, 'really the work of God'.[89] If faith is a glad confidence, then Luther writes, 'Our confidence is built entirely on the fact that He [Christ] has arisen and that we have life with Him already and are no longer under the power of death'.[90]

Even the introductory passage on witnessing to the resurrection, confessing, and preaching, far from suggesting a 'break' in the logic, as Conzelmann proposes, promotes this theme. J.H. Johansen notes, 'Luther's emphasis on the saving quality of faith led directly to his high evaluation of preaching, one of the chief means by which faith is engendered'.[91] Moreover, preaching, like the sacraments, remains necessary because, as Johansen remarks in the same article, Luther could speak of the church simultaneously as 'the bride of Christ and the mother of all Christians' and 'as a wretched assemblage (*coetus miserrimus, armes*

87. M.E. Dahl, *The Resurrection of the Body* (London: SCM Press, 1962), pp. 76 and 77, cf. pp. 78-84 and 98-99.

88. LW 28.180 (WA 36.647).

89. LW 28.187 (WA 36.657).

90. LW 28.111 (WA 36.349).

91. J.H. Johansen, 'Martin Luther on Scripture and Authority and the Church, Ministry and Sacraments', *SJT* 15 (1962), p. 363; cf. pp. 350-68.

heufflin) plagued by the devil and the world'.[92] Similarly Paul's dual description of the church at Corinth as, on one side, 'God's temple' (3.16), and on the other as 'not spiritual but fleshly' (3.1-3), and as 'arrogant' (4.18; 5.2) reflects this double frame of reference. The two sides, in turn, correspond to the dual logic of *simul iustus simul peccator* in justification by grace. I have attempted in two studies to shed some light on the dual logic which is entailed.[93]

VI

5. Although the fifth and sixth theses may also belong together as a pair, more space is needed for comment on each, and we may therefore address them in two stages. Our discussion up to this point has, I hope, rendered increasingly precarious Schweitzer's claim that justification by grace constitutes no more than a 'subsidiary crater' within Paul's theology. J. Jeremias rightly rejects the claims of Schweitzer and Wrede, but nonetheless accepts the contention that 'the doctrine occurs exclusively where Paul is engaged in debate with Judaism'.[94] In 1 and 2 Corinthians, he argues, 'righteousness' usually means 'salvation', and the sense of 'justified' occurs only in 1 Cor. 6.11. Jeremias is right to urge that much of the issue depends on how broadly or how narrowly we define 'justification', and on the importance of the principle that 'the doctrine of justification should not be isolated'.[95] But this makes it all the more surprising that he appears to overlook that what Paul says *explicitly* about justification by grace in Galatians and Romans, he also says *implicitly* in 1 Corinthians.

There is also an important relationship between the emphasis on gift and grace in 1 Corinthians 15 and the move by Stendahl, Sanders, and others to interpret Romans in a more 'objective', 'historical', or 'social' way than that of 'existential inwardness' concerning guilt which many (rightly or wrongly) associate with a so-called 'Lutheran' approach to

92. Johansen, 'Luther on Scripture', pp. 357-58. He cites Luther's 'Sermons on Romans' in WA 49.684.

93. A.C. Thiselton, *The Two Horizons: New Testament Hermeneutics and Philosophical Description* (Grand Rapids: Eerdmans and Exeter: Paternoster Press, 1980, rpr. 1993), pp. 415-22; cf. further my *New Horizons in Hermeneutics* (London: Harper Collins, 1992), pp. 300-304.

94. J. Jeremias, *The Central Message of the New Testament* (London: SCM Press, 1965), p. 58.

95. Jeremias, *Central Message*, p. 60.

Romans.[96] Luther himself is less obsessed with 'inwardness' than many seem to suppose. Indeed such a claim is seriously weakened by Luther's very insistence that *God, not the human condition*, stands at the centre of the picture. This becomes transparent in his exposition of 1 Corinthians 15. We may go further. Luther sees the final, public, vindication and victory displayed in the cosmic event of the resurrection of the dead as the very paradigm of the notions of salvation, in the light of which the present is to be understood.

Luther and Barth stand together here. In the present, the church is on one side the temple of God, and on the other side utterly fallible and flawed; but an objective end lies ahead to which it is drawn. Luther writes, 'We will not only be enraptured and carried heavenward... We will be changed... The time will come when that which is *now always preached* and spoken about *will actually happen and be carried out...* He has transferred the victory to us.'[97] The Reformers do not, as Sanders seems to claim, miss this 'transference' aspect; they see that what in the *present* is *hidden* and appropriated by faith *becomes a public* event in the *public domain* at the future resurrection. These comments acquire still added point when we turn again to Barth. We noted that he sees 1 Corinthians 15 not only as a hermeneutical key to 1 Corinthians 1–14, but also as a key to other Pauline letters. Barth roundly asserts: 'The Epistles to the Romans, the Philippians and the Colossians cannot even be understood unless we keep in mind the sharp accentuation which their contents receive in the light of 1 Cor. XV, where Paul develops what elsewhere he only indicates and outlines'.[98]

Perhaps, however, we should ask whether Barth is here only carried along by his own study of this theme in 1924, or whether it maintains a firm place in the development of his theology. Further, how does this theme relate to that of justification in his other writings?

The early second edition of Romans (1922) stresses, as is well known, the limits of human self-achievement and knowledge not only in dialogue with Paul but also in dialogue with Kierkegaard. It has been urged that in the early Barth, the present hardly allows room for divine *deed*, only for *word*. F.W. Camfield, a sympathetic early interpreter, observes,

96. K. Stendahl, *Paul among Jews and Gentiles* (London: SCM Press, 1977), pp. 23-52 and 78-96; E.P. Sanders, *Paul and Palestinian Judaism* (London: SCM Press, 1977), esp. pp. 442-47 and 544-46.

97. LW 28.196, 201 213 (my italics); cf. WA 36.670-96.

98. Barth, *Resurrection*, p. 11.

'The final *deed* as it reaches the actual world can only reach it as final *word*; a message, an address...a promise... That which is new arises in faith, but strictly speaking *only in faith*: *not in actuality*, not in experience.'[99] This reflects part of Paul's own concern in addressing the problem of spiritual 'enthusiasm' and 'religious achievement' at Corinth, and it coheres with the background of earlier Barthian polemic against the 'religion' of liberal theology. Nevertheless, neither in Paul nor in Barth is a positive emphasis on new creation lost from view and this allows for an *interaction between word and deed*. In *Church Dogmatics* I.2 (1939, Eng. 1956) Barth speaks of the event of Christ's resurrection as 'the Archimedean point of the story and message of Easter', in which creative divine word is *grounded in creative divine deed*.[100] Still more strikingly, he repeats here his earlier theme: *'Not a line of the New Testament can be properly understood unless* it is read as a witness to *a finally achieved divine revelation and grace*, and therefore as the *witness to hope'*.[101]

As the thought of the *Church Dogmatics* proceeds, these themes never disappear. In volume II part 1 (1940) in which he stresses that 'God is known by God, and by God alone', he speaks at length of 'the hiddenness of God' in the present.[102] God expresses his love freely, independently of 'any conditioning from without', retaining his sovereign initiative as creator.[103] In volume II part 2 (1942) he expounds the theme found in Luther that only 'the *crucified* Jesus is the "image of the invisible God"'.[104] In this sense, in the period of the present, the identity of God himself remains cruciform, and is *not* disclosed as a *theologia gloriae*. Justification by grace and futurity of the resurrection promise bear this out. All of this coheres with 1 Cor. 2.11 (only the Spirit of God knows God); with 3.5 (God's 'choice' of his ministerial agents); and 15.38-56 (God *gives* it a body as he *chooses*). It is therefore entirely in keeping with the argument when, in volume III, part 2 (1945), he repeats his theme that resurrection promise holds 'the key to the

99. F.W. Camfield, *Revelation and the Holy Spirit: An Essay in Barthian Theology* (London: Elliot Stock, 1933), pp. 50 and 51 (my italics).
100. Barth, *CD*, I.2, p. 117.
101. Barth, *CD*, I.2, p. 117 (my italics).
102. Barth, *CD*, II.1, p. 179.
103. Barth, *CD*, II.1, p. 307; cf. pp. 256 and 321.
104. Barth, *CD*, II.2, p. 123 (Barth's italics).

whole'.[105] Because God remains sovereign and gracious, even someone under the illusion of strength and wisdom 'may let go of God, but God does not let go of him'.[106] The divine decree of creation and new creation remains the bulwark against the 'chaos' of non-existence, purpose, promise and futurity.[107]

In volume IV part 1 (1953) this pattern interacts with the doctrine of justification by grace as an issue of 'the right of God'. Barth asks, 'What kind of a right is this?' He replies: 'We cannot see it except in the judgment of God'.[108] But judgment constitutes an End event together with the resurrection, which, as a decisive act of God, also throws its light on the present. Weiss, we noted, described justification in Paul as a 'predating' of the verdict of the last day. Thus for Luther resurrection shares with justification in showing 'in brief, that God is God'.[109] Barth concludes in *Church Dogmatics* IV that in 1 Corinthians 15 'God has ratified and proclaimed...the alteration of the whole human situation, as it will finally be directly and everywhere revealed...That it has happened is our justification...It is itself the verdict of God...'[110] All this serves to add further weight to our fifth thesis. It may suggest that it is a pity that some biblical specialists who have recently called into question 'Lutheran' interpretations of Paul should have confined their attention, in effect, mainly to issues in Romans and Galatians, when they address this question of the assumption that 1 Corinthians concerns a quite different set of issues.

6. I have left little space to address my sixth thesis. But its validity has already been implied by much of the discussion up to this point. If the emphasis of Paul in 1 Corinthians lies on divine act, divine grace and divine gift, the logic remains unassailable: 'What have you that you did not receive? If then you received it, why do you boast as if it were not a gift?' (1 Cor. 4.7). What room is there for spiritual triumphalism, or for religious self-importance? In practical terms such self-importance leads only to obsessions about status within the church, and therefore, naturally enough, to potentially sectarian groups.

105. Barth, *CD*, III.2, p. 443.
106. Barth, *CD*, II.2, p. 317.
107. Barth, *CD*, III.3, pp. 302-349.
108. Barth, *CD*, IV.1, p. 529.
109. LW 28.95 (WA 36.526).
110. Barth, *CD*, IV.1, p. 334.

This may also distort a theology of ministerial function or office. As R.E. Davies remarks in his more popular study of this epistle, Paul wishes to save his readers 'from too high a doctrine of the Ministry—from supposing that the Minister is the person who makes the Church', but equally 'from too low a doctrine of the Ministry...Ministers are God's agents...' (3.5-15).[111] Yet all this faulty ecclesiology arises ultimately from a religious enthusiasm which has misconstrued the futurity emphasized in 1 Corinthians 15. As Moltmann rightly notes, whereas a *premature* anticipation of a divine 'no' generates *despair*, a *premature* anticipation of the divine 'yes' generates *presumption*. By contrast, Christian believers live on the basis of trustful hope in the promise of God.[112]

Luther had been forced to struggle with Carlstadt, with Müntzer, and the radical 'spiritual fanatics' over issues of ministerial office, of claims on the part of the self to speak with the voice of the Holy Spirit, and of a *theologia gloriae* which saw self-assertion and spiritual manipulation as a supposed way of promoting the gospel. It comes as no surprise, against such a background, to see how well the hermeneutical situation matches his exposition of Paul's eschatology of futurity in 1 Corinthians 15. He comments strikingly on 15.24: 'Then comes the end, when He [Christ] delivers the kingdom to God the Father'. Is Christ's kingdom, he asks, not present already now? He replies:

> He rules through the Word, and not in a visible and public manner. It is like beholding the sun through a cloud. To be sure, one sees light, but not the sun itself. But after the clouds have passed, both light and sun rule simultaneously... It is dark and hidden at present, or concealed and covered, comprehended entirely in faith and in the Word.[113]

In this present period 'God has hidden himself in Christ, so that we must seek God and acknowledge God only in Him'.[114] Luther anticipates Barth in seeing the very identity and character of God, as disclosed before the resurrection of the dead, as bound up with the humiliation of the cross of Christ. Here lies the death of 'spiritualistic enthusiasm'.

We do not have space to pursue this theme in other parts of Luther's writings. It is worth noting, however, that if Luther's commentary of

111. R.E. Davies, *Studies in 1 Corinthians* (London: Epworth Press, 1962), p. 42.
112. J. Moltmann, *Theology of Hope* (London: SCM Press, 1967), pp. 22-26.
113. LW 28.124; WA 36.569.
114. LW 28.126; WA 36.571.

1534 on 1 Corinthians 15 received added poignancy from the events between 1521 and 1525, the theme nevertheless occupied a central and explicit place in Luther's theology before any of these events took place, most especially in the *Heidelberg Disputation* of 1518. The *Heidelberg Disputation* is most readily accessible in *Luther: Early Theological Works*, edited by James Atkinson. Allusions to 1 Corinthians lie behind a number of Luther's statements. He speaks of the 'hinder parts of God' as his 'supposed weakness and foolishness (1 Cor. 1.25)'.[115] God is not to be found 'except in sufferings and in the cross' (cf. 1 Cor. 1.18; 4.9-13).[116] Christ is the believer's 'wisdom and righteousness... (1 Cor. 1.30)'. Love does not seek its own interests (1 Cor. 13.15).[117] It is worth noting here that *in recent social-historical readings of 1 Corinthians*, Ronald F. Hock and others have made much of Paul's deliberate decision to accept the term 'weak' as a (voluntary) designation of *low social status* on the basis of his decision to work as a tentmaker or artisan.[118]

In the more troubled waters of the Peasants' War we can see parallels between the radical enthusiasts at Corinth and in Germany: 'All things are lawful' (1 Cor. 6.12a); Paul and Luther reply: 'But not all things are helpful' (6.12b). In each case the opponents lay claim to γνῶσις, and to have gifts of prophetic insight. Yet neither Paul nor Luther could deny that effective proclamation depended on the Holy Spirit, without contradicting their own theologies. Both adopt the same strategy. The test of the Holy Spirit's agency is christological, and the fulness of the Spirit's power remains eschatological. These two streams of thought merge in Paul's resurrection chapter and in Luther's exposition of it.

Nothing can adequately translate the phrase 'spiritual body' (15.44), for neither term offers a one-to-one match with any English word. Modern biblical specialists agree that σῶμα, body, conveys human existence in its totality, regardless of the specific form which this 'totality'

---

115. 'Heidelberg Disputation', xx, in Atkinson (ed.), *Luther: Early Theological Works*, p. 290.

116. 'Heidelberg Disputation', xxi, p. 291.

117. 'Heidelberg Disputation', xxv, p. 294; and 'Further Proofs', p. 302.

118. R.F. Hock, *The Social Contexts of Paul's Ministry, Tentmaking and Apostleship* (Philadelphia: Fortress Press, 1990); cf. also E. Schüssler Fiorenza, 'Rhetorical Situation and Historical Reconstruction in 1 Corinthians', *NTS* 33 (1987), pp. 386-403; cf. further M. Carrez, 'With What Body do the Dead Rise Again?', in *Concilium* 10.6 (*Immortality and Resurrection*) (1970), pp. 92-102.

uses for self-expression. Bultmann calls it 'the most comprehensive term which Paul uses to characterize man's existence... A man does not *have* a *sōma*; he is *sōma*'.[119] M.E. Dahl plays safe, and adheres to the term, as the nearest English possible, 'somatic identity'.[120] We have moved away from the implausible suggestions of such writers as Weiss and Pfleiderer nearly a century ago who erroneously spoke of 'spiritual body' here as 'fine, imperishable, heavenly fabric'(!).[121] C.K. Barrett convincingly sums up the issue: '*Spiritual* does not describe a higher aspect of man's life; the noun spirit...refers to the Spirit of God, and the *spiritual body* is the new body, animated by the Spirit of God, with which the same man will be clothed and equipped in the age to come...by way of resurrection'.[122]

Luther anticipates this exegesis which became partly lost from view in the nineteenth century. Rather than restate any of our six theses, it is appropriate in this volume, of all volumes, to give to Luther himself the last word. Those who claim already to be wholly 'spiritual' are invited to recall, in Luther's own words, that only at the resurrection the raised entity 'becomes completely new and spiritual and lives solely of and by the Spirit'.[123] This raised mode of existence will be 'strong and vigorous, healthy and happy...more beautiful than the sun and moon...we shall all have spiritual gifts'.[124]

We cannot doubt a double allusion to those who claimed in 1 Corinthians 12–14 and in Luther's own time to possess 'all spiritual gifts' before the resurrection. But the resurrection creation will entail both transformation and continuity of identity. It will be 'endowed with a more beautiful and better form than the present one'.[125] Yet 'each body will have its own peculiar glory'.[126] This transformation, above all, is achieved by the power of God through the agency of the Holy Spirit in accordance with the image of Christ. For the ground on which the new creation now comes to be 'endowed with beauty', whereas in its

119. R. Bultmann, *Theology of the New Testament* (London: SCM Press, 1952), pp. 193-94.

120. Dahl, *Resurrection*, p. 94.

121. Weiss, *Earliest Christianity*, II, p. 535.

122. Barrett, *First Corinthians*, pp. 372-73.

123. LW 28.192.

124. LW 28.142.

125. LW 28.181.

126. LW 28.183.

earthly existence it shared in the cross, is that in Luther's words, the raised new creation bears the image of the last Adam (15.47-49) and thus of 'another Man who can...bring it about, a Man who is called Christ'.[127]

127. LW 28.113.

'THE SAXONS BE SORE ON THE AFFIRMATIVE': ROBERT BARNES ON THE LORD'S SUPPER*

Carl R. Trueman

> Of the presence of Christ in the sacrament, meddle as little as you can, that there appear no division among us. Barnes will be hot against you. The Saxons be sore on the affirmative; whether constant or obstinate, I remit to God.[1]

This quotation is drawn from a letter written by William Tyndale, the Bible translator, to his friend and fellow Reformer, John Frith. In 1533, Frith was a prisoner in England awaiting trial for heresy. This somewhat restricted environment did not prevent him from attempting to help those Protestants in England who still enjoyed liberty but lacked strong theological leadership. It was for this reason that he decided to write a short tract on the eucharist in order to clarify a number of questions concerning the sacrament which 'the Brethren' had put to him.[2] News of Frith's intentions reached the ears of his friend and colleague William Tyndale, then in exile on the Continent, who was concerned at what he heard. It was in this context that he made the above comment. Though brief, the statement is extremely interesting for the light it sheds upon the nature of the English Protestant leadership at this time, and for the questions it raises about one leader in particular: Robert Barnes.

Tyndale's motive for writing is clear: he feared that if a leading

*   I am grateful to my colleague, Dr Mary Charles Murray for reading, and giving helpful comments upon, the first draft of this essay.
    1.   The text of the letter is quoted in N.T. Wright (ed.), *The Work of John Frith* (Appleford: Courtenay Reformation Classics, 1978), p. 493.
    2.   'Brethren' was a title used by members of the popular Protestant movements originating in Lollardy: see A.G. Dickens, *The English Reformation* (London: Fontana, 1967), p. 106.

English Reformer was to compose a tract on the eucharist which upset the Lutherans, then English Protestant unity would be jeopardized and the movement as a whole would suffer. After all, it was only four years since Reformed and Lutheran theologians had failed to reach agreement on the eucharist at Marburg and had thus formally divided the Protestant cause. Knowing that Frith's own sacramental sympathies lay with the Reformed cause, Tyndale must have felt that raising the issue at this point in time could only be counter-productive.

This, of course, brings up the question of the extent to which a disagreement over the eucharist would have ruptured English Protestantism as a whole. Certainly Luther's emphasis on the real, physical presence of Christ in the eucharist did not find English soil conducive. Popular movements of lay piety, whose origins lay in crudely sacramentarian Lollard groups, would have no time for Luther's high view of the sacramental presence. It has also been suggested that Lollardy, with its 'literalistic and unscholarly biblicism' provided fertile soil for a theology built around the idea of covenant which 'is always inimical to a sacramental theology'.[3] Whatever the reason, there is little evidence to suggest widespread acceptance of Luther's sacramental theology among England's earliest Protestants. It therefore seems likely that when Tyndale here expresses fears about divisions, he is referring to the intellectual leadership of the English Protestants, in particular Robert Barnes, and not to the movement as a whole.

Robert Barnes's Lutheran credentials are, superficially at least,

3.   B. Hall, 'The Early Rise and Gradual Decline of Lutheranism in England (1520–1600)', in D. Baker (ed.), *Reform and Reformation: England and the Continent c1500–c1750*, (Oxford: Ecclesiastical History Society, 1979), p. 110. It is not clear exactly what Hall means when he says that 'a covenant theology is always inimical to a sacramental theology'. If he simply means that covenant theology is inimical to a realist view of the sacraments, then his statement is correct. However, it is most strange to single out federal theology as being particularly responsible for the English rejection of sacramental realism. It is true that Tyndale advocated a strongly covenantal theology, but federal theologians did not come to exert a significant influence in England until the latter part of the sixteenth century. Far more influential in the formulation of anti-realist English sacramental theology were non-federal theologians, such as Cranmer and Ridley. If, on the other hand, Hall means that covenant theology, by its very nature, allows no significant role to the sacraments, he is wrong. Federal theologians can maintain a high view of the personal and ecclesiological importance of the sacraments within the structure of a covenant theology, as is clearly shown in ch. 29 of *The Westminster Confession of Faith*.

impeccable. Born near Lynn in Norfolk in 1495, he joined the Augustinian priory at Cambridge before studying at Louvain. On returning to Cambridge, he was made prior and instituted a number of cultural reforms, including the introduction of the reading of Terence, Plautus and Cicero. He then became involved in the White Horse group and was exposed both to Pauline theology and to various Reformation writings. On Christmas Eve, 1524, he preached a sermon at St Edward's Church, Cambridge, which upset the authorities. He was then constantly in trouble until, in 1528, he faked his own death and fled to the continent. Enrolling at the University of Wittenberg, he engaged in theological study for some time before returning to England to act as Henry VIII's go-between with Luther and the continental Lutheran movement. Falling out of favour, he perished at the stake in 1540. Luther, deeply shaken that one who had eaten at his table should come to such an end, wrote and published an obituary for him as a token of respect.

Recent scholarship on Barnes has focused on the extent to which his theology was consistent with that of Luther. The traditional view, from Thomas More to Gordon Rupp, was that Barnes was indeed a thoroughgoing Lutheran.[4] However, more recent scholarship has dismissed this view, arguing that he may have started as a Lutheran but he finished life as, partially at least, Reformed. While this interpretation sees the shift primarily in terms of Barnes's doctrine of justification, it also detects a parallel modification within his sacramental theology.[5] It is this question with which the present essay is concerned.

There are three works by Barnes which are relevant to this question: a collection of patristic quotations on particular theological subjects,[6] and two editions of one work in English, *A Supplication unto Henry VIII*.[7]

---

4.   E.G. Rupp, *Studies in the Making of the English Protestant Tradition* (Cambridge: Cambridge University Press, 1947).

5.   The major advocate of this thesis is W.A. Clebsch in *England's Earliest Protestants* (Yale: Yale University Press, 1964). He is followed by Hall, 'Lutheranism in England', p. 110. Hall's reference to Barnes as a Franciscan is incorrect. He was actually an Augustinian, like his mentor, Luther. For a critique of Clebsch's interpretation of Barnes's doctrine of justification, emphasizing the doctrinal continuity between the two editions of the *Supplication*, see C. R. Trueman, *Luther's Legacy: Salvation and English Reformers 1525–1556* (Oxford: Clarendon Press, 1994), pp. 156-97.

6.   *Sentenciae ex doctoribus collectae quas papistae valde impudenter hodie damnant* (Wittenberg, 1530).

7.   The two editions of the *Supplication* were published, in Antwerp in 1531 and

The argument for Barnes's movement away from Lutheranism is based upon changes in content between the 1531 and the 1534 editions of the *Supplication*, but before turning to an examination of these texts, it is necessary to make a few preliminary observations.

The first, and most obvious, point is that the eucharistic theologies of Lutherans and Reformed are formally distinguished by their differing views of Christ's presence in the bread and wine. Luther argued that Christ was present according to both his humanity and his divinity, while the Reformed considered his presence to be solely spiritual, that is, according to his divinity. Behind this basic difference lies a multitude of other points upon which the two sides disagreed, both christological and soteriological. However, these subsidiary issues are not dealt with by Barnes: whether he is, or is not, Lutheran in his view of the eucharist can be determined only on the basis of his view of the sacramental presence.

The second point is that Clebsch's argument for a fundamental change in Barnes's eucharistic theology is determined to a large extent by his interpretation of Barnes's understanding of justification. According to Clebsch, the *Supplication* of 1531 contains a theology of salvation which is in substantial agreement with that of Luther, placing a single-minded emphasis on faith, not imparted righteousness, as the formal cause of justification. By 1534, however, Clebsch regards Barnes as having shifted to a bipolar doctrine whereby both faith in Christ and the believer's own works form coordinate bases for justification. This shift indicates the impact of Reformed thought upon Barnes's theology and forms the framework within which textual variations between the two editions of the *Supplication* are to be understood.[8]

Clebsch's argument here is vulnerable to criticism even before the relevant texts have been examined. The doctrines of justification and of the eucharist are not so inextricably linked that it is possible, for example, to predict a particular individual's view of the sacramental presence of Christ simply through reference to his or her understanding of

---

in London in 1534. Foxe's edition of the work, which appeared as part of *The Whole Workes of W. Tyndall, Iohn Frith, and Doct. Barnes* (London, 1573), is useless as a scholarly tool because its text is a conflation of the two editions.

8.   Clebsch, *England's Earliest Protestants*, pp. 58-73. In fact, Barnes's view of justification is always shaped to a certain extent by his background in Erasmian Humanism, and is thus more open to a positive view of good works than Luther even in the *Supplication* of 1531.

justification. During the Medieval period, belief in the Real Presence was not inhibited by an emphasis upon justification through the impartation of righteousness; conversely, during the Reformation, adherence to a symbolic presence did not preclude belief in a justification based upon the imputation of Christ's extrinsic righteousness. Thus, Barnes's development of the doctrine of justification between 1531 and 1534 is not directly relevant to an understanding of his eucharistic theology over this same period. Whether one argues for continuity or fundamental change in his view of justification, one cannot use this as a basis for prejudging the eucharistic question: change or continuity in the one doctrine need not be reflected in the other. Examination of the texts is the only legitimate basis for drawing conclusions about Barnes's eucharistic thought.

That Barnes was a Lutheran in terms of eucharistic doctrine in 1530 is not disputed: section 17 of the *Sentenciae* is entitled 'In the sacrament of the altar there is the true body of Christ'. Given the fact that the work was published in Wittenberg in 1530, the year after the Marburg Colloquy, and had an introduction written by Luther's colleague, Bugenhagen, there is no possible way that it can be considered as espousing anything but a Lutheran view of Christ's eucharistic presence. Indeed, the book proved so popular and useful to Lutherans that Bugenhagen translated it into German and this, along with the Latin text, went through various editions.[9] The Barnes of 1530 was obviously in agreement with the post-Marburg Lutheran establishment.

A year later, in 1531, the first edition of the *Supplication* was published, consisting of an appeal to Henry VIII, a list of the articles for which Barnes had been condemned, and eight theological 'common places'. While the appeal to Henry and the discussion of his condemnation indicate that the exiled Barnes intended the work as something of a personal appeal for clemency, the common places give important insights into his personal theological convictions at this time.

It is interesting to compare the articles dealt with in 1531 with those which occur in the *Sentenciae*. Six of the eight articles in the *Supplication* have direct counterparts in the earlier work: that only faith justifies before God; what the Church is, who be thereof, and whereby men may know her; what the keys of the Church be, and to whom they were given; that the freewill of man after the Fall can do nothing but sin; that men's constitutions which be not grounded in Scripture bind not

9. For the bibliographical history of the work, see Clebsch, *England's Earliest Protestants*, p. 49.

the conscience of man under the pain of deadly sin; and that all manner
of Christian men, both spiritual and temporal, are bound when they are
able to receive the sacrament in both kinds under the pain of deadly
sin.[10] While there is some variation in the order of the arguments,
justification by faith alone is first in both works, indicating the axiomatic
nature of the doctrine and Barnes's conscious fidelity to the emphases of
Luther.

In addition to these repetitions, there are two articles in the
Supplication which have no counterpart in the *Sentenciae*. The first,
that it is lawful for all manner of men to read Holy Scripture, can be
understood in terms of the specific English situation, where the most
pressing theological issue for English Protestant exiles was the need for
official recognition of Tyndale's efforts to translate the Scriptures. Such
an article would have been superfluous in the *Sentenciae* since its
Wittenberg audience already enjoyed access to a vernacular Bible.

The second additional article, that it is against Scripture to honour
images and to pray to saints, is in part an expansion of the article on the
mediation of saints which was present in the *Sentenciae*. However,
Barnes's wider application of this principle to the notion of honouring
images takes him beyond the position of Luther and closer to that of
Reformed thought which was always more iconoclastic, in the literal
sense of the word, than that of the Lutherans. Nevertheless, deviation on
this point is probably more to do with Barnes's Erasmian background
than with a sudden penchant for a more radical approach to reform.

A more interesting and, for our purposes, a more significant difference between the two works concerns those articles present in 1530 but
absent in 1531. There is now no separate article to discuss Christ's satisfaction for all sins; the impossibility of obeying God's commands; the
fact that in all good works the righteous sin; that councils can err; that
priests should marry; that auricular confession is not vital for salvation;
that monks are no more holy than laymen; that fast days are not binding; that everyday is a sabbath for the Christian; that unjust papal
excommunications are of no effect; that the saints are not to be invoked
as mediators; and a discussion of the origins of the mass. Many of these
issues are dealt with, or at least presupposed, in the articles which are
retained in 1531, indicating that a desire for conciseness may be the
primary cause for their omission. However, the most significant change
as far as Barnes's sacramental theology is concerned is the complete

10. *Supplication*, ii.a.

omission of article 17 as a separate section: that in the sacrament of the altar there is the true body of Christ. There are a number of ways in which this omission could be interpreted. It is possible that Barnes omitted the article because he had come to reject the Lutheran view of Christ's presence, but, as we shall see, subsequent events more or less disprove this idea. It is more likely that Barnes was motivated either by ecumenical or by political considerations. Ecumenically, he may have been worried about alienating himself from the mainstream of English Protestant exiles who were overwhelmingly sacramentarian in their sympathies. This view receives some support from Tyndale's comment to Frith. It may well have been that an uneasy truce existed between the exiles over the eucharistic presence whereby neither side raised the issue in order to avoid provoking conflict. However, Tyndale's letter could easily be interpreted to mean the exact opposite: that Barnes was such a combative character that he could not bear to be contradicted over eucharistic doctrine.

A more likely reason for the omission is the political purpose of the *Supplication*. It was intended primarily as a direct attempt to persuade Henry VIII of the catholicity of Lutheranism and thus of the orthodoxy of Barnes himself. As such, it would most certainly have been taking unnecessary risks to raise the subject of the eucharistic presence with a monarch who found that area of Luther's teaching particularly repugnant.[11] A Lutheran tract could hardly avoid justification by faith, but, if circumstances demanded, a discreet silence could be maintained over the eucharistic presence without fundamentally betraying the theology of Luther.

Whatever the reason for this interesting change, it means that our only textual evidence for Barnes's eucharistic theology in 1531 is article 7, on the need to receive the eucharist in both kinds. It is the subsequent absence of this article in 1534 that is, for Clebsch, the decisive evidence for Barnes's fundamental change on this issue. As such, only detailed examination of the content of the article will enable us to assess the strength of Clebsch's claim.

11. Henry VIII's major attempt at theological polemic was his *Assertio septem sacramentorum adversus M. Lutherum* (London, 1521). There has been considerable debate as to how much of the work was actually written by Henry and how much assistance he received from the likes of John Fisher and Thomas More: see Rupp, *Studies*, p. 90. The work was even reprinted as part of Fisher's corpus: see his *Opera Omnia* (Wirceburg, 1597), cols. 6-79.

Barnes opens his discussion of utraquism with a declaration that attention to the plain words of Scripture and the teaching of 'old doctors' (i.e. the patristic authors) would have prevented the erroneous idea that, while the consecrating priest could receive the sacrament in both bread and wine, the laity should only partake of the bread. As Barnes himself notes, this idea was formalized by the Church at the thirteenth session of the Council of Constance, 15 June 1415, in opposition to the teachings of Wyclif and Hus.[12] The reasoning behind the Church's teaching is rigorously logical: if the whole Christ is fully contained in each of the two species, then one need only receive the one species in order to enjoy the full benefits of Christ's presence.[13] Why this logic should not apply to priest as much as to people is not made clear in the article; we are simply told that this restriction was placed on lay participation in order to avoid 'certain scandals and dangers' of an unspecified nature. What is clear, however, is that while this issue might seem to be primarily concerned with Church practice, its roots actually lie in Christology. Therefore we might reasonably expect Barnes's critique of the Church's position to betray something of his own views on the relationship between the incarnate Christ and the eucharistic elements.

Martin Luther had himself attacked the withholding of the cup from the laity in *The Babylonian Captivity of the Church* (1520). However, Barnes's essay does not appear to be textually dependent on Luther's work and is tailored specifically towards an English audience, as demonstrated by his choice of John Fisher, bishop of Rochester, as his major opponent. This choice of Fisher is significant not only because it offered Barnes the opportunity of criticizing the views of a contemporary Englishman, but also because it had potential advantages for Protestants given the political climate at that time. Fisher had been open in his opposition to Henry's divorce, and, by 1531, was already moving towards a confrontation with the king concerning royal supremacy over the Church. By directing his arguments against Fisher, Barnes was not only attacking Catholic doctrine, he was also pointing out to Henry that the Lutheran cause might well prove to be a formidable stick with which

12. *Supplication* (1531 edn), cxxiii.b–cxxiiii.a. The text of the Council of Constance's decree can be found in Denzinger (23rd edn), 626.

13. 'cum firmissime credendum sit et nullatenus dubitandum, integrum Christi corpus et sanguinem tam sub specie panis, quam sub specie vini veraciter contineri...' Denzinger 626. For a more thorough statement of this christological position, see Aquinas, *Summa Theologiae* 3a.76.

to beat his domestic enemies. Such a political motive will become highly significant when we come to assess the omission of the utraquist plea from the 1534 edition of the *Supplication*.

Barnes's argument for communion in both kinds is fundamentally christological, not in terms of arguments about the communication of properties but in terms of the relationship between Christ's words and God's truth. At the start of the essay, he declares that no-one would ever have erred concerning communion if they had followed the words of Scripture, the practice of Christ's holy Church, and the teaching of the old doctors.[14] In fact, it is the words of Scripture which have decisive importance for Barnes, with the other two only possessing authority as they coincide with what Scripture teaches. This emphasis on the absolutely binding authority of Christ's words underpins the whole of Barnes's discussion, and is itself directly dependent upon his doctrine of the incarnation:

> Now wylle I exhorte alle christen men in the glorious name of oure myghty lorde Jesus christe (which is bothe their redemer and shall be their judge) that they wylle indifferently here thys artykel discussed by the blessed worde of oure Master Christe Jesus whiche wasse not alonly of god, but also very god him selfe; and all that he dyd was done by the counselle of the whole trynyte…by whose counselle alle counsels, both in heven and erthe, must be ordered.[15]

For Barnes, the divinity of Christ means that all that Christ says or does represents the single will of the Trinity. As a result, his words take on a singular importance. First, at a propositional level, they form the basic criterion of truth. As such, they stand in judgment over the Church's teaching, which must be consistent with Christ's teaching if it is to possess any authority. Secondly, Christ's words take on profound existential significance, with their acceptance or rejection being decisive for the individual's relationship with God: acceptance of Christ's words is no less than acceptance of God; consequently, rejection of Christ's words amounts to rejection of God.[16] This view of Scripture obviously has important consequences for the Church's view of the eucharist. In light of the fact that eucharistic doctrine must take the words of Christ as its basic starting point, Church teaching and practice on this issue therefore

---

14. *Supplication* (1531 edn), cxxiii.b.
15. *Supplication* (1531 edn), cxxiiii.a-b.
16. *Supplication* (1531 edn), cxxiii.b.

function as fundamental indicators of whether the Church accepts Christ or rejects him.

Closely allied to this emphasis upon Christ's words of institution is Barnes's rejection of rational argumentation in this matter. His opponents argue that if the whole Christ, both flesh and blood, is fully contained in both the bread and the wine, then one need only receive communion in one kind to experience the full benefit of partaking of Christ. While the christological assumptions behind this conclusion cannot be regarded as rational in the accepted sense of the word, the conclusion based upon these assumptions owes more to logic than to biblical exegesis, and Barnes regards this as an unwarranted rationalization of theology. Indeed, in his rejection of the Roman position, he explicitly sets the 'sure anchor' of the Scriptures and Christ's word against 'the carnal reason' of the papists.[17]

Barnes's fear of 'carnal reason', along with his emphasis upon the radical importance of Scripture provide the basic impulses behind his argument for utraquism which is, as a result, marked by an emphasis upon the plain meaning of the words of Scripture. Indeed, Barnes clearly feels he has little need to engage in detailed exegesis of the relevant passages because the scriptural basis for his case is conceded by the majority of his opponents. Indeed, as he is not slow to point out, the Catholic Church accepts that utraquism was the practice of the early Church even though it has now forbidden it on pragmatic grounds.[18] As such, the issue is as much one of the nature of ecclesiastical authority as of the interpretation of Scripture.

What is interesting is that Barnes does not expend a great deal of energy dealing with the dogmatic underpinnings of either the Catholic or the utraquist position. Indeed, he makes no comment whatsoever on his opponents' crucial christological assumption concerning the existence of the whole Christ in both species. This, of course, does not necessarily mean that Barnes accepts a corporeal presence of Christ in the sacrament, although it does point towards such a conclusion. Indeed, when coupled to his espousal of the Lutheran position just twelve months previously, there can be little doubt that Barnes's views have remained fundamentally the same. However, his silence becomes more significant in the light of Clebsch's claim that the omission of this essay in the 1534 edition indicates a fundamental shift away from a Lutheran view of the

17. *Supplication* (1531 edn), cxxvi.a.
18. *Supplication* (1531 edn), cxxv.b.

sacrament. In fact, it is clear from studying this essay that its omission in 1534 does not necessarily tell us anything about a shift in Barnes's eucharistic Christology simply because the actual inclusion of the essay in 1531 does not tell us very much about this aspect of his thought either. If, therefore, Christology is not the reason for the essay's omission, the change must be explained on other grounds. There appear to be two plausible reasons why Barnes may have omitted the essay on utraquism from the 1534 edition. First, the essay could have lost its relevance because of changes in the polemical context; secondly, as Clebsch asserts, Barnes could have changed his mind concerning the essay's theological content. Of course, these two reasons are not necessarily mutually exclusive, and so it is worthwhile examining the evidence for both.

As far as the polemical context goes, the world of 1534 was far removed from that of 1531. Between these two points lay the series of steps by which Henry VIII had unshackled England from the Church of Rome, culminating in his assumption of the headship of the Church. While these changes were primarily political rather than theological, it was inevitable that many Protestants would have been cautiously optimistic about how far the reforms would extend. The Lutheran states of northern Europe now appeared as potential partners in an anti-Habsburg alliance, and, if foreign policy developed in such a direction, there would be obvious dividends for those in England with Lutheran sympathies. However, in 1534 it was still not possible to judge with great certainty which way events would develop, and so any attempts to encourage Henry in a Lutheran direction would have to be cautious at best.

This caution is evident throughout Barnes's 1534 espousal of the Lutheran cause: the abuse of opponents which was so prominent in 1531 is, to a large extent, moderated, and Barnes frequently uses the sympathetic pronoun 'we' when talking of those who have been guilty of error. Nor is this moderation restricted solely to tone: content too undergoes transformation, as Barnes now includes a detailed account of his disputation with the bishops. More significant are the sections which he omits all together: the essays on the keys, on the vernacular Scriptures, on men's constitutions, on image worship, and on utraquism. Each of these essays was fundamentally ecclesiological, and their omission gives the 1534 *Supplication* a somewhat less radical tone in terms of its doctrine of the Church. Two new sections are added, on the true Church and on priestly celibacy, but they are scarcely revolutionary in the context. While the latter is perhaps a radical stance for an

Englishman to adopt at this time, the former is addressed to Thomas More, who had already fallen foul of Henry because of his views on papal supremacy. Thus, it is hard not to see Barnes's contribution on this issue as an attempt to ingratiate himself with the king.

In the light of these observations, it is difficult not to conclude that Barnes's omission of the utraquist plea from his 1534 *Supplication* was influenced, at least in part, by political considerations. Henry was well-known for being particularly sensitive on sacramental issues, and the intrusion of even the slightest hint of sacramental radicalism into any document aimed at winning his approval would most certainly have proved self-defeating. It was therefore imperative that the contents of the 1531 essay should not be allowed to ruin Barnes's hopes for a return from exile in 1534.[19] His purpose in the treatise as a whole is clear: to show Henry that he was unjustly treated by the old, corrupt Church authorities, and that he could be a useful, and theologically orthodox, worker in the new climate. Drawing unnecessary attention to his sacramental views could only jeopardize his plans.[20]

Having established that the omission of the utraquist plea in 1534 is explicable in terms of the changing political situation, we now come to see what evidence there is that Barnes may have omitted the section for reasons of theological substance. In this context, the first thing to note is that even if Barnes had indeed come to repudiate the content of the 1531 essay on utraquism, this would still not support claims that he no

19. Clebsch, *England's Earliest Protestants*, p. 69, makes the bizarre claim that 'Barnes removed from the 1534 tract the points of Reformation thought and action that were regarded in England as specifically Lutheran'. This immediately begs the question as to why he retained essays with the titles, 'Only faith justifieth before God', and 'Freewill of man, after the fall of Adam, of his natural strength can do nothing but sin'. The latter essay even contains passages borrowed directly from Luther's *On the Bondage of the Will*. While Clebsch's argument is undergirded by his claim that Barnes does not hold to a Lutheran notion of justification in 1534, this is based upon a fundamental misreading of the documents: see Trueman, *Luther's Legacy*, pp. 156-97.

20. The 1531 essay had also lost some of its polemical relevance by 1534. Barnes's chosen opponent in 1531 had been John Fisher, who had attacked utraquism in his 1525 reply to Luther's *Babylonian Captivity*. However, by 1534, John Fisher was a spent political force because of his opposition to the Royal Supremacy. While the same applies to More, for whom Barnes writes a whole new section in the second *Supplication*, this new essay is only just under four folios in length, a somewhat dismissive treatment of a man of More's stature: see *Supplication* (1534 edn) xliii.b –xlvi.b. For Fisher on utraquism, see *Opera Omnia*, cols. 131-56.

longer held to a real, physical presence of Christ in the eucharist. While the 1531 essay was Lutheran in tone, with its emphasis upon taking Christ at his word and rejecting the competence of 'carnal reason' in matters theological, it contains no explicit statement about the physical presence of Christ in the elements or any discussion of the communication of properties in the Incarnation. Up until 1534, the only indications we have so far seen that Barnes was Lutheran on these matters are the chapter in the *Sentenciae* of 1530 entitled 'In the sacrament of the altar is the true body of Christ', and Tyndale's reference to Barnes in his letter to Frith. If one is going to argue that omission of a subject treated previously indicates rejection of an earlier position, one would have to conclude that Barnes changed his views on the eucharistic presence either in late 1530 or early 1531, since this issue is conspicuously absent from the first edition of the *Supplication*. At best, such an approach can only point to the possibility of a change of mind; at worst, it is utterly nonsensical. Evidence on this issue must, therefore, be sought elsewhere, and fortunately there is sufficient available to enable us to draw firm conclusions about Barnes's eucharistic theology in the years between 1531 and his death at the stake in 1540.

The first piece of evidence against seeing Barnes as in any way sacramentarian is provided by one of his most implacable foes, Sir Thomas More. In the third book of his vast and tedious polemical work, *The Confutation of Tyndale's Answer*, More makes the following statement about Barnes:

> For frere Barons [Barnes] was of zwynglius secte agaynste the sacrament
> of the auter, bylyvynge that it is nothynge but bare brede.[21]

Indeed, More then goes on to assert that it was Barnes who persuaded Tyndale of the truth of the Zwinglian position. Of course, if this was More's only statement on the matter, we would have good grounds for at least having some doubts about the historical accuracy of what he says, since it appears to contradict Tyndale's later fears about Barnes's reaction to Frith's proposed work on the sacrament. However, we do not have to depend upon inferences from Tyndale's letter in order to refute More: Barnes himself disputed the accuracy of More's claims in a letter written to him sometime during 1532. In this letter, Barnes sought to distance himself from the views of Zwingli, and this provided More

21. *The Complete Works of St Thomas More*, VIII (Yale: Yale University Press, 1973), p. 302.

with just the material he needed to bait his current opponent, John Frith. With obvious delight, he taunted English Protestants with the letter's content in his 1533 work, the *Letter against Frith*:

> And also frere Barnes, albe it that as ye wote well he is in many other thinges a brother of thys yonge mannes secte, yet in thys heresye [i.e., sacramentarianism] he sore abhorreth hys heresye or ellys he lyeth hym selfe. For at hys laste beynge here, he wrote a letter to me of hys own hand wherin he wryteth that I lay that heresye wrongfully to his charge and therin he taketh wytnesse of god and his conscyence and sheweth hym self so sore greved therwyth that any man should so repute hym by my wrytyng, that he sayth he will in my reproche make a boke against me, wherin he wyll professe and proteste hys fayth concernyng thys blessed sacrament. By whych boke it shall he sayth appere, that I have sayd untrewly of hym, and that he abhorreth thys abomynable heresy.[22]

That Barnes was so outraged by More's accusation that he wrote such a letter is surely indicative of a man for whom purity in sacramental doctrine, especially in terms of the Real Presence, was of greater importance than unity with persecuted colleagues of a sacramentarian persuasion. The echoes of Luther's split with Zwingli and Oecolampadius at Marburg are too strong to be ignored, and we cannot credibly argue that Barnes held to anything less than a Real Presence in the year following his first *Supplication*. That the promised book was never written might be interpreted as indicating a subsequent change of mind on this issue. However, Barnes may well have felt either that More's published reference to his letter was sufficient to clarify his differences with Tyndale and Frith, or that More's own loss of political power rendered a full-scale reply unnecessary.

The next event of significance in Barnes's life certainly suggests that his decision not to reply in full to More was not motivated by a conversion to Zwinglianism: on 20 June 1533, he matriculated under the name Antonius Anglus at the University of Wittenberg and remained there while he prepared the second edition of the *Supplication*. Now, university allegiance does not necessarily tell us a great deal about Barnes's theology at this time, but, in the absence of evidence to the contrary, the fact that he chose to study at the intellectual centre of Lutheranism and was happy to stay there until mid-1534 must at least suggest something about the general tenor of his intellectual convictions. Indeed, even his

22. *The Complete Works of St Thomas More*, VII (Yale: Yale University Press, 1990), pp. 255-56.

departure from Wittenberg in 1534 was the result of the political climate, not some personal theological crisis: from 1534 until his falling out of favour, he was used extensively by Henry in his negotiations with the continental Lutherans as England pursued the idea of an anti-Habsburg alliance. All of this, while obviously suggesting that Barnes remained a faithful Lutheran, is not in itself conclusive. However, there is a piece of evidence about his mature eucharistic theology which is far less equivocal in nature: the John Lambert incident.

John Lambert was born in Norwich and educated at Cambridge, where, like Robert Barnes, he was converted to vital Christianity through the ministry of Thomas Bilney.[23] After being persecuted for his beliefs, he fled to Antwerp, where he became friendly with Tyndale and Frith, and then engaged in the work of Bible translation. At some point in the early 1530s, he returned to England, where his religious radicalism led to his prosecution in 1532, by Thomas More, and, in 1536, by the then staunchly orthodox Hugh Latimer. Fortunately for Lambert, on neither occasion did he suffer the usual fate of those charged with heresy. However, in 1538 his good fortune was to come to an end.

In this year, Lambert heard the bishop of Lincoln, Dr Taylor, preach a sermon where he made references to the doctrine of the Real Presence. Lambert challenged him about this and thus set in motion the chain of events that led to his own death at the stake. It is here that Robert Barnes enters the story, as John Foxe relates:

> [Dr Taylor] also conferred with Dr Barnes: which Barnes, although he did otherwise favour the gospel, and was an earnest preacher, notwithstanding seemed not greatly to favour this cause; fearing, peradventure, that it would breed among people some let or hinderance to the preaching of the gospel (which was now in good forwardness), if such sacramentaries should be suffered. He persuaded Taylor, by and by, to put up the matter to Thomas Cranmer, archbishop of Canterbury.[24]

23. Thomas Bilney (?1495–1531) was responsible for the conversion of several prominent Reformers, including Hugh Latimer. However, while embracing justification by faith, he still held to papal supremacy, the mass, and the Catholic view of the keys. Thus, it is important not to overestimate his importance in radicalizing the views of the young men with whom he had contact: see Dickens, *English Reformation*, pp. 117-19.

24. Foxe, *Acts and Monuments*, V (London: Seeley, Burnside & Seeley, 1847), pp. 227-28. One might object that Foxe is not always that reliable a witness because of his underlying hagiographical agenda. However, this incident scarcely sets Barnes in a good light and could easily have been omitted had Foxe's sole concern been for

Having been brought before Cranmer, Lambert made the suicidal decision to appeal to the king, a man renowned for his hatred of sacramentarianism. The subsequent disputation, presided over by Henry himself, led to the inevitable outcome: Lambert was burned at the stake on 22 November 1538.

The significance of this event for our understanding of Barnes's eucharistic theology can scarcely be overestimated. Lambert's own views, like those of his late friends, Tyndale and Frith, were Reformed in orientation. In a letter to Lord Lisle, dated 16 November 1538, John Husee, an eyewitness at the disputation, summed Lambert's position up as follows:

> [Lambert] held to his opinions, denying the very body of God to be in the said Sacrament in corporal substance, but only to be there spiritually.[25]

These were the very views which, in 1532, More had imputed to Barnes and which the latter had so vigorously repudiated. In the year 1538, had Barnes abandoned his belief in the Real Presence, he would have had to keep his views secret in order to avoid the wrath of the Church establishment. If this was the case, one might have expected him simply to have ignored Lambert. It defies credibility to think that he would have brought a man holding the same views as himself to the attention of the authorities. The explicit recommendation that Lambert be brought before Cranmer to answer for his sacramental beliefs can only have been motivated by personal theological conviction. Perhaps there was also a certain cynical desire to ingratiate himself with the authorities, but he does not seem to have needed to do so prior to the collapse of Henry's flirtatious relationship with the continental Lutherans. His position only becomes insecure after the disastrous Anne of Cleves affair and Stephen Gardiner's assertion of control over Church policy, as embodied in the passing of the Six Articles. In fact, Barnes's action is only really comprehensible if we accept that he was himself an adherent to the doctrine of the Real Presence. We noted earlier that the relationship he drew between Christ's words and the will of the Trinity made the doctrine of the eucharist a fundamental test of fidelity to God. It is surely

good Protestant propaganda. It is perhaps not surprising that this distasteful event is recounted by Foxe only in his life of Lambert and that, in his life of Barnes, he maintains a discreet silence about the whole affair.

25. *Letters and Papers of Henry VIII* (London: Eyre & Spottiswood, 1892), 13 i, no. 851.

this same principle which lies behind Barnes's actions in 1538: Lambert denied the Real Presence and was therefore not a Christian. Any other view of Barnes's eucharistic beliefs at this time precludes a satisfactory explanation of this incident. Barnes clearly believed in the Real Presence, and did so to such an extent that he could find no common bond of Christian unity or love with Lambert to prevent him from ensuring that the latter paid for his beliefs with his life.

The Lambert incident is surely the decisive piece of evidence against any view of Barnes which sees him as abandoning a high view of the eucharist. However, at the risk of introducing a level of 'overkill' into the argument, there is one more fact which speaks eloquently about his views in this matter: the reason for his execution. The Six Articles of 1539 were specifically intended to reimpose the doctrines of Catholic orthodoxy, with the exception of papal supremacy, upon an England which had enjoyed a certain trend towards Protestantism under Thomas Cromwell. A key element of the Six Articles was the declaration that rejection of the Real Presence was to be punished by death. When Barnes and his two colleagues, Garrard and Jerome, were condemned to death, the heresies for which they were to suffer death were not specified. Such an omission was most significant in an age when there was good propaganda to be made from cataloguing the heresies of one's opponents. Had Barnes been at all tainted with sacramentarianism, it is unthinkable that this should not have been used as a weapon against him. In fact, the real reason for his execution was an ill-timed public attack which he had made on Stephen Gardiner. This, coupled with his association with Cromwell, whose own fortunes were by now in rapid decline, was enough to seal his fate. It was not heresy, and certainly not denial of the Real Presence, which actually brought about his downfall, but his links with discredited foreign and domestic policies.

Conclusion

When the evidence for Barnes's view of the eucharist is assembled, it is quite clear that there is nothing to suggest that his view of the sacrament changed in any way that led either to an outright denial, or even to a devaluing, of the Real Presence. The case for such a change is based upon the correlation of alleged shifts in his doctrine of justification between 1531 and 1534 with his omission of the utraquist plea in the second edition of his *Supplication*. Such an argument from silence, based upon unjustified inferences from misinterpretations of the sources, is scarcely a sound basis for assertions of radical discontinuity in Barnes's theology. Furthermore, this argument is not just methodologically unsound but is actually contradicted by Barnes's own personal history. His love of the Lutheran teaching on salvation, his early assertion of the Real Presence, his subsequent failure to attack the christological underpinnings of communion in one kind, his anger at More's accusations of sacramentarianism, his matriculation at Wittenberg, his persecution of John Lambert, the fact that the heresies for which he died were unspecified—taken individually, each of these incidents is at least suggestive; taken as a whole, they are surely decisive. Barnes's life simply does not make sense if he did not hold to the Real Presence of Christ within the sacrament. It is arguable that this conclusion is of more significance for understanding the thought of Robert Barnes himself than for any more general conclusions about the English Reformation as a whole. It certainly make Barnes himself a much more interesting figure. In a way, he was England's own answer to Martin Luther, for he too was prepared to break with his fellow Protestants simply over the issue of the eucharistic presence. It also contradicts the view that English Protestantism, for whatever reason, was inherently predisposed to Reformed theology and that even those who started off spiritually in Wittenberg ended up in Zürich. Finally, it is a clear sign that English Protestantism was no unified movement with a common agenda. Indeed, the Protestants themselves were clearly aware of this, and Lambert's death in 1538 serves merely to underline the fact that, unlike some modern scholars, Tyndale had been under no illusions about the nature of Barnes's beliefs and the strength with which he held them. In this context the words which he wrote to John Frith in 1533 take on a horribly prophetic quality:

> Of the presence of Christ in the sacrament, meddle as little as you can, that there appear no division among us. Barnes will be hot against you.

ERASMUS AND MARSILIUS OF PADUA

Robert C. Walton

1. *Introduction*

This essay considers the origin of certain aspects of the political thought of Erasmus. The main argument of the paper is that Marsilius of Padua's *Defensor Pacis* played a central role in the development of Erasmus's conception of the relationship between the two powers which governed a Christian Republic or Society and in radicalizing his distaste for the Church's wealth and political power. Erasmus's concern for the relationship between the civil and spiritual power, which involved the Church's misuse of its authority and riches, was also typical of late mediaeval thought. Wilks has summed up the problem posed by this relationship very nicely, 'The question of the right relationship of powers, so necessary for the maintenance of the *harmonia mundi*, became a prime consideration of the age'.[1]

Erasmus was able to understand and use Marsilius's *Defensor*, because he shared many common assumptions with Marsilius and posed similar questions. Though Marsilius can hardly be called a humanist, he did return to the sources to seek arguments against the Church's abuse of its power and wealth.

Erasmus shared one other very basic assumption with mediaeval critics of the Church and indeed also with most mediaeval heretics. Along with so many others, he believed that the primitive Church represented the golden age of Christianity and was normative for the Western Church. G. Leff describes this belief as one of the important foci for late mediaeval heretics and other critics of the Church.[2]

---

1. M. Wilks, *The Problem of Sovereignty in the Later Middle Ages: The Papal Monarchy with Augustinus Triumphus and the Publicists* (Cambridge, 1963), p. 15.

2. G. Leff, *Heresy in the Later Middle Ages: The Relation of Heterodoxy to Dissent* (2 vols.; Manchester, New York, 1967), I, p. 7.

Erasmus, like his late mediaeval predecessors, spoke often of Christ and the Apostles' conduct and goals, and constantly compared them with those of Popes, Bishops and the Lower Clergy. Indeed, long before Erasmus's birth, a consensus had been reached that the proper authority for the Church in the golden age as well as the present was the New Testament, which recounted the teaching and acts of Christ and the Apostles,

> From the eleventh to the fifteenth centuries, its aspirations were common to all religious reform, namely, the desire to emulate the life and teachings of Christ and his Apostles; and more particularly to seek a return to the precepts of the gospel through a life of poverty—or one of complete simplicity—and preaching.[3]

The application of the golden age of the Church and the use of the norms established by Christ and the Apostles, which were to be found in the New Testament, inevitably fed anticlericalism in the late mediaeval period. Any comparison between the Church of the golden age and the Church as it was in the fourteenth or fifteenth century was bound to raise serious criticism, particularly of the clergy. There can also be no doubt that Marsilius's radically critical approach nourished anticlericalism for almost two centuries before the coming of the Reformation. Speaking of Marsilius, Leff asserts that he

> took the example of the primitive Church as model for what the present Church should be.[4]

> Marsilius seems to have been the first to make it a serious argument against the power of pope and cardinals that in the primitive Church there had only been two orders—those of priests and deacons; bishop and priest had been synonymous, and correspondingly pope and cardinals are nonexistent. They had no coercive power over bishop and priest... The second facet was far more far-reaching and of incalculable influence upon Wycliff and Hus, namely, a denial of the primacy of Rome. All the apostles, Marsilius averred, had been under the authority of Christ, they had all been equal with one another, and Peter had never tried to make himself pre-eminent or exercised coercive authority over them.[5]

The idea of a golden age was part of a series of general assumptions made by late mediaeval thinkers. The same idea was of course also present in the thought of the Conciliarists, and the Renaissance-Reformation

3. Leff, *Heresy*, I, 3 (the Bible), II, pp. 414ff.
4. Leff, *Heresy*, II, pp. 416.
5. Leff, *Heresy*, II, pp. 416-17.

period, as people looked back to the glory and norms of the Graeco-Roman civilization. The conception of reform championed by Erasmus, and especially his idea of a *renascantur bonae literae* was widely accepted.[6]

However, this conception of reform could not have developed without the prior existence of the late mediaeval idea of the Golden Age and the norms set by Christ and the Apostles. If it was really possible, Renaissance-Reformation thinkers took an even more negative view of the Medieval Church than had their late mediaeval predecessors. It should never be forgotten that the arsenal for the attack launched against the Medieval Church during the Reformation had been fashioned during the fourteenth and fifteenth centuries. The use of the idea of a golden age of the Church and the norms of Christ and the Apostles found in the New Testament, which, among other things, were believed to demand a return to poverty and the end of the exercise of coercive jurisdiction, represented the continuation of a vitally important late medieval heritage. Erasmus's 1516 edition of the New Testament, the *Novum Organum*, as well as his *Adnotationes* and above all the *Paraphrases* represented a systematic effort to make the norms and teaching of Christ and the Apostles contained in the New Testament available to the students of sacred philology.[7] Later *The Paraphrases of the New Testament* as well as the New Testament itself were also made available in the vernacular, thanks to the labor of Erasmus's friends, for example, Leo Jud at Basel and Zürich. His Paraphrase of the Book of Revelation even found a place in the second volume of the English edition of the *Paraphrases*. The work of translating the *Paraphrases* into English was largely carried out by the court circle around Henry VIII's wife, Catherine Parr, which included both the future Queens Mary and Elizabeth. Under the reign of Edward VI Catherine Parr was replaced by Anne Seymour, Duchess of Somerset.[8]

6.   See W.K. Ferguson's now somewhat dated discussion in *The Renaissance in Historical Thought: Five Centuries of Interpretation* (Cambridge, MA, 1948), pp. 39, 41-44, 372-85.

7.   In using the term sacred philology, this essay follows P.O. Kristeller, *Renaissance Thought: The Classic, Scholastic, and Humanistic Strains* (New York, 1955, 1961 [1955]), pp. 78-79.

8.   K.-H. Wyss, *Leo Jud: Seine Entwicklung zum Reformator 1519–1523* (Bern, 1976), pp. 60-62, 63ff., 76, 160-61. J.K. McConica, *English Humanists and Reformation Politics under Henry VIII and Edward VI* (Oxford, 1965), pp. 200ff., 213-32, 232-33, 246ff.

By using the tools of sacred philology to confirm the mediaeval conception of the central authority of the New Testament, Erasmus laid the foundation for the Reformation polemic. The frequency with which he and Marsilius agreed is surprising. The two centuries which divided them still left them in communication. It is well to remember here that Marsilius was a fourteenth-century polemicist in the service of the Emperor Lewis the Bavarian, and Erasmus, though a noted polemicist, was the Prince of Humanists, and honorary councillor to the Emperor Charles V in the early sixteenth century.

2. *Erasmus and Marsilius*

a. *Erasmus and the Manuscripts of the Defensor Pacis*
Our aim in this section of this essay is to see whether or not it is possible to prove that Erasmus had had access to and had read Marsilius's *Defensor Pacis*. The problem of answering this question is complicated by the fact that Marsilius's teaching concerning the constitution of the Church had been condemned by Pope John XXII in the bull *Licet iuxta doctrinam* which was issued on 23 October 1327. Subsequently Clement VI (1342–1352) condemned 250 errors found in Marsilius's *Defensor*.[9] Condren asserts that despite these condemnations, 'it was translated into the vernacular wherever there were strong centers of anticlericalism'.[10] Nevertheless, in many parts of Europe one could not always look to anticlericalism for protection. As a result, even those who had carefully read one of the manuscripts or vernacular excerpts of them would have hardly been willing to cite him as a source. It was simply dangerous to cite a man whose basic teaching had been condemned by the Church. For a man like Erasmus who relied upon both lay and clerical patronage, there were good reasons to be cautious. This explains his failure to cite Marsilius, especially in the *Paraphrases*. However, before the entire issue of those who used Marsilius without admitting it is considered, it is necessary to have a look at the locations of the various manuscripts of the *Defensor*, where Erasmus might have

9. 'Marsilii Patavini de constitutione Ecclesiae', in H. Denzinger, A. Schoenmetzer, SJ (eds.), *Symbolorum Definitionum et Declarationum De Rebus Fidei et Morum*, Editio XXXIII (Barcinone, Freiburgi Brisgoviae Romae Neo-Eboraci, 1965), pp. 289-90. Denzinger does not cite Clement's bull.

10. C. Condren, *The Status and Appraisal of Classic Texts: An Essay on Political Theory, its Inheritance, and the History of Ideas* (Princeton, 1985), p. 190.

been able to read them. After that, citations from the *Defensor* which reappear in Erasmus's works, in particular the *Paraphrases*, will be considered.

In the first place there were fragmentary translations of the *Defensor* in French and Italian, as well as excerpts from his Latin manuscripts. According to Scholz, Marsilius owned an original manuscript of the *Defensor* completed in 1324 from which two copies were made. The copies became the sources for two differing manuscript groups—the French group designated as A and the German group of manuscripts as B. Scholz assumes that the cause of the variations between the two manuscript groups was the fact that Marsilius had later corrected and altered the B manuscript, probably in preparation for a new edition. Scholz identified the oldest manuscript of the B group, Tortosa, as the crucial link to the revised copy. He even speculated that the T manuscript might even be the original Marsilian manuscript which was later revised.

The possible places where Erasmus may have had access to one of the manuscripts are of greater importance, but here it is necessary to be cautious. So far I have not been able to check the accession records of the various manuscripts, in order to be sure what manuscripts were really available to Erasmus in the early sixteenth century. It is known that these manuscripts moved about Europe and were copied. For instance, the seventeen manuscripts in the A group were copied between 1400 and 1416.

Today there are six copies of the A group of manuscripts in Paris and one each in Oxford and Cambridge. Oxford also owns one manuscript of the B group. Two other A group manuscripts are also in England and three others of the A group are in Turin, Florence, and the Vatican Library, respectively. Could Erasmus have read any of these manuscripts?

Erasmus may have had opportunities to read the *Defensor* at Oxford or Cambridge during his stays there. This is a question which requires further research. Paris was also a good possibility, and, considering Erasmus's long stay in the Low Countries, between 1514 and 1522, so is Bruges.[11]

There must also have been a manuscript of the *Defensor* at or near Basel which the editors of the first printed editions of the work were

11. *Marsilius von Padua, Der Verteidiger des Friedens—Defensor Pacis* (2 vols.; ed. H. Kusch; Darmstadt, 1958), I, xviii-xx. Hereafter referred to as DP with the appropriate discourse, chapter and paragraphs.

able to use, but so far it has not been possible to identify its location. As will be demonstrated, this was the manuscript which Erasmus certainly did read. Piaia has rightly suggested that it was at some time during Erasmus's frequent journeys from the Low Countries to Basel, in order to settle various publishing problems with Froben, that Erasmus became acquainted with the *Defensor*. He believes that it was Rhenanus and other members of the humanist circle at Basel who made him aware of the Paduan's work.[12]

It is noticeable that between 1514 and 1522 Erasmus's attacks upon the wealth and power of the higher clergy also grew more relentless. They, he repeatedly asserted, were also the ones responsible for disturbing the peace of Europe. His comparisons of the ways of Popes, Cardinals and Bishops with those of Christ and the Apostles became ever less charitable. However, it is also possible to argue that on the eve of the Reformation there was a general increase of hostility towards the higher clergy. Von Hutten's pamphlets, *De unitate Ecclesiae conversanda et schismate quod fuit inter Henricum IV et Gregorium VII papam,* and *De schismate extinguendo*, and his publication of Valla's attack on the Donation of Constantine, *De Falso credita et ementita donatione Constantini declamatio*, written and published between 1519 and 1520, give us a very vivid example of the vituperative nature of the polemic directed against the wealth and power of the Church. Thanks to Hutten and earlier Celtis, it was widely believed in the Empire that the Church's unrightful interference in the affairs of the Empire had destroyed its political power. The question of whether or not von Hutten had also read Marsilius cannot be considered here, but the question should at some time be addressed.

Erasmus gave his humanist friends in Basel the chance to read *Julius Exclusus* before its publication. They enjoyed the book greatly. Indeed this work simply expanded upon a Marsilian theme, as did the *Querela Pacis*. The story of the translation of the *Querela Pacis* into German is of particular interest for anyone seeking to demonstrate closer links between Erasmus and Marsilius.

Erasmus's friend, Leo Jud, had been persuaded by Zwingli to interrupt his translations of the *Paraphrases* into German, in order to translate the the *Querela* and, as it turned out, Erasmus's *Expostulatio Jesu ad mortales* and Luther's *De votis monasticis*. Another close friend of

12. G. Piaia, *Marsilio da Padova nella riforma e nella controriforma fortuna ed interpretazione* (Padova, 1977), pp. 20ff.

314   *The Bible, the Reformation and the Church*

Zwingli, Abbot Joner of the cloister of Kappel, took Jud's German translation of the *Querela* to Basel for publication, but Zwingli intervened. He was in the midst of an assault upon the signing of the mercenary treaty between Francis I and all the Confederates (1521), except Zürich, which still remained loyal to its papal treaty, and continued to provide Pope Leo X with soldiers for the Swiss guard. The more influential of the two mayors of Zürich, Marx Roeist, was the titular head of the Swiss guard. The guard was actually commanded at Rome by the mayor's son, Kaspar. Ironically, Marx Roeist was Zwingli's closest ally in introducing the Reformation at Zürich.[13] The *Querela* provided ideal propaganda for Zwingli, but he wanted it published by the Zürich printer, Froschauer, and not in Basel.

Soon afterwards, Froschauer took over other of Jud's translations, such as the second German edition of the *Institutio Principis Christiani*.[14] It appears that Zwingli deliberately drew Jud away from Erasmus, but in fact he continued to translate Erasmus's works into German under Zwingli's supervision. The German translation of the *Paraphrase of Matthew* appeared early in 1522; the dedication to the Emperor and the letter to the reader were dated respectively January 13th and 14th, 1522. As has already been indicated, having completed his translations of the Paraphrases of Ephesians and Philippians, Jud interrupted his work upon the *Paraphrases* to translate the *Querela Pacis*. He then took on the job of translating the *Paraphrase of Matthew* and at the same time he also translated Luther's *De Libertate Christiana* and after that Erasmus's *Paraphrase of the Epistle to the Romans*. It is also well worth noting Wyss's observation that Leo Jud asserted Zwingli took over from Luther the ideal of justification by faith alone and the belief that faith was the cause of good works. Jud however was convinced that the remainder of the theological basis for the Reformation at Zürich came from Erasmus. 'Alle übrigen theologischen Grundlagen der Reformation glaubte er in der kritischen, auf die Quellen der Heiligen Schrift bezogene Haltung des Erasmus vorgefunden zu haben.'[15] The entire story demonstrates how involved with the work of

13. M. Hass, *Huldrych Zwingli* (Zürich, 1969, 1976), p. 73.
14. Wyss, *Leo Jud*, pp. 61ff, 109-11, 113-14.
15. Wyss, *Leo Jud*, pp. 70-73. After 1523 Jud was gradually drawn into the Zürich sodalitas and eventually became one of Zwingli's closest co-workers (pp. 116-19).

the Basel humanists Zwingli's future friend was.[16] The next question is was Erasmus directly involved in the publication of the *Defensor* at Basel? The answer is, as far as we know, 'no', but those who were responsible for the two early editions were all close to Erasmus. In the late autumn of 1521 the printer, Valentin Curio, published the first edition of the *Defensor Pacis*. Zwingli was not the editor of this volume as some have surmised, but it is believed that Leo Jud, though by now Zwingli's successor as People's Priest at Einsiedeln, was in fact the editor. Jud was close friend of both Erasmus and Zwingli. Froben purchased the composed print from Curio and published two more editions of the *Defensor Pacis* in the course of 1522. Beatus Rhenanus was the editor, and the Hebraist, Conrad Pellican, Zwingli's fellow reformer at Zürich after 1526, was responsible for the Index.[17]

The work of editing Marsilius was carried out by men who either belonged to or had close contacts with the humanist circle at Basel and in some cases at Zürich. Erasmus had for many years been a very influential member of the Basel circle and Zwingli had also been drawn into it by Rhenanus. If Erasmus had never before read the *Defensor Pacis*, then he certainly must have come into contact with the work between 1521 and early 1522, when Rhenanus and Froben were involved in the publication. Piaia is probably right that the acquaintance came earlier. It seems safe to say that late 1521 and early 1522 set the 'terminus ad quem' for Erasmus's acquaintance with the *Defensor Pacis*. Incidentally, the same can also be said of Zwingli, long a member of the Basel humanist circle, and a frequent correspondent with Erasmus. Zwingli had probably read the *Defensor Pacis* by mid-1522, and doubtless derived his earliest acquaintance with it from his friends in the Basel humanist circle.

To strengthen this argument, it is worth noting that from 1520 on

16. R.C. Walton, 'Der Streit zwischen Thomas Erastus und Caspar Olevian über die Kirchenzucht in der Kurpfalz in seiner Bedeutung für die internationale reformierte Bewegung', in H. Faulenbach, D. Meyer, R. Mohr (eds.), *Caspar Olevian 1536–1587, ein evangelisch-reformierter Theologe aus Trier: Studien und Vorträge anlässlich des 400. Todesjahres, Im Auftrage des Vereins für Rheinische Kirchengeschichte* (Köln, 1989), pp. 224-25, 234-36.

17. L. Weisz, *Leo Jud, Ulrich Zwingli's Kampfgenosse 1482–1542* (Zürich, 1942), p. 31. Walton, 'Der Streit', pp. 235, 235 n. 85. Among others Potter lists Rhenanus, Heinrich Loritis, Glarean, Conrad Pellican, Conrad Zwick, and Caspar Hedio as members of the Basel humanist circle (G.R. Potter, *Zwingli* [Cambridge, 1976], p. 19).

Zwingli and Jud bought their books together and Zwingli took responsibility for the transport of Jud's share to Einsiedeln.[18] It is likely that this joint book-buying eventually brought to Zürich the first of the three copies of the *Defensor* which eventually were at Zürich. It is tempting to ask why Jud never translated the *Defensor* into German. The answer is that this would have been a foolish and dangerous thing to do, in view of the political tensions which the introduction of the Reformation at Zürich and its spread had caused throughout the Confederacy. The general mistrust with which Marsilius's *Defensor* was viewed in official circles would have given the defenders of the old faith a powerful weapon against Zwingli and his followers.[19]

b. *The Paraphrases and the Defensor Pacis*
The question which this section will try to answer is whether or not the *Paraphrases* contain evidence demonstrating that Erasmus knew and used the *Defensor Pacis*. However, before doing this section of the paper, it is necessary to mention a discovery which emerged from an earlier article concerning the conflict between Caspar Olevian and Thomas Erastus over the question of the introduction of a Calvinist excommunication into the Church of the Rhineland Palatinate.[20] Erastus relied heavily upon antistes, that is, Bishop, Heinrich Bullinger of Zürich, for advice. Among other things, the article surmised that the Züricher sent Erastus a copy of the *Defensor* with additional citations from other authors copied on the fly leaves. The volume in question belonged to the future antistes, Johannes Rudolf Stumpf, who had most probably inherited it from his father, the humanist historian, who had belonged to the intimate circle of Zwingli's friends.

In the course of examining the sources of the Zürich conception of excommunication, it became evident that Zwingli and then Bullinger had drawn heavily from Erasmus's *Paraphrases* in considering the problem. In the *Paraphrases* Erasmus had interpreted Mt. 16.13-20, Mt. 18.15-19 and 1 Corinthians 5 to argue that the proper form of excommunication which the congregation should exercise was ostracism which followed a period of admonition by the pastor and others. The use of coercion in this matter was left to the secular authorities. Zwingli, Bullinger and Erastus followed Erasmus, but this argument was not one first developed

18. Wyss, *Leo Jud*, p. 69.
19. Wyss, *Leo Jud*, pp. 32, 61ff., 74-80, 116-19.
20. See footnote 16.

by Erasmus. Erasmus appears to have taken the argument from part two, ch. 6 of the *Defensor Pacis*. Zwingli, Bullinger and Erastus most probably knew that Marsilius was the original source, but preferred to cite Erasmus.[21] In sum, the Zürichers and Erastus used Marsilius's arguments to deny the clergy any coercive power in the matter of excommunication. They also followed him in arguing that the decision of human beings to excommunicate a sinner was certainly not a confirmation of a decision already made by God. The assumption that it was a confirmation was made by Thomas Aquinas, Calvin, Beza, and many others; and Bullinger and Erastus never ceased to warn the Elector Frederic III that the form of excommunication used by the Calvinists resembled that of the Donatists and Anabaptists, and would totally disrupt the peace of the Rhineland Palatinate. It was doubtless Erasmus's *Paraphrases* which first made them aware of the value of the Marsilian source. He was the mediator. The Zürich Reformation as a whole remained remarkably Erasmian, but at the same time was far more Marsilian than we have previously realized. Zwingli's letter to Ambrosius Blarer in 1528 in which he described the constitution of the city as the visible Church is certainly Marsilian. Indeed, Erastus's *Seventy-Five Theses* were also largely Marsilian.[22] The influence of the reappearance of Marsilius was not confined to Erasmus. Also recently attention has been drawn to Aventinus's knowledge of Marsilius.[23]

Mt. 22.17-21 and Rom. 13.1-7 are the two important Bible texts which will be discussed in this section. Indirectly, Erasmus twisted the tail of the Papal lion when considering Mt. 22.17-21 which continued a theme begun in Mt. 17.26—the money for the payment of taxes having been drawn from a fish's mouth. John XXII had condemned Marsilius's interpretation of this verse in the bull *Licet iuxta doctrinam*, because Marsilius's interpretation made the payment of taxes to the Emperor obligatory. He had argued 'that all the temporalia of the Church were

---

21. DP II.VI §§3, 4, 6, 7, 9, 11-12, 13-14. Walton, 'Der Streit', pp. 222-42; DP III.II §§16-17. Cf. *Desiderii Roterdami Opera Omnia* (10 vols.; repr. 1706, Hildesheim edn 1962), VII, pp. 92-93, 99-101, 872-74. Hereafter referred to as OO with the appropriate volume and page.

22. Walton, 'Der Streit', pp. 234-35; 236b, 237-39. I intend to continue my study of this issue by a closer study of Lk. 22.38 and Jn 21.15-17.

23. G. Piaia, *Marsilio da Padova*, p. 15.

subject to the Emperor and that he was able to receive these things as his own'.[24]

Mt. 22.21 elaborated upon the same theme. In interpreting the passage Erasmus followed the general humanist historical approach to the verse. Erasmus made it clear that it has to be understood in the context of the question posed to Christ in v. 17: was it lawful for a Jew who kept the law to pay taxes to Caesar or not? According to the account, the purpose of the agents of King Herod and the Pharisees, who posed the question, was to trap Jesus by asking him for a ruling on the question whether it was lawful or not, according to Jewish law, to pay taxes to the Emperor at Rome. Jesus clearly sensed the real purpose behind the question and openly called his questioners hypocrites. His counter to their enquiry was to pose another question. He asked for a silver coin, probably a denarius or a sesterce which the account says was used for the purpose of paying taxes or tribute. Then he very simply asked them whose head and inscription were on the coin. They had to answer that Caesar's head and Caesar's inscription were on the coin. This gave Jesus the opening for which he had been waiting. According to the New English Bible, he then said to them, 'Then pay to Caesar what belongs to Caesar and to God what belongs to God'. People of my generation are still more used to the words, 'render therefore unto Caesar...'

Erasmus interpreted the apparently simple story in terms of the sharp and very clear distinction between a 'censum pietatis', that is, an assessed payment of piety to God, and the obligatory regulations governing a secular assessment and payment of a tax, not just to Caesar, but to any ruler. This distinction was obviously very important to Erasmus: secular matters and spiritual matters should not be confused. To make this very clear, Erasmus also stressed the fact that Jesus said that he had not come into the world to make secular laws. The Latin words *lex* and *idiom lex ferre* which Erasmus put in Jesus' mouth, when he claimed that he had not come to frame laws concerning these things ut leges ferret hisce de rebus demonstrates Erasmus's knowledge both of classical Latin and Roman law. Erasmus's argument was clear enough and he repeated it more succinctly in the *Adnotationes*.[25] Jesus refused to play the role of a magistrate, for this was not his domain. To make this

24. 'Quod omnia temporalia Ecclesiae subsunt Imperatori, et ea potest accipere velut sua.' Denzinger, p. 289; cf. DP II.IV §§10-11; DP II.XV, XVI §§5, 8, 9, 22; XXVIII; cf. DP II.XXIX §§5-10.
25. *OO*, VII, p. 116.

argument 'liquide clarus' Erasmus presented the reader with a portrayal of Jesus looking at the coin as if, as Erasmus says, he had no knowledge of the inscription or of the significance of the Emperor's profile on the coin, for he was concerned with heavenly things, that is spiritual matters. In the letter to Paul Volz which was first included as an introduction to the *Enchiridion Militis Christiani* in the 1518 Froben edition, Erasmus also used the example of Mt. 22.17-21, in order to make the same case. Erasmus's argument was that Christ's Church should confine itself to spiritual matters.

Erasmus took care in the latter part of the paraphrase of v. 21 to assert that those who rendered unto Caesar his due did no harm whatsoever to their own piety, if only they first rendered unto God the things which were God's. He closed his paraphrase by clearly stating the limits of God's, and the magistrate's, authority. God could command anyone to give homage to Caesar, even when such a person was not required to do so and the homage made him or her poorer. It is simply unwise, Erasmus said, not to do so, for disobedience would anger both God and Caesar. However, if the secular ruler requires that we return to godlessness, this command is not a properly assessed tribute to Caesar, but rather to the devil.[26]

The classic statement of the division of power in the world can be found in the 13th chapter of Paul's Epistle to the Romans. Erasmus's paraphrase of it is extensive, and there is unfortunately no time for a full discussion here. Erasmus paraphrased the first verse of ch. 13 in a very interesting way. He discussed v. 1, 'Let every soul be subject unto the higher power for there is no power, but of God, the powers that be are ordained of God', in terms of the passive acceptance of persecution—he did not speak even of passive resistance—at the hands of the magistrate or prince for the sake of the faith. He argues that that is what God has told us to do, since a republic or better said a civil government is always in accord with order. This order should not be shaken on the pretext of religion, and those who do so are simply desirous of evil and are wicked. Erasmus added that such unruly people should be avoided by Christians and indeed be resisted. When it came to resistance it even might be necessary to work together with 'gentiles' rather than to accept the activities of those who would disrupt the peace of civil society in the name of religion.[27] These remarks are of particular interest, for Luther's theses

26. *OO*, VII, pp. 116-17.
27. See nn. 21-23.

had only very recently been posted, and the *Paraphrase of the Epistle to the Romans* went to the press in late November, 1517. Erasmus's admonition was probably directed at the radical humanist Ulrich von Hutten, and some of his friends, such as mercenary leader Franz von Sickingen, or at the foreign policy of Leo X. Still it is interesting to note that Erasmus sensed the tension which was in the air and feared exactly what did happen. The events of the following years marked the failure of his reform program.

The prince of the humanists then went on to explain the three categories of values which were present in a peaceful community. Divine matters, that is religious affairs, were peculiar to Christ alone and always had to come first. Then there were the things of this world which involved greed and wickedness. The third category which stood between the affairs of Christ and the wickedness of this world was neither good nor evil in itself; it was neutral or *adiaphoron*, but also essential for maintaining the harmony of the *res publica*. This, Erasmus explained, was the reason he admonished Christians not to cause unrest for the sake of religion; they should obey the magistrate and the laws, because however imperfectly, the ruler bears the image of God, is ordained by him, and acts for God when he punishes the wicked. The neutral category is really the Christian's willingness to be obedient to the ruler, even if persecuted. In this discussion Erasmus recognizes, as he did in the paraphrase of Mt. 22.17-21, that some forms of obedience can serve the devil. Nevertheless, he remains convinced of the necessity of obedience for the existence and survival of the *res publica*. It is indeed very hard to find the basis for any kind of right of resistance in Erasmus.[28]

In paraphrasing Rom. 13.4 Erasmus applauds the Pauline description of the magistrate as a minister of God, when he properly performs his duties. In this respect Erasmus is very traditional and we do not find in him the type of radically Marsilian argument which Wolfgang Musculus of Bern later developed. Musculus maintained that the minister of God is rightly subordinated to the magistrate, because the word minister comes from *minus*, that is, 'small', and magis, the root of the word magistrate, comes from *magis*, 'in a higher degree', or 'greatly'. What we find in Erasmus's paraphrase of this verse, however, is the clear separation of

28. *OO*, VII, 116, pp. 820-21: 'Brief an Paul Volz'; cf. *Erasmus von Rotterdam: Ausgewählte Schriften*, I, p. 23.

divine and worldly things, as well as the assertion that the things of Christ always come first.[29]

The constant theme of the necessity of the separation of the heavenly things from the affairs of the magistrate and a world of evil certainly appears in other works of Erasmus. He never ceased to complain about the Church's exercise of secular power and pursuit of wealth, which represented the interference of the spiritual realm in the affairs of the secular and was the cause of constant war and disruption in Europe—one should say the lack of peace. In the *Praise of Folly*, which probably appeared first in 1511, Erasmus had the following to say about the clergy:

> Our Popes, cardinals and bishops for some time now have earnestly copied the state and practice of princes, and come near to beating them at their own game... Nor do they keep in mind the name they bear, or that the name 'bishop' means, labour, vigilance, solicitude. Yet in raking in moneys they truly play the bishop, overseeing everything and overlooking nothing.[30]

He also complained bitterly about the Supreme Pontiff's usurpation of the place of Christ. In this criticism Christ becomes a type which stands for the simplicity, poverty and spirituality of the early Church. Indeed, in Erasmus's works references to Christ become a code word for the criticism of the Church and its rulers.

> As to the Supreme Pontiffs who take the place of Christ, if they tried to emulate His life, I mean his poverty, labors, teaching, cross and contempt for safety, if even they thought upon the title of Pope—that is, Father, or the addition 'Most Holy', who on earth would be more afflicted... It would lose them all that wealth and honor, all those possessions, triumphal progress, offices... In the place of these it would bring...a thousand troublesome tasks.[31]

Erasmus's solution to the problem of the Pope's usurpation of Christ's position and the misuse of the wealth of the Church by the higher clergy was simple. Erasmus looked to the prince to right the wrongs of the Church's abuse of wealth and power. 'There is nothing in life better than a wise and good monarch...there is no greater scourge than a foolish and a wicked one... The studies and character of priests and bishops are a potent factor in this matter, I admit, but not merely as

29. *OO*, VII, p. 820: 'Quid sit magistratus, Loci communes sacrae Theologiae, iam recens recogniti et emendati per Wolfgang Musculum' (Basel, 1564), pp. 622-23.

30. D. Erasmus, *The Praise of Folly* (ed. W. Hudson; Princeton, 1941), pp. 85-86.

31. *Praise of Folly*, pp. 98-99.

much so as are those of princes.'[32] Do we find similar ideas in Marsilius's *Defensor Pacis*? The answer is yes, but most of the things Erasmus said about the Church's wealth and power had been so often said by the beginning of the sixteenth century that it was certainly not necessary for Erasmus to have read all or part of the *Defensor Pacis* to come to the conclusions he made public. Indeed, it is very difficult to find a specific mention of Marsilius in any of Erasmus's writings. The main reason for this is that it was still dangerous to cite Marsilius.

In Discourse I, ch. V, Paragraph 11 Marsilius argues that the establishment of religion had also stabilized society, even where it was not Christian, and served the peace of society, 'As a consequence, many disputes and injuries ceased to threaten communities'. Religion defended peace. This is a theme which Erasmus discussed in the Paraphrase of Romans 13. In describing the function of Christian priests in Discourse I, ch. VI, Paragraphs 7 and 8, Marsilius explained the priest's function:

> As teacher of this law, and as ministers of its sacraments, certain men in communities were chosen, called priests and deacons or levites. It is their office to teach the commands and counsels of Christian evangelical law, as to what must be believed, done and spurned, to the end that a blessed status be attained in the future world, and the opposite avoided.[33]

It is clear that he assigned no other function than this one to the clergy. Erasmus certainly defended the same position in his writings.

In Discourse II, ch. IV Marsilius attacked the Coercive Rulership of Bishops (for which John XXII later condemned him), and denied that they should exercise it. In Paragraph 9 he interpreted Mt. 22.21 at length. The first few lines of his consideration also touched on themes which today we call Erasmian and are reflected in the two citations from the *Praise of Folly*, which compare the actual office of a priest which Christ established and for which he provided the model with that of the present Popes, Bishops and Lower Clergy. At the same time Marsilius stressed the importance of the subordination of all people to the authority of the secular ruler. He wrote,

---

32. D. Erasmus, *The Education of a Christian Prince* (ed. L.K. Born; New York, 1936, 1964, 1968), pp. 156-57; cf. DP II.IV §1.

33. *Marsilio of Padua: The Defender of Peace: The Defensor Pacis* (trans. A. Gewirth; New York, 1956, 1967), pp. 19, 23 (= DP I.VI §§7, 8; cf. DP II.XVI). From here on the Gewirth edition of the *Defensor Pacis* will be employed.

> It now remains to show that not only did Christ himself refuse rulership or
> coercive judgement in this world, whereby he furnished an example for his
> apostles and disciples and their successors to do likewise but also he
> taught by example that all men, both priests and non-priests, should be
> subject in property and in person to the coercive judgement of the rulers of
> this world.

Marsilius later returned to his argument in Discourse II, ch. XXVIII,
Paragraph 24 and came to the same conclusion. Erasmus was not slow
to use this argument but declined to acknowledge his source.[34]

The remainder of Erasmus's paraphrase of verse Mt. 22.21 was an
unacknowledged word-for-word copy of Marsilius's discussion of the
verse. It followed faithfully the order of citations originally used by
Marsilius. In both the *Paraphrases* and the *Adnotationes* Erasmus failed
to acknowledge that Marsilius was his source and he used the citation
from Chrysostom which asserted that rendering unto Caesar the things
that are Caesar's was not harmful to piety without the acknowledge-
ment of either Chrysostom or Marsilius, who had been very careful to
cite his source. The same is true for Marsilius's brief citation from
Ambrose at the end of paragraph. Still it does seem that Erasmus knew
Ambrose's works and could have used them independently. Erasmus
was guilty of plagiarism, because he followed the sequence in which
Marsilius had used the citations. If nothing else, it did confirm that
Erasmus knew and read the *Defensor Pacis* for the *Paraphrases*—that
is, 5 to 6 years before the publication of the *Defensor* at Basel.

In Paragraph 1 and 10 of Discourse II, ch. IV Marsilius considered once
again the question of rendering unto Caesar that which was Caesar's.
This time he directed his attention to Mt. 17.24-27. The story was about
finding the coin required for the tribute to the authorities in the mouth
of a fish, but he used the passage to claim that bishops and priests
should not be exempt from such tribute. In Paragraph 12 he carefully
demonstrated that Christ was anxious to make it clear to his disciples
that his property and his person were subject to the *merum imperium*,
that is, the 'capital jurisdiction' of the 'Roman legislator'. Marsilius
asserted that Jesus himself had recognized that Pilate had 'power from
above' and could judge Jesus, as well as execute the judgment.

To strengthen further his argument, as he had already done in ch. V,
Paragraph 4, Marsilius cited Augustine's exegesis of Rom. 13.1-7.
Augustine had claimed that the power of jurisdiction could only come

34. DP II.IV §§10-13, XXVIII §24.

from God. He added that 'he who acts out of malice and hands over an innocent man to the authorities to be killed, sins more than do those in authority, or if he kills the man for fear of another's greater power'. Citing both Augustine and Bernard of Clairveaux, Marsilius argued that if Pilate had coercive judiciary power over Christ, how much more did he have it over the Apostles, their successors and also Bishops and Priests. Not only did Christ wish to exclude himself from secular ruler-ship or coercive judicial power, but he also barred his apostles from it, both among themselves and with respect to others: 'Why then do priests have to interfere with coercive secular judgements? For their duty is not to exercise temporal lordship, but rather to serve by example and com-mand of Christ.' Marsilius ended the chapter by repeating that Christ 'in word and deed' cut himself off from worldly rulership and coercive power. He desired to be subject to the 'governance, judgment, or coercive power'.[35] Erasmus's paraphrase of Rom. 13.1-7 shows more originality, but remains dependent upon Marsilius's arguments, as a look at ch. IX, Paragraph 9 also demonstrates.

The discussion which Marsilius carried on in ch. V, Paragraphs 4, 10-13 and in ch. IX, Paragraph 9 is reflected in the two citations from the *Praise of Folly* noted above. Marsilius's discussion also demonstrates the very clear emphasis upon the sovereignty of the ruler and can be clearly seen again in Erasmus's *The Education of a Christian Prince*. Marsilius cites Rom. 13.1, Mt. 22.17-21 and Mk 12.13-17. Here Marsilius's view of the prince's importance as a moral example is again to be seen in Erasmus. He copies Marsilius's discussion and his citations of Ambrose, Peter Lombard's *Collectanea*, and Bernard of Clairveaux's letter to the archbishop of Sens in the same order. It is true that Erasmus knew these works, but then why has Marsilius's order been employed? He also cites Augustine in Discourse II, ch. V, Paragraph 4, just the way Marsilius has. The first citation from the *Praise of Folly* advances the same argument and is a direct copy of Marsilius's description of clerical corruption given in *Defensor Pacis* II, ch. II, Paragraph 7.[36] The citations in the *Praise of Folly*, which probably came from Marsilius, bring the date at which Erasmus had read some or all of the *Defensor Pacis* down to 1510 or 1511. Both men truly believed that the example of the monarch was more valuable than that of bishops and priests. More important than that is the fact that Erasmus uses Christ as the type

35. DP II.IV §§10-13; II.V §8.
36. DP II.V §§4, 10-13; II.IX §9; see nn. 30-32; DP II.II §7.

of purity and spirituality exactly as Marsilius does. Christ and the Apostles are also the type of the primitive Church and the standing model of piety which both men used against the Popes who usurp Christ's position and the Bishops who seek to become wealthy. Erasmus was very much a Marsilian.

Conclusion

The *Paraphrases* of Erasmus were directly influenced by Marsilius of Padua's *Defensor Pacis*. Erasmus had probably begun to read the Paduan as early as 1511; he had certainly read him by 1521. Marsilius's *Defensor Pacis* was a central component in the development of Erasmus's critique of the Church and his plans for reform.

PUBLICATIONS OF JAMES ATKINSON

Books

Luther's Early Theological Works (Library of Christian Classics, XVI; London: SCM Press, 1962).

Rome and Reformation (London: Hodder & Stoughton, 1966).

Luther's Works (vol. 44; American Edition; Philadelphia: Fortress Press, 1966).

Luther and the Birth of Protestantism (Harmondsworth: Pelican, 1968).

Lutero y el Naciento del Protestantismo Alianza (Madrid: Editorial Madrid, 1971 [translation into Spanish]).

Lutero: La Parola Scatenata (trans.) (L'uomo e il Penserio; Turin: Claudiana, 1982).

The Great Light (Paternoster Church History, IV; Exeter: Paternoster, 1968).

The Trial of Luther (London: Batsford, 1971).

Martin Luther: Prophet to the Church Catholic (Exeter: Paternoster, 1983, 500 year anniversary).

The Darkness of Faith (London: Darton, Longman & Todd, 1987).

Contributed to

J.T. McCord and T.H.L. Parker (eds.), *Service in Christ: Essays Presented to Karl Barth on his Eightieth Birthday* (London: Epworth, 1966).

O. Thulin (ed.), *Reformation in Europe* (Leipzig: Heinrichs, 1967).

A. Richardson (ed.), *Dictionary of Christian Theology* (London: SCM Press, 1967).

A. Richardson and J. Bowden, *New Dictionary of Christian Theology* (London: SCM Press, 1983).

D.F. Poellot (ed.), *Studies in Commemoration of the 450th Anniversary of the Reformation* (St Louis: Concordia, 1967).

T. Dowley (ed.), *The History of Christianity* (Oxford: Oxford University Press, 1990).

C. Meyer (ed.), *Luther for an Ecumenical Age* (St Louis: Concordia, 1967).

A.B. Clarke and A. Linzey (eds.), *Dictionary of Theology and Society* (London: Routledge, 1994).

Latimer Studies: Rome and Reformation (Oxford: Latimer House, 1982).

Church and State under God (Oxford: Latimer House, 1982).

Christianity and Judaism (Oxford: Latimer House, 1984).

Articles and Reviews

Journal of Theological Studies
Theology
Scottish Journal of Theology
Churchman
Anvil
Evangelical Quarterly
Church of England Newspaper
Church Times

INDEXES

INDEX OF REFERENCES

OLD TESTAMENT

NEW TESTAMENT

INDEX OF AUTHORS

INDEX OF SUBJECTS

JOURNAL FOR THE STUDY OF THE NEW TESTAMENT

Supplement Series